REAL ESTATE VALUATION THEORY

RESEARCH ISSUES IN REAL ESTATE

Sponsored by the
AMERICAN REAL ESTATE SOCIETY

REAL ESTATE VALUATION THEORY

edited by

Ko Wang
California State University, Fullerton
U.S.A.

Marvin L. Wolverton
University of Nevada Las Vegas
U.S.A.

KLUWER ACADEMIC PUBLISHERS
Boston / Dordrecht / London

Distributors for North, Central and South America:
Kluwer Academic Publishers
101 Philip Drive
Assinippi Park
Norwell, Massachusetts 02061 USA
Telephone (781) 871-6600
Fax (781) 681-9045
E-Mail: kluwer@wkap.com

Distributors for all other countries:
Kluwer Academic Publishers Group
Post Office Box 322
3300 AH Dordrecht, THE NETHERLANDS
Telephone 31 786 576 000
Fax 31 786 576 474
E-Mail: services@wkap.nl

 Electronic Services <http://www.wkap.nl>

Library of Congress Cataloging-in-Publication Data

Real estate valuation theory / edited by Ko Wang and Marvin L. Wolverton.
    p.cm. – (Research issues in real estate ; v. 8)
  Includes bibliographical references.
  ISBN 0–7923–7663–3 (alk. paper)
    1. Real property – Valuation. I. Wang, Ko, 1955-II. Wolverton, Marvin L. III.Series.

HD1387 .R394 2002
333.33′2–dc21   2002022580

2001 American Real Estate Society

President's Council

AIG Global Real Estate Investment*
Appraisal Institute
Fannie Mae Foundation
Fidelity National Title Insurance Company
John Hancock Real Estate Investment Group
Institutional Real Estate, Inc.
LaSalle Investment Management

Legg Mason
Lend Lease Real Estate Investments
PricewaterhouseCoopers
Prudential Real Estate Investors
The Roulac Group
RREEF

Regents

Cornerstone Real Estate Advisers Inc.
CoStar Group
Ferguson Partners
International Council of Shopping Centers (ICSC)

MIG Realty Advisors
National Association of Real Estate Investment Trusts (NAREIT)

Sponsors

AEW Capital Management
Association of Foreign Investors in U.S. Real Estate (AFIRE)
Ballard, Biehl & Kaiser
BDO Seidman
BRE Properties*
CIGNA Investments
Citadel Realty
Counselors of Real Estate (CRE)
Dearborn Real Estate Education
The Dorchester Group
Exel Logistics
Freddie Mac
GE Capital Real Estate
Government of Singapore Investment Corporation (GSIC)
Heitman Capital Management Corporation
Kennedy-Wilson International
Management Reports, Inc. (MRI)

Mortgage Banker's Association (MBA)
National Association of Industrial and Office Properties (NAIOP)
National Association of REALTORS® (NAR)
National Investment Center for the Seniors Housing & Care Industries (NIC)
National Multi Housing Council (NMHC)
New York University Real Estate Institute
Real Estate Center at Texas A&M University
Realty One
Research Institute for Housing America
Society of Industrial and Office REALTORS® (SIOR)
South-Western Thomson Learning*
SSR Realty Advisors
Steven L. Newman Real Estate Institute
Torto Wheaton Research
UBS Brinson Realty Investors
Urban Land Institute (ULI)

*New for 2001

THE AMERICAN REAL ESTATE SOCIETY

Officers

Board of Directors

IRES Board Members

2001 Membership
Academic ($110), Professional ($225), Academic Library ($350), Company Library ($450), Student ($55), Corporate ($450), Sponsor ($1,500), Regent ($3,000) and President's Council ($6,000). Checks should be made payable to ARES and correspondence should be addressed to: Helen Murphy, ARES, University of North Dakota. College of Business & Public Administration, P. O. Box 7120, Grand Forks, ND 58202-7120. Phone: 701-777-3670; Fax: 701-777-6380. Website: www.ARESnet.org or Helen Murphy at helen_murphy@und.nodak.edu.

*Past President

2001 Fellows of the American Real Estate Society

Endowed Doctoral Sponsorships

Glenn R. and Jan H. Mueller
Theron R. and Susan L. Nelson
James R. and Anais B. Webb

Fellows

Joseph D. Albert
James Madison University

Brent W. Ambrose
University of Kentucky

Randy J. Anderson
Prudential Real Estate Investors*

Michael A. Anikeeff
Johns Hopkins University

John S. Baen
University of North Texas

John D. Benjamin
American University

Donald H. Bleich
California State University – Northridge

Amy Bogdon
Fannie Mae Foundation

Waldo L. Born
Eastern Illinois University

James H. Boykin
Virginia Commonwealth University

Nicholas Buss
PNC Bank*

Todd A. Canter
ABKB / LaSalle Securities

James Carr
Fannie Mae Foundation

Lijian Chen
Lend Lease Real Estate Investments

Ping Cheng
Salisbury State University

Mark S. Coleman
Bondspace

James R. Cooper
Georgia State University

Glenn E. Crellin
Washington State University

Charles G. Dannis
Crosson Dannis

Karen G. Davidson
Davidson & Associates

James R. DeLisle
Georgia State University

Gene Dilmore
Realty Researchers

Geoffrey Dohrmann
Institutional Real Estate Inc.

Mark G. Dotzour
Texas A & M University

John T. Emery
Louisiana Tech University

Donald R. Epley
Washington State University

Robert A. Ernst
RAE Securities

Jack P. Friedman
Jack P. Friedman & Associates*

S. Michael Giliberto
J. P. Morgan Investment Management

John L. Glascock
George Washington University

Paul R. Goebel
Texas Tech University

Richard B. Gold
Lend Lease Real Estate Investments

William C. Goolsby
University of Arkansas – Little Rock

Jacques Gordon
LaSalle Investment Management

G. Hayden Green
University of Alaska – Anchorage

D. Wylie Greig
RREEF

Karl L. Guntermann
Arizona State University

Otis E. Hackett
Otis E. Hackett & Associates

Thomas Hamilton
Indiana State University

Jun Han
John Hancock Real Estate Investments Group

Richard L. Haney
Texas A & M University

William G. Hardin, III
Mississippi State University

William T. Hughes
MIG Realty Advisors

Jerome R. Jakubovitz
MAI

G. Donald Jud
University of North Carolina – Greensboro

Ronald W. Kaiser
Ballard, Biehl & Kaiser*

Steven D. Kapplin
University of South Florida

George R. Karvel
University of Saint Thomas

William N. Kinnard. Jr.
Real Estate Counseling Group of Connecticut

Richard Knitter
Great Realty Advisors

Phillip T. Kolbe
University of Memphis

Steven P. Laposa
PricewaterhouseCoopers

Youguo Liang
Prudential Real Estate Investors

Frederick Lieblich
SSR Realty Advisors

Joseph B. Lipscomb
Texas Christian University

Marc A. Louargand
Cornerstone Realty Advisers Inc.

Emil Malizia
University of North Carolina – Chapel Hill

Christopher A. Manning
Loyola Marymount University

Richard Marchilelli
Appraisal Institute

John F. McDonald
University of Illinois – Chicago Circle

Willard McIntosh
AIG Global Real Estate Investment Corporation

Isaac Megbolugbe
Fannie Mae Foundation

Ivan J. Miestchovich, Jr.
University of New Orleans

Norman G. Miller
University of Cincinnati

William Mundy
Mundy Jarvis & Associates

F. C. Neil Myer
Cleveland State University

Graeme Newell
University of Western Sydney

Joseph L. Pagliari, Jr.
Citadel Realty

Joseph D. Pasquarella
Joseph D. Pasquarella & Co.

Edward F. Pierzak
Henderson Investors North America

Steven A. Pyhrr
Kennedy-Wilson International

R. Malcolm Richards
Texas A&M University

Rudy R. Robinson, III
Austin Valuation Consultants*

Stephen E. Roulac
The Roulac Group & University of Ulster

Ronald C. Rutherford
University of Texas–San Antonio

Anthony B. Sanders
Ohio State University*

Karl-Werner Schulte
European Business School

Arthur L. Schwartz, Jr.
University of South Florida

David Scribner
Scribner & Associates

M. Alef Sharkawy
Texas A&M University

Leon Shilton
Fordham University

Robert A. Simons
Cleveland State University

Pelros Sivitanides
Torto Wheaton Research

C. Ray Smith
University of Virginia

Simon A. Stevenson
University College–Dublin*

Stephen F. Thode
Lehigh University

Robert Thompson
King Sturge

Grant I. Thrall
University of Florida

Raymond Torto
Torto Wheaton Research

Raymond Y. C. Tse
Hong Kong Polytechnic

Jorge I. Vallejo
Vallejo & Vallejo

Stephen M. Verba
Realty One

Ko Wang
California State University–Fullerton

R. Bryan Webb
UBS Brinson Realty Advisors

John E. Williams
Morehouse College

Larry E. Wofford
C & L Systems Corporation

Marvin Wolverton
University of Nevada–Las Vegas

Elaine M. Worzala
Colorado State University

Charles H. Wurtzebach
Henderson Properties

Tyler Yang
Freddie Mac

Michael S. Young
RREEF

Leonard V. Zumpano
University of Alabama

*New for 2001

Contents

Section III: Appraising Contaminated Property

Section IV: Property Tax Assessment

Section V: New Perspectives on Traditional Appraisal Methods

About the Editors

Ko Wang

Ko Wang is currently a professor in the Department of Finance and co-director of the Real Estate and Land Use Institute at the California State University – Fullerton. Prior to this appointment, Professor Wang was an assistant professor in the Department of Finance at the University of Texas at Austin and a chaired real estate professor at The Chinese University of Hong Kong. He had also worked full time for several leading real estate consulting and development firms in the U.S. and Asia. Professor Wang holds an MS degree in Community and Regional Planning (1982), an MBA degree with a real estate concentration (1984), and a Ph.D. degree in real estate and finance (1988). All the degrees are from the University of Texas at Austin.

Professor Wang publishes both in real estate and finance journals, which include *Real Estate Economics* and *Journal of Real Estate Research* (10 publications each), *Journal of Urban Economics, Journal of Real Estate Finance and Economics, International Real Estate Review, Journal of Finance, Journal of Financial Economics, Journal of Financial and Quantitative Analysis*, and *Review of Financial Studies*. He also co-authored a book on Real Estate Investment Trusts (Oxford University Press, New York) and co-wrote 18 teaching cases and teaching notes on real estate and finance issues faced by firms in Asia (distributed by Harvard Business School Publishing and European Case Clearing House). He is the editor of the *Journal of Real Estate Research* and the founding editor of the *International Real Estate Review*. Professor Wang is a Fellow of the Homer Hoyt Institute and the Hong Kong Institute of Real Estate.

Marvin L. Wolverton

Marvin L. Wolverton is currently a visiting associate professor in the Department of Finance at the University of Nevada Las Vegas. He holds a Ph.D. in Business Administration with Real Estate and Decision Science concentrations from Georgia State University in Atlanta, Georgia, and he holds the Appraisal Institute's MAI designation. He also has a M.S. in Economics from Arizona State University in Tempe, Arizona, and a BSEM in Mining Engineering from the New Mexico Institute of Mining and Technology in Socorro, New Mexico. Professor Wolverton taught in the Department of Finance, Insurance, and Real Estate at Washington State University for five years prior to his present affiliation with UNLV, where he held the positions of Alvin J. Wolff Professor of Real Estate and Director of Real Estate Research. Prior to his university affiliations, he worked for many years as a practicing real estate appraiser and consultant, and continues to engage in consulting assignments as time permits.

Dr. Wolverton is on the editorial boards of *The Appraisal Journal* and the *Journal of Real Estate Research*. He is also the editor of the *Journal of Real Estate Practice and Education*. He has written numerous articles appearing in *The Appraisal Journal*, the *Journal of Real Estate Research, Real Estate Economics*, the *Journal of Real Estate Finance and Economics*, the *Assessment Journal*, the *Journal of Property Research*, the *Journal of Property Investment and Finance*, and *Real Estate Review*. He and his wife Mimi now reside in Las Vegas, Nevada.

Foreword

The Appraisal Institute is pleased to join with the American Real Estate Society in cosponsoring this monograph entitled "Real Estate Valuation Theory." Since its inception the Appraisal Institute has strongly supported research and theoretical thought as a means to expand our body of knowledge. In that regard we have long supported the efforts and undertakings of the American Real Estate Society.

As with most fields of research and investigation, the ultimate goal is to refine our modes of practice. Those of us who work on the frontlines of valuation practice look to theoreticians to discover new ways of thinking, new approaches and new applications that change and improve the way we solve our clients' problems. Theory, combined with technology, has created a new dimension for us to work in, which is pointed up in the range of articles presented in this monograph.

The Appraisal Institute appreciates the opportunity to participate in the publication of "Real Estate Valuation Theory," and we look forward to continuing our close relationship with the American Real Estate Society and its members in the future.

Brian A. Glanville, MAI
2001 President
Appraisal Institute

Introduction

Is real property appraisal evolving, or have all of the "big ideas" already been conceived? This question has been circulating among the leaders of the Appraisal Institute during the past several annual meetings, usually encountering little in the way of satisfying answers. This isn't too surprising, because grand ideas and new knowledge don't usually evolve from off-hand conversation. They are the product of focused intellectual activity and hours of difficult work.

This unquenched thirst for new knowledge is the primary reason for assembling this collection of new manuscripts dealing with valuation theory, which was financially underwritten by the Appraisal Institute. Their generosity and willingness to partner with the American Real Estate Society made this collection of thoughtful and thought provoking essays possible. They are the result of a global response to a worldwide call for papers, and demonstrate that real estate valuation is indeed an international discipline. The United States, Australia and New Zealand, Southeast Asia, the Pacific Rim, and Europe are all represented by this impressive collection of authors. Together, the eighteen essays that make up this volume demonstrate that there are a sufficient number of "big ideas" to challenge and improve the appraisal profession for years to come.

The monograph is organized around five categories of intellectual contribution to the whole – appraiser decision making and valuation accuracy, application of nontraditional appraisal techniques such as regression and the minimum-variance grid method, appraising contaminated property, ad valorem tax assessment, and new perspectives on traditional appraisal methods. One common thread is that all of the papers are exceptionally well written and thought provoking.

Section I: Appraiser Decision Making and Valuation Accuracy

This section begins with a paper written by Julian Diaz III and J. Andrew Hansz titled "Behavioral Research into the Real Estate Valuation Process: Progress Toward a Descriptive Model." The authors rightly claim that a descriptive model must be derived to fully understand expert appraiser problem-solving and decision-making behavior, hence the appraisal process. They set the scene for this section and for the monograph by stressing the human element of appraisal. Fortunately for the appraisal discipline, much of the behavioral research done in the field of real estate has been focused on appraisers. Their paper reviews this research, most of which deals with common cognitive biasing influences on appraisers. They discuss the underlying behavioral theories, organize extant research findings and the techniques employed, and take a small but crucial initial step toward development of a descriptive model of the valuation process. In their descriptive model the appraisal process varies with appraiser experience, market familiarity, the regulatory environment, client relationships, and the cultural context of the work environment.

Section I's second paper is titled "Are Appraisers Statisticians." Here R. Kelley Pace, C.F. Sirmans, and V. Carlos Slawson, Jr. look at the phenomenon of "statistically challenged [human] appraisers following ad hoc procedures" oftentimes exhibiting prediction errors substantially less than those exhibited by hedonic pricing models resting on a foundation of "statistical and economic theory." They note that rather than relying on the human equivalent of a statistical hedonic model, appraisers seem to focus on the comparable sale selection process. They investigate a spatial-temporal model based solely upon distance and time and a multi-dimensional model adding baths, bedrooms, area, and age as exemplars of what appraisers do (focus on comparable sales), and compare the results of these models to a simple form and a complex form of hedonic model. The two models designed to capture what appraisers do both outperformed the two hedonic pricing models derived for comparison purposes. This leads the authors to the conclusion that "the statistically naïve practice of appraisers may have a more sophisticated basis than a casual examination would reveal." They suggest that prediction in statistical models could be improved by incorporation of elements of what appraisers actually do.

Paul Gallimore completes this section with his paper, "The Components of Appraisal Accuracy." He points out the correspondence between the concepts of appraisal accuracy (comparison of appraised values and market values) and appraisal variance (agreement among appraisers valuing the same property) and the research design conditions of validity and reliability. He presents a framework – the lens model – that provides insight into elements of appraisal accuracy. The lens model's strength is its applicability to problem solving by use of cues (i.e., comparable sales) to make judgments about events that cannot be observed directly (i.e., property value). This theoretical framework, borrowed from psychology, uncovers three avenues for improving appraisal accuracy – predictability of the real property environment, the match between valuation models and the real property environment, and consistency in application of valuation models. Gallimore concludes that appraisal accuracy can be improved by recognizing appraisers as being "forcasters of unobservable events." He then suggests that this perspective leads to the realization that improvements in data, monitoring of external influences, and greater consistency in application of valuation models may all be fruitful means to the goal of improving appraisal accuracy.

Section II: Regression, Minimum-Variance Grid Method, and Other Valuation Modeling Techniques

Kicki Björklund, Bo Söderberg and Mats Wilhelmsson's massive undertaking, "An Investigation of Property Price Studies," appropriately leads off this section of the monograph. They systematically examine 145 articles appearing in 13 high ranking American and European real estate, housing, and urban economics journals during the 1990–1995 period, assessing how well the researchers adhered to "general methodological guidelines associated with the treatment and reporting of empirical econometric research." They also provide an overview of real estate economics topics covered in these papers and classify the articles into subcategories.

The 145-article sample represents distillation of 1,882 articles, leaving only those manuscripts incorporating estimates of price or rent equations using regression techniques. The 145 articles are assessed from four perspectives, including the relation to previous research, modeling procedures, the data, and how the results are presented and interpreted. Their analysis reveals that there is room for improvement in hedonic modeling and reporting of research results. Two particularly troubling findings are (i) residual analysis, a fundamental element of regression modeling, was omitted from 75% of the articles studied, and (ii) motivation for choice of functional form was omitted from 73% of the articles. Clearly, real estate and housing practitioners and researchers can improve on reporting of their work, and the 18-item checklist found in this paper represents a good source of guidance.

The second article in this section is "Comparison of the Accuracy of the Minimum-Variance Grid Method and the Least Squares Method – a Non-Linear Extension" by Kwong Wing Chau, Wei Huang, Fung Fai Ng, and Hin

Man Louise Ng-Mak. They take on the question of comparing the accuracy of the least squares method to the relatively new minimum-variance grid method, extending the work in this area of inquiry to include the non-linear least squares estimator case. Importantly, these authors derive the necessary and sufficient conditions under which $\sigma^2_G < \sigma^2_{NLS}$ (conditions where the minimum-variance grid method is more accurate than the non-linear least squares method based on prediction accuracy). They note, however, that the results for the non-linear case are asymptotic, requiring a large number of observations, which limits application to liquid markets with readily available market data. They conclude by calling for empirical tests of their mathematical result.

In "Error Tradeoffs in Regression Appraisal Methods," Max Kummerow and Hanga Galfalvy conduct an empirical study of an issue related to the preceding paper by Chau, et al., and the Pace, et al., paper from Section I. That is, do market sales data become so heterogeneous as sample size grows that the errors stemming from such heterogeneity more than offset the asymptotic benefits derived from a large sample? They argue that one would expect measurement errors and omitted variables to become more problematic as sample size grows, perhaps leading to greater prediction error in large samples. They demonstrate error tradeoffs between decreasing random error and growing adjustment errors as sample size increases, and test their models using data consisting of more than 2,000 sales derived from Perth, Australia. Kummerrow and Galfalfy postulate a "U" shaped prediction error function based on analysis of their data, consistent with accepted industry practice of basing an analysis on a small number of most comparable sales.

In this section's fourth article, "Automated Valuation Models," R. Kelley Pace, C.F. Sirmans, and V. Carlos Slawson, Jr. examine the prospect of adapting computer aided mass assessment (CAMA) used in property tax assessment to traditional appraisal settings. They contrast the accuracy of manual and CAMA appraisals, discuss issues of moral hazard, unbundling appraisal services, the market for low-cost, automated appraisals, and the possibility of integrating traditional and automated appraisal services. The article then explores implementation of an automated valuation system, dealing with a variety of related issues such as data needs, omitted variables, model construction, model diagnostics, and the spatial and temporal nature of real estate data. They note also that the last item – dealing with spatial and temporal information – constitutes the major computational problem for adapting CAMA to traditional appraisal work. The authors conclude that an ideal system in terms of competitive pricing combined with objective and acceptably accurate results might involve appraisers as property examiners and data collectors along with CAMA techniques being employed to estimate property values.

Bo Söderberg narrows the focus of the hedonic modeling discussion to income property in this section's fifth paper, "A Note on the Hedonic Model

Specification for Income Properties." The study is developed in the context of Stockholm, Sweden where a mixed-use assumption consisting of residential and commercial property components underlies the analysis. Using a 282-observation sample, the author compares results derived from a Cobb-Douglas type, log-linear value estimation model (Model I) with results of a semi-log linear estimation model resulting from underlying exponential relationships (Model II). The estimation equations include variables controlling for proportions of residential and commercial space, building age, distance from the central business district, nature of the buyer, and temporal variation over 12 quarters. Although regression results were nearly identical in terms of goodness of fit, age and distance effects vary substantially between the two models. There was also a difference in out-of-sample prediction accuracy, with Model I being inferior to Model II in these measures. Appendices to the article provide valuable theoretical insight into the observed superior performance of the Model II functional form.

K.C. Wong, Albert T.P. So, and Y. C. Hung wrote the final paper in this section. In "Neural Network vs. Hedonic Price Model: Appraisal of High-Density Condominiums," they select a sample of 216 residential condominium units in Hong Kong as a training set to value 35 units held out as a test set. These data are used to compare the results of a neural network with two alternative specifications of the hedonic pricing model. They find that the neural network may appeal to a "risk averse appraiser" wanting to reduce maximum error on individual property appraisals, although the neural network did not significantly reduce average prediction error. They note the drawbacks to neural networks, including long computation time and the absence of indicators of implicit prices of property characteristics. Conversely, in addition to underscoring the reliability of, and potential for, neural networks as a valuation tool, their paper provides important insight regarding neural network design decisions concerning the number of iterations and hidden nodes.

Section III: Appraising Contaminated Property

Valuing contaminated property and estimating real property damages resulting from contamination represent a relatively new, yet substantial, aspect of modern appraisal practice. According to William N. Kinnard, Jr., Elaine M. Worzala, Sandy Bond, and Paul J. Kennedy, in "Comparative Studies of United States, United Kingdom and New Zealand Appraisal Practice: Valuing Contaminated Commercial Property," U.S. literature on this topic began recently in approximately 1984. These authors trace this literature in order to compare how appraisers have dealt with contamination related valuation assignments in the U.S., U.K. and New Zealand. They also report on surveys of appraisers in the three countries (and Canada) in order to analyze the extent to which practice adheres to techniques recommended in published articles and conference papers. Lastly, they review practice standards relating to valuing contaminated property in light of their research findings regarding practice and the literature. Their research reveals dramatic between-country differences in contaminated property valuation experience and practice. Additionally, data availability varies widely by country. These two factors lead to divergent opinions and little agreement regarding best practices. While this lack of agreement may be unsettling, it underscores the need to develop better methods for dealing with contaminated property. It also clearly identifies a need to build a better understanding of the analysis tools currently being used. The remaining two articles in this section are a first step toward meeting this need.

"Hedonic Modeling in Real Estate Appraisal: The Case of Environment Damages Assessment," by Alan K. Reichert is a thorough primer on applying the hedonic modeling technique to contamination appraisal assignments. The paper confronts practical problems that must be addressed "to ensure accurate and reliable results." The issues discussed include variable selection, functional form, and sample size effects—viewed from multiple perspectives including goodness of fit, prediction error, number of significant variables, and average independent variable significance level. Also discussed are control sample selection and double-counting problems that can arise from over-modeling. Three differing data sources (MLS, PACE and METROSCAN) are evaluated on the basis of data limitations and prediction accuracy in the context of an actual valuation case, and accuracy of longitude and latitude coordinates derived from mapping software is assessed. Other important and insightful topics include the interaction of multicollinearity and sample size, heteroskedasticity, and interpretation of regression coefficients. The author concludes that an appropriately designed and estimated hedonic model can produce median absolute percentage errors small enough to compete "with maximum error rates achieved by appraisers and tax assessors."

In this section's last paper, "Do Market Perceptions Affect Market Prices? A Case Study of a Remediated Contaminated Site," Sandy Bond compares perceptions uncovered by survey to the structure of a hedonic pricing model. The study is focused on post-remediated vacant residential land in Perth, Australia. The opinion survey questionnaire consisted of 50 response items developed specifically for the research project. The survey results revealed perceptions and attitudes concerning location quality, river view, access to public transportation, and proximity to a remediated site with contaminants buried on-site. The hedonic model was employed in the study to investigate the degree to which the perceptions and attitudes uncovered by the survey actually impacted upon market prices. The opinion survey results were shown to be "at least consistent with those of the market sales analysis," showing similar directions of impact. One important finding was that the stigma associated with a remediated site's contamination history can be offset by location and site amenities. Another insight to be gained from this article is the importance of fully understanding prevailing perceptions and attitudes and identifying variables that capture these for use in a price estimation model.

Section IV: Property Tax Assessment

Mark A. Sunderman and John W. Birch take on the issue of estimating land value when there are a limited number of available land sales in "Valuation of Land Using Regression Analysis." Noting that improved property sale price is composed of land value and improvement value, they reason that a multiple regression model can be used to isolate and estimate the value of the land, improvements, or both. For improved property, land value is estimated by deducting market-derived estimates of improvement value from the estimated market value of the total property (land and improvements). Land sales are included in the model along with improved sales by setting all land-sale improvement characteristic variables equal to zero. Their model also creatively accounts for neighborhood effects such as systematic price-size nonlinearity within a given neighborhood and differences in price levels between neighborhoods. Based on a holdout sample, the model derive by the authors was more accurate at predicting land price than the conventional system in use at the time of the study. The practicality of this paper is enhanced by a thorough description of how the authors adapted their regression results to an existing system of neighborhood land value tables, which was restricted to six different lot sizes. The model, employed in an assessment context here, is applicable to land value appraisals in other contexts as well.

Shwu-huei Huang contributes this section's other paper, "Grid-Adjustment Approach – Modern Appraisal Technique." The paper describes inefficiencies and inequities in the existing land declared price system of estimating the value of the tax base for Taiwan's land value tax, and then proposes two methods for improving the system. Inefficiency is evident in current assessment-to-sale-price ratios (A-S Ratio) averaging from .10 to .13 citywide over the study period. Inequity is revealed in the form of unacceptably high coefficients of variation and failure of a progressivity test. One proposed cure is a hedonic model, derived after extensive experimentation with functional form and heteroskedasticity correction. This method improved citywide A-S Ratios to an average of 1.08 over the five-year study period, reduced the average coefficient of variation to within 10% of Back's criterion, and removed all evidence of progressivity or regressivity. The grid-adjustment approach is the second proposed cure. The results were similar to the hedonic modeling approach, with improvements in the three metrics used to measure efficiency and equity. The author recommends the grid-adjustment approach for the practical reason that assessors are more likely to be accepting of it due to similarities with the familiar market comparison approach.

Section V: New Perspectives on Traditional Appraisal Methods

In "The Unit-Comparison Approach in Residential Appraisal" Peter F. Colwell and David W. Marshall develop a non-tabular approach to construction cost estimation. They derive a three-component function that incorporates constant, linear, and square root elements. Constant elements are those that are found in a base house regardless of size. Examples include a minimum number of plumbing fixtures, a front door, and elements of the heating and cooling systems. Linear elements are those that vary directly with house size such as floors and ceilings. Square root elements include components that increase in cost with size at a decreasing rate such as exterior walls. The cost function developed in their paper is the sum of these three components, and is shown to be quite adaptable. The cost estimating equation developed in this paper has potential to be used in practice to evaluate the accuracy of cost manuals. Another application might be to replace cost tables with cost functions imbedded into a computerized cost program. Additionally, as the authors note, the results here have theoretical implications regarding the expected concavity of hedonic functions in square footage. Finally, in an appendix to the paper, the authors develop additional and interesting cost details, including separation of the heating and cooling equipment from the air circulation system and incorporation of roof pitch variation into the cost function.

Michael Devaney examines integration of equity capitalization rates in "The Long-Run Equilibrium Relationship among Equity Capitalization Rates for Retail, Apartment, Office, and Industrial Real Estate." He utilizes a vector error correction model to investigate if and how equity capitalization rates converge toward a long-run equilibrium. Equity capitalization rates are derived from American Council of Life Insurance overall rate data spanning a 23-year period using the band of investment technique. Results indicate that retail, apartment, and industrial equity capitalization rates exhibit a long-run equilibrium relationship attained primarily through adjustments in apartment and retail pricing. Office equity capitalization rates were, on the other hand, segmented from rates determined in the other three property type markets.

The office anomaly could have been a consequence of market imbalance in office properties during the 1980s and early 1990s, as the author notes, and may be less apparent during more normal periods. The findings in the retail, apartment, and industrial markets is consistent with the principle of substitution, which suggests that mispricing of a given property type will be corrected by market activity. The paper's empirical evidence of cointegration has implications for appraisers and investors confronting markets demonstrating deviations from their long-run relationships.

In "A Fuzzy Discounted Cash Flow Analysis for Real Estate Investment," Tien Foo Sing, David Kim Hin Ho, and Danny Poh Hat Tay explore application of fuzzy set theory to real property cash flow modeling. As one of the few papers dealing with application of fuzzy mathematics to financial modeling, this paper represents a first step into uncharted waters for the real property valuation discipline. The authors provide a case illustration as a means of demonstrating the insight gained by fuzzy discounted cash flow analysis compared to the traditional, deterministic discounted cash flow (DCF) technique. They guide the reader through unfamiliar fuzzy mathematical concepts, fuzzy financial modeling, and the development of a fuzzy DCF model. This new knowledge is then applied to an office development case in Singapore as a means of comparing fuzzy DCF and traditional DCF results. They conclude that the fuzzy DCF model "provides a natural and intuitive way of dealing with cognitive uncertainty associated [with] vague and imprecise information."

The final paper in this section is "Real Options and Real Estate: A Review and Valuation Illustration" by Steven H. Ott. The author notes that application of the discounted cash flow "NPV decision rule ignores the changing dynamics of the actual marketplace." Specifically, traditional DCF models ignore a property owner's inherent flexibility to make future choices in order to adapt to changing market conditions. Real option analysis takes into account future investment opportunities imbedded in real estate investment decisions. Incorporation of real options analysis into analytical models can enhance real estate decision-making and value estimation. This paper provides a practical illustration of how this can be done using an actual Charlotte, North Carolina land development project, linking the value of a growth option to the value derived through the traditional DCF method. The imbedded growth option turns what would be traditionally viewed as an unfeasible, negative NPV project into a project viewed as a feasible, positive NPV project. This paper provides new insight into the highest and best use issue, which appraisers frequently encounter. Indeed, when option value is included in overall real property value, it may become more difficult to justify a change in an existing use.

Conclusion

The editors thank the Appraisal Institute, the American Real Estate Society and all of the contributing authors and referees for their combined and individual efforts, without which this volume would have never existed. We also acknowledge the efforts of Wayne Archer for handling 3 of the papers that ultimately were accepted for publication here. We are pleased to have had the opportunity to edit this volume, and hope that it proves to be a useful resource for years to come.

I

APPRAISER DECISION MAKING AND VALUATION ACCURACY

Chapter 1

Behavioral Research into the Real Estate Valuation Process: Progress Toward a Descriptive Model

Julian Diaz III
Department of Real Estate, Robinson College of Business, Georgia State University, Atlanta, Georgia

J. Andrew Hansz
Department of Real Estate and Finance, College of Business Administration, University of Texas at Arlington, Arlington, Texas

1.1 Introduction

The Appraisal Institute (2001) prescribes an eight-step real estate valuation process in *The Appraisal of Real Estate*, *12th* Edition (see Appendix A for a summary of this process).[1] This process model, pioneered by George Schmutz (1941), has appeared in the Institute's valuation text in various forms since the first edition was published in 1951. The Appraisal Institute's valuation process is a normative model because it suggests how appraisers should proceed, step-by-step, when addressing a valuation problem. This model is a cookbook or recipe approach to valuation. However, expert appraisers, like master chefs, do not appear to follow a normative, systematic process or recipe.

The Appraisal Institute raises the question as to "... how applicable the [normative] valuation model is to actual appraisal assignments, how well it analyzes the forces that affect value, and how accurately it interprets the actions and motivation of market participants."[2] A descriptive valuation model would explain how appraisers actually do their work. Although no definitive descriptive valuation model exists (and developing such a model is beyond the scope of this paper), for approximately a decade descriptive research into appraiser problem solving behavior has been conducted.

Many have recognized that the essence of real estate, including property valuation, is human behavior. Ratcliff appreciated this and incorporated behavioral concerns into his normative writings (Ratcliff, 1972). Graaskamp (1991) argued that the real estate discipline is applied social science. In the late 1980s, Diaz (1987) pioneered contemporary human problem solving behavior in a real estate context with theories and research techniques rooted in the cognitive psychology literature. At approximately the same time, Gallimore introduced a similar epistemology to the British property valuation literature. Although others have subsequently joined Diaz and Gallimore, this type of valuation research is still in the early stages of a research paradigm.[3]

Although a definitive descriptive model, or models, of the valuation process is premature and beyond the scope of this paper, behavioral research has produced some important insights concerning appraiser decision-making behavior and the valuation process. This paper reviews and organizes the behavioral research findings relevant to appraiser decision-making behavior. To begin, the underlying human problem solving theories and research methodologies are discussed in order to form a better understanding of the conclusions and limitations presented here.

1.2 Human Problem Solving Theories

The field of cognitive psychology has abundant research concerning human information processing and heuristics behavior. Newell and Simon (1972) and Simon (1978) developed a general theory of human problem solving that forms the foundation for behavioral real estate valuation research. See Appendix B for a diagram representing the general theory of human problem solving. This theory states that behavior is a function of two major components, the task environment and the human information processing system.

The task environment is the complex external environment in which the appraiser operates. The human information processing system consists of two components: short-term memory and long-term memory.

The appraiser's task environment includes all market data such as comparable sales information, rental income and operation expense data, vacancy information, capitalization rates, pending sale prices, list prices, and other market information. Often this data is incomplete and/or inaccurate contributing to the complexity of the environment. Typically, the appraiser is working on several appraisal assignments in various phases of completion (the normative valuation model may imply that an appraiser focuses on a single assignment). Other cues in the task environment include feedback in the form of transaction prices, opinions from other experts, and client influence (and potential coercion). Indeed, the appraiser operates in an information rich and complex environment.

All interaction between the task environment and the human information processing system is filtered through short-term memory. Short-term memory is important because it is the link to the task environment and is the location where human problem solving takes place. Short-term memory functions as an information filter because the task environment is complicated, continuous, and information rich, and short-term memory has limited storage capacity and processing capabilities. Short-term memory is composed of a language interpreter and the problem space. The language interpreter's function is to understand the problem. The problem space, which controls short-term memory, is the information processing system's representation of the task environment and is where actual problem solving occurs. The problem space has significant structure and size limitations. First, the problem space capacity is limited to approximately four to nine "chunks" (pieces) of information. These chunks are serially processed (one chunk at a time) from either the language interpreter or long-term memory. Second, problem space processes information serially which is a severe limitation to processing speed.

Long-term memory can be thought of as a large database, called semantic memory, with an indexing system composed of recognition memory and associative structures. Semantic memory has unlimited storage capacity; however, the serial recognition memory indexing system is slow and tedious. Associative memory establishes quicker "smart" shortcuts to the semantic information and associative links from among the semantic information.

Simon (1978) states that this general model of human information processing is robust for both novice and expert problem solvers who are solving both well-structured and ill-structured problems. However, significant differences between novice and expert information processing systems exist. In short-term memory, an expert forms larger and richer data chunks (sometimes referred to as nested chunks) which expands the processing capabilities of the problem space.

Novices access semantic memory through the slow, serial recognition memory index. Experts develop associative structures that provide efficient indexing, list structures, and intelligent links between information. Novices have not yet developed that store of knowledge from which to draw information.

Because of the limited amount of storage and processing capacity in short-term memory, humans develop simplifying cognitive shortcuts or production rules to solve complex problems. These simplifying production rules are commonly know as cognitive heuristics or simply heuristics. Although heuristic behavior is an efficient means of information processing, heuristic behavior can lead to systematic error (judgmental bias).

For example, an experienced appraiser valuing a residential property located in a mature neighborhood may skip steps in the normative valuation process, such as the market analysis, highest and best use, and/or land value opinion, and proceed directly to the sales comparison approach. If any unusual market indications are found in the comparable sales data, the appraiser might return to prior steps in the valuation process and consider further investigation into the market area or possibly a change in highest and best use.

Departure from the normative valuation model is not erroneous; in fact, departure is the result of experience and expertise development. A student appraiser attempting to value a mature residential property for the first time does appear to carefully follow each step in the normative valuation process, possibly giving equal time and careful consideration to all steps. After a semester of work, the student may produce an impressive valuation report, however this slow and systematic approach will not prosper in a competitive business environment.

The expert appraiser realizes that the key to the mature residential property valuation assignment is the sales comparison approach and focuses on the critical sales data and the sales comparison valuation technique. Through experience and education, the appraiser develops efficient production rules or heuristics that simplify the valuation problem (i.e., when facing a residential valuation assignment in a mature neighborhood, place primary focus on the sales comparison approach and return to prior steps in the valuation process if warranted). Although the expert appraiser has developed an efficient production rule, the appraiser may miss an important demographic trend or change in highest and best use by not proceeding systematically through the normative process step-by-step.

Tversky and Kahneman (1974) identify several different types of cognitive heuristics often employed in problem solving. Representativeness, availability, and anchoring and adjustment are examples of common cognitive heuristics identified by Tversky and Kahneman. Although humans can employ any combination of heuristics, the anchoring and adjustment heuristic has been ubiquitous in many problem-solving situations. Generally, anchoring occurs in situations where people make value judgements by starting from some initial value (a reference point) and make adjustments from that point to yield a final answer. Typically, insufficient adjustments are made to the anchor and as a result lead to judgmental bias. In a valuation context, anchoring occurs when an appraiser relies (or anchors) on some reference point, for example a pending contract sale price, and fails to make sufficient adjustments from that anchor.

Hogarth (1981) argues that the conditions under which dysfunctional, judgmental heuristics are found need to be clearly identified. Tversky and Kahneman's experiments used novice subjects solving simple, discrete problems. In a discrete experiment, subjects are presented a problem and asked to commit to a solution. However, in the natural environment, problem solving occurs in steps, commitment to a solution is a gradual process as alternatives are explored and information is gathered. The problem solver learns and develops expertise from redundancy (experience) and feedback. Humans operate in a dynamic, continuous environment; and interaction between organism and environment is critical for successful performance. Hogarth states, "several biases revealed through such discrete evaluations are, in fact, indicative of mechanisms that are functional in more prevalent continuous environments."[4]

It is important to emphasize that the limitations on human information problem solving identified by Simon, Newell, and Hogarth and the findings of Tversky and Kahneman that humans tend to compensate for these cognitive limitations by the use of heuristic behavior apply to *all* humans, not to real estate appraisers in particular. Heuristic behavior has been found in the problem solving behaviors of a variety of subject groups from card players to physicians making medical diagnoses.[5] The psychology literature primarily uses novices, often students, solving relatively simple problems. Diaz et al. have built upon this literature by using expert problem solvers (appraisers) solving complex problems (a valuation assignment).

1.3 Human Problem Solving Research Methodologies

Behavioral valuation researchers have employed three distinct research methods in studying problem solving in a real estate valuation context: process tracing,[6] controlled experiments, and field surveys. Table 1 provides an overview of the methodologies and samples used in behavioral real estate valuation research.

Gallimore (1994, 1996), Kinnard et al. (1997), Wolverton and Gallimore (1999), Levy and Schuck (1999), and Wolverton (2000) surveyed or interviewed appraisers to investigate bias in the valuation process. As identified in Table 1, the survey methodology can generate large sample sizes. The large sample size surveys are conducted by mail. Levy and Schuck (1999)

Table 1: Overview of Research Methods and Samples Used in Behavioral Real Estate Valuation Literature

Methodology	Author(s)/Date	Sample
Survey	Gallimore (1994)	Experiment 1: 210 expert English valuers
Survey	Gallimore (1996)	Experiment 2: 221 expert English valuers 41 expert English valuers
Survey	Kinnard et al. (1997)	927 expert appraisers
Survey	Wolverton/Gallimore (1999)	376 expert appraisers
Survey/Interviews	Levy/Schuck (1999)	5 expert New Zealand valuers
Survey	Wolverton (2000)	293 expert appraisers
Controlled experiment/ process tracing	Diaz (1990a,b)	12 residential expert appraisers and 12 novices
Controlled experiment	Wolverton (1996)	24 expert residential appraisers
Controlled experiment	Gallimore/Wolverton (1997)	16 expert residential American appraisers and 16 expert residential English valuers
Controlled experiment	Northcraft/Neale (1987)	Experiment 1: 48 novices; 21 sales agents Experiment 2: 54 novices; 47 sales agents
Controlled experiment	Diaz (1997)	28 apprentices and 30 expert commercial appraisers
Controlled experiment	Diaz/Hansz (1997)	44 expert commercial appraisers
Controlled experiment	Diaz/Wolverton (1998)	30 expert commercial appraisers
Controlled experiment	Hansz/Diaz (2001)	40 expert commercial appraisers

conducted in-depth face-to-face interviews, explaining the smaller sample size. The survey is a useful tool for identifying attitudes, opinions, and states of being which may lead to potential areas of fruitful research; however, no manipulation or treatment is made to the subjects so inferences regarding causality are not possible. Also, one has to carefully consider the possibility of non-response bias and who actually complete these surveys (i.e., the actual appraiser identified in the sample frame or the appraiser's assistant).

Process tracing, another research method, attempts to follow the thought processes, typically through verbal protocol, information boards, or eye fixation techniques. However, these techniques have been criticized for interrupting and altering natural cognitive processes. Requiring subjects to verbalize their thought process or to frame a problem in an information board is likely to alter behavior. Additionally, wearing iris-tracing headgear is awkward for the subjects, makes the subjects fully aware of an experimental setting, and is of significant expense to the researcher. Another criticism of process tracing is that no inference testing is possible so it is limited to a case study methodology.

Diaz (1990a) used a process tracing methodology to test hypotheses that expert problem solvers do not follow normative models. Diaz overcame the limitations of process tracing by developing an alternate process tracing methodology, consisting of a system of folders, and creating a statistical test. The folder system eliminated the need for intrusive verbal protocol and impractical eye tracing. Subjects were asked to solve an appraisal problem and could request information as needed. The data required to solve the problems was held for the subjects in a series of folders. Diaz traced the thought process in experimental sessions by carefully recording the sequence of information requested in these experimental sessions.

Transition scores were used to measure degree of adherence to the normative model. Subject scores were aggregated to establish an observed cumulative distribution of transition scores. With statistical comparisons, Diaz made inferences to the experiment's population of expert problem solvers. With creative protocol collection methods and the development of a statistical test, process tracing in a controlled experimental setting has become an established method in behavioral valuation research for measuring departure from the normative valuation process.

Controlled experiments have been the method of choice for most behavioral valuation research. Wolverton (1996), Diaz (1990a,b), Diaz and Hansz (1997), Diaz and Wolverton (1998), Gallimore (1994), and Hansz and Diaz (2001) all used controlled experiments. An experiment has three basic components, a research instrument, a random sample, and a manipulation.

The research instrument in these studies is typically a valuation case containing information appraisers typically use in their normal course of business. For example, the valuation case used in Hansz and Diaz (2001) was thirteen pages and included many exhibits and photographs. This particular case, with vacant industrial land as the subject property, was divided into five sections: Identification of the Subject, Purpose of the Appraisal, Neighborhood Data (including neighborhood map), Property Data (including subject plat and subject photos), and Comparable Land Sales (including descriptions of five comparable sales, a sales map, and comparable sales photos).

A sampling frame is developed from a population of expert appraisers. "Experts" are differentiated from novices by screening potential participants for a certain number of years of valuation experience or the acquisition of an advanced appraisal designation or degree. A random sample is taken from the sampling frame and the selected appraisers are contacted and asked to participate. Typically, the researcher travels to the appraisers place of business to administer the experiment.

Participants are also randomly assigned to *either* a control or treatment group. The control group receives the experimental valuation case exclusively. This group is the benchmark for comparison to a treatment group, or groups. In addition to the experimental valuation case, the treatment group receives an additional piece of information, a manipulation, before or during the experiment. An example of manipulation used in a past study is a pending contract price on a subject property (Wolverton, 1996).

Because the information the participants receive is carefully controlled and all participants are randomly assigned to groups, the researcher can attribute differences between the control group's typical response and the treatment group's typical response (as measured by the mean or median). Because the experiment is carefully designed to control extraneous variability, evaluative statistical methods are quiet straight forward. Typically, simple parametric and non-parametric tests are used to compare measures of central tendency between groups. With a carefully constructed experiment, a researcher can randomly assign participants to groups and control exogenous influences. Therefore, controlled experiments can establish strong causal relationships between manipulation and response.

Criticisms of controlled experiments focus on issues of external validity, claiming that results using "laboratory" data may not be generalized across settings, persons, and times. Cook and Campbell (1976) explain that tradeoffs exist between validities, "some ways of increasing one kind of validity will decrease another kind." They emphasize the importance of internal validity in experiments:

> Since experiments are conducted to make causal statements, internal validity assumes a particular importance because it relates to whether a relationship – of whatever strength – is unambiguously causal or not. The primacy of internal validity does not stand out where true experiments are concerned because the random allocation procedure rules out almost all the experiment threats.[7]

Controlled experiments are necessary to establish internal validity even though external validity maybe limited. Sacrificing some degree of generalization to a population in order to establish a solid causal relationship is a prudent tradeoff at this stage of the behavioral research paradigm. Furthermore, the experimental instruments used are carefully designed to have a high degree of fidelity to the appraisers natural work environment.

1.4 Behavioral Real Estate Valuation Literature

Behavioral, real-estate-valuation literature is classified as follows: departures from normative models Diaz (1990a), selection of comparable sales

[Diaz (1990b), Wolverton (1996), Wolverton and Gallimore (1997)], bias in value estimates [Northcraft and Neale (1987), Diaz (1997), Diaz and Hansz (1997), Diaz and Wolverton (1998), Gallimore (1994), and Gallimore (1996)], and client valuation feedback issues [Kinnard et al. (1997), Wolverton and Gallimore (1997), Levy and Schuck (1999), Wolverton (2000), and Hansz and Diaz (2001)]. Table 2 provides an overview of this behavioral real estate literature.

Departure from normative models. Diaz (1990a) investigated the practical use of the normative appraisal process by expert residential real estate appraisers in both familiar and unfamiliar settings (task environment). The research hypothesis was that expert appraisers would deviate from the normative appraisal process when solving valuation problems. By using a process tracing methodology in an experimental setting (previously described), strong support was found for the research hypothesis in both familiar and unfamiliar geographical settings.

Diaz formulated a descriptive five-step residential appraisal model: (1) appraisal objective, (2) description of the subject site and improvements, (3) comparable sales selection, (4) sales comparison approach, and (5) reconciliation or final value judgement. Experts skipped steps in the normative appraisal process, using optional information only if needed. Furthermore, experts reversed the prescribed order of data selection. The normative model suggests a general-to-the-specific data collection strategy (for example, collection of regional, neighborhood, and site/improvements data, respectively). However, experts used a more efficient specific-to-general data selection strategy (for example, requesting site and improvement information and referencing regional or neighborhood information only if needed).

The importance of the Diaz (1990) study is twofold. First, it established that expert appraisers deviate from the normative appraisal model, and it proposes an initial descriptive model. This finding provides the foundation for subsequent descriptive research of appraiser behavior (and behavior of other real estate professionals). Second, this study made contributions to the process tracing methodology (previously noted).

Comparable sale selection. Diaz (1990b) investigated how novice and expert residential appraisers select comparable sales. The experimental task was a residential valuation problem. The researcher held twelve sales grouped into four sets (three sales per set) and subjects were free to request any sales data set as needed. Diaz found that novice appraisers examined more sales data (3.58 sets per novice), as compared to experts (2.96 sets per expert). Novices used cognitively demanding search strategies (for example, adjusting all sales) and postponed final selection judgement until they had examined all sales. Experts used a less cognitively demanding selection strategy and

Table 2: Overview of Behavioral Literature in Real Estate

Subject	Author(s)/Date	Findings
Departure from normative models	Diaz (1990a)	Residential appraisers depart from the normative appraisal process.
Comparable sale selection	Diaz (1990b)	Expert residential appraisers search strategy differs from novices in nature and amount of data examined. Experts use screening strategies and examine less data as compared to novices.
Comparable sale selection	Wolverton (1996)	Prior knowledge of sale price influences the selection of comparable sales resulting in comparable sale selection bias by residential appraisers.
Comparable sale selection	Gallimore/Wolverton (1997)	Cross cultural comparison of English valuers and American appraisers. Valuers are highly susceptible to sale price knowledge, but exhibit sales selection bias to a lesser degree than appraisers in a residential appraisal problem.
Bias in valuations (anchoring)	Northcraft/Neale (1987)	Students and real estate agents are influenced by list price knowledge in a "real world" residential setting.
Bias in valuations (anchoring/recency)	Gallimore (1994)	Evidence of anchoring and *recency* effects in valuation judgement.
Bias in valuations (confirmation bias)	Gallimore (1996)	Survey of English valuers investigated confirmation bias. No evidence found.
Bias in valuations (anchoring)	Diaz (1997)	No evidence that expert commercial appraisers are influenced by the previous value judgements of anonymous experts in areas of geographic familiarity.

Bias in valuations (anchoring)	Diaz/Hansz (1997)	Found evidence that expert commercial appraisers operating in areas of geographic uncertainty do rely on previous judgements of anonymous experts.
Bias in valuations (anchoring)	Diaz/Wolverton (1999)	Expert commercial appraisers make insufficient temporal adjustments when re-appraising or updating a prior value judgement. Anchoring on a previous value judgement contributes to appraisal smoothing.
Client valuation feedback	Kinnard et al. (1997)	Survey of appraisers found evidence of client pressure in appraisal assignments.
Client valuation feedback	Wolverton/Gallimore (1999)	Survey of appraisers found the client valuation feedback has significant impact on appraiser's role perception.
Client valuation feedback	Levy/Schuck (1999)	Interviews with New Zealand valuers confirm existence of client pressure in task environment and suggest primary factors affecting the degree of client influence.
Client valuation Feedback	Wolverton (2000)	Survey of appraisers to develop a structural model of the client feedback/role perception constructs developed in Wolverton/Gallimore (1999) and Levy/Schuck (1999).
Client valuation feedback	Hansz/Diaz (2001)	Pervasive agent-client concerns may subconsciously over-sensitize appraisers to valuation judgments which are "too low" compared to those which are "too high."

focused on key attributes (such as location). Furthermore, experts appeared to use a multiple stage selection strategy. First, a compensatory search was used to look for one or two of the best sales in the first data set examined. Second, a non-compensatory screen was employed to compare these "best" sales to other candidate sales. Diaz concluded that expert appraisers develop shortcuts or heuristics in comparable sales selection, and, over time, these heuristics become subconscious production rules imbedded in the problem-solving schema. Although heuristics can be an efficient means of information processing, these shortcuts may cause appraisers to overlook relevant comparable sales data and can lead to systematic bias.

Wolverton (1996) examined the impact of pending sales price knowledge on comparable sales selection by expert residential appraisers. The control group was presented a valuation case and asked to select the three best sales from 15 candidate comparable sales. An experimental group was presented the same case with one additional piece of information – a hypothetical pending sale price. He gave a third group the same valuation task and a hypothetical list price (and no hypothetical pending sale price). Sales data was arranged so that the sales most similar to the subject property's pending sale price and listing price were most dissimilar in terms of physical features. Wolverton found strong evidence supporting the research hypothesis that knowledge of the subject property sale price will bias comparable sales selection by expert appraisers. The biasing influence of sale price knowledge has important policy implications because the Uniform Standards of Professional Appraisal Practice (USPAP) require lenders to give appraisers the pending contract sale price prior to performing the appraisal. No statistically significant evidence was found for the premise that listing price knowledge affects comparable sale selection.

Ancillary to his research hypotheses, Wolverton found that the control group selected most of the same comparable sales with little variation. However, when a hypothetical pending sale or listing price was introduced, a greater variety of sales were selected.

Gallimore and Wolverton (1997) extended the Wolverton (1996) investigation by looking at cultural differences in the sale selection strategy of American *appraisers* and English *valuers*. A replication of the Wolverton (1996) study was conducted using English valuers.

American *appraisers* and English *valuers* operate in different task environments. First, appraisers use pre-approved standardized summary forms (the Uniform Residential Appraisal Report) to report values. On this form, the comparable sales are identified and described and adjustments explicitly reported. Conversely, valuers have minimal reporting requirements. Valuers rarely identify or described comparable sales and adjustments are not explicitly reported. Second, American appraisers have access to data from Multiple Listing Services (MLS). Because most American residential properties are sold through a multiple listing, these databases provide a comprehensive sample of market data. Valuers have no databases comparable to the American MLS. English lenders and valuers keep separate in-house transaction databases. English residential sales data is scarce and fragmented; therefore, valuers operate in a data poor environment relative to Americans. Third, English lenders are not required by law to provide a pending sale price to the appraiser.

Sale price knowledge significantly influenced the English valuers. Statistical differences were found between the control (no prior sale price knowledge) and treatment groups (prior sale price knowledge) in both comparable sale selection and final value estimate. These results were similar to the findings for American appraisers. However, valuers' sale selection bias was weaker than the appraisers' sale selection bias and the valuers' final value estimate bias was stronger than the appraisers' final value estimate bias. When estimating market value, valuers anchored heavily on the contract sale price but were only moderately biased in their selection of comparable sales. Conversely, prior sale price knowledge moderately biased value estimates by appraisers but their sales selection bias was quite high. Finally, the valuers examined far fewer sales than the appraisers.

It should be noted that this quasi-experiment consists of intact groups (valuers and appraisers) and does not control for all possible differences between these two groups (i.e. differences in public education systems, differences in professional licensing requirements, etc.). However, a tenable explanation for differences between valuer behavior and appraiser behavior is attributed to differences in the task environment. The valuers, having minimal reporting requirements and operating in a data poor environment, are not as concerned with the link between comparable data and value estimate. Valuers are accustomed to working with poor sales data and making large adjustments. When selecting comparable sales, valuers appear to "satisfice" or settle with the data provided where appraisers are more concerned with the relationship between comparable sales and the value estimate. These findings suggest that the data environment and reporting requirements influence the appraisal process.

Bias in valuations. Two psychologists, Northcraft and Neale (1987), conducted an experiment to investigate the robustness of the anchoring and adjustment heuristic in laboratory settings using simple, discrete problems. The "real world" problem selected was to estimate the value of a residential house. The research hypothesis was that subjects' would anchor on listing price and fail to make sufficient adjustments to arrive at market value. A second research hypothesis stated that the biasing influence of the listing price on estimates of market value would decrease as the listing price becomes a less credible reference point. In other words, the listing price will lose credibility as a legitimate anchor as the list price is set very high or low from market value.

Participants, comprised of undergraduate business students and volunteer real estate sales agents, were transported to a residential neighborhood to inspect an actual house and comparable sale properties. The treatment variable was the list price at four levels, low-price, moderately low-price, moderately high-price, and high-price. Researchers found that list price knowledge did have a strong biasing influence on both groups – undergraduate business majors and real estate sales agents. Furthermore, findings were consistent among all four list price levels. Northcraft and Neale stated that, "These findings clearly point to the importance of laboratory findings on biases and heuristics – even to theorizing about decision behavior in considerably more information-rich, real world settings."[8] This conclusion is well justified by their experimental results; however, the authors are on less-solid solid ground when they extend their discussion to examine problem-solving differences between novices and experts in general.

Novices were operationalized as "undergraduate business students" and experts as "real estate sales agents." Real estate sales agents, experts in marketing real estate, are not experts in valuing real estate. The typical real estate agent is neither trained in the appraisal process nor has substantial appraisal experience. Therefore, real estate sales agents cannot be considered "expert" problem solvers in a valuation context. Northcraft and Neale confounded expert and novice problem solving behavior with two levels of novice problem solving behavior and their discussion of novice versus expert behavior must be discounted.

Gallimore (1994) investigated anchoring and data presentation effects in a survey distributed to English valuers. He found strong evidence of anchoring and a data presentation order effect known as recency. The recency effect suggests that when data is provided sequentially, the most recent data is given the greatest weight. Valuers gave the greatest weight to recent positive supporting evidence. Gallimore (1996) investigated confirmation bias in a survey of English valuers. Confirmation bias is when valuers form an initial 'gut feeling' opinion of value in the early stages of the appraisal process and seek information to confirm that initial estimate. Gallimore concluded that the case for confirmation bias remains unproven.

Diaz (1997), Diaz and Hansz (1997), and Diaz and Wolverton (1998) defined, or operationalized, a valuation expert as an appraiser who holds the MAI (Member of the Appraisal Institute) designation to study the appraisal smoothing phenomena in valuation based real estate return indices. These research questions were addressed:

- Diaz (1997) addressed the question, do expert appraisers anchor on an anonymous expert opinion in areas of geographic familiarity?
- Diaz and Hansz (1997) addressed the question, do expert appraisers anchor on an anonymous expert opinion in areas of geographic unfamiliarity?

- Diaz and Wolverton (1998) addressed the question, do expert appraisers anchor on their own previous value judgements?

To test the first two questions, Diaz (1997) designed a valuation task involving the valuation of a vacant industrial parcel of land in Atlanta, Georgia. The 15-page self-contained valuation problem consists of the following sections: problem statement, worksheet, identification of the subject property, purpose of the appraisal, neighborhood data, property data, and comparable sale data (five sales). The prices of the five comparable sales ranged from $80,187 to $90,006 on a price per acre basis with a mean and median of $85,061 and $85,001, respectively. Diaz designed the transaction data so no obvious patterns in the data existed. For example, the highest and lowest per acre sale prices were assigned to the two tracts most similar to the subject property. The control group received a valuation case and no additional information (the no reference point group). The treatment group received the same valuation case and a letter of transmittal from an anonymous expert (MAI) stating that a MAI recently appraised the property for $88,000 per acre (the reference point group).

He administered the case to 28 apprentice (novice) appraisers and 30 expert commercial appraisers practicing in the Atlanta area (geographic familiarity). The results indicated differences between the treatment and control group means for both apprentices and experts; however, these differences were not statistically significant. These findings led to the conclusion that expert appraisers, operating in an area of geographic familiarity, do not rely on anonymous value estimates of other experts. This finding is consistent with normative behavior, because appraisers are taught to form their own independent value estimates.

Diaz and Hansz (1997) replicated Diaz (1997) but used expert commercial appraisers *unfamiliar* with the Atlanta market. In this study, a significant difference was found between the control and treatment groups that led to the conclusion that the previous value judgements of anonymous experts did influence appraisers operating in unfamiliar geographic areas. Combining the findings from the two studies, it appears that geographic unfamiliarity increases the complexity of the valuation problem (a more ill-structured problem). Subsequently, appraisers are more likely to rely on the opinion of an anonymous expert to deal with this greater uncertainty.

Diaz and Wolverton (1998) recruited 30 expert commercial appraisers to participate in a longitudinal study. The appraisers were asked to provide a value estimate from a case involving a residential apartment complex in a geographically unfamiliar area (Phoenix, Arizona). Six months later, the appraisers were asked to reappraise the property. The second valuation case had some updated information reflecting changing economic conditions in the market. A control group was also asked to value only the second, updated case. The authors attribute differences between the two groups to the reappraisal group anchoring on their previous value judgement. The reappraisal group anchored on their initial value estimate and made insufficient adjustments to reflect changing market conditions. The findings from these three studies suggest the existence of a behavioral component of appraisal smoothing phenomena.

Client valuation feedback. Kinnard et al. (1997) and Wolverton and Gallimore (1999) surveyed appraisers to investigate the effects of client valuation feedback on the appraisal process. Kinnard surveyed MAI designated commercial real estate appraisers to measure the amount of client pressure they perceived in their task environment. The survey explored the nature and frequency of client pressure. Kinnard developed a scenario where a hypothetical client (lender) was requesting an adjustment to a value estimate and the appraisers were asked to change a value estimate. Forty-one percent of the subjects revised the value conclusions when requested to do so by clients. The appraiser's decision to readjust was significantly and directly related to client size but not significantly related to the size of the adjustment requested. The results of this survey suggest that appraisers feel pressure to support a pending contract sale price as opposed to providing an unbiased opinion of market value.

Wolverton and Gallimore (1999) identified three possible forms of client feedback: environmental perception feedback, coercive feedback, and positive reinforcement of the normative appraisal model. The survey samples were composed of Appraisal Institute designated appraisers and non-designated appraisers listed on a national appraisal registry. The appraisers perceived that the *clients (lenders)* viewed the appraiser's role in the lending process as that of validating the pending sale price. Generally, appraisers did not perceive *their own* role as validating pending sale price. However, appraisers receiving high levels of environmental perception feedback and coercive feedback represent a sub-population who is more likely to perceive its role as loan validators and depart from normative training. Conversely, positive reinforcement feedback has a constructive impact on the appraiser's role perception, and appraisers receiving high levels of positive reinforcement represent a sub-population who has not abandoned its normative training. This study suggests that feedback from the environment influences appraiser behavior and the valuation process. Furthermore, the type of feedback can discourage or reinforce normative behavior.

Levy and Schuck (1999) conducted in-depth interviews with five senior New Zealand Registered Valuers to investigate the client influence on valuations. This study confirmed the anecdotal evidence that client pressure does exist in New Zealand. Furthermore, the authors suggest elements of client influence or primary factors affecting the degree of client influence. These elements include the type of client, characteristics of the valuer and valuation firm, purpose of the valuation, and information endowments of clients and valuers.

Wolverton (2000) found many consistencies between the role perception and feedback constructs explored in Wolverton and Gallimore (1999) and the elements of client influence developed by Levy and Schuck (1999). Using findings from both of these previous studies, he developed an initial descriptive structural model of the relationship between client influence and appraiser behavior, and urges further research on this complex relationship.

Hansz and Diaz (2001) set up a series of experiments to examine the impact of transaction price feedback on valuation judgment. Among expert appraisers participating as subjects, evidence of asymmetrical response was found. The expert group receiving transaction price feedback indicating that current judgments were "too low" responded with judgments in subsequent, unrelated valuations that were significantly higher than the expert group that received no feedback. The response from "too high" feedback was in the expected direction (lower value judgments) but was not significant. Pervasive agent-client concerns may subconsciously over-sensitize appraisers to valuation judgments which are "too low" compared to those which are "too high."

Summary of human behavioral real estate research. The literature reviewed in this section extends the human problem solving research from using novices solving simple problems to real estate appraisers operating in complex and real world environments. Research into the behavior of real estate appraisers has found that appraisers depart from normative models and demonstrate heuristic behavior.

The anchoring and adjustment heuristic has been robust in real estate valuation problem solving. Expert appraisers anchor early in the appraisal process and search for confirming data. Evidence has been found that appraisers anchor on pending contract sale price, biasing comparable sale selection and subsequent final value estimates. No evidence was found in an early study that appraisers operating in areas of geographic familiarity anchor on an anonymous expert opinion. However, a subsequent study indicated that geographic unfamiliarity may trigger the use of an anonymous expert opinion as a reference point, and, from Diaz and Wolverton (1998), appraisers fail to make sufficient adjustment from their own previous value estimates. This failure to make a sufficient adjustment leads to bias and may contribute to appraisal smoothing. Preliminary findings concerning the recency effect in data presentation and confirmation bias warrants additional research in these areas of valuation problem-solving behavior.

Kinnard et al. (1997), Wolverton and Gallimore (1999), Levy and Schuck (1999), and Wolverton (2000) have used surveys and interviews to establish that client feedback is a part of the appraiser's task environment and has implications for appraiser behavior and the valuation process. Hansz and Diaz (2001) found evidence that client feedback may over-sensitize appraisers to arriving at judgments that result in "low" value estimates. Appendix C provides a complete overview of both the methodologies and samples from Table 1 and a summary of the research findings from Table 2.

1.5 Conclusion and Potential Areas for Future Behavioral Valuation Research

Conclusion. The attractiveness of the Appraisal Institute's prescribed eight-step normative valuation model is its simplicity. Behavioral research into how expert appraisers actually do their work indicates that appraisers do not follow the normative valuation model and a descriptive valuation model or models may be complex. A descriptive model should consider the following behavioral findings.

- More experienced appraisers develop shortcuts and screening strategies compared to the structured and systematic approaches employed by novices.
- Geographic familiarity appears to be an important determinant in appraiser behavior, as appraisers operating outside of their area of geographic expertise appear to be susceptible to potential anchors.
- Pending sales price knowledge appears to influence residential appraisers comparable sale selection.
- Coercive client feedback appears to influence the appraiser's role perception and over-sensitize the appraiser to potentially low value estimates.
- Evidence from a cross-cultural comparative study indicates that a behavioral model of American appraisers may not be transferable to British valuers.

A descriptive model may first be dependent on the appraiser's level of experience and familiarity with the local market. The regulatory environment appears to have an impact on appraiser behavior, for example, current banking regulations, requiring the lender to report a pending sale price, tends to influence the appraiser's valuation process and may have unintended policy consequences. The agent-client relationship may influence the appraiser's role perception and subsequent judgment. Finally, cultural differences appear to influence the decision-making behavior. A descriptive model may include level of experience, geographic familiarity, regulatory environment, agent-client relationship, and culture.

These findings contribute to a better understanding of how appraisers actually do their work and make valuation judgments. Identifying conditions under which appraisers may be susceptible to judgmental bias is an important step toward understanding the valuation process and subsequently improving appraiser decision-making behavior.

Future research. Future behavioral studies will improve upon current data collection techniques, measurement instruments, investigate a variety of heuristic behaviors, and integrate and building upon the current behavioral body of knowledge. Behavioral experimental data collection techniques can be made more efficient. Experimental work requires primary data collection which is time consuming and costly. For example, recruiting and conducting an experiment with 40 appraisers can take several months devoted solely to data collection. Mail surveys increases efficiency but low response rates and instrument integrity are legitimate concerns. Advances in Internet and communication technologies will likely result in more efficient data collection techniques.

Improvement can be made in measurement instruments and research methodologies. Measurement instruments can be improved to simulate the appraiser's natural environment. An interesting approach to pursue is the use of field experiments in addition to the traditional self-contained paper cases. A field experiment must be carefully designed and implement to reduce potential contaminants. Most experiments, with the exception of the Diaz and Wolverton's (1998) longitudinal study and the Hansz and Diaz's (2001) experiment incorporating transaction price feedback, have utilized discrete problems. Future studies may use panel groups and incorporate feedback and redundancy into the experiments.

Most behavioral real estate valuation studies have focused on the anchoring and adjustment heuristic. Other heuristics such as representativeness, availability, and recency found in general human behavior and the cognitive psychology literature[9] have not been fully investigated in a real estate context. Behavioral perspectives such as over-reaction, over-confidence,[10] and sentiment[11] have received attention in the finance literature.[12] These human tendencies may have important implications for research concerning appraisers and other real estate decision-makers.

In an early study, Diaz (1990a) has proposed a general descriptive model of residential appraiser behavior. More recently, Wolverton (2000) developed an initial structural model of client influence on commercial appraiser behavior. With these exceptions, behavioral research has focused on very specific heuristic behaviors. The paradigm has progressed to the point that past discoveries, reviewed in this paper, can be linked to future studies in order to develop general models of how appraisers actually do their work.

Finally, behavioral research has spread to investigate the problem solving behavior of other real estate decision makers. This paper has focused exclusively on research concerning valuation issues and appraiser behavior. Other areas of real estate decision-making behavior have been pioneered. For example, Hardin (1997) conducted an interesting experiment with real estate lenders and Gallimore et al. (2000) have studied the decision-making behavior of property investors in the United Kingdom. There are certainly a multitude of real estate decision-making questions yet to be addressed and under-explored areas to study in this evolving research paradigm.

APPENDIX A: The Valuation Process

The eight steps in the "normative" valuation process are as follows:[13]

1. *Definition of the Problem*: identification of client/intended users, intended use of the appraisal, purpose of the appraisal (including definition of value), date of opinion of value, identification of characteristics of property (including location and property rights to be valued), extraordinary assumptions, hypothetical conditions.
2. *Scope of Work*
3. *Data Collection and Property Description*: Market Area Data (general characteristics of region, city, and neighborhood), Subject Property Data (specific characteristics of land and improvements, personal property, business assets, etc.), Comparable Property Data (sales, listings, offerings, vacancies, cost and depreciation, income and expenses, capitalization rates, etc.).
4. *Data Analysis*: Market Analysis (demand studies, supply studies, marketability studies), Highest and Best Use Analysis (site as though vacant, ideal improvement, property as improved).
5. *Land Value Opinion*
6. *Application of the Approaches to Value*: cost, sales comparison, income capitalization.
7. *Reconciliation of Value Indications and Final Opinion of Value*
8. *Report of Defined Value*

APPENDIX B: Simon's General Theory of Human Problem Solving

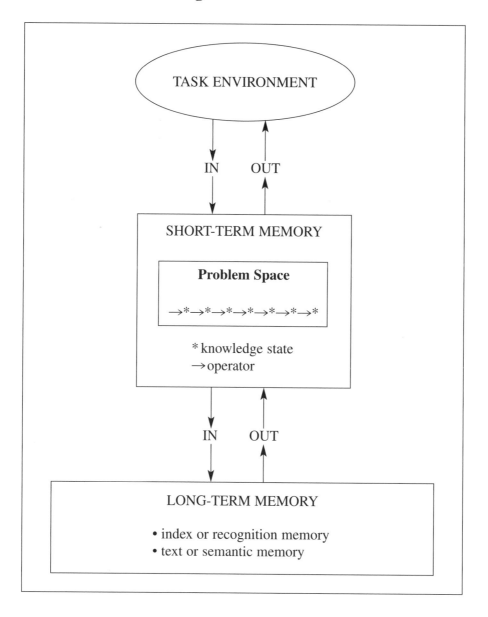

TASK ENVIRONMENT

IN   OUT

SHORT-TERM MEMORY

Problem Space

→*→*→*→*→*→*

* knowledge state
→ operator

IN   OUT

LONG-TERM MEMORY

• index or recognition memory
• text or semantic memory

APPENDIX C: Overview of Research Methods, Samples, and Behavioral Literature in Real Estate

Subject	Author(s)/Date	Methodology	Sample	Findings
Departure from normative models	Diaz (1990a)	Controlled experiment/process tracing	12 residential expert appraisers and 12 novices	Residential appraisers depart from the normative appraisal process.
Comparable sale selection	Diaz (1990b)	Controlled experiment/process tracing	12 residential expert appraisers and 12 novices	Expert residential appraisers search strategy differs from novices in nature and amount of data examined. Experts use screening strategies and examine less data as compared to novices.
Comparable sale selection	Wolverton (1996)	Controlled experiment	24 expert residential appraisers	Prior knowledge of sale price influences the selection of comparable sales resulting in comparable sale selection bias by residential appraisers.
Comparable sale selection	Gallimore/Wolverton (1997)	Controlled experiment	16 expert residential English valuers and 16 expert residential American appraisers	Cross cultural comparison of English valuers and American appraisers. Valuers are highly susceptible to sale price knowledge, but exhibit sales selection bias to a lesser degree in a residential appraisal problem.
Bias in valuations (anchoring)	Northcraft/Neale (1987)	Controlled experiment	Experiment 1: 48 novices and 21 sales agents; Experiment 2: 54 novices and 47 sales agents.	Students and real estate agents are influenced by list price knowledge in a 'real world' residential setting.

Topic	Author	Method	Sample	Findings
Bias in valuations (anchoring/recency)	Gallimore (1994)	Survey	Experiment 1: 210 expert English valuers; Experiment 2: 221 expert English valuers.	Evidence of anchoring and recency effects in valuation judgement.
Bias in valuations (confirmation bias)	Gallimore (1996)	Survey	41 expert English valuers	Survey of English valuers investigating confirmation bias. No evidence found.
Bias in valuations (anchoring)	Diaz (1997)	Controlled experiment	28 apprentices and 30 expert commercial appraisers	No evidence that expert commercial appraisers are influenced by the previous value judgements of anonymous experts in areas of geographic familiarity.
Bias in valuations (anchoring)	Diaz/Hansz (1997)	Controlled experiment	44 expert commercial appraisers	Evidence that expert commercial appraisers operating in areas of geographic uncertainty do rely on previous judgements of anonymous experts.
Bias in valuations (anchoring)	Diaz/Wolverton (1998)	Controlled experiment	30 expert commercial appraisers	Expert commercial appraisers make insufficient temporal adjustments when re-appraising or updating a prior value judgement. Anchoring on a previous value judgement contributes to appraisal smoothing.
Client valuation feedback	Kinnard et al. (1997)	Survey	927 expert appraisers	Survey of appraisers found evidence of client pressure in appraisal assignments.

APPENDIX C: (*Continued*)

Subject	Author(s)/Date	Methodology	Sample	Findings
Client valuation feedback	Wolverton/Gallimore (1998)	Survey	376 expert appraisers	Survey of appraisers found the client valuation feedback has significant impact on appraiser's role perception.
Client valuation feedback	Levy/Schuck (1999)	Survey	5 expert New Zealand valuers	Interviews with New Zealand valuers confirm existence of political pressure in task environment and suggest primary factors affecting the degree of client influence.
Client valuation feedback	Wolverton (2000)	Survey	293 expert appraisers	Survey of appraiser to develop a structural model of the client feedback/role perception constructs developed in Wolverton/Gallimore (1999) and Levy/Schuck (1999).
Client valuation feedback	Hansz/Diaz (2001)	Controlled experiment	40 expert commercial appraisers	Pervasive agent-client concerns may subconsciously over-sensitize appraisers to valuation judgments which are "too low" compared to those which are "too high."

NOTES

[1] *The Appraisal of Real Estate, 12th* Edition is organized following the normative valuation model and Chapter 4, pages 49 to 66, is dedicated to describing the valuation process.

[2] Appraisal Institute. *The Appraisal of Real Estate 11th Edition.* Chicago, IL: Appraisal Institute, 1996, p. 80.

[3] For a discussion of the framework and philosophy of the behavioral research paradigm see Diaz (1993). Also, see Diaz (1999) for an overview of the behavioral research findings from the first decade of behavioral research.

[4] Hogarth, p. 204.

[5] For example, see H. H. Keren. (1987). "Facing Uncertainty in the Game of Bridge: A Calibration Study." *Organizational Behavior and Human Decision Processes* 39, 98–114; and J. J. J. Christensen-Szalanski and J. B. Bushyhead (1981). "Physicians' Use of Probabilistic Information in Real Clinical Settings." *Journal of Experimental Psychology: Human Perception and Performance* 7, 928–935.

[6] To date, real estate behavioral researchers have used the process tracing methodology only in a controlled experimental setting. An exciting area for advancement of the paradigm would be to employ the process tracing methodology in a field experiment.

[7] Cook and Campbell, p. 245.

[8] Northcraft and Neale, p. 95.

[9] For example, see Daniel Kahneman and Amos Tversky. (1982). *Judgment Under Uncertainty: Heuristics and Biases,* New York: Cambridge University Press; and Sarah Lichtenstein and Baruch Fischhoff. (1977). "Do Those Who Know More Also Know More About How Much They Know?" *Organizational Behavior and Human Performance* 20, 159–183.

[10] For example, see Werner F. M. De Bondt and Richard H. Thaler. (1987). "Does the Stock Market Overreact?" *Journal of Finance* 40, 793–808; and Kent D. Daniel, David Hirshleifer, and Avanidhar Subrahmanyam (1998). "Investor Psychology and Security Market Under- and Over-reactions." *Journal of Finance* 53, 1839–1886.

[11] For example, see Nicholas Barberis, Andrei Shleifer, and Robbert Vishny. (1998). "A Model of Investory Sentiment." *Journal of Financial Economics* 49, 307–343.

[12] For an overview of behavioral research in finance see Hersh Shefrin. (2000). *Beyond Greed and Fear: Understanding Behavioral Finance and the Psychology of Investing,* Boston: Harvard Business School Press; Meir Statman. (1999). "Behavioral Finance: Past Answers and Future Questions." *Financial Analysts Journal* 55, 18–27; and Richard H. Thaler. (1993). *Advances in Behavioral Finance,* Russell Sage Foundation.

[13] Appraisal Institute. *The Appraisal of Real Estate 12th Edition.* Chicago, IL: Appraisal Institute, 2001, p. 51.

REFERENCES

Appraisal Institute. (1996). *The Appraisal of Real Estate 11th Edition.* Chicago, IL: Appraisal Institute.

Appraisal Institute. (2001). *The Appraisal of Real Estate 12th Edition.* Chicago, IL: Appraisal Institute.

Cook, Thomas and Donald Campbell. (1976). "The Design and Conduct of Quasi-Experiments and True Experiments in Field Settings." in Marvin Dunnette *The Handbook of Industrial and Organizational Psychology,* Chicago: Rand-McNally.

Diaz, Julian III. (1987). *Processing Tracing Investigation into Problem Solving within Residential Real Estate Appraisal*, Dissertation, Georgia State University.

——. (1990a). "How Appraisers Do Their Work: A Test of the Appraisal Process and the Development of a Descriptive Model." *The Journal of Real Estate Research* 5:1, 1–15.

——. (1990b). "The Process of Selecting Comparable Sales." *The Appraisal Journal* 58:4, 533–540.

——. (1993). "Science, Engineering and the Discipline of Real Estate." *Journal of Real Estate Literature* 1:2, 183–195.

——. (1997). "An Investigation into the Impact of Previous Expert Value Estimates on Appraisal Judgment." *Journal of Real Estate Research* 13:1, 57–66.

——. (1999). "The First Decade of Behavioral Research in the Discipline of Property." *Journal of Property Investment and Finance* 17:4, 326–332.

Diaz, Julian III and J. Andrew Hansz. (1997). "How Valuers Use the Value Opinions of Others." *Journal of Property Valuation and Investment* 15:3, 256–260.

——. (2001). "How Valuers Use the Value Opinions of Others." *Journal of Property Research* forthcoming.

Diaz, Julian III and Marvin L. Wolverton. (1998). "A Longitudinal Examination of the Appraisal Smoothing Hypothesis." *Real Estate Economics* 26:2, 349–358.

Gallimore, Paul. (1994). "Aspects of Information Processing in Valuation Judgment and Choice." *Journal of Property Research* 11:2, 97–110.

——. (1996). "Confirmation Bias in the Valuation Process: A Test for Corroborating Evidence." *Journal of Property Research* 13:4, 261–273.

Gallimore, Paul, J. Andrew Hansz, and Adelaide Gray. (2000). "Decision Making in Small Property Companies." *Journal of Property Valuation and Investment* 18:6, 602–612.

Gallimore, Paul and Marvin Wolverton. (1997). "Price-knowledge-induced Bias: A Cross-cultural Comparison." *Journal of Property Valuation and Investment* 15:3, 261–273.

Graaskamp, J. A. (1991). "The Failure of the Universities to Teach the Real Estate Process as an Interdisciplinary Art Form." in Jarchow, S.P. (Ed.), *Graaskamp on Real Estate* Washington D.C.: ULI-the Urban Land Institute.

Hansz, J. Andrew and Julian Diaz III. (2001) "Valuation Bias in Commercial Appraisal: A Transaction Price Feedback Experiment." *Real Estate Economics* 29:4, 553–565.

Hardin, William G., III. (1997). "Heuristic Use, Credit Constraints and Real Estate Lending." *Journal of Property Valuation and Investment* 15:3, 245–255.

Hogarth, Robin. (1981). "Beyond Discrete Biases: Functional and Dysfunctional Aspects of Judgment Heuristics." *Psychological Bulletin* 90, 197–217.

Kinnard, William N., Margarita M. Lenk, and Elaine M. Worzala. (1997). "Client Pressure in the Commercial Appraisal Industry: How Prevalent is It?" *Journal of Property Valuation & Investment* 15:3, 233–244.

Levy, Deborah and Edward Schuck. (1999). "The Influence of Clients on Valuations." *Journal of Property Valuation and Investment* 17:4, 380–400.

Newell, A. and Herbert Simon. (1972). *Human Problem Solving*, Englewood Cliffs, NJ: Prentice-Hall.

Northcraft, Gregory, and Margaret Neale. (1987). "Experts, Amateurs, and Real Estate: An Anchoring Perspective on Property Pricing Decisions." *Organizational Behavior and Human Decision Processes* 39:1, 84–97.

Ratcliff, R. U. (1972). *Valuation for Real Estate Decisions*, Santa Cruz, CA: Democrat Press.

Slovic, Paul and Sarah Lichtenstein. (1971). "Comparison of Bayesian and Regression Approaches to the Study of Information Processing and Judgement." *Organizational Behavior and Human Performance* 6:6, 649–744.

Schmutz, George L. (1941). *The Appraisal Process*, North Hollywood, CA. the author.

Simon, Herbert A. (1978). "Information-processing Theory of Human Problem Solving." in W. K. Estes, *Handbook of Learning and cognitive Processes: Vol.5: Human Information Processing* Hillsdale, NJ: Erlbaum, 271–295.

Tversky, A. and D. Kahneman. (1974). "Judgement Under Uncertainty: Heuristics and Biases." *Science* 185:4157, 1124–1131.

Wolverton, Marvin. (1996). Investigation into Price Knowledge Induced Comparable Sale Selection Bias, Dissertation. Georgia State University.

——. (2000). "Self-Perception of the Role of the Appraiser: Objective Opinions or Price Validation?" *The Appraisal Journal* 68:3, 272–282.

Wolverton, Marvin, and Paul Gallimore. (1999). "Client Feedback and the Role of the Appraiser." *Journal of Real Estate Research* 18:3, 415–432.

Chapter 2

Are Appraisers Statisticians?

R. Kelley Pace
*E.J. Ourso College of Business Administration, Louisiana State University,
Baton Rouge, Louisiana*

C.F. Sirmans
Center for Real Estate and Urban Economic Studies, Storrs, Connecticut

V. Carlos Slawson, Jr.
*E.J. Ourso College of Business Administration, Louisiana State University,
Baton Rouge, Louisiana*

2.1 Introduction

Traditional hedonic pricing models, based upon an impressive corpus of statistical and economic theory, often exhibit prediction errors with a standard deviation in the range of 28–50%.[1] In contrast, statistically challenged appraisers following *ad hoc* procedures often exhibit prediction errors with a standard deviation around 10%.[2] The juxtaposition of these purported facts suggests the fruitfulness of examining elements of appraisal practice from a statistical perspective. In this vein Pace and Gilley (1998) showed the grid adjustment estimator employed by appraisers is a restricted version of the simultaneous autoregressive (SAR) estimator from spatial statistics. They suggest spatial statistics provides a unifying intellectual framework for reconciling appraisal practices with statistical theory.[3]

For the hedonic pricing approach to perform optimally, a reasonable number of independent variables should model the dependent variable well enough to produce nearly independent regression residuals in large samples. The history of hedonic pricing, however, suggests a large number of variables can significantly affect the quality of model predictions. Attempts to simultaneously use many of the suggested variables lead to serious multicollinearity problems whereby the regression may predict adequately within the sample, but presents interpretation difficulties and may have trouble with ex-sample performance. Finally, data quality and quantity limit the specification of the hedonic pricing model. Many data sets may not contain all the relevant variables or may do so only for a portion of the observations (missing values). It requires few resources to accurately collect information on variables such as the number of bedrooms, but may strain resources to accurately collect information on variables measuring the quality of construction.

Statistics presents a continuum of choices between the specification of conditional mean (*i.e.*, in linear regression $X\beta$) and the dependence in the errors among observations. Conventional hedonic pricing concentrates solely upon specification of conditional mean while appraisers seemingly concentrate upon specification of the dependence among observations (*e.g.* selection of comparables).

Appraisers select comparables using a number of dimensions such as space, time, and physical characteristics such as the number of bedrooms, number of bathrooms, and age. As a simplified characterization of their activities, appraisers prefer to select comparables located as close as possible to the subject property subject to the constraints that the comparables sold within recent months, match the number of subject bedrooms, match the number of subject bathrooms, and do not differ greatly in age from the subject. In section 2.2, we develop a simple model of multi-dimensional dependence among observations mimicking some of these key elements of appraiser behavior.

Having developed an alternative means of estimating house prices based upon the multi-dimensional dependence among observations, we proceed in section 2.2 to contrast the performance of that approach versus the more conventional hedonic pricing models. If modeling the multi-dimensional dependence among observations produces superior performance relative to hedonic pricing models, this would aid in the understanding of conventional appraisal practice. As an alternative perspective, we believe that real estate appraisers have gradually developed effective techniques for processing real estate information. We wish to develop a statistical model incorporating some of these tested techniques.

Specifically, in section 2.3 we conduct a number of empirical specification comparisons using data from Baton Rouge. First, we examine the predictive performance of both a very simple (two parameter) and a very complicated (98 parameter) hedonic pricing model to provide a performance benchmark. The performances of these extreme models should span those of more reasonable hedonic models. Second, we present the results from estimating a three parameter spatial-temporal model (comparables based only upon distance and time) and a five parameter multi-dimensional model (comparables based upon distance, time, baths, beds, area, and age). While the spatial-temporal model does model dependence in multiple dimensions (distance and time), for clarity we will reserve the term multi-dimensional to apply to the modeling of the dependence in distance, time, baths, beds, area, and age.

As a brief overview of the findings presented at the end of section 2.3, the multi-dimensional dependence model displays the lowest sample errors (6.06% median absolute proportional errors), followed by the three parameter spatial-temporal model (6.67% median absolute proportional errors), the 98 parameter complicated hedonic pricing model (8.19% median absolute proportional errors), and the two parameter simple hedonic pricing model (14.36% median absolute proportional errors).

Hence, we conclude that modeling the multi-dimensional dependence among observations does seem to provide a parsimonious way of accurately predicting house prices and provides a framework for understanding various appraisal practices.

2.2 Simple Dependence Models

Two basic approaches exist for specifying regressions. First, one can attempt to include all relevant variables (with concomitant attention to functional form) in a relatively elaborate model of the conditional mean (*e.g.*, $X\beta$) and hope the residuals are approximately independent. Second, one can use a simpler model, but specify the dependence among errors and use this to correct the prediction from the simple model. Both approaches are commonly used in time series analysis whereby some regressions use dummy variables to account for time or seasonality while other regressions use corrections for temporal autocorrelation. Many specifications use both approaches. For example, a regression of house prices over time might include a substantial number of variables and use an autocorrelation adjustment as well.[4]

Subject matter considerations and the purpose of the regression can dictate whether to focus upon the model or the error dependence. For subjects where the model has a specific theoretical functional form, directly using this form has appeal. For subjects where the true model depends upon many variables without a specific and simple functional form, using a simple model and correcting its faults by modeling the dependence among errors has appeal (provided one can specify the dependence sufficiently well).

Modeling the errors as opposed to the conditional mean may have additional appeal for independent variables that have a complicated, non-monotonic effect on the conditional mean. For example, time by itself does not necessarily have a deterministic effect upon house prices. House prices could rise and fall over time. Similarly, space does not have a simple effect upon prices. Prices do not rise or fall monotonically and smoothly as one follows a particular direction across the urban landscape. The year of the house's construction does not by itself imply a lower or higher price. Like wine, some years were better than others (*e.g.*, pre-war versus post-war construction). The confounding of this vintage effect with age, remodeling activities, and the effects of survivorship (structures with aesthetic appeal or structures in superior locations tend to attract maintenance funds) results in potentially non-monotonic influences of age upon the conditional mean (see Goodman and Thibodeau (1995)). Holding the size of the house constant, more bedrooms or bathrooms do not imply higher prices. Good design sets an optimal number of bedrooms and bathrooms for a house of a given size. Hence, these design variables have a non-monotonic, potentially complicated effect upon the conditional mean.

While researchers could use flexible functional forms in the conditional mean to capture these variables' complicated effect upon price, this leads to many parameters with associated estimation problems. Modeling the dependence among errors can mitigate the effects from omitted variables as well as imperfections in the functional form as long as these pertain to both the observation and the group of observations identified as having errors correlated with the observation (*i.e.*, comparables). Appraisal practice suggests guidelines for choosing such groups of observations (the subject and the comparables). In practice, appraisers try to minimize the differences among the subject and comparable properties in (a) location; (b) time of sale; (c) bedrooms; (d) bathrooms; (e) living area; and (f) age. Note, these are the variables which do not necessarily have a simple effect upon price. Naturally, appraisers can not simultaneously minimize each of these differences. However, they could pick the closest comparables conditional upon some restrictions on the differences in the other variables.

To test the utility of some of the restrictions motivated by appraisal practice, we must first introduce some form of housing price model with a form amenable to such restrictions. Fortunately, Pace, Barry, Clapp, and Rodriguez (1998) and Pace, Barry, Gilley, and Sirmans (forthcoming) proposed some relatively general spatial-temporal hedonic pricing models which can easily be simplified. A simplified version of their model can be written as,

$$(I - S)(I - T)Y = (I - S)(I - T)X\beta + \varepsilon \qquad (1)$$

where Y represents the n element vector of observations on the dependent variable, X represents the n by k matrix of observations on the independent variables, S represents an n by n spatial weight matrix with positive entries in each row for the m_S spatially nearest, previously sold comparable properties, I represents the n by n identity matrix, and T represents an n by n matrix with positive entries in each row for the m_T most recent sales prior to the sale of the subject property. The rows in both S and T sum to 1. This version of the spatial weight matrix S conditions only upon previously sold observations. This avoids some computational problems and facilitates forecasting.

Essentially the matrices S, T function like spatial lag (or local average) and temporal lag operators. For example, SY represents the local average of property values and TX represents the lagged values or temporally smoothed values of the independent variables. Hence, $(I - S)Y$ measures the deviation of the subject properties' values from the relevant local averages (average of the prices of comparable sales). Also, $(I - T)Y$ measures the deviation of the subject properties' prices relative to the average of recently sold properties. Let $\Delta Y = (I - T)Y$ and $\Delta X = (I - T)X$. We can rewrite (1) as,

$$(I - S)\Delta Y = (I - S)\Delta X\beta + \varepsilon \qquad (2)$$

Pace and Gilley (1998) showed the adjustment grid estimator could be written in matrix form as,

$$(I - S)Y = (I - S)X\beta_{grid} + \varepsilon \qquad (3)$$

where β_{grid} represents the appraiser's estimate of the characteristic values. Hence, the simple model in (2) simply generalizes the familiar adjustment grid estimator by (a) using temporally differenced prices and characteristics and (b) estimating β as opposed to using an appraiser's estimate. If S and T only involve previously sold properties (assured by construction), one can estimate (2) by applying OLS to the transformed variables $\hat{Y} = (I - S)\Delta Y$ and $\hat{X} = (I - S)\Delta X$. Hence, one simply estimates the equation $\hat{Y} = \hat{X}\beta + \varepsilon$ via OLS.

The transformation $(I - S)(I - T)$ of the variables equates to estimating generalized least squares (EGLS) as opposed to OLS. Hence, the assumed covariance matrix equals,

$$'\Omega = \sigma^2((I - T)'(I - S)'(I - S)(I - T))^{-1} \tag{4}$$

where σ^2 is the variance of the errors. In small, repeated samples, OLS on the transformed variables (EGLS) will outperform OLS on the untransformed variables when the assumed covariance structure matches reality better than the OLS assumption of $\Omega = \sigma^2 I$ (assumed independence). Asymptotically, both OLS and EGLS will have the same parameter estimation efficiency, but EGLS will predict better if the errors have the assumed dependency structure. In technical terms, the OLS predictor is not the best linear unbiased predictor (BLUP) in the presence of dependent errors. OLS fails to use the information contained in the correlated errors. Hence, better specification of the variance-covariance matrix should aid prediction (Cressie (1993)).

2.3 The Performance of Different Pricing Models

In this section we examine the performance of the simple hedonic model, the complex hedonic model, the spatial-temporal model, and the multi-dimensional model. In section 2.3.1 we discuss the data common to all the models, section 2.3.2 presents both the simple and complex hedonic pricing models used for comparisons with the spatial-temporal models, section 2.3.3 details the parts of the temporal specification used in the spatial-temporal modeling, section 2.3.4 provides information on the spatial weight matrices used in the unrestricted spatial-temporal model, section 2.3.5 describes the construction of the restricted spatial weight matrix, section 2.3.6 provides more information on the partitioning of the sample, section 2.3.7 presents the unrestricted spatial-temporal model, section 2.3.8 presents the multi-dimensional model, and finally section 2.3.9 compares the results from the hedonic pricing and spatial-temporal models.

2.3.1 Data

We began with 3,095 observations on homes in Baton Rouge which sold during 1996 and 1997 which had complete data on number of bedrooms, number of bathrooms, list price, sales price, year built, latitude, longitude, date-of-sale and an MLS area identification code. In addition, we only considered houses with a list price between \$35,000 and \$250,000, with at least one bedroom and one bathroom, and with a sales price within 15% of the list price. We used this as a proxy for unusual properties (houses in the Baton Rouge MLS tend to sell for a discount of only a few percent relative to the list price). In a few cases, we observed very large differences between the list price and the sales price which suggested some other forms of consideration may have been part of the sale.

We ordered the observations by date of sale with the oldest observation as the first element in Y and the first row in X. Also, we reserved the first 999 observations sold in 1996 for potential comparables as described in more detail in section 2.3.6 below. Hence, all the models used a sample of 2,096 observations. The sample period ran from September 1996 until December 1997.

2.3.2 Simple and Complex Linear Hedonic Models

We fit both a simple and more complex hedonic pricing model via OLS. The simple model was,

$$\ln(\text{sales price}) = \beta_1 + \beta_2 \ln(\text{living area}) + \varepsilon$$

Naturally, this model is too simple to serve as an accurate model.

In contrast, the more complex model included (a) dummy variables for each month in the sample (15); (b) dummy variables for each MLS area with 50 or more sales (11); (c) the MLS area dummy interacted with living area, squared living area, age, squared age, age times living area (55); (d) a polynomial in latitude and longitude (5); (e) dummy variables for the number of baths (4); (f) dummy variables for the possible half bath combinations (3); and (g) dummy variables for the number of bedrooms (5). This amounts to 98 variables. Naturally, this model seems overly parameterized. However, the results from the simple and complex models fitted by OLS should span the results of more realistic models.

2.3.3 Specification of the Temporal Weight Matrices

To fit the spatial-temporal models below we need to compute the quantities $(I - T)Y = Y - TY$ and $(I - T)X = X - TX$. For data sorted by the date-of-sale, TY and TX correspond to computing a running average (or a nearest neighbor estimate over time) of the previously sold price and characteristics. Naturally, one must choose how many observations to use to form this running average, which we symbolize as m_T. A priori we chose $m_T = 499$, which corresponds to about four months of past sales.

2.3.4 Specification of the Unrestricted Spatial Weight Matrices

The spatial weight matrix S specifies which other observations are comparables for each observation (subject). For the unrestricted spatial weight matrices, only physical proximity to previously sold observations matters. Consequently, we computed the Euclidean distance d_{ij} between every pair of observations j and i where $(i > j)$. We used unprojected decimal latitude and longitude coordinates to compute these distances. We subsequently sorted these distances and formed the set of individual neighbor matrices $S_1, S_2, \ldots$, S_{m_S}, where S_1 represents the closest previously sold neighbor (shortest distance), S_2 represents the second previously sold neighbor (second shortest distance) and so on. The first rows of these matrices may have all zeros due to a lack of previously transacted neighbors. These very sparse matrices have a 1 in each row and contain zeros otherwise (apart from the initial rows). *A priori*, we decided that 15 neighbors ($m_S = 15$) should capture the vast majority of the spatial effects.

To make the approach more flexible, we introduced a parameter λ which governs the weight the closest comparables receive relative to the more distant comparables. We computed the overall spatial matrix S via,

$$S = \frac{\sum_{l=1}^{m_S} \lambda^l S_l}{\sum_{l=1}^{m_S} \lambda^l} \tag{5}$$

where λ^l weights the relative effect of the lth individual neighbor matrix. Hence, S depends upon the parameters λ and m_S. Thus, (5) imposes an autoregressive distributed lag structure on the spatial variables. By construction, each row in S sums to 1, S is lower triangular, and has zeros on the diagonal.

The use of the individual neighbor matrices, S_l, greatly speeds up investigation of the sensitivity of the results to different forms of S. The individual neighbor matrices themselves require some expense in computation. However, reweighting these as in (5) requires very little time.

2.3.5 Restricted Spatial Weight Matrix

The restricted spatial weight matrix, denoted by S_{rest}, requires the neighboring observations obey a series of restrictions. Specifically,

$$|\text{Subject Baths} - \text{Comparable Baths}| \leq R_1$$
$$|\text{Subject Beds} - \text{Comparable Beds}| \leq R_2$$

$$|\text{Subject } \ln(\text{living area}) - \text{Comparable } \ln(\text{living area})| \le R_3$$

$$|\text{Subject } \ln(\text{age}) - \text{Comparable } \ln(\text{age})| \le R_4$$

where R_1, R_2, R_3, and R_4 are the restrictions. The first two restrictions we set to 1 *a priori*. We estimated R_3 and R_4 from the data via minimizing the sum-of-squares of the errors from the multi-dimensional model. Apart from the restrictions, one constructs the restricted spatial weight matrix identically to the unrestricted spatial weight matrix.

2.3.6 Treatment of Initial Observations

We form all the quantities (*e.g.*, *TY, SY, TX, SX, STX, TSX, STY, TSY*) needed in computing the estimates for the entire sample. We subsequently drop 999 initial observations from these quantities for use in the actual estimation sample. Without retaining some prior observations, the spatial-temporal estimator could perform poorly initially as it would have a very small selection of previously sold neighbors to use in the first predictions. Dropping the first 999 observations allows about an eight month period for comparable sales selection prior to making the first prediction. Of course, predictions towards the end of the sample have almost two years of data for comparable sales selection that gives them a mild advantage. Naturally, we could adjust the number of dropped observations. To facilitate comparison with the conventional hedonic pricing models, we use the same sample for all the models.

2.3.7 Unrestricted Spatial-Temporal Covariance Model

The unrestricted spatial-temporal model uses living area as the only independent variable (although S and T specify spatial and temporal effects).

$$(I - S)\Delta \ln(\text{sales price}) = \beta_1 + \beta_2 (I - S)\Delta \ln(\text{living area}) + \varepsilon$$

2.3.8 Multi-dimensional Covariance Model

The multi-dimensional model differs from the unrestricted spatial-temporal model only in the choice of the spatial weight matrix, S_{rest}.

$$(I - S_{rest})\Delta \ln(\text{sales price}) = \beta_1^{rest} + \beta_2^{rest} (I - S_{rest})\Delta \ln(\text{living area}) + \varepsilon$$

The multi-dimensional model is very parsimonious in the usual independent variables, using only living area. However, it does model space and time though S and T. Moreover, S and T depend upon R_1, R_2, R_3, R_4, λ_{rest}, m_S, and m_T, although we picked R_1, R_2, m_S, m_T based on experience with other data. Hence, modeling the spatial-temporal dependency of the errors receives more attention than the more common modeling of $X\beta$.

2.3.9 A Comparison of Results

Table 1 contains some of the parameter estimates and sample error performances across the four models considered. First, the simple hedonic model (min mean model) had the worst error performance with a median absolute proportional error of 14.36%. We use the term proportional error for the models examined to denote the error in predicting the log of price.[5] However, this very simple model only included an intercept and the living area variable. Second, the complex hedonic model (max mean model) had a substantially better performance with a median absolute proportional error of 8.19%. However, this model employed 98 variables. Third, the unrestricted spatial-temporal model had an even better error performance with a median absolute proportional error of 6.67%. This model only employed three variables

Table 1: Estimates and Sample Error Statistics Across Models

	Min Mean Model	Max Mean Model	Unrestricted ST Covariance Model	Restricted ST Covariance Model
Intercept	3.8129		−0.0065	−0.0054
	(32.8761)		(−2.2116)	(−1.8714)
Log(Area)	1.0257		0.7974	0.7316
	(65.7859)		(54.4453)	(31.6532)
m_t			499	499
m_s			15	15
λ			0.65	0.65
$|\Delta Baths| \leq$				1
$|\Delta Beds| \leq$				1
$|\Delta \log(Area)| \leq$				0.3702
$|\Delta \log(Age)| \leq$				0.8634
R^2	0.6739	0.8473	0.8752	0.8812
Median$|e|$	0.1436	0.0819	0.0667	0.0606
Mean$|e|$	0.1703	0.1084	0.0946	0.0897
Log-Likelihood	−4831.55	−4036.54	−3824.65	−3773.00
n	2096	2096	2096	2096
k	2	98	3	5

$(\beta_1, \beta_2, \lambda)$ and yet outperformed the complex hedonic model. Finally, the multi-dimensional model displayed the best error performance with a median absolute proportional error of 6.06%. This model only employed five variables $(\beta_{1rest}, \beta_{2rest}, \lambda_{rest}, R_3, R_4)$.

The estimated coefficients also illustrate some interesting points. First, the estimated coefficients for the simple hedonic model seem plausible, with an estimated elasticity of the price with respect to the living area not significantly different from 1. In contrast, the corresponding elasticity for the unrestricted spatial-temporal model is a much lower 0.7974. The difference in the estimated values stems from a difference in interpretation. The unrestricted spatial-temporal model holds the neighborhood constant and hence the estimate is the price elasticity with respect to living area holding the neighborhood constant. As is well known, if one doubled the size of a house (relative to the average) in a given neighborhood, one would expect less than a doubling of the price. In contrast, the simple hedonic pricing model examines the effect of doubling size without holding the neighborhood the same. By conditioning even further on number of bedrooms, number of bathrooms, and age, the estimated price elasticity with respect to living area falls slightly to 0.7316 for the multi-dimensional model.

The estimated restrictions appear plausible. One should use as comparables houses with living areas between approximately 69% and 145% of the living area of the subject property $(\exp(-0.3702), \exp(0.3702))$. One should use as comparables houses with ages approximately between 42% and 241% of the age of the subject property $(\exp(0.8634), \exp(-0.8634))$. These are not very restrictive bounds. Successful specifications of the other parts of the model should make the restrictions less important. For example, if the unrestricted model could produce a perfect performance, the restrictions would not improve performance.

2.4 Conclusion

The statistically naïve practice of appraisers may have a more sophisticated basis than a casual examination would reveal. As discussed in Pace and Gilley (1998), the grid adjustment estimator can be thought of as a restricted spatial autoregression. As this paper discusses, the common appraisal practice of limiting comparable properties to those whose characteristics resemble the subject property characteristics may serve as an easy-to-implement adjustment for multi-dimensional error dependence. Specifying the error dependence as opposed to the conditional mean $(X\beta)$ may have appeal when the variables have non-monotonic, non-smooth effects upon housing prices. Time, space, age, and design fall into this category.

In the example studied, imposing the restrictions, at the cost of two additional parameters (five total parameters), reduced median absolute proportional errors from 6.67% to 6.06%, a substantial reduction. In contrast, the complex hedonic model with 98 parameters displayed a median absolute proportional error of 8.19%.

The multi-dimensional nature of the error dependence suggests that when viewing the comparables selected from any single dimension, the pattern of dependence may not seem very clear. Specifically, the selected comparables may be located in more complicated patterns over space as opposed to comparables selected strictly by proximity to the subject. Hence, modeling the non-spatial dimensions may provide a way of implicitly modeling anisotropy (error dependence not depending strictly upon distance among observations).[6]

In conclusion, parsimonious modeling of space, time, and the property characteristics can produce models with good predictive performance. Incorporating elements of standard appraisal practice into the statistical model not only increases our understanding of appraiser behavior, but also can lead to improved prediction in statistical models of house prices.

ACKNOWLEDGEMENTS

We also gratefully acknowledge the generous research support provided by the University of Connecticut and Louisiana State University as well as the valuable comments provided by two anonymous reviewers and Wayne Archer.

NOTES

[1] This figure comes from Case, Pollakowski, and Wachter (1997) where they compute the standard deviations of the prediction errors from a plausible hedonic pricing model for four different markets. The numbers provided come from computing a weighted average of their results. Naturally, other hedonic pricing models may provide more or less accurate predictions. However, many studies do not report statistics on absolute accuracy as opposed to relative accuracy (*e.g.*, R^2). Also, this study did examine the same model across large samples in four markets and hence provides some idea of typical predictive accuracy.

[2] Dotzour (1988) obtained this by looking at appraiser accuracy in home relocation programs.

[3] A variety of recent studies have documented the power of spatial statistics when applied to real estate data (*e.g.*, Can and Megbolugbe (1997), Pace and Gilley (1997), Basu and Thibodeau (1998), and Dubin (1998)). The same remarks apply to the value of spatial-temporal statistics (*e.g.*, Gelfand, Ghosh, Knight, and Sirmans (1998), Pace, Barry, Clapp, and Rodriguez (1998), and Pace, Barry, Gilley, and Sirmans (forthcoming)).

[4] This modeling choice has different names across the literature. In panel data studies, fixed effect models usually involve elaborate specification of the conditional mean while random

effect models usually involve careful specification of the correlation structure. Mixed models incorporate both fixed and random effects (Kennedy, pp. 226–228). See Cressie (1993, p. 25) for a discussion of this topic in the context of spatial models.

[5] As well-known, when attempting to transform the predicted value of log(Price) back into the original space, one must allow for the asymmetry of the log-normal density. To arrive at unbiased predicted values, one must use the formula $E(\hat{P}_i) = \exp(\hat{Y}_i)\exp(-\hat{\sigma}^2/2)$ where $\hat{Y}_i$ denotes the predicted value of the log(Price) for observation i and $\hat{\sigma}^2$ is the estimated variance of the errors (Kennedy (1998, p. 37)). The correction factor $\exp(-\hat{\sigma}^2/2)$ is very small for these models, since the variance of the errors are small. For example, the correction factor for the multi-dimensional model is 0.9913. If one does not employ the correction factor, the prediction is unbiased for the median and not the mean price given the independent variable values (Kennedy, p. 115).

[6] See Meyers (1997) for more upon isotropy (dependence as a function of proximity alone) and anisotropy (dependence a function of location as well as distance). Note, geostatistics provides some standard methods such as directional variograms for explicitly modeling anisotropy.

REFERENCES

Basu, Sabyasachi and Thomas Thibodeau. "Analysis of Spatial Autocorrelation in House Prices," *Journal of Real Estate Finance and Economics* 17 (1998), pp. 61–86.

Can, A. and Megbolugbe, I. "Spatial dependence and House Price Index Construction," *Journal of Real Estate Finance and Economics* 14 (1997): 203–222.

Case, Bradford, Henry Pollakowski, and Susan Wachter. "Frequency of Transaction and House Price Modeling," *Journal of Real Estate Finance and Economics* 14 (1997), pp. 173–188.

Cressie, Noel A.C. *Statistics for Spatial Data.* Revised ed. New York: John Wiley, 1993.

Dotzour, Mark G. "Quantifying Estimation Bias in Residential Appraisal," *Journal of Real Estate Research* 3 (1988), pp. 1–12.

Dubin, Robin. "Predicting House Prices Using Multiple Listing Data," *Journal of Real Estate Finance and Economics* 17 (1998), pp. 35–60.

Gelfand, Alan E., Sujit K. Ghosh, John R. Knight, and C.F. Sirmans. "Spatial-Temporal Modeling of Residential Sales Data," *Journal of Business and Economic Statistics,* 16 (1998), pp. 312–321.

Goodman, Allen C., and Thomas G. Thibodeau. "Age-Related Heteroskedasticity in Hedonic House Price Equations." *Journal of Housing Research* 6 (1995), pp. 25–42.

Kennedy, Peter. *A Guide to Econometrics,* Fourth ed. Cambridge, MA: MIT Press, 1998.

Myers, Jeffrey. *Geostatistical Error Management,* New York: Van Nostran Reinhold, 1997.

Pace, R. Kelley, Ronald Barry, John Clapp, and M. Rodriguez. "Spatio-Temporal Estimation of Neighborhood Effects," *Journal of Real Estate Finance and Economics* 17 (1998), pp. 15–33.

Pace, R. Kelley, Ronald Barry, O.W. Gilley, and C.F. Sirmans. "A Method for Spatial-Temporal Forecasting with an Application to Real Estate Prices," *International Journal of Forecasting,* forthcoming.

Pace, R. Kelley, and O.W. Gilley. "Using the Spatial Configuration of the Data to Improve Estimation," *Journal of the Real Estate Finance and Economics* 14 (1997), 333–340.

Pace, R. Kelley, and O.W. Gilley. "Optimally Combining OLS and the Grid Estimator," *Real Estate Economics* 26 (1998), pp. 331–347.

Chapter 3

The Components of Appraisal Accuracy

Paul Gallimore
Nottingham Trent University, Nottingham, England

3.1 Introduction

In the past decade or so, there has been growing attention paid to the question of appraisal, or valuation, accuracy. Studies that encompass this question have principally been driven by concerns over how appraisal *in*accuracy may adversely affect the validity of appraisal-based real estate indices and of the portfolio management policies that draw inferences from them. Such studies have been pursued in the US (e.g. Webb, 1994; Fisher, Miles and Webb, 1999; Clayton, Geltner and Hamilton, 2000), the UK (e.g. Matysiak and Wang, 1995; Blundell and Ward, 1997; Drivers Jonas/IPD, 1997) and Australia (Parker, 1998; Newell and Kishore, 1998). Given the nature of the concerns, these studies have generally focused on commercial appraisals, especially of institutional grade real estate, although accuracy is a wider issue that surrounds all forms of appraisals.

This wider view is reflected in a different, somewhat subsidiary, strand of enquiry that encompasses the more general question of the degree of accuracy that may be expected of appraisers by the public. Investigation from this perspective has centred on situations where court actions have been taken against appraisers for arguably substandard professional behavior leading to client financial loss. Work taking this angle is confined largely to the UK (Crosby, Lavers and Murdoch, 1998; Crosby, 2000).

Both these kinds of study involve not only the concept of appraisal accuracy: i.e. the extent to which valuation differs from actual market values; but also the concept of appraisal variance: the extent to which appraisers differ amongst themselves, as might be observed when several appraisers value the same property. These concepts are analogous to those of validity and reliability in the design of research measurements. In the same way that reliability is a pre-condition to, but does not guarantee, validity; appraisal variance affects, but does not itself determine, the level of appraisal accuracy. The discussion in this paper encompasses both concepts but is directed at the larger issue of validity. It addresses the theoretical foundation for evaluating this, analysing what determines appraisal validity, using a framework that enables consideration of its constituent components. The paper suggests ways in which this analysis may contribute to improvements in appraisal accuracy.

3.2 Appraisal Accuracy and Real Estate Indices

In strict terms, appraisal accuracy cannot in practice be measured because true market values are unobservable. Empirical studies of appraisal accuracy therefore utilize comparisons of valuations against market prices, as proxies for underlying true market value. This practical and inevitable limitation has led investigators to adopt different criteria for deciding which market prices may be regarded as proxies for true value, most notably with respect to the limits of the acceptable time lag between valuation date and corresponding transaction date. When comparing findings from different studies, the presence of such differences must be borne in mind, as must the differing databases, periods of analysis and market conditions.

These studies give some general indication of the level of appraisal accuracy and of the way that it may vary in different market conditions. In the US, for example, Webb (1994), examining the period between 1978 and 1992, discovered average differences between sale prices and appraisals that were positive (7.8%) in the rising market phase but negative (3.3% and 4.9%) in falling markets; with mean absolute differences being about 10%. As Fisher *et al.* (1999) point out, it is the mean absolute difference that is important in evaluating the general level of accuracy of appraisals whereas the average difference (with over-valuations compensating against under-valuations) is what matters in assessing the contribution of appraisals to producing indices that reflect actual market movements. Their study, covering the period from 1980 to 1998, points to a similar mean absolute level of difference as found by Webb. Their average differences were somewhat smaller, however, with sale prices exceeding appraised value by 4.5% and 4% in the upmarket phases and undershooting appraised values by 4.5% in the down market. These and other findings illustrate that, as markets move through cycles, the direction of the appraisal "error" shifts, implying that appraisals exhibit both a lagging of actual price movements and a dampening or smoothing of the track of these.

Similar studies have been conducted in the UK, although with somewhat different results as regards the magnitude of differences between appraisals and sale prices. A useful summary of these is provided by Crosby (2000). Although the methodology and presentation of findings in the UK studies differ somewhat from the US studies, Crosby's analysis concludes that the accuracy of valuations in the UK is about half that found in the US. Two unpublished Australian studies cited by Crosby (Parker, 1998; Newell and Kishore, 1998) suggest that Australian valuations have a similar level of accuracy to that found in the US.[1]

Something implicit in all these studies is that appraisal error is largely random (and hence, for investors, diversifiable with sufficiently large portfolios). This assumption has been questioned by Graff and Young (1999). They use sets of simultaneous independent appraisals of the same properties to investigate the magnitude of such error, conjecturing that the deterministic components of appraisal error for such pairs of appraisals are virtually identical. They accordingly treat the standard deviation for each set of simultaneous appraisals as the standard deviation of the random error component. They find that this is approximately 2%, well below the total error reported in previous studies. They suggest that this implies that the non-random component is correspondingly large, in contrast to studies that maintain that the total error of around 10% is largely random. In so doing they maintain that such studies misinterpret non-random error as random. Graff and Young's findings are illuminating of the nature of appraisal inaccuracies, being based, like most of the accuracy studies cited here, on institutional-grade real estate. They are not, of course, necessarily generalizeable beyond this class of property.

3.3 Lag-based Inaccuracies

Most of the foregoing studies focus upon appraisal lagging as a primary component of appraisal inaccuracy. This lag may in part be caused by appraisers using "old" comparables that fail fully to mirror market conditions current at the time of the appraisal. It may also be a function of uncertainty about current information, even when it is available. Trade-off of appraisers' relative levels of confidence in current as compared to prior market knowledge may result in appraisals that do not fully reflect the up-to-date situation and therefore lag behind it. This only-partial adjustment to new information is portrayed by Quan and Quigley (1991) as a rational updating strategy in the face of limited, "noisy", information. Though theoretically compelling, only one study to date has empirically investigated whether appraisers actually adopt such a strategy. This is reported in Clayton *et al.* (2000). They analysed a set of six consecutive appraisals each of 33 properties over periods between 1986 and 1996. Their findings confirm that appraisers' reliance on old information (i.e. previous appraisal reports or comparables used in those reports) increases with uncertainty about the current state of the market. Additionally, however, they find that this attraction to old versus new information increases in those cases where the appraiser undertakes successive valuations. This finding is consistent with Diaz and Wolverton's (1998) experimental results, which reveal a tendency for appraisers to "anchor", irrationally, on their previous appraisals. There are, therefore, three factors, at least (information-quality, "rational" behavioral and "irrational" behavioral), that contribute to lag-based inaccuracies in appraisals.

3.4 Objective Perceptions of Appraisal Accuracy

The foregoing discussion gives an indication of the overall level of appraisal inaccuracy as actually measured and of the possible causes of a probable major element of this (lagging). This is useful in the general sense of assessing the worth of appraisal-based indices and in the more specific tasks of producing and evaluating attempts to adjust indices to remove appraisal-induced inaccuracies and consequent formulation of investment strategy. A somewhat different approach to studying accuracy, however, is to examine what expectations those outside the appraisal profession may have of appraisal accuracy and the extent to which actual appraisals measure up to these expectations. This approach, as far as the author knows, exists only in the UK literature. Further, in contrast to most of the studies discussed so far, it is based upon consideration of appraisals conducted for loan purposes, rather than appraisals periodically conducted for portfolio management purposes.

This line of enquiry is principally attributable to the work of Crosby (Crosby, Lavers and Murdoch, 1998; Crosby, 2000), through an analysis of the reasoning in judicial cases in which the accuracy of individual valuations has been scrutinised to determine whether such valuations were conducted negligently. This analysis is largely confined to the UK, though more recently has been extended to include Australian cases. The principal issues are the perceived extent of allowable inaccuracy (the extent of the "margin of error" or "bracket") and the way that perceptions of this are derived (including the influence of valuers as expert witnesses). Crosby also tracks the as-yet-unresolved question of whether a valuation that falls outside the margins is indisputably treated by UK courts as *prima facie* evidence of negligence (and *vice versa*). He finds that the normal margin of error accepted in UK courts is "between ±10% and ±15%, rising to an absolute maximum of ±20% where the valuation is considered difficult" (Crosby 2000, 149). He suggests that, given the findings from UK valuation accuracy studies, the acceptable margin is being set at a level that is too rigorous (for the UK; though perhaps not for the US and Australia). He also points out that in helping to determine this level, valuers acting as expert witnesses deviate significantly in their opinions about accuracy from their actual performance as valuers, as reflected in UK accuracy studies. Crosby ponders on, but ultimately rejects, the idea that the wider margins implied in these studies could be adopted by the courts. Instead he argues for the UK courts to abandon the notion of the bracket.

Given that abandonment of the accuracy bracket by UK courts is unlikely, a clearer understanding of the determinants and components of valuation accuracy may assist in judicial judgements. Operationalising the lessons from this understanding may also be useful in the leading to improvements in valuation and appraisal behavior itself. It is the purpose of this paper to attempt some clarification of this understanding. This is done in the following sections by an examination of appraisal behavior through a theoretical framework – the Brunswik lens model – that separately identifies the principal components that determine appraisers' judgement accuracy. This includes consideration of components that are linked to characteristics of the market itself (such as inherent lags in the currency of information) and also those components that relate to behavior of appraisers within the market (such as a reluctance to fully absorb information to the extent suggested by appraisal models).

3.5 The Lens Model

The ideas now discussed stem from the lens model derived from the work of Brunswik (1956) and developed by Hursch *et al.* (1964) and Tucker (1964). This is by no means the only model in the cognitive psychology literature that can be used to examine appraiser behavior. Diaz (1999) provides a comprehensive summary of these as applied in the developing field of behavioral real estate analysis. The particular attraction of the lens model, however, is that it provides a framework that is both entirely consonant with the appraisal task but can also accommodate many of the findings from the behavioral literature.

In the literature of cognitive psychology itself, there is an abundance of descriptions of the lens model and its diagrammatic representation (for appraiser-oriented versions of this, see Wolverton and Gallimore, 1999). The description presented here is somewhat simplified, because the purpose of this paper is not to investigate the validity of the model itself[2] but rather to draw from the model a framework that is helpful in analysing the concept of appraiser accuracy.

The lens model applies to situations when people have to make judgements about an event that cannot be directly observed. The inability to see the event may be, for example, because it will occur in the future; or it may be because it is a hypothetical event and thus will not occur at all. An obvious instance of the former is a forecast of future interest rates. An illustration of the latter is a present day judgement of the market value of some real estate, where no actual sale is contemplated. In these circumstances, the person making the judgement has to rely on various indicators of the outcome of the event: what the model terms "cues". These "cues", taken in combination, form the "lens" through which the person making the judgement attempts to see the outcome.[3]

The potential applicability of this simple model to appraisal is clear. Appraisers have to make judgements about one aspect of an unobservable event – the price on the transaction hypothesised in the market value definition. They use the "cues" supplied by the market to make that judgement. Thus far, however, correspondence of the appraiser's task with the model is largely of academic interest. Its potential usefulness becomes clearer in its translation (Hursh *et al.*, 1964; Tucker, 1964) into the lens model equation, and especially the distillation from this equation of the key factors contributing to an individual's forecasting[4] accuracy. The lens model equation captures the truism that the correspondence between a forecast (e.g. an appraised value) and an event (e.g. the true market value) is essentially the product of three terms, respectively representing:

(a) the inherent predictability of events in the environment, as reflected in an "environmental" forecasting model;
(b) the match between the forecaster's (i.e. appraiser's) model and the environmental model; and
(c) the consistency with which the forecaster (appraiser) applies his or her model.

A frequent assumption in lens model studies is that relationships in the environment are essentially linear and therefore that environmental predictability can effectively be represented by the explanatory power of a regression model. The lens model equation, however, does not require the use of regression.[5] In fact, the equation contains a fourth term, which recognises the possible presence of non-linear components and that improvement in accuracy that may ensue from a forecaster's capacity to perceive and utilize these (Hursch *et al.* 1964, 46–47). Generally, however, this fourth factor has been regarded as small and thus able to be ignored (Stewart, 1999). Putting aside this added complication, the three principal components of the equation – predictability, match, and consistency – can theoretically be "perfect" but are unlikely ever to be so. A better insight into these factors, and what causes them to fall short of perfection in the particular context of appraisal, should help advance an understanding of the limits of appraisal accuracy.

Despite the ease with which the lens model translates to the appraisal task it has not been generally utilized to analyse appraisal behavior. The exceptions to this are Langfield-Smith and Locke (1988) and the studies by Wolverton and Gallimore (1999; Gallimore and Wolverton, 2000). The latter studies use the lens model to explore the interaction of appraiser and client behavior, in particular the extent to which client feedback causes appraisers and valuers to "re-learn" their problem-solving goal. Wolverton and Gallimore focus more on appraiser-client interaction than upon appraiser accuracy. They illustrate, however, that in applying the lens model to the appraisal task, account needs to be taken of its two-stage complexity (i.e. a prediction is required not only of market value, but also of the comparables that best support that value). By contrast, Langfield-Smith and Locke (1988) address directly the application of the lens model to the appraisal task, although their interest pre-dates the full emergence of the appraisal accuracy issue. Nonetheless, their suggestions, for ways in which the lens model could be applied to help evaluate appraiser performance, partially anticipate the theme developed in this paper. Their proposals for this evaluation, however, are conjectured only at the theoretical level of the lens model and, as far as the author is aware, have not since been developed to apply to practical circumstances.

3.6 Environmental Predictability

The first constraint on appraisal accuracy is the extent to which the real estate environment, and specifically the relationships between price and property attributes in that environment, is less than perfectly predictable. With complete certainty in the environment, it would be possible to interpret available data so as to construct an "environmental" model with perfect forecasting ability. Since there is likely to be some uncertainty in all environments, complete accuracy is a vain hope. A relevant question here, however, is that of the level of uncertainty that exists in the real estate environment and, correspondingly, how well can the dynamics of such an environment be captured in a model determined solely by the inter-relationships in the available data?

In considering these questions, it must be borne in mind that in any one locality there is frequently more than one "environment". Although it is possible to conceive of the real estate market as a single environment, it is in practice more sensibly viewed as composed of a set of unique though sometimes overlapping environments. Thus, the determinants of the value of a condominium will include its physical characteristics and will also extend to wider demographic factors such as metropolitan income levels, unemployment rates and so on. The equivalent factors for retail real estate in the same city will encompass a wholly different set of physical variables but may include the same demographic factors, albeit perhaps weighted differently. Even within discrete property types, sub-markets exist, although specifying the boundaries of these sub-markets, even where they are stable over time, is not always easy. Ensuing discussion of the real estate environment assumes that this problem is recognized.

As previously noted, environmental models in the wider lens model literature are typically conceived of within the framework of multiple regression analysis. Whether this is the most appropriate form of environmental model for real estate is a moot point. At best, such models generally fail to explain much more than 80% of the variation in real estate prices with corresponding levels of accuracy in price prediction (as reflected, for example, by the coefficient of dispersion). They have been used more extensively with residential property than with commercial forms of real estate, for which the level of price explanation is generally poorer. Moreover, their application, in isolation at least, is generally to multiple appraisal rather than single appraisal tasks. In the latter circumstances, simpler approaches used by appraisers, such as comparable sales adjustment grid models, can display higher levels of price fidelity than more sophisticated regression models. This is reflected in the classic paradox where several virtually identical comparables sales are available. A regression analysis will extract relatively little from this information, in trying to explain price variability. A comparables sales analysis will derive far more, by making inferences about the implications of the information for the distribution of possible prices (Matysiak, 1991).

Comparables sales analysis tends to perform relatively better in markets composed of substantially homogeneous properties in broadly similar locations, but falls away as markets become more diversified. In the former kind of market these approaches appear to represent the optimum environment model. To work successfully, however, they generally require some "human" intervention in the form of appraiser judgement and for this reason are perhaps better regarded as "forecaster" models (*infra*) than "environmental" models. More autonomous – though not wholly autonomous – versions of comparable sales adjustment models have been advanced (Vandell, 1991; Gau, Lai and Wang, 1992). These may better represent environmental models, in relatively uncomplex markets, than do either appraisers' simpler models (because these are not sufficiently autonomous) or regression models (because of the typical limits on their performance). Accordingly, levels of inherent predictability may go well beyond that produced by regression models, perhaps to approach closer to 100%. This is speculative, however, and the author is unaware of any testing of such techniques on actual data, by comparison of the resulting value estimates against those produced by more conventional means, to indicate what levels of achievement are possible.

The difficulty in apprehending the ideal form of predictive model for an environment is also related to the definition or delineation of the market or sub-market of which that environment is composed. This, in turn, is a function of the relative heterogeneity of real estate characteristics within these markets. In any particular market, the choice of model – as between regression, simple adjustment, some variant, or some hybrid – is really an empirical problem. What is clear, however, is that the level of predictability as embodied in the concept of an environmental model is not easy to assess. While the explained variance in the better performing regression studies – say 80–85% – gives an indicator of inherent market predictability its seems probable that for relatively homogeneous markets something better can be expected. Conversely, as markets become more heterogeneous, the figure is likely to move below those bounds.

As well as market heterogeneity, variations in inherent predictability are also explainable by information quality. Stewart, Roebber and Bosart (1997) show that weather forecasters can perform significantly better than other groups (e.g. psychologists) because the level of task predictability is enhanced by the high quality of information available to them. Information quality in real estate markets is often well below that desired, and some real estate variables often measured only with imprecision (e.g. location variables). It is therefore in the area of information quality that advances in the level of market predictability may most likely be secured. Overall, however, the foregoing discussion suggests quite wide variation in environmental predictability for real estate markets. Generalisations in the debate about appraisal accuracy usually overlook this fact.

3.7 The Match of Appraisers' Models and Environmental Models

The second component that determines forecast accuracy is the match between the forecaster's model and the environmental model. Since the latter is regarded as setting the higher bound for predictive accuracy, any deviation from this in the actual model used will erode accuracy. Since it is difficult to define, for real estate markets, the ideal environmental model, it is equally difficult to generalise about the degree to which appraisers adopt such models. Even with a clearer grasp of the latter, this would remain an empirical question. One important respect, however, in which appraisers' models may diverge significantly from environmental models is through behavioral and agency related biases. Diaz (1999) reviews the work that has been done in the last decade to uncover the former kind of bias. Examples of the latter are provided by Hendershott and Kane (1995) and Graff and Webb (1997). Both can operate to systematically produce appraisal figures that are at odds with those which should emerge from appraisers' overt models.

As discussed above, the ideal environmental model may embody some non-linear feature, which may or may not be correspondingly reflected in the appraiser's model. While non-linear features have been treated in the lens model literature as small and insignificant, this seems unlikely to be the case in real estate markets. Appraisers may improve their performance by taking into account non-linear factors, while at the same time failing to capture linear factors as optimally as a desired environmental model would imply.

This discussion cannot lead to definite conclusions about the typical closeness of fit of the models that appraisers use, compared to what would be maximally predictive. What it does is to highlight what needs to be considered in assessing the level of accuracy to be expected in an appraisal. There must be some consideration of what is ideally possible and how this might be achieved, coupled with some evaluation of how close the model actually used is to this ideal, and where differences exist whether these are likely to reduce or improve performance in relation to the ideal. Without consideration of these questions, and the way that they may vary in different market conditions, views about expected levels of accuracy, or the acceptability of actual levels of accuracy, are at best limited and at worst blind.

3.8 Appraiser Consistency

This is the third component of appraiser accuracy. Even if an appraiser's model has maximum predictive capacity for a given environment, the overall accuracy of the appraiser's predictions (as measure by the mean absolute "error") will be undermined if the model is employed inconsistently. Therefore, irrespective of the contribution of the other two components, accuracy will be directly impacted by inconsistency in the application of the appraiser's model. This inconsistency in behavior, if random, may be treated as compensating, especially in cases where appraisals are pooled, such as large portfolios or in index construction. In other cases, it is clearly more of a problem.

Several factors may determine the level of consistency that people display in performing repeated tasks, although measurement of this is generally difficult, if not impossible, outside the laboratory. This is true for appraisers, largely because they are virtually never in a position in which they repeat an appraisal under identical conditions.[6] This precludes a test-retest approach to assessing consistency. Theoretically, it might be possible to estimate consistency as the R^2 of the regression model of appraisers' valuation figures against available "cues". If the model were a good representation of how prices are determined, then the extent of the failure of the model to explain variation in valuations would be an indicator of the inherent inconsistency in those figures. As far as the author is aware, this approach has not been applied to appraisals. Another approach to estimating consistency, or at least its lower bound, would be to discover the degree of correlation between appraisers conducting the same appraisals (an approach that is analogous to that adopted by Graff and Young (1999)).

A useful distinction, in discussing inconsistency, is that made by Stewart (1999), as between inconsistency in information acquisition and inconsistency in information processing. Information acquisition is the state of going from what cues are available to be observed, to what cues are actually extracted from the observation. For example, a weather forecaster may have to judge the size of an approaching storm by looking at its apparent size on a radar screen. In making this judgement, the forecaster may display inconsistency. Following this, he or she then has to process this judgement about the storm's size into implications for upcoming weather conditions. This provides a second opportunity for inconsistency in judgement.

The problem in the first stage, that of information acquisition, arises in part because people have to infer subjective cues – how big is the storm? – from objectives cues – the storm's apparent size on the radar (Stewart and Lusk, 1994). Stewart (1999) contends that inconsistency in this stage is pervasive across many tasks. This appears more likely, however, in tasks that require interpretation of images or recognition of complex patterns in data. Appraisal tasks are generally not of this nature. The information acquisition stage in appraisal may therefore not be a serious source of inconsistency. Where this might arise, however, is where, for instance, the appraiser is confronted with data about a series of transactions and has to infer the way in which the market is moving. Studies of human behavior suggest that appraisers may in repeated similar circumstances reach different conclusions. Other scenarios, such as when an appraiser has to infer a capitalisation rate from data on transaction price and income stream, seem less likely to lead to inconsistency.

The extent of inconsistency in the second stage, information processing, depends to a large degree on the mode of processing – i.e. the extent to which it is intuitive as compared to analytic. It is not that one form of processing is overall inherently superior to the other.[7] It is that intuitive processes are generally less reliable than analytical processes, in that they typically produce a wider spread of answers. The greater precision of analytical processing comes, however, at a cost, since when errors do occur they are usually much larger than those present in intuitive forecasts. Of course, treating these two processes as a strict dichotomy is false, since much judgment is likely to be a combination of both modes. The last point is true of appraisal judgement. Though based on formal procedure and rules of reasoning, appraisal judgements are often described as requiring the application of "market insight", "experience" or "feel" – arguably all forms of intuitive cognition. Nonetheless, a more analytic approach to the appraisal task may improve this component in appraisal accuracy.

3.9 Conclusion

Appraisal accuracy is an important issue, with effects across a spectrum of real estate activities. These effects essentially center on what is an acceptable margin of deviation of appraisals from true value, and what factors contribute to this deviation. Perceptions of what is acceptable in these contexts frame the worth that users ascribe to actual appraisals and may also influence the formulation of investment decision-making strategies. Better understanding of what determines appraisal accuracy should help in identifying how improvements in appraisal accuracy might be brought about and the extent to which such improvements are realistically possible.

Enhancing this understanding can come in part from empirical studies and from the analysis and reflection that they stimulate. It must also be aided by a consideration of theoretical aspects of the underlying processes that appraisers engage in, as perceived through a framework that views appraisers as forecasters of unobservable events. This is the approach taken in this paper, using the lens model equation to focus attention on the principal components of appraisal accuracy. Applying this framework reveals some difficulties, such as that of identifying appropriate environmental models and hence apprehending the level of inherent predictability in particular real estate environments. Nevertheless, this very fact underlines the dangers in making generalisations about appraisal accuracy that fail to acknowledge the complexity of real estate markets. The discussion also highlights the need for appraisers to review their models against the concept of maximum market predictability. In particular, it suggests a focus on those aspects of *de facto* behavior that would not be embodied in an environmental model because they relate to the human facets of judgment (i.e. behavioral bias, susceptibility to agency pressures).

There is also a need to monitor the consistency with which appraisal judgements are made. This is likely to arise more in the processing of information than in its acquisition. Research in other fields implies that a more analytic, as compared to intuitive, approach to information processing will reduce variation in individuals' forecasting behavior. It is tempting, for example, to speculate that the significant apparent differences in accuracy as between US appraisers and UK valuers may in large part stem from differential inclinations to adopt intuitive reasoning, with training in the UK generally less quantitative in its nature and arguably, therefore, less oriented to analytic processing. Both appraisers and valuers naturally take pride in their intuitive insights and correspondingly have been shown to develop less formalised but more efficient decision-making processes than those learned in initial training (Diaz, 1990; Diaz, Gallimore and Levy, 2000). The ultimate trade-off for this efficiency, however, may be a greater level of inconsistency in performing their appraisals, and consequent erosion in accuracy.

In many respects, appraisals are imperfect attempts to hit an unattainable goal. This paper seeks, by analysing the different components of this process, to provide a clearer understanding of why this is and to suggest ways in which further research and changes in practice can help to improve this position. Research would be particularly worthwhile to devise means to investigate further the relationships between education, behavior and outcomes, as between the US and the UK, as they affect the consistency component in appraiser behavior. If improvements in appraisal practice are also to be made, however, this analysis implies that they must come through a combination of means. First, data improvements (to advance inherent market predictability); second, vigilance in monitoring for the kind of external influence and bias that has been identified already in behavioral real estate studies (to improve appraiser-environmental model match); and finally, by limiting inconsistencies in the application of appraisal models, through reduced reliance on intuitive reasoning, at least where alternative analytical procedures are available and feasible in use.

NOTES

[1] Accuracy studies can be biased in various ways. For example, the phenomenon by which appraisers doing residential mortgage loan appraisals tend in substantial numbers to report values at or slightly above pending sale price sale (e.g. Cho and Megbolugbe, 1996) obviously undermines the assumptions underlying objective appraised value/sale price comparisons. The studies referred to here have generally taken steps to reduce or eliminate this form of contamination. Another way in which accuracy study samples may be biased stems from the greater likelihood that properties will be selected for sale if prospective price exceeds a previous appraisal (biasing the sample of properties sold as representative of properties appraised). This phenomenon has recently been reported in Baum *et al.*, 2000.

[2] The model's validity has typically been investigated by studying the way in which people use "cues" to make judgements and how feedback may be used to help them improve their performance.

[3] Although the conceptualisation of the judgement process as analogous to a seeing through a lens is an elegant representation, it is not important for the purpose of this paper to appreciate this visual depiction.

[4] "Forecast" here refers to predictions about both current (possibly hypothetical) events and to future events. Where, elsewhere in the paper, the term is used in the real-estate context, it generally refers to the former.

[5] Hursch *et al.* (1964), which provided the stimulus for many later studies, used a regression-based approach. Their analysis, however, was specifically directed at an examination of the statistical characteristics of forecasting achievement.

[6] A second reason has already been noted, namely that appraisers have to estimate an unobservable figure, true market value, preventing direct testing of both accuracy and reliability. This can be circumvented by using transaction prices as proxies for true market value.

[7] Such contentions are, however, made. Dawes (1988), for example, seeks to demonstrate that intuitive cognition leads to judgement that is inferior to that of analytic cognition.

REFERENCES

Baum, A. E., Crosby, N., Gallimore, P., McAllister, P., and Gray, A. The Influence of Valuers and Valuations on the Workings of the Commercial Property Investment Market, 2000, London, Research report published by the Royal Institution of Chartered Surveyors Research Foundation.

Blundell, G. F. and Ward, C. W. R. The accuracy of valuations – expectation and reality, unpublished paper, 1997, The University of Reading, England.

Brunswik, E. Perception and the representative design of psychological experiments, 1956, Berkeley, CA., University of California Press.

Cho, M. and Megbolugbe, I. An empirical analysis of property appraisal and mortgage redlining, *Journal of Real Estate Finance and Economics*, 1996, 13, 45–55.

Clayton, J., Geltner D., and Hamilton, S. W. Smoothing in commercial property valuations: evidence from individual appraisals, 2000, University of Cincinnati, Department of Finance working paper.

Crosby, N. Valuation accuracy, variation and bias in the context of standards and expectations, *Journal of Property Investment and Finance*, 2000, 18:2, 130–161.

Crosby, N., Lavers A., and Murdoch, J. Property valuation variation and the "margin of error" in the UK, *Journal of Property Research*, 1998, 15:4, 303–330.

Dawes, R. M. *Rational choice in an uncertain world*, 1988, New York, Harcourt Brace Jovanovich.

Diaz, J. How appraisers do their work: a test of the appraisal process and the development of a descriptive model, *Journal of Real Estate Research*, 1990, 5:1, 1–15.

Diaz, J. The first decade of behavioural research in the discipline of property, *Journal of Property Investment and Finance*, 1999, 17:4, 326–332.

Diaz, J. and Wolverton, M. A longitudinal examination of the appraisal smoothing hypothesis, 1998, Real Estate Economics, 26:2, 349–358.

Diaz, J., Gallimore, P., and Levy, D. Residential valuation behavior in the United States, the United Kingdom, and New Zealand, 2000, RICS Property Research Conference, London.

Drivers Jonas/IPD. *The variance in valuations: interim report*, 1997, Drivers Jonas/Investment Property Databank, London.

Fischer, J. D., Miles, M.E., and Webb, R. B. How Reliable are commercial appraisals? Another look, *Real Estate Finance*, 1999, 16:3, 9–15.

Gallimore, P. and Wolverton, M. The objective in valuation: a study of the influence of client feedback, *Journal of Property Research*, 2000, 17:1, 47–57.

Gau, G. W., Lai, T.-Y., and Wang, K. Optimal Comparable Selection and Weighting in Real Property Valuation: An Extension, *Journal of the American Real Estate and Urban Economics Association*, 1992, 20:1, 107–123.

Graff, R. A. and Webb, J. R. Agency costs and inefficiency in commercial real estate, *Journal of Real Estate Portfolio Management*, 1997, 3:1, 19–36.

Graff, R. A. and Young, M. S. The magnitude of random appraisal error in commercial real estate valuation, *Journal of Real Estate Research*, 1999, 17:1/2, 33–54.

Hendershott, P.H. and Kane, E. J. US office market values during the pasr decade: how distorted have appraisals been?, *Real Estate Economics*, 1995, 23:2, 101–116.

Hursch, C. J., Hammond, K. R., and Hursch, J. L. Some methodological considerations in multiple-cue probability studies, *Psychological Review*, 1964, 71:1, 42–60.

Langfield-Smith, K. M. and Locke, S. M. A lens on valuation, *Journal of Valuation*, 1988, 6:1, 365–381.

Matysiak, G. Comment on: valuation by comparable sales and linear algebra, *Journal of Property Research*, 1991, 8:1, 21–27.

Matysiak, G. and Wang, P. Commercial property market prices and valuations: analysing the correspondence, *Journal of Property Research*, 1995, 12:3, 181–202.

Newell, G. and Kishore, R. The accuracy of commercial property valuations, 4th Pacific Rim Real Estate Society Conference, 1998, Perth.

Quan, D. C. and Quigley, J. M. Price formation and the appraisal function in real estate markets, Journal of Real Estate Finance and Economics, 1991, 4:2, 127–147.

Parker, D. Valuation accuracy – an Australian perspective, 4th Pacific Rim Real Estate Society Conference, 1998, Perth.

Stewart, T. R. Improving reliability of judgmental forecasts, in Scott Armstrong, J. (ed), *Principles of forecasting: a handbook for researchers and practitioners*, 1999, Norwell, MA., Kluwer Academic Publishers.

Stewart, T. R. and Lusk, C. M. Seven components of judgmental forecasting skill: implications for research and improvement of forecasts, *Journal of Forecasting*, 13, 579–599.

Stewart, T. R., Roebber, P. J., and Bosart, L. F. The importance of the task in analysing expert judgment, *Organizational Behavior and Human Decision Processes*, 1997, 69:3, 205–219.

Tucker, L. R. A suggested alternative formulation in the developments by Hursh, Hammond and Hursch, and by Hammond, Hursch and Todd, *Psychological Review*, 1964, 71:6, 528–530.

Webb, R. B. On the reliability of commercial appraisals: an analysis of properties sold from the Russell-NCREIF index, *Real Estate Finance*, 1994, 11:1, 62–5.

Wolverton, M. and Gallimore, P. Client Feedback and the Role of the Appraiser, *Journal of Real Estate Research*, 1999, 18:3, 415–431.

Vandell, K. Optimal Comparable Selection and Weighting in Real Property Valuation, *AREUEA Journal*, 1991, 19:2, 213–239.

II

REGRESSION, MINIMUM-VARIANCE
GRID METHOD, AND OTHER VALUATION
MODELING TECHNIQUES

Chapter 4

An Investigation of Property Price Studies

Kicki Björklund, Bo Söderberg, and Mats Wilhelmsson
Section of Building and Real Estate Economics, Royal Institute of Technology, Stockholm, Sweden

4.1 Introduction

4.1.1 Background and Purpose

Several delicate issues are connected to the question of how to compose scientific papers. A number of rules and guidelines apply – some interdisciplinary, others common for all sciences. The scientific policies of the academic journals, but also their space constraints, play an important role in forming the rules. Still, in several situations the question regarding what should be explained and interpreted explicitly and what may be left for the reader to understand is open. In the present paper, we address one area of economic science where we believe some guidelines regarding the reporting of scientific research are well established. In particular, we consider a number of general methodological guidelines associated with the treatment and reporting of empirical econometric research.

We empirically investigate whether this belief is well founded. We turn to a specific field of applied scientific research, to see to what extent these guidelines appear to have influenced the researchers when writing their papers. The body of research addressed is the vast sub-discipline of real-estate economics (including housing as well as urban economics) that deals with the empirical estimation of property-price equations by regression techniques. The selection of papers investigated contains articles published in leading peer reviewed journals.

The purpose of the present paper is twofold. Firstly, we aim at providing an overview of the prevalence of property-price studies, and roughly classifying the articles of the sample into a number of subgroups. In what journals are these kinds of articles found and in what frequency? What topics are addressed? Secondly, we investigate the adherence to good scientific practice when reporting the econometric issues of property-price studies. Is the modeling explicitly motivated? Is the data set presented? Are the empirical findings put in perspective?

It is reasonable to assume that if a particular issue (for example, a discussion of data reliability) is reported in a paper, then this indicates its authors are aware of its importance and in turn, that they have considered its importance when carrying out their analysis, although one cannot be certain that they did. On the other hand, an issue may have been thoroughly considered during the research process without that being explicitly reported in the paper. Having this in mind, we want to stress that the present paper investigates what is *reported* in the sample of articles. We do not speculate further over what the authors may or may not have considered.

4.1.2 Method

A review of the literature by McCloskey and Ziliak (1996) inspired the present study. Our work resembles their analysis in some respects, we do not try to replicate their study. What McCloskey and Ziliak focused on was the distinction between economic and statistical significance. Their main point was that a difference can be statistically significant without being significant or of consequence in economic terms or for science or policy. According to McCloskey and Ziliak, a key element in any empirical investigation is the interpretation in economic terms of its findings. The analysis must be placed in its proper context and the relevance of the results for policy and science discussed. In particular, statistical and economic significance must not be confused.

McCloskey and Ziliak investigated how this issue was treated in leading textbooks in econometrics as well as in articles using regression analysis that had been published in *American Economic Review* between 1980 and 1990.

"... We here examine the alarming hypothesis that ordinary usage in economics takes statistical significance to be the same as economic significance. We compare statistical best practice against leading textbooks of recent decades and against the papers using regression analysis in the 1980s in the *American Economic Review* ..." (McCloskey and Ziliak, 1996, p. 98).

They confronted their selection of articles with nineteen "yes"/"no" questions, in which a "no" signified that statistical significance is not distinguished from economic relevance. Their findings indicate that largely the authors misunderstand statistical significance. Even though the focus of McCloskey and Ziliak was statistical significance vs. economic significance, they included in their analysis of the papers several related important concepts and present a series of steps that represents adherence to proper econometric practice and good scientific procedure in general.

Methodologically the present paper follows that by McCloskey and Ziliak, but we consider a number of issues that fall into the category of good scientific practice, rather than focusing on the sole issue of statistical significance. Instead of focusing on articles from a single journal, we focus on articles from several.

Our selection of journals includes the leading ones on real estate, housing and urban economics and our choice of articles includes those on property-price (or rent) studies that apply regression techniques. The articles were published during the six years from 1990 to 1995. The 145 articles we selected were all empirical studies.

We discuss a number of basic guidelines for reporting research in general and econometrics in particular and for each, we have formulated a question that when it elicits a positive answer indicates that the article under examination has made a scientifically accurate treatment of its subject, or adheres to good econometric practice. The following key aspects are considered. (1) Identification of the sub-disciplines to which the paper belongs; (2) presentation of the model and the modeling process; (3) explanation of the sample and sampling process; and (4) completeness in the presentation and interpretation of the results. The resulting questionnaire contains 18 questions. (A few of our questions are similar or identical to some of the questions posed by McCloskey and Ziliak.)

Some of the guidelines addressed apply equally well to all kinds of econometric studies. These guidelines were obtained from standard textbooks in econometrics or from McCloskey and Ziliak. Other guidelines addressed are perhaps more specific to the research area we are investigating. These were derived from a number of review studies, briefly examined below. Finally, a few of the guidelines are very general and apply to any kind of scientific writing.

We then tried to answer all the questions in the questionnaire for each of the articles we had selected. If our questions are all well received by other researchers and if these researchers share our views, we would expect the results to include only high frequencies of "yes" replies. However, there are several reasons why this need not necessarily be the case, some of which are discussed below.

We do not single out individual articles for public flogging. Rather, we discuss how key aspects in the investigative process have been treated in the articles investigated as a whole. Our analysis of one particular aspect is not meant to detract from the contributions made in other aspects. Consequently, the evaluation of the questionnaire responses should not be interpreted as an instrument for disqualifying individual papers. Rather, one ought to regard the results as a starting point in an attempt to revive the previous frank debate concerning the role of, and the form for presenting, applied econometrics in property price studies. Furthermore, the questionnaire itself may serve as a checklist, though limited, for writers of papers of the kind as well as for editorial referees.

The rationale of focusing on how econometric research is presented in practice is the growing importance of statistics within scientific research in general, and within economics in particular. Furthermore, as summarized below, many of the earlier reviews have recommended improvements to specific econometric issues. It may therefore be of some interest to investigate whether these recommendations, or any of them, have affected research published after these reviews.

4.1.3 Organization

The remainder of the paper is organized in the following way. Firstly, we briefly review some of the classic papers as well as some of the early reviews of property-price studies. Then follows a section describing the sample-generating process, and discuss our selection of journals and some descriptive statistics on the selected articles in the sample. We then present the questionnaire and our arguments for the relevance of each question. The results follow next. The paper closes with a short discussion of major conclusions.

4.2 Literature Review

4.2.1 Some Classic Papers

The first work, in which a real estate price equation is estimated by multiple regression analysis, is probably that by Haas (1922). This paper is an excellent piece of research that appears very modern in most of its aspects. The paper adheres remarkably well to good econometric practice as defined by our questionnaire and it was the forerunner of a first period of interest in this particular kind of research. All studies during this period of the real estate market were done before the term "hedonic price" was introduced by Court (1939) in a study of the prices of automobiles.

The increasing availability of computing power after the Second World War supported the wave of price equation studies that followed. A third wave of research included the work that followed upon the development of the theoretical framework. This was done primarily by Rosen (1974), who formulated a theory for hedonic prices applied to heterogeneous goods in general, but also in a major empirical work with real estate market application, namely Kain and Quigley (1970).

The term "hedonic technique" has gradually been established as more or less synonymous with the application of regression analysis in the study of real estate prices. However, many of the various studies categorized as "hedonic analyses" may have little in common scientifically. The studies that build on Rosen aim generally at estimating the *demand* for housing or for specific attributes, with the estimation of hedonic prices being more of an inevitable introductory step. However, other studies aim at estimating the *marginal price effect* of different attributes and predicting market prices.

In principle, the use of the hedonic technique as a means for holding the quality of attributes constant when creating price index series for heterogeneous products falls within yet another research area. In his seminal work, Griliches (1961) revived the ideas put forward by Court and created the theoretical foundation for this field. A fourth group of property price studies where regression analysis is applied consists of work aiming at explaining the general price movements on the market in terms of macroeconomic variables and other market fundamentals. In practice however, there are no clear borders between the groups. Many papers belong in two or more of them.

The empirical literature has a long history and a vast number of studies have been published. In fact, there is much more than one can possibly survey, which emphasizes the need for literature reviews that summarize the state of the literature and help to put individual papers into perspective. However, over the years only a few reviews covering the area have been written, and the latest traditional reviews date back some ten to fifteen years. Thus, it still seems legitimate to conduct further reviews of the area. Such reviews may examine what has happened within the field during the past ten to fifteen years. Furthermore, the literature may be reviewed from a number of fundamentally different viewpoints, addressing both empirical and theoretical aspects.

4.2.2 Earlier Reviews

We have found eight reviews or review-like papers on regression analyses of property prices, but excepting Miller (1982) who worked from findings by Ball (1973), none builds on any of the others. The eight reviews are briefly summarized below. The first three were published before Rosen's article and so none refers to the concept of "hedonic".

The earliest known review is Salter (1948), which examines American research in rural land economics up to the mid 1940s. A minor part of this comprehensive review discusses the role, within the evolving discipline, of the early regression analyses applied to land price equations. However, Salter provides no details as to how these early studies were designed, nor does he summarize the empirical findings of the various studies. Furthermore, his review does not touch upon urban applications.

Lessinger (1969) discusses and criticizes the widespread use of linear models in real estate price regressions. He argues that apart from the much ignored multicollinearity problem, the researchers do not recognize that the true functional relation between attributes and the price is rarely additive, nor do they discuss their choice of model specification. Lessinger briefly presents 17 studies published between 1958 and 1966, as representatives of the second wave of regression analysis of real estate appraisal.

Ball (1973) presents a thorough and detailed review of 11 papers (6 of them UK studies, 5 US) published between 1965 and 1973. This is the first traditional review, where empirical studies are systematically compared. Ball examines the papers in following technical aspects: data sources, dependent variable, sample size, statistical method, significant parameters and degree of fit. He could not conclude which approach and what variables are preferable, as all studies produce high R^2 values in spite of their being very different in these aspects.

Maclennan (1977) discusses a number of theoretical problems related to housing price studies, rather than investigating empirical findings. In particular, the implicit assumptions that usually underlie hedonic studies are questioned. Generally, the market is assumed to be in equilibrium, though this is often unlikely. The possible existence of sub-markets is ignored as well as the role of search costs and the supply side of the market. The functional forms used in hedonic estimations also reveal implicit assumptions that are not likely to be realistic. For example, the linear form implies that the marginal valuation of an attribute is invariant with the quantity level. Maclennan also stresses the risk that the omission of important variables causes estimation bias.

Miller (1982) presents a traditional review of the literature that builds on Ball's review. Miller makes an effort to classify the many studies in the field into different categories. This paper has the longest reference list of all the reviews; most of the 118 studies reviewed are empirical, but most of them appear only in the overall categorization exhibit, and are not analyzed in detail in the text. In reviewing the studies Miller focuses firstly on the current understanding of factors that affect property values and secondly on current limitations of the hedonic method. He concludes that the understanding of how fundamental factors (physical and location attributes) influence property values is well established and that the attention must now focus on financial factors and transaction costs. Regarding the limitations, he especially emphasizes that the problem with multicollinearity must be fully recognized.

Follain and Jimenez (1985) made an extensive traditional review of studies that aimed at estimating the demand for housing and location attributes. This review differs from those discussed above in taking Rosen (1974) as a natural theoretical starting point. Follain and Jimenez reviewed only post-Rosen articles that intended to estimate the effect of *demand* rather than *price*. They distinguished five groups among the studies according to the econometric procedures used in the estimations. They argued that the two-step technique proposed by Rosen seems to be the best. These studies empirical findings showed little regularity, particularly the estimates of willingness to pay for various attributes. The income and price elasticity of demand also varied considerably, but revealed some patterns. The income elasticity of demand was generally low for space but high for quality.

Mark and Goldberg (1988) made an extensive survey of the application of regression analysis in appraisal and assessment in an article that is not a traditional review of other studies, but is a review of issues, techniques available and likely problems. These include topics such as model specification, choice of statistical estimator, stepwise techniques, interaction, non-linearity, stratification, and multicollinearity, as exemplified by several empirical papers.

Smith and Huang (1995) made an untraditional analysis of hedonic studies published between 1967 and 1988 that contained empirical estimates of marginal willingness to pay for better air quality. They did not review how the studies were done, but utilized the various hedonic estimates as new observations in a meta-analysis. They examined 37 papers, chose 20 of them, and could reconstruct 86 hedonic estimates from them. The estimates of marginal willingness to pay are regressed by Smith and Huang on income, vacancy, level of air pollution and variables capturing the modeling technique of the reviewed papers. They found several independent variables to be significant in the meta-analysis.

To summarize, we can state that the reviews we found are not particularly well coordinated, nor do they build further on each other chronologically or focus on the same issues. In perhaps two respects it is possible to infer that there is a tendency towards consensus among the earlier reviews. Firstly, they criticize the theoretical aspects of the studies they examined, as well as their use of econometric tools, how their models are built and how the work is founded in underlying theory. Secondly, though we may now know rather well what determines relative prices, little is still known about demand.

4.3 The Sample Generating Process

4.3.1 Journals Examined

The initial tasks in the sampling procedure are those of delimiting the discipline of real estate economics and identifying the relevant academic journals. Two studies, Webb and Albert (1995) and Diaz, Black and Rabianski (1996), that ranked the real estate journals helped us with this task. We decided to include journals that deal primarily with real estate, housing and urban economics. The articles investigated should be original research presented according to academic publishing principles. To limit the initial screening process we excluded journals that specialize in planning, policy and regional science.

Of American journals, we relied on the classification into an Academic and a Professional group proposed by Diaz, Black and Rabianski (1996). We included all the academic journals listed in that review except the *Journal of Regional Science* (*JRS*) on account of limitations mentioned above; the *Housing Finance Review* (*HFR*), which has ceased publication and the *Journal of Real Estate Literature* (*JREL*), which we found contained no articles of the particular kind we were looking for. We added one journal that Diaz, Black and Rabianski (1996) did not mention – the *Journal of Housing Research* (*JHR*) – as it has all the usual attributes of an academic journal. Furthermore, we added one of the professional journals, *Appraisal Journal* (*AJ*), as it was highly ranked in both ranking articles.

The European real estate journals are perhaps not so well known in America and neither ranking study considered them. We selected European journals using ordinary literature searches and in the light of our own experiences. We included any journal with a policy of publishing original research work, a double-blind review procedure and an editorial board dominated by researchers. Eight European journals met these standards but we excluded four because their major topics are planning, policy and regional science: *Urban*

Table 1: Journals Used for Generating the Sample of Articles

Journal		UK Journals	Year Founded	Volumes Searched	Total Number of Articles
Appraisal Journal	*AJ*		1932	58–63	357
Housing Studies	*HS*	UK	1986	5–10	125
Journal of Housing Economics	*JHE*		1991	1–4	73
Journal of Housing Research	*JHR*		1990	1–6	70
Journal of Property Finance	*JPF*	UK	1990	3–6	93
Journal of Property Research	*JPR*	UK	1984	7–12	86
Journal of Property Valuation and Investment	*JPVI*	UK	1982	9–12	48
Journal of Real Estate Finance and Economics	*JREFE*		1988	3–11	186
Journal of Real Estate Research	*JRER*		1986	5–10*	193
Journal of Urban Economics	*JUE*		1974	27–38	266
Land Economics	*LE*		1925	66–71	224
Real Estate Economics	*REE*		1973	18–23	161
Total					1,882

* Volume 10: Issues 1–4.

Studies (*US*), *Regional Science and Urban Economics* (*RSUE*), the *Netherlands Journal of Housing and the Built Environment* (*NJHBE*) and *Scandinavian Housing and Planning Research* (*SHPR*). Of the remaining four, two have a section for academic papers and another for professional papers, namely the *Journal of Property Finance* (*JPF*) and the *Journal of Property Valuation and Investment* (*JPVI*). We used only articles from their academic sections. The other two European journals are *Housing Studies* (*HS*) and the *Journal of Property Research* (*JPR*).

With a few minor exceptions, the total population is then all full-length articles published in these 12 journals during the period 1990–1995. The journals and volumes examined are listed in Table 1. The total number of articles found is 1,882. The next step was to read all these articles to select those that included estimations of price or rent equations by regression techniques; however, we excluded articles on unimproved land.

4.3.2 The Sample of Articles Studied

The procedure resulted in a sample of 145 articles, i.e., almost 8% of the population. The distribution of the sample over the journals and over the different years of the period is shown in Table 2. Only 10 came from the four British journals. Six of the journals yielded 12 articles or more each, and together yielded 122 articles, i.e., some 84% of the sample. For two of the

Table 2: Articles in the Sample by Journal and Year of Publication

Journal	Year						Total	Share of Sample (Percent)	Share of Articles in Respective Journals (Percent)
	1990	1991	1992	1993	1994	1995			
AJ	1	3	4	3	5	0	16	11.0	4.5
HS	1	0	0	0	0	0	1	0.7	0.8
JHE	–	5	3	–	1	2	11	7.6	15.1
JHR	0	0	0	2	0	0	2	1.4	2.9
JPF	–	–	0	0	0	1	1	0.7	1.1
JPR	2	0	0	1	0	4	7	4.8	8.1
JPVI	0	0	0	1	0	–	1	0.7	2.1
JREFE	2	2	1	9	3	4	21	14.5	11.3
JRER	14	2	5	5	1	3	30	20.7	15.5
JUE	2	4	8	3	5	3	25	17.2	9.4
LE	3	2	3	1	1	2	12	8.3	5.4
REE	4	5	6	2	0	1	18	12.4	11.2
Total Share of Sample (Percent)	29	23	30	27	16	20	145	100.0	7.7
	20.0	15.9	20.7	18.6	11.0	13.8	100.0		

journals, nearly half of the articles appeared in one particular year. Thus, there are 14 articles in the *Journal of Real Estate Research* (*JRER*) 1990, and 9 articles in the *Journal of Real Estate Finance and Economics* (*JREFE*) 1993. The two journals that yielded most articles of the particular kind were the *Journal of Real Estate Research* (*JRER*) and the *Journal of Urban Economics* (*JUE*), at 30 and 25 respectively. The two journals with the greatest yield percentually were the *Journal of Real Estate Research* (*JRER*) and the *Journal of Housing Economics* (*JHE*), with around 15% each.

Within the sample, we can identify a number of subsets: (i) two classes of main purposes of the studies, being either (a) the estimation of coefficients for individual attributes, or (b) the search for a model as a whole; (ii) the dependent variable can be (c) a price (or value) estimate, or (d) a measure of return (or revenue); (iii) the kinds of real estate in question are (e) owner-occupied or (f) income (investment) properties. Figure 1 shows the distribution of the

Figure 1: Articles in the sample, by main Purpose, type of Dependent Variable and Type of Property studied

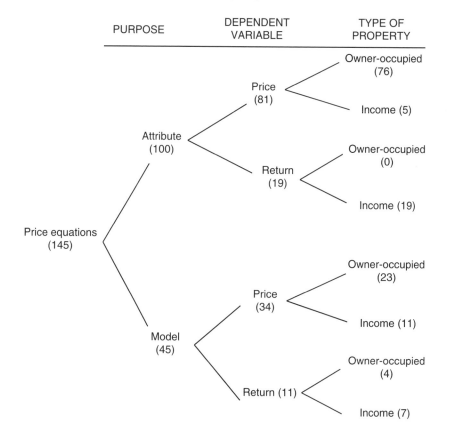

sample over different conjunctions of these subsets. Surprisingly little work has been done in some areas. For example, the hedonic technique is rarely applied to income properties.

It is interesting to see the distribution of the researchers that have produced these studies. Many papers are jointly written and the total number of authors behind the 145 articles is 207. As many as 163 of them have participated in only one of the articles, whereas 26 wrote two, 11 three, and 7 authors wrote or contributed to four or more articles. In other words, it seems that researchers who do not regularly produce articles of this particular kind wrote most of the studies reviewed in the present paper. However, it may also be that the present review only traced a small part of the total stock of articles within this sub-topic of real estate published during the period in question, or that a six-year period is too short to be a basis for drawing such conclusions.

4.3.3 Applying the Questionnaire

The last step in the data-generating process was to answer our 18 questions with respect to each of the 145 articles. This we did by using a printed form with a check box for each of the 18 questions, as well as category alternatives used for sub-group classifications. We read each article with a questionnaire at hand and, when we deemed a part of its text provided an answer to one of our questions, checked the appropriate box and marked the text appropriately.

The 145 studies reviewed are a heterogeneous group of articles. They are all reports of empirical work, only partly using the same analytical tool, but they cover a wide range of sub-disciplines within economics. The sample contains both time series and cross-section analyses. Furthermore, there is a scientifically fundamental difference between studies that aim at estimating and explaining economic phenomena in terms of the individual variables, and those where models are constructed to predict general tendencies.

Being aware of the possibility that the heterogeneity in the sample could confuse the results, we also applied the analysis to a sub-sample of methodologically homogenous articles. The results obtained from the whole sample and from the sub-sample hardly differ. (The results from the sub-sample are not reported here, but are available upon request.) The sub-sample consists of the traditional hedonic studies where the implicit prices of individual attributes are estimated, where the application is to owner-occupied housing, and where the theory was considered to be microeconomic. The sub-sample is, therefore, more homogeneous than the whole sample in terms of the terminology, purpose and standard literature references, and supposedly also in terms of the authors' views of what is econometrically appropriate. The size of the sub-sample is 59. These articles all belong to the group of 76 articles found at the top right of Figure 1.

4.4 The Questionnaire

The questionnaire consists of 18 questions, all of which were chosen subjectively. Consequently, we have subjectively chosen *not* to consider an uncountable number of *other* questions that are just as important when examining the over-all quality of empirical research presented in academic articles. Furthermore, we are aware that it is impossible to weigh and rank the scientific importance of the individual questions, and that the relative importance of a specific question depends on the nature of the study investigated. Thus, the results of applying the questionnaire are not to be regarded as a quality index.

We have tried to avoid all difficulties that follow from having to interpret the intention of the authors when looking for answers to our questionnaire. Thus, our questions were formulated so as to enable us to find concrete answers to them in the studies. However, this has not always been easy, and this circumstance remains a possible source for bias in the results.

There is one general principle that is fundamental for understanding the relevance of almost all the 18 questions. The general reason for using statistical or econometric methods in applied research is that these tools make it possible to draw conclusions about a (large) *population* from observations of a (smaller) *sample*, i.e., to make statistical inferences. To be able to draw such conclusions properly it is essential that the studies be carried out in accordance with the assumptions under which the econometric tools are derived. The standard textbooks in econometrics discuss these issues thoroughly and recommend the users to control for possible violation of assumptions. However, regression techniques may also be used for out of sample predictions, regardless of what the underlying theory may look like or what the statistical interpretations may be. From that perspective, the discussion in this section of the paper becomes less relevant. However, having that perspective means that the results from a regression analysis largely lack scientific interpretability.

The 18 questions presented and discussed below are clustered together in four groups. Two questions (1 and 2) are related to the presentation of how the work is connected to previous research. Six questions (3 through 8) are related to how the considerations underlying the modeling procedure are presented and four questions (9 through 12) to how the data is presented. Finally, six questions (13 through 18) are related to how the results are presented and interpreted. Appendix 1 presents citation examples, which indicate what we required for a "yes" answer to each question.

Though it is impossible to weigh the importance of the questions, from a purely econometric point of view, some may be regarded as more fundamental. Thus, we propose that for five of the questions a negative answer may be more severe from an econometric point of view than for the remaining questions. The questions, referred to below as the "five most important questions", are 6, 7, 10, 17 and 18. The reason for emphasizing these questions is that each relates to one or more issues where methodological shortcomings may bias empirical results.

4.4.1 Questions about Relation to Previous Research

The following two questions address the relationship, if any, of the paper to previous research:

(1) *Does the paper contain any theoretical discussion that permits it to be assigned to an established scientific tradition?*
(2) *Does the paper refer to any similar study that facilitates its comparison of its method, its data and its results?*

Research in general aims to contribute to existing knowledge of its discipline. The results of a regression analysis have little meaning for a reader unless a researcher's theoretical framework is known. It may otherwise appear as measurement without theory. Though this is hardly the case in any research, and though it may be obvious in most cases what the relevant scientific tradition is, it is preferable that it not be left to the reader to make assumptions in this respect. Furthermore, it is generally regarded to be the responsibility of the author to facilitate critical examination of the work. Thus, it is preferable that the author put new contributions in perspective by making explicit some of the work he or she regards as representing the present state of the art.

4.4.2 Questions about Modeling Procedures

The six questions about modeling procedures are:

(3) *Is the choice of functional form for the equation motivated?*
(4) *Is the choice of independent variables in the equation motivated?*
(5) *Are hypotheses or assumptions about the most important independent variables expressed?*
(6) *Is there any discussion about the risk that relevant independent variables are omitted in the model?*

(7) *Does the author make any kind of judgment whether the parameter estimates are reasonable or not?*

(8) *Are variables allowed to remain in the equation even when they are statistically non-significant?*

The earlier reviews of the literature, briefly presented above, for the most part discuss the problems related to the choice of the functional form. Particularly, Lessinger (1969), Maclennan (1977) and Miller (1982) criticize the most commonly used model specification. Furthermore, several papers have stated that the choice of functional form cannot be derived from theory; see for example Cassel and Mendelsohn (1985). Thus, the topic is highly non-trivial. Similarly, the choice of independent, explanatory variables is never unimportant. The body of empirical research has established the general economic significance of a large number of price-affecting variables. However, some variables may be important in some sub-markets, but irrelevant in others. By selecting a particular explanatory variable, the researcher has implicitly announced that this variable is regarded important or potentially important. The reader would prefer to know the considerations that underlie these choices of the explanatory variables as well as how they mathematically enter the regression model.

Furthermore, it is preferable that it not be left for the reader to figure out the relevant hypotheses regarding the estimates for the explanatory variables, at least for the ones that are closely related to the main purpose of the study. This is not equally important for explanatory variables that just enter the model to control for potential effects. However, it is important to be aware of which variables are likely to have an effect, and in case data on such variables are missing, one would want the researcher to comment upon the situation. For non-biased and consistent parameter estimates, for example, each omitted relevant variable must be uncorrelated with each of the included or at least with the variables of interest.

As econometrics is measurement, it would be natural to apply standard guidelines related to measurement in general. This involves checking for possible measurement errors, including stochastic, large and systematic errors. One way to check for large errors is to examine the reasonability of the results, either by comparisons with other studies or by general judgments. This procedure may appear to be closely related to formulating hypotheses regarding the coefficients and economically interpreting the results, but it is in principle a different issue related to the modeling and the process of variable selection.

A variable that is explicitly considered in the initial stages of the modeling, presumably because of its theoretical reasonability, is sometimes spurned later in the analysis because of statistical non-significance. However, in case all explanatory variables are included in the model because the researcher really expects them to have a significant effect, one would assume the researcher regards a non-significant result equally interesting as a significant result. Thus, excluding non-significant variables may give the impression that the research is more of a hypothesis generating process, where the initial selection of explanatory variables is somewhat mechanical or determined by data availability. McCloskey and Ziliak (1996, p. 104) regard the exclusion of non-significant variables as an indication that economic relevance is confused with statistical significance. Therefore, the reader would prefer to see the results with respect to all variables.

4.4.3 Questions about the Data

Our four questions about the data used are:

(9) *Is the data source explicitly presented?*
(10) *Is there any discussion about the risk of the data not being valid or reliable?*
(11) *Are descriptive statistics for the variables presented, including one estimate of the central tendency and one estimate of the deviations?*
(12) *Can the number of observations be found explicitly in the paper?*

A fundamental issue in all sciences is that it should be possible for other scientists to check the analyses and results. Therefore it is highly relevant to expect researchers to provide the complete data set to other researchers (upon request), and many academic journals require that this be done as a condition for accepting papers. However, there are also plausible reasons for not providing the full data set used. Collecting or creating data is very time consuming, and the researcher would usually want to explore the full possibilities of his database (perhaps in future studies) before handing out detailed information to others. However, it should at least be possible to replicate a study reasonably well, which would require having similar data, or being able to examine critically the reliability of the data used. To be able to do so, one would want to know how the data set was generated and from what data source it was taken.

If the independent variables contain a measurement error, bias will trouble all estimated parameters; see Greene (1997). It is well known that data more or less always contain such errors. Thus, the reader would want to know something about the quality of the data used according to an investigation or to the researcher's judgment. Furthermore, it is elementary to include units of variables and then also to provide means, as empirical work in economics is measurement, see McCloskey and Ziliak (1996, p. 102).

Knowing the number of observations is useful when evaluating the results. One argument is that coefficients are likely to be statistically significant only if the sample is large enough, thus allowing the rejection of sound hypotheses; see McCloskey and Ziliak (1996, p. 99). On the other hand, Mark and Goldberg (1988, p. 93) argue that it is necessary to have a large sample to be able to use the results of regression analysis with confidence. In any case, the reader would be interested in this figure.

4.4.4 Questions about the Results

Our six questions about how the results are presented and interpreted are:

(13) *Can the explanatory power of the regression be found explicitly in the paper?*
(14) *Are there any comments or discussions that interpret the level of the explanatory power?*
(15) *Are estimates of individual coefficient parameters interpreted economically?*
(16) *Is there any discussion about the meaning of the estimated t-values, F-values or standard deviations?*
(17) *Are the results from a residual analysis presented, or does the author refer to a residual analysis that has been carried out though it is not presented?*
(18) *Is there any discussion about the risk of the independent variables being co-linear, or the possible consequences of some variables being co-linear?*

The coefficient of determination, or R^2-value, is often used as a measure of the goodness of fit of the model. It is a composite, benchmark figure that gives the reader a first hint of the overall performance of the model. However, nothing in the regression analyses requires the determination coefficient to be high, and a high explanatory power is not evidence in favor of the model. "In fact the most important thing about R^2 is that it is not important in the CR [classical regression] model" (Goldberger, 1991, p. 177). Therefore, a discussion about the meaning of R^2-value reveals a deeper understanding of the regression technique. Consequently, the reader would always want to see the R^2-value but would also prefer to have the value commented, interpreted or compared with that of similar studies.

Economic interpretations about individual parameters are important as they make it possible for the reader to judge whether the parameter estimates are reasonable or not, see McCloskey and Ziliak (1996, p. 102). Therefore, it is desirable that it not be left to the reader to recalculate the parameter estimates of the model into real-world interpretations. Furthermore, the *t*-test and the *F*-test usually only test whether coefficients (individually or jointly) are different from zero. However, this is not always the relevant hypothesis to test. Thus, it is preferable that the author explicitly expresses what hypotheses are tested, and what the interpretation of the test results should be. By so doing, any speculation about the tests having been applied, or reported, mechanically may be avoided.

The classical regression analysis relies upon a number of assumptions regarding the error term; e.g., see Goldberger (1991). If these are not fulfilled the interpretations of the estimated parameters are restricted. For example, ignoring the violation of the assumptions about constant variance and non-correlation between errors when applying OLS, yields estimators that are not efficient and hypothesis tests that are not valid. Thus, residual analysis is one of the most fundamental parts of regression analysis. Though residual analyses may be lengthy, and perhaps appear something of a sidetrack from the main analysis, it is preferable for the major results from the residual analyses to be mentioned.

An important implication of high multicollinearity is that the estimated standard error of each coefficient will be high, which lowers the *t*-values and may cause spurious non-significance. Multicollinearity may also considerably affect parameter estimates, thus biasing the economic interpretation of individual variables. As discussed by Lessinger (1969) and Mark and Goldberg (1988) the problem of multicollinearity often occurs when variables are housing attributes. Thus, one would want the researcher to report the results from investigating the possible existence of multicollinearity, or at least to make judgments regarding the risks and the possible consequences of the results.

4.5 Results

4.5.1 General

The major results of the research in this paper are to be found in the simple descriptive statistics on the frequency of "yes" answers to the 18 questions. Table 3 presents the outcome of the questionnaire as a percentage of "yes" answers. The results for the different questions vary considerably. The frequency ranges from some 20% up to over 90%, with an average of 58%. The total number of "yes" answers per article ranges from 5 to 15, with an average of 10.4. Figure 2(a) illustrates the distribution graphically.

Overall, the selected articles give recognition to the issues raised in our questionnaire. They explicitly address a major part of the topics discussed. Almost all

Table 3: Result from Applying the Questionnaire: Frequency of "Yes" Answers (in Percent)

Question	Frequency of "Yes" (Percent)
1. Does the paper contain any theoretical discussion that permits it to be assigned to an established scientific tradition?	84
2. Does the paper refer to any similar study that facilitates its comparison of its method, its data and its results?	70
3. Is the choice of functional form for the equation motivated?	27
4. Is the choice of independent variables in the equation motivated?	47
5. Are hypotheses or assumptions about the most important independent variables expressed?	61
6. Is there any discussion about the risk that relevant independent variables are omitted in the model?	**19**
7. Does the author make any kind of judgment whether the parameter estimates are reasonable or not?	**59**
8. Are variables allowed to remain in the equation even when they are statistically non-significant?	81
9. Is the data source explicitly presented?	83
10. Is there any discussion about the risk of the data not being valid or reliable?	**22**
11. Are descriptive statistics for the variables presented, including one estimate of the central tendency and one estimate of the deviations?	59
12. Can the number of observations be found explicitly in the paper?	93
13. Can the explanatory power of the regression be found explicitly in the paper?	93
14. Are there any comments or discussions that interpret the level of the explanatory power?	28
15. Are estimates of individual coefficient parameters interpreted economically?	78
16. Is there any discussion about the meaning of the estimated t-values, F-values or standard deviations?	77
17. Are the results from a residual analysis presented, or does the author refer to a residual analysis that has been carried out though it is not presented?	**25**
18. Is there any discussion about the risk of the independent variables being co-linear, or the possible consequences of some variables being co-linear?	**34**
Average, all 18 questions	58
Average, the five "most important questions"	32

The five "most important questions" in bold letters.
Source: Authors.

Figure 2: Distribution of articles over number of "yes"-answers per article to all 18 questions (a) as well as to the five "most important questions" (b)
Source: Authors

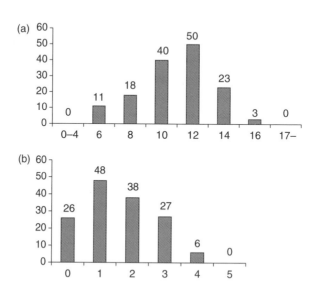

empirical work in the articles rests on a theoretical discussion. Comparisons to other studies are also frequently carried out, though not fully as often.

However, only a small share of the papers, 27%, explains the choice of functional form. The corresponding figure for articles using a linear function is even lower, namely 18%. Almost 50% motivate their choice of independent variables and a slightly larger group presents assumptions for the chosen variables. However, they do not discuss the risks connected to excluding possibly relevant variables to the same extent.

The presentations of the data are generally rather substantial. Almost every article presents the number of observations and the data sources. The number of articles that present descriptive statistics is lower, and only one out of five papers discusses the validity of the data, possibly indicating the assumed absence of measurement error in the data.

Nearly all articles present the explanatory power, but less than one third of them say anything about their interpretation of this figure. In many cases the explanatory power is very high (e.g. over 0.80) or very low (e.g. lower than 0.10) without being commented upon. A large number of articles comment on significant figures and discuss the economic interpretation of estimated coefficients. However, only a third of the papers explicitly give recognition to the multicollinearity problem, and only one out of four presents a residual analysis.

If we separately examine the results for the five "most important questions" the over-all impression is less notable. The frequency ranges from some 20% up to some 60%, with an average of 32%. The total number of "yes" answers per article to these five questions ranges from 0 to 4, with an average of 1.6. Figure 2(b) illustrates the distribution graphically.

A common aspect of the five "most important questions" is that they all relate to econometric issues where shortcomings may lead to biased results. From an econometric point of view, one would expect a systematically "better" result with respect to these questions. On the other hand, the studies reviewed are all applied research where econometrics is a tool rather than the main attraction. Therefore, it is also reasonable to expect that space constraints in combination with adaptations to what is supposed to be the focal interest of the readers, cause the econometric issues be kept to a minimum.

We made various attempts to isolate sub-groups within the sample regarding differences in the results. We found almost no tendencies towards explainable variation between different sub-samples. In particular, an attempt to rank the journals based on the results from the questionnaire and compare it with results found in the two ranking articles referred to above, gave no results.

4.5.2 Two Surprising Results

The outcome of the questionnaire varies considerably and there are arguments for this being plausible, although a positive response to the individual questions would be desirable. However, there are two questions, where the results are rather poor, and where this is somewhat more surprising.

One of them is number 17 ("...*Are the results from a residual analysis presented*..."), one of the five "most important questions". The other four questions in that group ask for comments, judgments and discussions and as such, matters may possibly be regarded as slightly "speculative" in nature; they are probably more likely to be excluded from a paper than are "concrete" and "objective" results. Residual analysis on the other hand can hardly be excluded from a paper on similar grounds. Furthermore, as emphasized in the textbooks as well as in the statistical packages, residual analysis is indisputably one of the most fundamental parts of the regression technique. Therefore, it is hardly possible that space constraints would ever be raised as an argument for leaving it out of an article. However, one possibility would be that it is generally understood that as long as there are no reports or comments regarding residual analysis, then all premises for the regression technique are fulfilled.

The rather poor result reported for question number 3 ("*Is the choice of functional form...motivated?*") is also a bit surprising. We observe that the linear functional form dominates the sample. Furthermore, we recall that for more than twenty years there has been a continuous discussion going on, in both theoretical and empirical papers, concerning the choice of functional form. Several of the review papers referred to above, which are assumed to be well known among researchers in the field, emphasize this topic as one of the most important problems within the sub-discipline. In many of these discussions, serious objections to the use of linear models have been made. Yet, the vast majority of the articles in the sample do not motivate the choice of functional form.

4.6 Conclusion

Some of the results from this investigation are of practical importance. Firstly, we review a number of earlier reviews within the discipline. We find that there is little connection among these reviews, and that several years have passed since the last conventional review was written. This calls for further reviews of the subject. Our investigation only touches upon a few of the issues brought to focus by some of the earlier papers. By so doing, we hope we have revitalized a previously well established discussion. The questionnaire presented here may serve as a (limited) checklist for writers of empirical price studies, but also as a starting point for further academic debate.

Secondly, there are results related to the categorizations of the articles studied. We notice that though this research area is well established and has been thoroughly investigated for decades, it still offers promising opportunities for researchers. A number of real estate sub-markets appear to have been sparsely investigated using the hedonic technique. This is particularly true for applications to income properties. The growing importance of financial economics and the increasing interest in the role of real estate in this matter also provides support for the idea that income properties should be studied individually using the hedonic technique.

Thirdly, there are results to be found in the descriptive statistics from the assessment of the articles in the sample. Under the assumption that all researchers follow the recommendations found in econometric textbooks, critical reviews and general guides to writing scientific papers, one would expect the frequency of "yes" answers to come rather close to 100% for most of the 18 questions. However, this is not what we find. The result is in some cases much lower. If we match the results with those obtained by McCloskey and Ziliak (1996), we get the impression that the shortcomings are of a comparable nature. However, we should remember that the two studies have not been carried out identically.

The results should not be interpreted to mean that the studies investigated, or the journals where the sample is collected for that matter, are not high quality research. There are a number of circumstances, some of which have been discussed above, that can explain why it is reasonable not to find only "yes" answers to the questionnaire. In light of these objections, we find the overall result to be reasonably good. However, in two respects we found the results surprisingly poor, taking into account the emphasis that has been put on these topics in standard textbooks and earlier reviews.

ACKNOWLEDGEMENTS

This paper has benefited considerably from the support given by professors Roland Andersson, Austin Jaffe, Christian Janssen, Hans Lind, John Quigley and Nancy Wallace. We are very grateful for all their valuable suggestions. Remaining errors and shortcomings are naturally our own responsibility. We are grateful for financial support from Lundbergs Scholarship Foundation, the Swedish Council for Building Research and the Swedish Transport & Communications Research Board.

REFERENCES

Ball, M. J. (1973). Recent Empirical Work on the Determinants of Relative House Prices, *Urban Studies*. 10:213–233.

Cassel, E., and Mendelsohn, R. (1985). The Choice of Functional Forms for Hedonic Price Equations: Comment, *Journal of Urban Economics*. 18:135–142.

Court, A. T. (1939). Hedonic Price Indexes with Automotive Examples, in *The Dynamics of Automobile Demand*, pp. 99–117, General Motors Corporation.

Diaz III, J., Black, R. T., and Rabianski, J. (1996). A Note on Ranking Real Estate Research Journals, *Real Estate Economics*. 24:551–563.

Follain, J. R., and Jimenez, E. (1985). Estimating the Demand for Housing Characteristics: A Survey and Critique, *Regional Science and Urban Economics*. 15:77–107.

Goldberger, A. S. (1991). *A Course in Econometrics*. Cambridge, Massachusetts: Harvard University Press.

Greene, W. H. (1997). *Econometric Analysis*. New Jersey: Prentice Hall.

Griliches, Z. (1961). On an Index of Quality Change, *Journal of the American Statistical Society*. 56:535–548.

Haas, G. C. (1922). *Sales Prices as a Basis for Farm Land Appraisal*. (Technical Bulletin 9, Agricultural Experimental Station). St. Paul, Minnesota: The University of Minnesota.

Kain, J. F., and Quigley, J. M. (1970). Measuring the Value of Housing Quality, *Journal of the American Statistical Association*. 65:532–548.

Lessinger, J. (1969). Econometrics and Appraisal, *Appraisal Journal*. 37:501–512.

Maclennan, D. (1977). Some Thoughts on the Nature and Purpose of House Price Studies, *Urban Studies*. 14:59–71.

Mark, J., and Goldberg, M. A. (1988). Multiple Regression Analysis and Mass Assessment: A Review of the Issues, *Appraisal Journal*. 56:89–109.

McCloskey, D. N., and Ziliak, S. T. (1996). The Standard Error of Regressions, *Journal of Economic Literature*. 34:97–114.

Miller, N. (1982). Residential Property Hedonic Pricing Models: A Review, in Sirmans (Ed.) *Research in Real Estate*. 2:31–56. Greenwich, CT: JAI Press.

Rosen, S. (1974). Hedonic Prices and Implicit Markets: Product Differentiation in Pure Competition, *Journal of Political Economy*. 82:34–55.

Salter, L. Jr. (1948). *A Critical Review of Research in Land Economics*. Minneapolis, Minnesota: University of Minnesota Press.

Smith, V. K., and Huang, J.-C. (1995). Can Markets Value Air Quality? A Meta-Analysis of Hedonic Property Value Methods, *Journal of Political Economy*. 103:209–227.

Webb, J. R., and Albert, J. D. (1995). Evaluating the Real Estate Journals: The Mainstream Finance Perspective, *Journal of Real Estate Research*. 10: 217–226.

APPENDIX 1

Citation examples from articles in the sample that demonstrate the requirements for being awarded a "yes" answer.

1. "Following these observations, we will study a search model where a home seller employs a broker to search for a potential buyer. The model presented here is a simple extension of Yavas (1992) to incorporate the role of listing price. The objective is to examine the strategic choice of the listing price by the seller, and the impact of listing price on the search and trading behavior of the players in the market (the seller, the seller's broker and the buyer)."

2. "While some of these studies have investigated the diseconomy associated with negative location-specific externalities, other studies have shown that a property's proximity to positive, location-specific externalities, such as schools (Clotfelter, 1975; Jud, 1985), greenbelts (Correll et al., 1978), neighborhood parks (Weicher and Zerbst, 1973), and travel times (Nelson, 1977) add value."

3. "There are obvious reasons why the specific functional form represented by equation 1 is employed. Firstly, we are principally interested in measuring the percentage price discount associated with cash financing. Secondly, the relationships between sales price and several property characteristics (bedrooms, bathrooms, lot size, and age, etc.) have generally been found to be chronically nonlinear (see Kowalski and Colwell, 1986; Colwell and Sirmans, 1978)."

4. "Edmonds (1984, 73) asserts that 'only those utility-affecting characteristics that are components of the purchased [unit] should be included as dimensions' of X. This article considers the role of unit age as a utility-affecting characteristics."

5. "The hypothesis of this study is that the final sale price of the property would be influenced by the settlement period (all other influential factors constant). Specifically, it is hypothesized that settlement periods longer than the 'norm' would be associated with price premiums."

6. "If these omitted neighborhood attributes are negatively correlated with distance, then a positive rent gradient can be estimated due to this specification error, even when the monocentric model is true."

7. "This would seem to be on the low end of previously estimated time costs (Deacon and Sonstelie, 1985)."

8. (Our interpretation of figures presented in tables.)

9. "The data are single-family house transactions in Washington, DC during 1992. These houses were sold through the Multiple Listing service operated by Washington, DC Association of Realtors."

10. "Such measurement errors in the independent variables can introduce bias or inconsistency into regression coefficient."

11–13. (Figures presented in table.)

14. "The adjusted coefficient of determination for the equations in Table 1 range from 0.73 to 0.86. These indicate that between 73 and 86 percent of the variance of the dependent variable Ln (Value) is explained by the regression. This is generally considered a good fit, especially when explaining cities with the size and diversity of Halifax."

15. "Another bedroom leads to the seller asking 9,6% more for a house, while another bathroom increases the list price by 12,6%."

16. "The joint hypothesis that the coefficients on all of the expenditure's variables are zero is rejected at the 10% level of significance."

17. "Both the Goldfeld-Quandt and Park-Glejser test were employed to test for the presence of heteroscedasticity."

18. "The danger always exist that important indicators of unit condition are omitted from Z but reflected in β. This misspecification exists only when the following three conditions hold: (1) there are omitted utility-affecting variables, (2) the omitted variables are orthogonal to X and Z, and (3) the omitted variables are correlated with AGE."

19. (Figures presented in table.)

APPENDIX 2

Articles in the sample

Adair, A., Berry, J., and McGreal, S. (1995). "Property Investment in Peripheral Regions." *Journal of Property Finance* (6), 43–55.

Allen, M. T., Springer, T. M., and Waller, N. G. (1995). "Implicit Pricing Across Residential Rent Submarkets." *Journal of Real Estate Finance & Economics* (11), 137–151.

Ambrose, B. W. (1990). "An Analysis of the Factors Affecting Light Industrial Property Valuation." *Journal of Real Estate Research* (5), 355–370.

Arimah, B. C. (1992). "An Empirical Analysis of the Demand for Housing Attributes in a Third World City." *Land Economics* (68), 366–379.

Asabere, P. K. and Huffman, F. E. (1994). "Historic Designation and Residential Market Values." *Appraisal Journal* (62), 396–401.

Asabere, P. K. and Huffman, F. E., (1994). "The Value Discounts Associated with Historic Facade Easements." *Appraisal Journal* (62), 270–277.

Asabere, P. K., Huffman, F. E., and Mehdian, S. (1992). "The Price Effects of Cash versus Mortgage Transaction." *Real Estate Economics* (20), 141–150.

Asabere, P. K. (1990). "The Value of a Neighborhood Street with Reference to the Cul-de-Sac." *Journal of Real Estate Finance & Economics* (3), 185–193.

Asabere, P. K. and Huffman, F. E. (1993). "The Impact of Settlement Period on Sales Price." *Journal of Real Estate Finance & Economics* (7), 213–219.

Asabere, P. K. and Huffman, F. E. (1993). "Price Concessions, Time on the Market, and the Actual Sale Price of Homes." *Journal of Real Estate Finance & Economics* (6), 167–174.

Atterberry, W. L. and Rutherford, R. C. (1993). "Industrial Real Estate Prices and Market Efficiency." *Journal of Real Estate Research* (8), 377–385.

Benjamin, J. D. and Lusht, K. M. (1993). "Search Cost and Apartment Rents." *Journal of Real Estate Finance & Economics* (6), 189–197.

Benjamin, J. D., Coulson, E. N., and Yang, S. X. (1993). "Real Estate Transfer Taxes and Property Values: The Philadelphia Story." *Journal of Real Estate Finance & Economics* (7), 151–157.

Benjamin, J. D., Boyle, G. W., and Sirmans, C. F. (1992). "Price Discrimination in Shopping Center Lease." *Journal of Urban Economics* (32), 299–317.

Benjamin, J. D., Sa-Aadu, J., and Shilling, J. D. (1992). "Influence of Rent Differentials on the Choice between Office Rent Contracts with and without Relocation Provisions." *Real Estate Economics* (20), 289–302.

Benjamin, J. D., Shilling, J. D., and Sirmans, C. F. (1992). "Security Deposits, Adverse Selection and Office Leases." *Real Estate Economics* (20), 259–272.

Benjamin, J. D. and Chinloy, P. T. (1995). "Technological Innovation in Real Estate Brokerage." *Journal of Real Estate Research* (10), 35–44.

Bernes, G. L. and Mitchell, P. S. (1992). "An Analysis of Indicators of Multi-Family Complex Values." *Appraisal Journal* (60), 379–385.

Bialaszewski, D. and Newsome, B. A. (1990). "Adjusting Comparable Sales for Floodplain Location: The Case of Homewood, Alabama." *Appraisal Journal* (58), 114–118.

Black, R. T. and Nourse, H. O. (1995). "The Effect of Different Brokerage Modes on Closing Costs and House Prices." *Journal of Real Estate Research* (10), 87–98.

Blackley, D. M. and Follain, J. R. (1991). "An Econometric Model of the Metropolitan Housing Market." *Journal of Housing Economics* (1), 140–167.

Bleich, D. H., Findlay, M. C. III, and Phillips, G. M. (1991). "An Evaluation of the Impact of a Well-Designed Landfill on Surrounding Property Values." *Appraisal Journal* (59), 247–252.

Brown, P. M. (1990). "United Kingdom Residential Price Expectations and Inflation." *Journal of Property Research* (7), 57–67.

Brown, P. M. (1990). "The Changing United Kingdom Residential Real Estate Market." *Journal of Property Research* (7), 119–132.

Cannaday, R. E. (1994). "Condominium Covenants: Cats, Yes; Dogs, No." *Journal of Urban Economics* (35), 71–82.

Case, K. E. and Shiller R. J. (1990). "Forecasting Prices and Excess Returns in the Housing Market." *Real Estate Economics* (18), 253–273.

Chambers, D. N. (1992). "The Racial Housing Price Differential and Racially Transitional Neighborhoods." *Journal of Urban Economics* (32), 214–232.

Cho, M., and Linneman, P. (1993). "Interjurisdictional Spillover Effects of Land use Regulations." *Journal of Housing Research* (4), 131–163.

Clapp, J. M., Giaccotto, C., and Tirtiroglu, D. (1991). "Housing Price Indices Based on All Transactions Compared to Repeat Subsamples." *Real Estate Economics* (19), 270–285.

Clapp, J. M. and Giaccotto, C. (1994). "The Influence of Economic Variables on Local House Price Dynamics." *Journal of Urban Economics* (35), 161–183.

Clapp, J. M. and Giaccotto, C. (1992). "Estimating Price Trends for Residential Property. A Comparision of Repeat Sales and Assessed Value Methods." *Journal of Real Estate Finance & Economics* (5), 357–374.

Coate, D. and Vanderhoff, J. (1993). "Race of the Homeowner and Appreciation of Single-family Homes in the United States." *Journal of Real Estate Finance & Economics* (7), 205–212.

Colwell, P. F. (1990). "Power Lines and Land Value." *Journal of Real Estate Research* (5), 117–127.

Coulson, E. N. (1991). "Really Useful Tests of Monocentric Model." *Land Economics* (67), 299–307.

Crone, T. M. and Voith, R. P. (1992)."Estimating House Price Appreciation: A Comparison of Methods." *Journal of Housing Economics* (2), 324–338.

Dale-Johnson, D. and Yim, H. K. (1990). "Coastal Development Moratoria and Housing Prices." *Journal of Real Estate Finance & Economics* (3), 165–184.

Do, A. Q. Wilbur, R. W., and Short, J. L. (1994). "An Empirical Examination of the Externalities of Neighborhood Chuches on Housing Values." *Journal of Real Estate Finance & Economics* (9), 127–136.

Do, A. Q. and Grudnitski, G. (1995). "Golf Courses and Residential House Prices: An Empirical Examination." *Journal of Real Estate Finance & Economics* (10), 261–270.

Dodgson, J. S. and Topham, N. (1990). "Valuing Residential Properties with Hedonic Method: A Comparison with Results of Professional Valuations." *Housing Studies* (5), 209–213.

Doiron, J. C., Shilling, J. D., and Sirmans, C. F. (1992). "Do Market Rents Reflect the Value of Special Building Features? The Case of Office Atriums." *Journal of Real Estate Research* (7), 147–155.

Dokko, Y., Edelstein, R. H., Pomer, M., and Urdang, E. S. (1991). "Determinants of the Rate of Return for Nonresidential Real Estate: Inflation Expectations and Market Adjustment Lags." *Real Estate Economics* (19), 52–69.

Dotzour, M. G. and Levi, D. R. (1993). "The Impact of Corporate Ownership on Residential Transaction Prices." *Appraisal Journal* (61), 198–205.

Dotzour, M. G. and Levi, D. R. (1992). "The Impact of Corporate Ownership on Residential Transaction Prices." *Journal of Real Estate Research* (7), 207–216.

Eckert, J. K., O'Connor, P. M., and Chamberlain, C. (1993). "Computer-Assisted Real Estate Appraisal: A California Savings and Loan Case Study." *Appraisal Journal* (61), 524–532.

Fehribach, F. A., Rutherford, R. C. and Eakin, M. E. (1993). "An Analysis of the Determinants of Industrial Property Valuation." *Journal of Real Estate Research* (6), 25–54.

Fisher, J. D. and Lentz, G. H. (1990). "Business Enterprise Value in Shopping Malls: An Empirical Test." *Journal of Real Estate Research* (5), 167–175.

Fisher, J. D., Geltner, D. M., and Webb, B. R. (1994). "Value Indices of Commercial Real Estate: A Comparision of Index Construction Methods." *Journal of Real Estate Finance & Economics* (9), 137–164.

Follain, J. R., Leavens, D. R., and Velz, O. T. (1993). "Identifying the Effects of Tax Reform on Multifamily Rental Housing." *Journal of Urban Economics* (34), 275–298.

Forgey, F. A. Goebel, P. R., and Rutherford, R. C. (1993). "Implicit Liquidity Premiums in the Disposition of RTC Assets." *Journal of Real Estate Research* (8), 347–363.

Forgey, F. A. and Goebel, P. R. (1995). "The Use of Locational Factors by Tenants in Shopping Centre Space Selection." *Journal of Property Research* (12), 149–156.

Frew, J. R., Jud, D. G., and Winkler, D. T. (1990). "Atypicalities and Apartment Rent Concessions." *Journal of Real Estate Research* (5), 195–201.

Galster, G. and Williams, Y. (1994). "Dwellings for the Severely Mentally Disabled and Neighborhood Property Values: The Details Matter." *Land Economics* (70), 466–477.

Gatzlaff, D. H. and Smith, M. T. (1993). "The Impact of the Miami Metrorail on the Value of Residences Near Station Locations." *Land Economics* (69), 54–66.

Giannias, D. A. (1991). "Housing Quality Differentials in Urban Areas." *Journal of Urban Economics* (29), 166–181.

Giliberto, S. M. (1990). "Equity Real Estate Investment Trust and Real Estate Returns." *Journal of Real Estate Research* (5), 259–263.

Gilley, O. W. and Pace, K. R. (1990). "A Hybrid Cost and Market-Based Estimator for Appraisal." *Journal of Real Estate Research* (5), 75–88.

Giussani, B., Hsai, M., and Tsolacos, S. (1993). "A Comparative Analysis of the Major Determinants of Office Rental Values in Europe." *Journal of Property Valuation & Investment* (11), 157–173.

Glascock, J. L., Sirmans, C. F., and Turnbull, G. K. (1993). "Owner Tenancy as Credible Commitment under Uncertainty." *Real Estate Economics* (21), 69–82.

Glascock, J. L., Jahanian, S., and Sirmans, C. F. (1990). "An Analysis of Office Market Rents: Some Empirical Evidence." *Real Estate Economics* (18), 105–119.

Goodman, J. L. and Ittner, J. B. (1992). "The Accuracy of Home Owners' Estimates of House Value." *Journal of Housing Economics* (2), 339–357.

Hamilton, S. W. and Schwann, G. M. (1995). "Do High Voltage Electric Transmission Lines Affect Property Value?" *Land Economics* (71), 436–444.

Herrin, W. E. and Kern, C. R. (1992). "Testing the Standard Urban Model of Residential Choice An Implicit Market Approach." *Journal of Urban Economics* (31), 145–163.

Hughes, W. T. (1995). "Brokerage Firms' Characteristics and the Sale of Residential Property." *Journal of Real Estate Research* (10), 45–56.

Hughes, W. T. and Sirmans, C. F. (1993). "Adjusting House Prices for Intra-Neighborhood Traffic Differences." *Appraisal Journal* (61), 533–538.

Jud, D. G. and Winkler, D. T. (1991). "Location and Amenities in Determining Apartment Rent: An Integer Programming Approach." *Appraisal Journal* (59), 266–275.

Jud, D. G., Winkler, D. T., and Kissling, G. E. (1995). "Price Spreads and Residential Housing Market Liquidity." *Journal of Real Estate Finance & Economics* (11), 251–260.

Kask, S. B. and Maani, S. A. (1992). "Uncertainty, Information and Hedonic Pricing." *Land Economics* (68), 170–184.

Kiel, K. A. (1995). "Measuring the Impact of the Discovery and Cleaning of Identified Hazardous Waste Sites on House Values." *Land Economics* (71), 428–435.

Kiel, K. A. and Carson, R. T. (1990). "An Examination of Systematic Differences in the Appreciation of Individual Housing Units." *Journal of Real Estate Research* (5), 301–318.

Kiel, K. A. and McClain, K. (1995). "The Effect of an Incinerator Sitting on Housing Appreciation Rates." *Journal of Urban Economics* (37), 311–323.

Kim, K.-H. (1993). "Housing Prices, Affordability, and Government Policy in Korea.." *Journal of Real Estate Finance & Economics* (6), 55–71.

Kim, K.-H. and Suh, S. H. (1993). "Speculation and Price Bubbles in the Korean and Japanese Real Estate Markets." *Journal of Real Estate Finance & Economics* (6), 73–87.

Kinzy, S. (1992). "An Analysis of the Supply of Housing Characteristics by Builders within the Rosen Framework." *Journal of Urban Economics* (32), 1–17.

Kluger, B. D. and Miller, N. G. (1990). "Measuring Residential Real Estate Liquidity." *Real Estate Economics* (18), 145–159.

Knight, J. R., Sirmans, C. F., and Turnbull, G. K. (1994). "List Price Signaling and Buyer Behavior in the Housing Market." *Journal of Real Estate Finance & Economics* (9), 177–192.

Kohlhase, J. (1991). "The Impact of Toxic Waste Sites on Housing Values." *Journal of Urban Economics* (30), 1–26.

Larsen, J. E. (1991). "Leading Residential Real Estate Sales Agents and Market Performance." *Journal of Real Estate Research* (6), 241–249.

Lim, G.-C. and Lee, M.-H. (1993). "Housing Consumption in Urban China." *Journal of Real Estate Finance & Economics* (6), 89–102.

Lin, S. C.-C. (1993). "The Relationship Between Rents and Prices of Owner-Occupied Housing in Taiwan." *Journal of Real Estate Finance & Economics* (6), 25–54.

Linneman, P. and Voith, R. (1991). "Housing Price Functions and Ownership Capitalization Rates." *Journal of Urban Economics* (30), 100–111.

Lipscomb, J. B. and Gray, J. B. (1990). "An Empirical Investigation of Four Market-Derived Adjustment Methods." *Journal of Real Estate Research* (5), 53–66.

Matysiak, G. and Wang, P. (1995). "Commercial Property Market Prices and Valuations: Analyzing the Correspondence." *Journal of Property Research* (12), 181–202.

McAllister, P. (1995). "Valuation Accuracy: a Contribution to the Debate." *Journal of Property Research* (12), 203–216.

Michaels, R. G. and Smith, V. K. (1990). "Market Segmentation and Valuing Amenities with Hedonic Models: The Case of Hazardous Waste Sites." *Journal of Urban Economics* (28), 223–242.

Miles, M., Cole, R., and Guilkey, D. (1990). "A Different Look at Commercial Real Estate Returns." *Real Estate Economics* (18), 403–430.

Mills, E. S. (1992). "Office Rent Determinants In the Chicago Area." *Real Estate Economics* (20), 273–287.

Mok, H. M. K., Chan, P. P. K., and Cho, Y.-S. (1995). "A Hedonic Price Model for Private Properties in Hong Kong." *Journal of Real Estate Finance & Economics* (10), 37–48.

Mooney, S. P. (1990). "Cash Equivalency in Dichotomous Residential Markets." *Journal of Real Estate Research* (5), 89–106.

Moorehouse, J. C. and Smith, M. S. (1994). "The Market for Residential Architecture: 19th Century Row Houses in Boston's South End." *Journal of Urban Economics* (35), 267–277.

Murdoch, J. C., Singh, H., and Thayer, M. (1993). "The Impact of Natural Hazards on Housing Values: The Loma Prieta Earthquake." *Real Estate Economics* (21), 167–184.

Nelson, A. C., Genereux, J., and Genereux, M. (1992). "Price Effects on Landfill on House Values." *Land Economics* (68), 359–356.

Newsom, B. A. and Zietz, J. (1992). "Adjusting Comparable Sales Using Multiple Regression Analysis – The Need for Segmentation." *Appraisal Journal* (60), 129–135.

Newsome, B. A. (1991). "Adjusting Comparable Sales for Vinyl Siding." *Appraisal Journal* (59), 92–95.

Palmquist, R. B. (1992). "Valuing Localized Externalities." *Journal of Urban Economics* (31), 59–68.

Parsons, G. R. and Yangru, W. U. (1991). "The Opportunity Cost of Coastal Land-Use Controls: An Empirical Analysis." *Land Economics* (67), 308–316.

Peek, J. and Wilcox, J. A. (1991). "The Measurement and Determinants of Single-Family House Prices." *Real Estate Economics* (19), 353–382.

Peek, J. and Wilcox, J. A. (1991). "The Baby Boom, "Pent-Up" Demand, and Future House Prices." *Journal of Housing Economics* (1), 347–367.

Phillips, R. A. and Vanderhoff, J. H. (1991). "Two-Earner Households and Housing Demand: The Effect of the Wife's Occupational Choice." *Journal of Real Estate Finance & Economics* (4), 83–91.

Pogodzinski, J. M. and Sass, T. R. (1994). "Zoning and Hedonic Housing Price Models." *Journal of Housing Economics* (5), 263–291.

Pollakowski, H. O., Wachter, S. M., and Lynford, L. (1992). "Did Office Market Size Matter in the 1980s? A Time-Series Cross-Sectional Analysis of Metropolitan Area Office Market." *Real Estate Economics* (20), 303–324.

Pollakowski, H. O. and Wachter, S. M. (1990). "The Effects of Land-Use Constraints on Housing Prices." *Land Economics* (66), 315–324.

Pollakowski, H. O., Stegman, M. A., and Rohe, W. (1991). "Rates of Return on Housing of Low and Moderate-Income Owners." *Real Estate Economics* (19), 417–425.

Potepan, M. J. (1994). "Intermetropolitan Migration and Housing Prices: Simultaneously Determined?" *Journal of Housing Economics* (3), 77–91.

Powe, N. A., Garrod, G. D., and Willis, K. G. (1995). "Valuation of Urban Amenities Using an Hedonic Price Model." *Journal of Property Research* (12), 137–147.

Quigley, J. M. (1995). "A Simple Hybrid Model for Estimating Real Estate Price Indexes." *Journal of Housing Economics* (4), 1–12.

Rauch, J. E. (1993). "Productivity Gains from Geographic Concentration of Human Capital: Evidence from the Cities." *Journal of Urban Economics* (34), 380–400.

Reichert, A. K., Small, M., and Mohanty, S. (1992). "The Impact of Landfills on Residential Property Values." *Journal of Real Estate Research* (7), 297–314.

Rinehart, J. R. and Pompe, J. J. (1994). "Adjusting the Market Value of Coastal Property for Beach Quality." *Appraisal Journal* (62), 604–609.

Rodriguez, M. and Sirmans, C. F. (1994). "Quantifying the Value of a View in Single-Family Housing Markets." *Appraisal Journal* (62), 600–603.

Roistacher, E. A. (1992). "Rent Regulation in New York City: Simulating Decontrol Options." *Journal of Housing Economics* (2), 107–138.

Rose, L. A. (1992). "Land Values and Housing Rents in Urban Japan." *Journal of Urban Economics* (31), 230–251.

Rosenthal, S. S. and Helsley, R. W. (1994). "Redevelopment and the Urban Land Price Gradient." *Journal of Urban Economics* (35), 182–200.

Rubin, G. M. (1993). "Is Housing Age a Commodity? Hedonic Price Estimates of Unit Age." *Journal of Housing Research* (4), 165–184.

Schafer, S. M. (1994). "Bank Branch Valuation: An Empirical Approach." *Appraisal Journal* (62), 171–180.

Scock, J. L., Kim, M., and Sirmans, C. F. (1993). "An Analysis of Office Market Rents: Parameter Constancy and Unobservable Variables." *Journal of Real Estate Research* (8), 625–637.

Shilling, J. D., Sirmans, C. F., and Dombrow, J. F. (1991). "Measuring Depreciation in Single-Family Rental and Owner-Occupied Housing." *Journal of Housing Economics* (1), 368–383.

Shilling, J. D., Benjamin, J. D., and Sirmans, C. F. (1990). "Estimating Net Realizable Value for Distressed Real Estate." *Journal of Real Estate Research* (5), 129–140.

Shilling, J. D., Sirmans, C. F., Turnbull, J. D., and Benjamin, J. D. (1992). "Hedonic Prices and Contractual Contingencies." *Journal of Urban Economics* (32), 108–228.

Simons, R. A. (1992). "Site Attributes in Retail Leasing: An Analysis of a fast-food restaurant Market." *Appraisal Journal* (60), 521–531.

Singell, L. D. and Lillydahl, J. H. (1990). "An Empirical Examination of the Effect of Impact Fees on the Housing Market." *Land Economics* (66), 82–92.

Sirmans, C. F. and Guidry, K. A. (1993). "The Determinants of Shopping Center Rents." *Journal of Real Estate Research* (8), 107–115.

Sirmans, C. F., Turnball, G. K., and Benjamin, J. D. (1995). "The Markets for Housing and Real Estate Broker Services." *Journal of Housing Economics* (6), 25–42.

Sirmans, C. F., Turnball, G. K., and Dombrow, J. (1995). "Quick House Sales: Seller Mistake or Luck?" *Journal of Housing Economics* (4), 230–243.

Sirmans, S. G., Sirmans, C. F., and Benjamin, J. D. (1990). "Rental Concessions and Property Values." *Journal of Real Estate Research* (5), 141–151.

Sirmans, S. G. and Sirmans, C. F. (1991). "Property Manager Designations and Apartment Rent." *Journal of Real Estate Research* (7), 91–98.

Sirpal, R. (1994). "Empirical Modeling of the Realtive Impacts of Various Sizes of Shopping Centers on the Values of Surrounding Residential Properties." *Journal of Real Estate Research* (9), 487–505.

Sivitanidou, R. (1995). "Urban Spatial Variations in Office-Commercial Rents: The Role of Spatial Amenities and Commercial Zoning." *Journal of Urban Economics* (38), 23–49.

Smith, B. A. and Tesarek, W. P. (1991). "House Prices and Regional Real Estate Cycles: Market Adjustment in Houston." *Real Estate Economics* (19), 396–416.

Smolen, G. E., Moore, G., and Conway, L. V. (1992). "Economic Effects of Hazardous Chemical and Proposed Radioactive Waste Landfills on Surrounding Real Estate Values." *Journal of Real Estate Research* (7), 283–295.

Speyrer, J. F. and Ragas, W. R. (1991). "Housing Prices and Flood Risk: An Examination Using Spline Regression." *Journal of Real Estate Finance & Economics* (4), 395–407.

Stull, W. J. and Stull, J. C. (1991). "Capitalization of Local Income Taxes." *Journal of Urban Economics* (29), 182–190.

Sunderman, M. A., Birch, J. W., Cannaday, R. E., and Hamilton, T. W. (1990). "Testing for Vertical Inequity in Property Tax Systems." *Journal of Real Estate Research* (5), 319–334.

Sunderman, M. A., Cannaday, R. E., and Colwell, P. F. (1992). "The Effect of Listing Price on Cash Equivalence." *Appraisal Journal* (60), 275–282.

Sunderman, M. A., Cannaday, R. E., and Colwell, P. F. (1990). "The Value of Mortgage Assumptions: An Empirical Test." *Journal of Real Estate Research* (5), 247–257.

Taylor, L. L. (1995). "Allocative Inefficiency and Local Government." *Journal of Urban Economics* (37), 201–211.

Thayer, M., Albers, H., and Rahmatian, M. (1992). "The Benefit of Reducing Exposure to Waste Disposal Sites: A Hedonic Housing Value Approach." *Journal of Real Estate Research* (7), 265–282.

Thibodeau, T. G. (1990). "Estimating the Effect of High-Rise Office Buildings on Residential Property Values." *Land Economics* (66), 403–408.

Vanderporten, B. (1992). "Strategic Behavior in Pooled Condominium Auctions." *Journal of Urban Economics* (31), 123–137.

Voith, R. (1993). "Changing Capitalization of CBD-oriented Transportation Systems: Evidence from Philadelphia, 1970–1988." *Journal of Urban Economics* (33), 361–376.

Walden, M. L. (1990). "Magnet Schools and the Differential Impact of School Quality on Residential Property Values." *Journal of Real Estate Research* (5), 221–230.

Wang, K. O., Grissom, T. V., Webb, J. R., and Spellman, L. (1991). "The Impact of Rental Properties on the Value of Single-Family Residences." *Journal of Urban Economics* (30), 152–166.

Webb, B. R., Miles, M., and Guilkey, D. (1992). "Transaction-Driven Commercial Real Estate Return: The Panacea to Asset Allocation Models?" *Real Estate Economics* (20), 325–357.

Wheaton, W. C. and Torto, R. G. (1994). "Office Rent Indices and Their Behavior over Time." *Journal of Urban Economics* (35), 121–139.

Willis, K. G. and Garrod, G. D. (1993). "Not From Experience: A Comparison of Experts' Opinions and Hedonic Price Estimates of the Incremental Value of Property Attributable to an Environmental Feature." *Journal of Property Research* (10), 193–216.

Yavas, A. and Yang, S. (1995). "The Strategic Role of Listing Price in Marketing Real Estate: Theory and Evidence." *Real Estate Economics* (23), 347–368.

Chapter 5

Comparison of the Accuracy of the Minimum-Variance Grid Method and the Least Squares Method – a Non-linear Extension

Kwong Wing Chau, Wei Huang, and Fung Fai Ng
Department of Real Estate and Construction, The University of Hong Kong, Hong Kong

Hin Man Louise Ng-Mak
Department of Applied Mathematics, The Hong Kong Polytechnic University, Hong Kong

5.1 Introduction

The Minimum-Variance Grid method developed by Vandell (1991) has laid down the theoretical foundation for the selection of a set of optimal weights for property valuation based on transaction prices of comparables. This method has also been shown by Lai and Way (1996) to be more accurate compared with valuation based on linear multiple regression. However, Lai and Wang's results do not hold universally. The paper identifies the necessary and sufficient conditions for Lai and Wang's results to hold.

Since the linear hedonic price model is too restrictive and is unlikely to represent the true hedonic price function in reality, it is necessary to analyze the case when the linearity assumption is relaxed. Halvorsen and Pamlquist (1981), for example, have shown that a nonlinear specification is preferred over a linear specification in describing a hedonic price model. This paper also extends Lai and Wang's comparison to the non-linear case.

5.2 Nonlinear Least Squares Estimator and the Adjustment-Grid Estimator

Consider a general hedonic price model (including the non-linear case) with an additive error term:

$$V = f(Z, \beta) + \varepsilon, \tag{1}$$

where V is a m-dimensional vector variable representing the observed transaction prices, Z is a k-dimensional vector which represents the observable price influencing attributes of the comparable properties. β is a p-dimensional vector of unknown parameters, which is assumed to lie in a compact set Θ, and f is a known nonlinear function.

The model is assumed to be correctly specified and the error term ε is assumed to be independently and identically distributed with mean zero and constant variance σ^2, and f is twice continuously differentiable with respect to β and continuous with respect to Z, the Jacobian of f is written as

$$F(\beta) = (\partial/\partial\beta')f(Z, \beta). \tag{2}$$

Given the hedonic price equation, the true subject property value can be specified as:

$$V_p = f(Z_p, \beta) + \varepsilon_p, \tag{3}$$

where Z_p represents the vector of attributes of a subject property, ε_p is the difference between the true property value V_p and the value predicted by $f(Z_p, \beta)$, and the model is assumed to be correctly specified as described above.

We specify the prediction of the subject property as

$$\hat{V}_p = f(Z_p, \beta). \tag{4}$$

The unknown parameter β can be estimated using the Nonlinear Least Squares Method based on the sample observations. (The maximum likelihood estimator is not considered here.)

Let the sum of squared deviations be:

$$SSE(\beta) = \sum_{i=1}^{n} [V_i - f(Z_i, \beta)]^2. \tag{5}$$

In vector notation it becomes:

$$SSE(\beta) = [V - f(Z, \beta)]' \, [V - f(Z, \beta)] = \|V - f(Z, \beta)\|^2. \tag{6}$$

The least square estimator is the value of $\hat{\beta}$ that minimized $SSE(\beta)$ over the parameter space Θ. If $SSE(\beta)$ is once continuously differentiable on some open subset Θ° with $\beta \in \Theta^\circ \subset \Theta$, then $\hat{\beta}$ satisfies the "normal equations" according to Gallant (1987):

$$F'(Z, \beta)[V - f(Z, \beta)] = 0. \tag{7}$$

Assuming the explicit solution to equation (7) exists, using Taylor's first order expansion of equation (6), Gallant (1987) has proved that

$$\hat{\beta} = \beta + (F'F)^{-1} F'\varepsilon + o_p\left(\frac{1}{\sqrt{n}}\right), \tag{8}$$

$$s^2 = \frac{\varepsilon'[I - F(F'F)^{-1} F']\varepsilon}{n} + o_p\left(\frac{1}{n}\right), \tag{9}$$

where s is the estimate of the variance of the errors ε corresponding to $\hat{\beta}$ and $F = F(Z, \beta)$. The notation $o_p(a_n)$ denotes a matrix valued random variable $X_n = o_p(a_n)$ with the property that each element satisfies

$$\lim_{n \to \infty} p\left[\left|\frac{X_{ijn}}{a_n}\right| \geq \xi\right] = 0, \tag{10}$$

for any $\xi > 0$.

The prediction of the subject property by the nonlinear least squares can also be specified as

$$\hat{V}_{NLS} = f(Z_s, \hat{\beta}). \tag{11}$$

5.3 An Examination of the Unbiasnesses

Now we can examine the asymptotic unbiasedness of the nonlinear least square estimator. From equation (8) and (9), when $n \to \infty$, we have

$$\hat{\beta} = \beta + (F'F)^{-1} F'\varepsilon, \tag{12}$$

$$s^2 = \frac{\varepsilon'[I - F(F'F)^{-1}]\varepsilon}{n}. \tag{13}$$

Assuming that the error terms are iid and approximately normal, $\hat{\beta}$ has the p-dimensional multivariate normal distribution with mean β and variance-covariance matrix $\sigma^2(F'F)^{-1}$, i.e.

$$\hat{\beta} \to N_p(\beta, \sigma^2(F'F)^{-1}). \tag{14}$$

If let $G = \partial f(Z_s, \hat{\beta})/\partial \hat{\beta}' = F_s(\hat{\beta})$, then by the Slutsky theorem,

$$p \lim f(Z_s, \hat{\beta}) = f(Z_s, \beta),$$

and

$$p \lim G = F_s(\beta) = F_s.$$

Thus

$$f(Z_s, \hat{\beta}) \xrightarrow{a} N[f(Z_s, \beta), F_s(\sigma^2(F'F)^{-1})F_s'], \tag{15}$$

and

$$\text{var}(f(Z_s, \hat{\beta})) = F_s(\sigma^2(F'F)^{-1})F_s'. \tag{16}$$

The mean of the limiting distribution of $\sqrt{n}(\hat{\beta} - \beta)$ is zero and the estimator in hand is asymptotically unbiased:

$$\lim_{n \to \infty} E(\hat{\beta} - \beta) = \lim_{n \to \infty} E[(F'F)^{-1}F'\varepsilon] = 0. \tag{17}$$

Since $E(\varepsilon_s) = 0$ and $\hat{\beta}$ is an asymptotically unbiased estimator, therefore

$$\begin{aligned} E(u_{NLS}) &= f(Z_s, \beta) + E(\varepsilon_s) - E[f(Z_s, \hat{\beta})] \\ &= f(Z_s, \beta) - f(Z_s, E(\hat{\beta})) \\ &= f(Z_s, \beta) - f(Z_s, \beta) \\ &= 0 \end{aligned} \tag{18}$$

That is, Nonlinear Least Squares estimation of the prediction error is asymptotically unbiased.

When applying the adjustment-grid method in the non-linear case, we use the Additive Percentage Adjustments Method (APAM) suggested by Colwell et al. (1983) to estimate the subject property value ($\hat{V}_G$):

$$\hat{V}_G = \sum_{i=1}^{n} w_i(f(Z_{ci}, \beta) + \varepsilon_{ci}) \frac{f(Z_s, \beta) - f(Z_{ci}, \beta)}{f(Z_{ci}, \beta) + \varepsilon_{ci}} + w'V_c \quad \text{(Due to the APAM)}$$

$$= \sum_{i=1}^{n} w_i(Z_s - Z_{ci}) \frac{f(Z_s, \beta) - f(Z_{ci}, \beta)}{Z_s - Z_{ci}} + w'V_c$$

$$= \sum_{i=1}^{n} w_i(Z_s - Z_{ci})f'(Z_{sci}, \beta) + w'V_c \quad (19)$$

where $n \times 1$ vector V_c represents the n observed comparable sales prices, Z_{ci} represents the attributes of the ith comparable, w_i is the weights on the ith comparable satisfying $\sum_{i=1}^{n} w_i = 1$ and w' is the weight of the comparables. Z_{sci} is a point between Z_s and Z_{ci} according to the Middle-Value Theorem, f' represents the first derivative of Z and $f'(Z_{sci}, \beta)$ is the adjustment factor according to the definition of the adjustment-grid method.

Both Colwell et al. (1983) and Vandell (1991) suggest that the hedonic-price coefficients ($\hat{\beta}$) estimated from a hedonic pricing equation can be used as the adjustment factors for the property attributes. We use the nonlinear least squares estimator $f'(Z_{sci}, \hat{\beta})$ to substitute for the adjustment factor $f'(Z_{sci}, \beta)$ in equation (19):

$$\hat{V}_G = \sum_{i=1}^{n} w_i(Z_s - Z_{ci})f'(Z_{sci}, \hat{\beta}) + w'V_c$$

$$= \sum_{i=1}^{n} w_i(f(Z_s, \hat{\beta}) - f(Z_{ci}, \hat{\beta})) + w'V_c$$

$$\left(\text{Since } f'(Z_{sci}, \hat{\beta}) = \frac{f(Z_s, \hat{\beta}) - f(Z_{ci}, \hat{\beta})}{Z_s - Z_{ci}} \right)$$

$$= f(Z_s, \hat{\beta}) + w'(f(Z_c, \beta) - f(Z_c, \hat{\beta}) + \varepsilon_c)$$

$$= \hat{V}_{NLS} + w'u_c. \quad (20)$$

where u_c is the prediction error of the comparable based on the regression method. The above representation is exactly the same as the result of the linear case derived by Lai and Wang.

The prediction error of the adjustment-grid estimator is the difference between V_s and $\hat{V}_G$,

$$u_G = V_s - \hat{V}_G = V_s - \hat{V}_{NLS} - w'u_c = u_{NLS} - w'u_c. \quad (21)$$

As in the linear case, equation (21) illustrates the relationship between the prediction error of the adjustment-grid method and the nonlinear least square method. In other words, the prediction error resulting from the adjustment-grid method must be equal to the prediction error of the subject property less the weighted average of the prediction errors of comparable properties. The asymptotic expectation of u_G can be specified as

$$\lim_{n\to\infty} E(u_G) = \lim_{n\to\infty} E(u_{NLS}) - w' \lim_{n\to\infty} E(u_c) = 0. \tag{22}$$

Since the asymptotic expectations of u_{NLS} and u_c are both zero, equation (22) shows that the adjustment-grid estimator is also asymptotic unbiased under the non-linear case.

5.4 A Comparison of the Prediction Errors

There are many ways to compare the accuracy of the different methods in appraised value estimates, following Lai and Wang, we compare the prediction errors of $\hat{V}_{NLS}$ and $\hat{V}_G$.

The variance of the prediction error of a nonlinear estimator (u_{NLS}) can be specified as:

$$\begin{aligned}
\sigma^2_{NLS} &= E[(u_{NLS})^2] = E[(V_s - \hat{V}_{NLS})^2] \\
&= E[(f(Z_s, \beta) - f(Z_s, \hat{\beta}) - \varepsilon_s)^2] \\
&= \mathrm{var}(f(Z_s, \hat{\beta})) + \mathrm{var}(\varepsilon_s). \tag{23}
\end{aligned}$$

From equation (16) and the independence of assumption about the error terms, we have

$$\sigma^2_{NLS} = \sigma^2(1 + F_s(F'F)^{-1}F'_s). \tag{24}$$

Suppose that all the covariances of the comparable and ε_{ci} are ε_s are equal to zero, then the variance of the prediction error of an non-linear adjustment-grid estimator (u_G) is

$$\begin{aligned}
\sigma^2_G &= E[(u_{NLS} - w'u_c)^2] = E[(u_{NLS} - w'u_c)(u_{NLS} - w'u_c)'] \\
&= E[u_{NLS}\,u'_{NLS} - w'u_c u'_{NLS} - u_{NLS}\,u'_c w + w'u_c u'_c w] \\
&= E[(u_{NLS})^2] - 2w' E[u_c u'_{NLS}] + w' E[(u_c)^2]w \\
&= \sigma^2_{NLS} - 2w' F_c(F'F)F'_s + \sigma^2\{w'[F_c(F'F)F'_c + I_n]w\} \tag{25}
\end{aligned}$$

where, $F_c = F_c(\beta) = \partial f(Z_c, \beta)/\partial \beta'$, n is the number of the comparable properties.

Comparing equation (25) here with equation (10) in Lai and Wang, we find that for the nonlinear case, the result is the same as the linear case. However, the results for the nonlinear case are asymptotic results, so it is necessary that the related regularity conditions hold (see, Prakasa Rao, B.L.S. (1987)). Since the results are asymptotic results, they are therefore more relevant for liquid markets where transaction prices are abundant and readily available.

With equation (25) in hand, we can began to compare the variances of the prediction errors of two different methods, *i.e.* σ_{NLS}^2 and σ_G^2. From equation (24), optimal weight w^* used to minimize σ_G^2 under the constraint $w'e_n = 1$ is:

$$w^* = A^{-1}B + \frac{1 - e_n'A^{-1}B}{e_n'A^{-1}e_n}A^{-1}e_n, \tag{26}$$

where $A = F_c(F'F)^{-1}F_c' + I_n$, $B = F_c(F'F)^{-1}F_s'$ and $w'e_n = 1$.

Substituting equation (26) into equation (25) we have

$$\sigma_G^2 = \sigma_{NLS}^2 + \sigma^2 \left[\frac{(1 - e_n'A^{-1}B)^2}{e_n'A^{-1}e_n} - B'A^{-1}B \right], \tag{27}$$

which is again the same as the result obtained in Lai and Wang. Therefore we have following proposition:

Proposition One: A necessary and sufficient condition for $\sigma_G^2 < \sigma_{NLS}^2$ is

$$\left(1 - \bar{e}_n'A^{-1}B\right)^2 < \left(e_n'A^{-1}e_n\right)\left(B'A^{-1}B\right). \tag{28}$$

5.5 An examination of the Necessary and Sufficient Condition

Lai and Wang did not provide a mathematical proof for $\sigma_G^2 < \sigma_{NLS}^2$, instead, they argued that the inequality should hold using numerical examples. They have used different examples of matrixes A and B to compare the values of $(1 - e_n'A^{-1}B)^2$ and $(e_n'A^{-1}e_n)(B'A^{-1}B)$. Their examples show that $(1 - e_n'A^{-1}B)^2$ is always less than $(e_n'A^{-1}e_n)(B'A^{-1}B)$. In fact, the there do exist such matrixes that violate that inequality.

Consider the following counter example:

If $B = \frac{1}{2n}e_n$, then $(1 - e_n'A^{-1}B)^2 > (e_n'A^{-1}e_n)(B'A^{-1}B)$.

Proof: We have $e_n' = (1, 1, ..., 1)$, $A = F_c(F'F)F_c' + I_n$, and $B = \frac{1}{2n}e_n$.

According to Greene, we have:

$$A^{-1} = I_n - F_c[(F'F)^{-1} + F_c'F_c]^{-1} F_c'.$$

Since $F'F$ and $F_c'F_c$ are both positive definite, therefore

$$F_c[(F'F)^{-1} + F_c'F_c]^{-1} F_c'$$

is also positive definite. So

$$
\begin{aligned}
e_n'A^{-1} e_n &= e_n'e_n - e_n'F_c[(F'F)^{-1} + F_c'F_c]^{-1} F_c'e_n \\
&= n - e_n'F_c'[(F'F)^{-1} + F_c'F_c]^{-1} F_c'e_n \\
&< n.
\end{aligned}
$$

Hence

$$
\begin{aligned}
(1 - e_n'A^{-1} B)^2 &= \left(1 - \frac{1}{2n}e_n'A^{-1} e_n\right)^2 \\
&= 1 - \frac{1}{n}e_n'A^{-1} e_n + \frac{1}{4n^2}(e_n'A^{-1} e_n)^2 \\
&> \frac{1}{4n^2}(e_n'A^{-1} e_n)^2 \\
&= (e_n'A^{-1} e_n)(B'A^{-1} B).
\end{aligned}
$$

This counter example shows that if $B = (1/2n)e_n = ((1/2n), (1/2n), \ldots, (1/2n))$, then $\sigma_G^2 > \sigma_{NLS}^2$. That is, the variance of the prediction error of the adjustment-grid estimator is bigger than that of a nonlinear least squares estimator when B equals $[(1/2n)e_n]$.

What is the necessary and sufficient condition for the inequality $(1 - \bar{e}_n'A^{-1} B)^2 < (e_n'A^{-1} e_n)(B'A^{-1} B)$ to hold?

We let $\langle e_n, B \rangle = e_n'A^{-1}B$ where $\langle,\rangle$ is the inner product.

Therefore $e_n'A^{-1} e_n = \|e_n\|^2$, $B'A^{-1}B = \|B\|^2$, where $\| \|$ is the corresponding norm.

Thus the inequality becomes:

$$|1 - \langle e_n, B\rangle|^2 < \langle e_n, e_n\rangle\langle B, B\rangle, \qquad \text{i.e.} \quad |1 - \langle e_n, B\rangle| < \|e_n\|\|B\|.$$

Now we present another proposition and its proof as follows:

Proposition Two: The sufficient condition for $(1 - \bar{e}_n'A^{-1} B)^2 < (e_n'A^{-1} e_n)(B'A^{-1} B)$ is $\langle e_n, B\rangle > 1/2$, while the necessary condition is $\|e_n\|\|B\| > 1/2$.

Proof: If $\langle e_n, B \rangle > \frac{1}{2}$, then

$$(1 - \bar{e}_n'A^{-1} B)^2 = |1 - \langle e_n, B\rangle|^2 = 1 - 2\langle e_n, B\rangle + \langle e_n, B\rangle^2 < \langle e_n, B\rangle^2.$$

By Schwarz Inequality, we have:

$$\langle e_n, B \rangle^2 < \langle e_n, e_n \rangle \langle B, B \rangle.$$

It follows that the inequality

$$(1 - \bar{e}_n' A^{-1} B)^2 < \langle e_n, e_n \rangle \langle B, B \rangle = (e_n' A^{-1} e_n)(B' A^{-1} B)$$

holds. Now let

$$(1 - \bar{e}_n' A^{-1} B)^2 < (e_n' A^{-1} e_n)(B' A^{-1} B).$$

Therefore

$$|1 - \langle e_n, B \rangle| < \|e_n\| \|B\|,$$

that is

$$\left| \frac{1}{\|e_n\| \|B\|} - \frac{\langle e_n, B \rangle}{\|e_n\| \|B\|} \right| < 1.$$

Since

$$\frac{\langle e_n, B \rangle}{\|e_n\| \|B\|} = \cos \theta$$

(θ is the angle of vectors e_n and B).
Thus we have

$$0 < \frac{1}{\|e_n\| \|B\|} < 2, \qquad \text{i.e. } \|e_n\| \|B\| > \frac{1}{2}.$$

It should also be noted that we cannot conclude that the variance of the prediction error of the nonlinear adjustment-grid estimator being lower than that of a non-linear least squares estimator still holds for those matrices B: $e_n' B \le 1/2$. However, we have derived the necessary and sufficient conditions for $\sigma_G^2 < \sigma_{NLS}^2$. Whether such condition is likely to happen in practice is an area for further research.

5.6 Conclusion

This paper extends the result of Lai and Wang in real property valuation from the linear case to the more general nonlinear case. We have shown that all results in Wang and Lai also hold in the non-linear case. The results for the non-linear case are asymptotic results and require a large number of observations and are therefore more relevant for real estate markets that are liquid markets where transaction prices are abundant and readily available.

We have also proved that, in theory, the inequality in Lai and Wang does not always hold. That is the adjustment-grid method is not always more accurate than the least square method for both the linear and non-linear case.

Finally, we have also specified the necessary and sufficient conditions under which the adjustment-grid method is more accurate than the non-linear least squares method. Whether such conditions are likely to occur in practice seems to be an empirical question that needs to be examined further.

REFERENCES

Colwell, P., Cannaday, E., and Wu, C. (1983). The Analytical Foundations of Adjustment Grid Methods. *The Journal of the American Real Estate and Urban Economics Association.* **11**, 11–29.

Gallant A. Ronald. (1981). *Nonlinear statistical models.* New York: Wiley.

Halvorsen, R. and Palmquist, R. (1981). Choice of Functional Form for Hedonic Price Equations. *Journal of Urban Economics* **10**, 37–49.

Prakasa Rao, B. L. S. (1987). *Asymptotic theory of statistical inference.* New York: Wiley.

Tsong-Yue Lai and Ko Wang. (1996). Comparing the Accuracy of the Minimum-Variance Grid Method to Multiple Regression in Appraised Value Estimates. *The Journal of the American Real Estate and Urban Economic Association.* **24**, 4, 531–549.

Vandell, K. D. (1991). Optimal Comparable Selection and Weighting in Real Property Valuation. *The Journal of the American Real Estate and Urban Economics Association.* **19**, 2, 213–239.

William H. Greene. (1997). *Econometric Analysis (3rd).* Prentice-Hall, Inc.

Chapter 6

Error Trade-offs in Regression Appraisal Methods

Max Kummerow
Department of Property Studies, Curtin University, Perth, Australia

Hanga Galfalvy
Department of Statistics, University of Illinois, Urbana-Champaign, Illinois

6.1 Introduction

This chapter presents a conceptualization of the problem of how many sales to use in a sales comparison method appraisal. We propose that the answer to this question depends on a tradeoff between different kinds of errors and is data dependent, varying across data sets. In hedonic regression appraisals, the law of large numbers does not necessarily hold. Increasing variance, omitted variables, and measurement errors in the sample may overwhelm the efficiency benefits of larger sample size. Heterogeneity within samples makes for the common problem of large standard errors in regression appraisal price predictions (Lenz & Wang, 1998) and suggests disaggregating data to improve the precision of price estimates. A "law of medium numbers" applies, meaning that heterogeneous data may yield smallest standard errors when subsets of data are used for estimates rather than the whole population of sales.

This view suggests that one "way forward" in automating appraisals is to mimic the sales comparison method as practiced by appraisers in the marketplace. Practitioners choose small subsets of sales (3 most often) and infer values from adjusted sale prices of these few sales. Consideration of the sources of errors in regression appraisal methods suggests that using a few comparables may lead to smaller prediction errors than hedonic regressions using larger sample sizes (Colwell Cannaday & Wu, 1983). Statistical data mining methods could be used to explore the optimum number, choice, and adjustment of comparables, reducing the potential for bias in ad hoc comparable selection methods. The optimum number of comparable sales and price prediction errors would vary depending on the characteristics of particular data sets.

We begin with a brief overview of the hedonic regression literature. We then examine four problems in developing models to predict house prices – submarkets, specification errors, measurement errors, and data costs. We then discuss regression versus sales comparison methods, following Colwell, Cannaday and Wu in noting their formal equivalence, as well as important differences. After discussion of comparable selection and weighting, we discuss four types of errors and show simulations to illustrate error tradeoffs. An empirical section then presents examples of error tradeoffs.

6.2 Literature

Hedonic regression appraisal methods have inspired a long and prolific literature extending back to the 1920s and still continuing vigorously today (Lusht, 1986; and Megbolugbe & Johnson, 1998, introduce special journal issues). There is space here to cite only a few papers as examples of major strands of this research.

Many papers investigate "effects of variable x" on house prices. Examples include the value of schools (Bogart & Cromwell, 2000), open space (Shultz & King, 2001), neighborhood diversity (McPherson & Sirmans, 2001), environmental contamination (Jackson, 2001) and so on through a long list of characteristics. Effects are estimated by their coefficients in hedonic pricing models. Another major strand of the recent literature constructs price indexes using hedonic modeling techniques to track constant quality prices over time (Cho, 1996; Meese & Wallace, 1997; Wolverton & Senteza, 2000). Another motive of the hedonic modeling literature is price estimation. Econometric methods promise low-cost, unbiased, and replicable "automated" property valuations, once a database of sales and property information is at hand (Vandell, 1991). The aim would be to use statistical methods to reduce transaction costs and increase transparency by making the appraisal process less dependent upon ad hoc and unreliable "judgment and experience" of the appraiser.

Decreasing costs of data storage and retrieval and GIS techniques enable analysts to use vastly larger databases than existed a few years ago. Recent literature explores techniques that allow incorporation of important spatial autocorrelation and location variables into models (Pace & Gilley, 1997; Pace, 1998; Dubin, Pace & Thibodeau, 1999). Spatial and neighborhood variables enrich the data available to explain price variation and reduce standard errors of pricing models (Des Rosiers & Therault, 1996). Other research looks to more sophisticated estimation methods or functional forms. Box-Cox transformations of variables (especially semi-log specifications), spline regressions, generalized least squares; Bayesian models and other techniques seek a better fit to data (Pace 1998a; Fletcher, Gallimore & Mangan, 2000). Disaggregation of data into submarket subsets to increase the homogeneity of samples and hence reduce standard errors has also received some attention (Lusht & Pugh, 1981; Watkins, 1999).

There are also papers on theory and methods per se, including some critical of what are perceived as major weaknesses in hedonic modeling methods (Lessinger, 1969, 1972). Rosen's (1974) critique of hedonic models pointed out identification problems arising from simultaneity of supply and demand. Rosen also noted that omitting the individual incomes of buyers could lead to biased estimates. Interaction effects, instability of data generating processes over time, complexity (large and variable numbers of salient hedonic candidate variables), non-linear or even non-functional relationships and other difficult econometric issues continue to challenge researchers and practitioners. Since hundreds of variables have been found to be significant in the pricing model literature, theory provides little guidance as to which variables should be included in pricing particular properties.

Four papers from this extensive literature are important foundations for this chaper. Colwell, Cannaday, and Wu, 1983 pointed out the formal equivalence of hedonic regression models and appraisers' traditional "adjustment grid" sales comparison methods and the possibility that sales comparison methods could be more accurate where there are misspecification biases. Lusht and Pugh's 1981 empirical paper was an early look at market segmentation or submarkets. They used prediction errors as their criterion for appraisal quality, a sensible choice in a world of uncertainty about the correctness of model specifications. Isakson (1986, 2001) discusses "near neighbors" criteria for choosing comparable sales.

Finally, Vandell's (1991) paper on comparable selection and weighting proposes a method for selecting and weighting comparable sales based on minimum variance of the resulting price estimate.

6.3 Decisions and Difficulties in Hedonic House Price Modeling

6.3.1 Submarkets

There is much more regression valuation literature testing alternative specifications for hedonic pricing models than addressing the questions of how to choose population and sample. Yet real estate is by nature heterogeneous as we learn early on in real estate texts and from observation. Variances both of price and predictor variables and hence variance of the subject property price estimate tend, therefore, to increase with submarket size. Defining a smaller, more uniform population could increase precision of price estimates relative to estimates from larger more heterogeneous samples. However, smaller, more uniform populations reduce feasible sample size. Scarcity of sales data is a major issue limiting the precision of regression methods, especially in thinly traded housing markets (Epley, 1997). Lusht and Pugh (1981) tested three alternative geographical strategies for comparable selection to try to expand the set of comparables. They tested single neighborhood, multiple similar neighborhoods, and community-wide samples. The wider choice of comparables from multiple similar neighborhoods gave more adequate sample sizes and smaller prediction errors than single neighborhoods. However, they found that expanding the population further to the whole community *reduced* precision of price estimates, despite increasing sample size.

Using more homogeneous data sets tends to reduce the range of predictor variables. For example, if all the houses on a street are the same size, house area will disappear as a useful price predictor in this sub-sample. Yet a regression model with low R^2 estimated from a very uniform sample could give a better price prediction (smaller errors, less bias) than a model with more explanatory power estimated from a more heterogeneous (i.e. higher variance) sample. Morton (1976) found this empirical result using Orange County, California data. Morton focused on R^2, that is, fit or explanatory power of the predictor variables, and therefore recommended using a diverse sample. Nevertheless, for price prediction purposes, Morton's more uniform samples had smaller standard errors of the estimate despite lower R^2.

Whipple (1995) maintains that appraisers should refer to market research, that is, they should interview buyers to find out which variables matter, and define sub-markets as homogeneous groups of buyers, rather than in terms of property types or neighborhoods. In this, Whipple follows Ratcliff's (1972) definition of appraisal as a prediction of behavior of buyers and sellers. Watkins (1999) used an F test to detect differences in coefficients estimated from different submarkets. He detected statistical evidence of submarkets in Scottish housing data.

Several papers discuss comparable sales selection criteria once the sub-market issue has been resolved. Tshira (1979) and Isakson (1986, 2001) approached the comparable selection process by defining "nearness" of comparables in terms of the similarity of property characteristics. The best comparables are those closest to the subject property in this vector space of hedonic variables. Dilmore, Robbins and Graaskamp in unpublished appraisal assignments conducted in the early 1980s used Euclidian distance as their nearness criterion, adjusting weightings of characteristics to minimize prediction errors. Isakson recommends Mahalanobis distance, a measure calculated from standardized property characteristics differences, variances and covariances. Vandell (1991) defines "nearness" of comparables in dollars, calculated by weighting hedonic characteristics differences with coefficients estimated from a submarket sample. He proposes an algorithm for selecting and weighting best comparables using minimum variance of the subject price estimate as the selection criterion. This improves on methods that define nearness in terms of physical characteristics without consideration of whether or not the market places any value on those characteristics. But, as Vandell pointed out, his method requires strong assumptions that the choice of submarket does not introduce bias, the model is correctly specified, and measurement errors are negligible. Vandell and follow up articles by Gau et al. (1992, 1994) and Green (1994) point out the need for empirical testing of these assumptions.

6.3.2 Correct Specification

In recent decades there has been considerable doubt raised about *a priori* models. All parsimonious (i.e. all useful) models leave things out, and so may be subject to omitted variable bias. Kennedy (1993) quotes G.P. Box: "All models are false, some are useful." In practice, it is possible to find better and worse models, but it is not possible to say that we have found the "correct" model.

Bruce and Sundell (1977) found that 141 variables had been used in hedonic house price papers they surveyed. Hundreds more variables have been included in models in subsequent papers. There is little or no theory to tell us whether in a particular case the market values swimming pools, or worries about the stigma of a contaminated site, distance from the CBD, quality of schools, etc. Moreover, interaction effects can be important. In hedonic pricing, there is no logical necessity that coefficients remain constant when the values of other variables change. All these issues make it doubtful that a "correct" model can be identified, or perhaps even that the concept of a uniform data generating process within or between samples has much meaning.

Most hedonic relationships are non-linear (Weirick & Ingram, 1990). In fact, the idea that there is a functional relationship may be only a convenient approximation (Ekeland, 1988; Giere, 1999). And as markets evolve, there is no reason for pricing criteria to remain constant – houses and preferences change. Context matters. There is little justification for regarding all buyers, even of similar houses in a restricted sample or sub-market, as having identical pricing models. For example, families with children may place a premium on good schools, while empty nesters may not consider schools relevant. Few hedonic regression models include buyer characteristics, that is, information on homogeneous *buyer* subgroups. Yet in marketing theory and practice, it is often homogeneous buyer characteristics, not characteristics of products, that define submarkets.

With little *a priori* theory to determine specifications, it is necessary to "let the data speak," that is, to test alternative specifications. But data mining results in pre-test biases. If C is the number of candidate variables tested and K is the number included, the corrected alpha level is approximately $(C/K)\alpha$, (Charemza & Deadman, 1992). For example, if ten variables are tested at the .05 significance level and two included, then the corrected alpha is $(10/2) \times .05 = .25$, not .05. Not surprisingly, if results are due to random effects found by data mining, out of sample prediction may be poor (Leamer, 1983). Hendry (1993) proposed a "general to specific" modeling strategy to avoid pretest bias. But general models may run into multicollinearity and efficiency problems, particularly in small samples. Hendry doesn't tell us what to do if we put all the variables into a model, estimate with a small sample and find that no predictors are significant. Or, if we have more candidate variables than data points, estimation may not be possible at all.

The relevant distribution is the possible sale prices of one particular house at a point in time, not the distribution of all house prices or even a subset of houses. This makes the heterogeneity of properties, buyers, and pricing models major concerns. Regression methods produce a predicted value that falls on a response surface, which is in a sense an average estimated from the sample. But in the region of a particular property's characteristics, the responses may differ from those that are estimated from a larger sample.

Another serious problem is data sets often omitting qualitative uncountable characteristics, such as neighborhood prestige, views, street appeal, or design quality that real estate agents and our own home buying experiences tell us are quite important in buyers' evaluations of properties.

Clearly the large number of possible candidate variables and heterogeneity of pricing processes suggest that misspecification bias can be a serious defect in hedonic regression models. Rather than assuming we have the *right* model, *a priori*, we might do better to admit that we always have the *wrong* model and not enough data to find the right one.

Because there is little theory, a specification search must test a number of alternative specifications (mine the data) and focus on prediction errors rather than calculated variances to test validity. However, testing more than one model creates pre-test bias increasing the possibility of spurious models. If the chosen model is wrong, the calculated variances and covariances are wrong and so are the minimum variance comparable selections and weightings recommended by Vandell (1991). Out of sample prediction errors are a better test of validity than statistics calculated within the sample when misspecification is suspected.

6.3.3 Measurement Errors

All physical measurements involve some degree of error. At the quantum level, Heisenberg's principle tells us that measurement error is a property of the universe. With housing data, measurement errors are much larger than the uncertainties in the location of electrons. For example, students in appraisal classes reported a distribution of house sizes, even though all of them measured the same building.[1] No doubt practicing valuers also sometimes forget to add a room, disagree about how to account for a finished attic, multiply incorrectly, hold the tape measure slightly crooked or have the batteries run low in a measuring device.

In addition, many of the variables we count and enter on spreadsheets that seem to be measured precisely are measured with error if one looks behind the simple number. A bathroom might be large with marble and a gold plated spa or a tiny closet with leaky forty-year-old toilet and rotting floorboards. Items recorded in a database as a particular number cover a range of property features with widely differing amenity values. Both bathrooms show up as an unambiguous, precise "1 bath" in the data, but the value implications are quite different. The concealed variation can be thought of as measurement error, since the data does not distinguish these price-affecting differences. These errors might be on the order of several hundred percent in some cases.

6.3.4 Cost of Data

Data is costly. In Western Australia tens of millions of dollars have been spent by the public sector to create property databases for use in the land records and property taxation systems and these data sets include only a fraction of the hedonic variables that an appraiser might wish to test in a pricing model. It would cost millions more to complete, clean and verify this data and 100% accuracy could never be attained so long as data is interpreted and entered by fallible humans.

For an individual appraiser, inspecting additional comparable sales adds to costs. With fees and profit margins kept low by competition, looking at a few more sales might easily mean a net loss on a valuation job. Cost pressures, therefore, send appraisers towards models and methods requiring a minimum of data.

6.4 Sales Comparison Adjustments versus Hedonic Regression Coefficients

Colwell, Cannaday, and Wu (1983) point out that regression appraisal models can be written so as to make them mathematically equivalent to a sales comparison adjustment grid (See also Kang & Reichert, 1991). If so, it would seem that larger sample size (more comparable sales) would decrease standard errors of house price estimates. Yet practicing appraisers usually use few comparable sales – perhaps 2–5 in most cases – while the standard form of the uniform residential appraisal report required by secondary mortgage markets and mortgage insurers specifies that three comparables are an adequate basis for the value estimate. Is this merely a cost-minimizing expedient, or do small samples yield more precise estimates?

A straight hedonic regression represents sale price as a function of a set of hedonic variables. In equation 1, $\hat{V}_s$ is the predicted price of the subject property, $\hat{b}_j$ is the estimated regression coefficient of the jth hedonic attribute, and X_{sj} is the measured value of the jth hedonic characteristic of the subject property. The coefficients are estimated from a sample of n sales with k hedonic characteristics.

$$\hat{V}_s = \sum_{j=1}^{k} \hat{b}_j X_{sj}. \tag{1}$$

Colwell, Cannaday, and Wu represent the "grid adjustment" sales comparison appraisal method as a form of regression model, but with one of the key predictors being the unadjusted sale price of a comparable property. The close substitute price proxies for an unknown complex hedonic pricing model. The advantage of this technique is that it sidesteps a host of difficult specification, measurement and estimation problems, albeit at the cost of using a proxy sold-property price to "indicate" the price of the subject. This is valuation by analogy. Only differences between subject and comparable sales need to be estimated

$$\hat{V}_s = V_o + \sum_{j=1}^{m} \hat{a}_j (X_{sj} - X_{oj}). \tag{2}$$

To distinguish the shorter list of characteristics from the k hedonic variables of equation 1, note that there are m adjustment factors, with $m < k$. The "s" subscript refers to the subject property, while "o" refers to the comparable observed sale property. $\hat{V}_s$ is therefore the "indicated" value of the subject property based on valuing a short list of m differences between the subject property and the comparable sale and adding these net adjustments to an observed sale price of a similar property. Characteristics that do not vary between subject and comparable are proxied by the sale price of the comparable. Subtracting the observed comparable sale price from both sides restates this model as a model to estimate the value of hedonic *differences* between subject and comparable sale. The value of these differences should be small relative to the total price, so even a large percentage error in estimating the differences leads to only a small percentage error in the subject property price estimate provided the comparable's price is a good proxy.[2]

Notice that there is no "hat" over the price of the comparable sale in equation 2 – this is an observed price, entered into the equation as a measured quantity, not a random variable. This observed price is, however, a realization of a random variable of possible prices that the comparable might have sold for, and therefore should be thought of as $V_{oi} = \mu_{oi} + e_{oi}$, where μ_{oi} is the mean of a random variable of possible sale prices for the ith comparable sale. Because we only observe one event from this distribution,[3] it is impossible to know precisely the distribution of V_{oi}, although we can make educated guesses based on circumstantial evidence (Kummerow, 1999).

Note that $a_j \neq b_j$ because the models are different. In equation 2 the coefficient is multiplied by an amenity characteristic's *difference* between two properties, a smaller number, while in equation 1 it is multiplied by the *full* measure of the characteristic for each individual property. Equality of coefficients in each equation is as unlikely as equality of marginal and average costs.[4] Additionally, $m < k$ means there are fewer adjustments in the sales comparison model. The observed comparable price proxies for omitted variables in a hedonic pricing process that may differ from the included variables in a straight regression model. Both the dependent variable and the predictors differ between the two approaches. Sales comparison coefficients therefore differ from straight regression coefficients even where predictor variables are the same.

6.4.1 Comparable Selection and Weighting

In selecting submarkets to comprise a uniform population of sales data and for choosing subsets of comparable sales, some criterion of "nearness" is required. Standardized Mahalanobis distances were proposed by Tchira (1979) and Isakson (1986) where D_{ij}, the "distance" between two sales, is calculated from

$$D_{ij} = (X_i - X_j) \, \Sigma^{-1} \, (X_i - X_j)' \tag{3}$$

where X_i and X_j are vectors of amenity characteristics for properties i and j, and Σ is a covariance matrix of these amenities. Tchira, points out, however, that these amenity characteristics are not necessarily translated into price effects. If buyers do not change their valuations of properties, it does not matter if physical characteristics differ.

Vandell's solution is to estimate a regression model from submarket data, then use a minimum variance subject property price estimate to find an optimal smaller set of comparables and their optimal weights. He uses the variances and co-variances of the adjustment factors estimated from the submarket regression equation to estimate the variance of the indicated values. One problem, as pointed out above, is that the levels and differences models have different dependent and independent variables, so the coefficients should differ.

Moreover, if the wrong submarket is used to estimate the sample, or if the submarket properties are not all priced by the same hedonic process (responses are heterogeneous across the sample space), then Vandell's method suffers from biased estimates. The exercise depends on the assumption of uniform hedonic structure throughout the submarket and unbiased choice of submarket in the first place.

Even if these assumptions were strictly true, a second criticism, pointed out to us by Peter Colwell, becomes operative – the Vandell procedure then becomes mathematically identical to a straight regression with results identical to simply estimating coefficients from the entire submarket sample and using these to calculate the predicted price of the subject. Vandell's finding that more comparable sales reduce standard errors simply means that precision of any regression estimate increases with sample size given a uniform data generating structure. Confusion in the notation in the 1991 Vandell paper leaves uncertainty about which criticism (ours from the preceding paragraph or Colwell's) is valid. An attempt to sort this out will set the stage for the reformulation presented in the following section of this chapter.

Let:

V_{oi} be the observed sales price of the ith comparable sale, which is one realization of V_i a random variable representing all possible sales prices on the date of sale for the ith comparable property,

μ_i be the expectation of this distribution, $E(V_i)$, so that $V_i = \mu_i + e$. (a random error).

$\hat{V}_{si}$ is the adjusted "indicated" price for the subject property, obtained by adjusting the ith comparable sale (an estimate derived from a pricing model, not an observation).

$\hat{V}_s$ (the final value estimate) will be a weighted average derived from q comparable sales, where q is a subset of n, the number of submarket sales.

Because we cannot observe the mean value (μ_i), we use V_{oi} in the equation 2 model to obtain an estimate of the subject price:

$$\hat{V}_{si} = V_{oi} + \sum^m \hat{a}_j(X_{sj} - X_{ij}). \tag{4}$$

If, on the other hand, we used a regression model (like equation 1) to estimate $\hat{V}_{si}$, then we would have

$$\hat{V}_s = \sum^m \hat{b}_j(X_{sj}). \tag{5}$$

We suspect that this is not a very good model due to misspecification since it was developed for the whole submarket and may not fit the subject property very well. Therefore, the $\hat{b}_j$ coefficients may be biased. In one equation Vandell uses the estimated value, $\hat{V}_{oi}$, rather than the observed value. Our equation 6 is equivalent to equation 2 in Vandell's paper (Ibid: 217).

$$\hat{V}_{si} = \hat{V}_{oi} + \sum^m \hat{b}_j(X_{sj} - X_{ij}). \tag{6}$$

The reason for preferring to use $\hat{V}_{oi}$ rather than V_{oi}, is presumably that the observed value may be an outlier, that is, not near the mean value, μ_i. If the equation 5 model is inadequate, which one must assume was the rationale for using the sales comparison method (equation 4) in the first place, then the use of the predicted comparable price in equation six also produces a poor prediction. Moreover, if we use the estimate rather than the observed price, then the estimate of the subject property price becomes, substituting the right side of equation 5 for $\hat{V}_{oi}$ into equation 6,

$$\hat{V}_{si} = \sum^m \hat{b}_j(X_{ij}) + \sum^m \hat{b}_j(X_{sj} - X_{ij}) = \sum^m \hat{b}_j(X_{sj}) = \hat{V}_s. \tag{7}$$

Equation 7 confirms if the estimated comparable price is used (as in Vandell's equation 2) rather than the observed comparable price and one assumes that the coefficients in both models are the same (i.e. follows Vandell's method of estimating sales comparison adjustment coefficients from the total submarket population of sales), the result is, as Colwell observed, merely a regression model, not sales comparison. Moreover, all of the estimates of the subject's price produced by different comparables will be equal.

Vandell's ensuing discussion shows (we think) that he really means instead to use the following pricing model

$$\hat{V}_{si} = V_{oi} + \sum_{j=1}^{m} \hat{b}_j(X_{sj} - X_{ij}). \tag{8}$$

Recall that $V_{oi} = \mu_i + e_i$ is a realization of the comparable sales price random variable V_i. The expectation of e_i is zero, meaning that it will disappear if we estimate $\hat{V}_{si}$ (indicated subject property price) for a large sample of comparable sales and average the results.

This Colwell et al. conceptualization of sales comparison uses the price of the comparable as a "black box" to avoid problems of efficiency and bias that arise in modeling the price of the subject directly from an incomplete and mismeasured list of hedonic characteristics. Misspecification problems are so serious, data so limited and property and people so heterogeneous that the sales comparison approach probably gives smaller prediction errors for many valuations. A black box observed price provides a more precise valuation model (especially after we adjust it to reflect differences from the subject) than an estimate from a misspecified model with unstable coefficients. This is not necessarily so due to any theory, it just so happens that in most cases data is scarce and mismeasured and samples are heterogeneous.

6.5 Four Types of Errors

It may be helpful to list four distinct types of errors in sales comparison methods. The comparable sale price is a random variable and rarely equals the mean value of the unobservable hypothetical distribution of possible prices, instead differing from the mean possible price by random error, e_{oi}, the deviation of the observed price of the ith comparable sale from the mean of the comparable sale's possible price distribution.

Next, there is error in the estimates of the a_m coefficients that we might call e_{am}. Then there are measurement errors in the hedonic characteristic differences between subject and comparable sale: $(X_{sm} - X_{im}) + e_{im}$. Each of the adjusted characteristics will have its own error, so there is a series of m measurement errors to worry about. Finally, there are omitted variables or other misspecification (e.g. wrong functional form, omitted interaction effects) resulting in an error, e_z. If we write the sales comparison equation with all these errors we have equation 9.

$$\hat{V}_{si} = V_{oi} + e_{oi} + \sum^{m}(a_m + e_{am})((X_{sj} - X_{ij}) + e_{mj}) + e_{zi}. \tag{9}$$

Only e_{oi} is likely to have an out of sample expectation of zero.[5] With heterogeneous sales, as the number of comparable sales, q, increases, errors in the adjustment factors may get larger due to increased likelihood of qualitative differences whose effects are harder to estimate. Measurement errors of the m hedonic characteristics also are an increasing function of the number of comparable sales. As properties become less similar, it becomes harder to measure differences that matter to buyers if only because there are likely to be more of them. For example, in Vandell's paper, Sale 7 has the same number of bedrooms and baths as the subject so errors in adjustment coefficients for these variables are irrelevant and only two variables (house area and lot size) must be measured. For sales 3 and 9, however, three factors must be adjusted, and for sale 10, all four variables differ between sale and subject.

Moreover, as the comparable and subject property become more dissimilar, it is likely that omitted variable biases increase. That is, the "black box" pricing model that produced the observed sale price V_{oi} becomes more unlike the process that will price the subject. In addition to the different characteristics of the houses themselves, less similar houses will attract buyers whose preferences and circumstances may differ. The comparable sale analogy for the subject property's hedonic structure becomes less valid. Citing Vandell's data, for example, one would expect a \$289,000 four bedroom home to be in a better neighborhood than a \$93,000 two bedroom home. On the other hand, sales with similar measured characteristics are more likely to also be similar in unmeasured variables such as neighborhood quality. As the set of comparable sales used gets larger, and more dissimilar, so do misspecification errors. If this were not true, we could simply use regression.

A preferable definition of "nearness" of comparable sales would be to rank order sales by the mean square error from all sources. Mean square error is defined as error variance + bias squared, where bias is the non-zero expectation of the error. MSE cannot be measured by calculated variances and co-variances because unknown measurement errors and omitted variables play important roles in determining total error. With four types of errors in the equation, error behavior as a function of sample size becomes very complicated unless we assume independence of the various types of errors and simple error functions as q and m increase. We do not think the errors are independent and moreover, at least two of the errors (measurement and omitted variables) are not directly measurable by definition.

Since a statistically complete treatment is not feasible, we propose to amalgamate errors in order to simplify analysis. We could write error for any particular estimate of the subject property price obtained from a sales comparison model (equation 2) to heuristically capture the idea that there are two classes of error. Total errors includes a random component, e_{oi}, and a possibly biased component, u_i, which represents some amalgamation of measurement and omitted variables errors:[6]

$$e_{si} = e_{oi} + u_i. \tag{10}$$

The above errors are realizations of random variables with mean square error reflecting random variation and bias:

$$\text{MSE}(V_{is}) = \text{Var}(e_{oi}) + \text{Var}(u_i) + E(u_i)^2. \tag{11}$$

$E(u_i)$ is the expectation of the non-random errors, that is, the bias resulting from these errors and V_s is the subject property price estimate. The expectation of the random error (sampling error) is zero, but the expectation of omitted variable and measurement error biases is not zero. Both variance and bias of these errors tend to increase with sample size.

Multiplying prices by weights when subject price estimates, V_{si}, indicated by different comparable sales are combined to produce a weighted average final value conclusion (V_s) does not eliminate the error tradeoff. Since measurement and omitted variables errors are by nature unknown, one cannot use calculated errors to determine proper weights.

The familiar relationship between the estimated population standard deviation $\hat{s}$ and the standard error of the sampling distribution of the mean, $\hat{s}/\sqrt{q}$ with sample size q, means that the random component of a price estimate standard error derived by averaging a sample of comparable sales decreases inversely to the square root of the number of comparables. If this standard error is 100 with sample size 1, it drops to 50 with sample size 4, to 33 with $q = 9$ and so on. Mean square error from the other sources however, may increase or decrease with q because both bias and variance of these errors increases as the properties become more heterogeneous. MSE $= f(q)$ where $f(q)$ is an increasing function. If the ratio $f(q)/\sqrt{q} > 1$, then mean square error increases with sample size. Therefore, if we order q comparable sales from most similar to least similar to the subject property in terms of measured characteristics then, $\text{MSE}(u_1) < \text{MSE}(u_2) < \text{MSE}(u_3) \cdots < \text{MSE}(u_q)$.

Optimal number of comparable sales depends on the relative size of the various kinds of error and how errors change as a function of increasing sample size q. Measurement errors and omitted variables vary between samples depending upon the characteristics of houses, buyers, and data gathering procedures so no general conclusion is possible.

Although we do not know the size of these errors, nor the function $f(q)$, which will vary between samples, we can use summary statistics of prediction errors to get an idea of the optimum number and weighting of comparables. Prediction errors tell us something about the sample distribution of errors from all sources. Total error is the sum of errors whose variance increases with number of comparables and errors whose sampling distribution variance decreases with number of comparables. Representing a disorderly process of increasing errors by a function $f(q)$ is clearly an oversimplification – the data (as we shall see) are not obliged to follow a simple functional form. Nevertheless, error variances calculated in this way give a stylized representation of the essentials of how total error variance varies with the number of comparable sales.

6.6 Error Trade-offs

If random errors in observed prices are large while mean square adjustment errors are small, that is, Var $e_{oi} > $ MSE (u_i), and $f(q)$ does not increase MSE(u_i) quickly, then increasing the number of comparable sales will reduce total error variance. For example in Figure 1, with \$10,000 as the standard deviation of the observed price and a slow linear increase of \$500 × q as a simplified guess of MSE from other sources, then a pattern like Figure 1 results. Under these stylized simple assumptions about the behavior of error variances, use of 20 comparable sales gives smallest total MSE. With fewer than 21 sales, the marginal decrease in random error is larger than the increase in MSE due to other sources of error. Both random variance and "other MSE" are divided by the square root of sample size, so the plotted MSE's represent sampling distribution statistics rather than population statistics, that is, they summarize error variances for the final subject property price estimate derived from a sample of q comparable sales.

Figure 1: Comparable Sale Price Errors Large Relative to Adjustment Errors

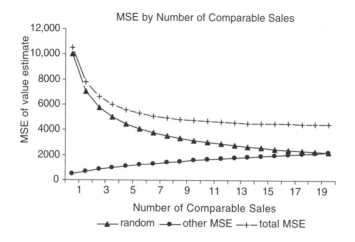

Figure 2: Comparable House Price Errors Small Compared to Adjustment Errors

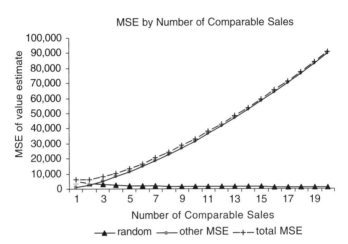

The Figure 1 scenario might be called "uninformed buyers, well-informed appraiser" because the former's pricing errors are large, while the latter's price adjustment errors are small. Figure 2 depicts the opposite, "well-informed buyers, uninformed appraiser" in that adjustment errors are big, but observed sales are correctly priced so the possible price distribution has a small variance. In this situation, the random house price error variance is small relative to adjustment variances and adjustment variances increase rapidly with q so the optimal number of comparable sales is fewer. For example, in Figure 2, standard deviation of observed prices is set at $5000 and adjustment related MSE at an exponentially increasing $1000 \times q^2$. Under these assumptions, the optimal number of comparables is reduced to one, that is, adjustment error variance increases are larger than random error variance decreases starting with the addition of the second comparable. No doubt this is an unrealistically pessimistic view of the size of adjustment errors in most cases, as shown by the large absolute size of total errors shown on the y-axis. Usually appraisers are not this uncertain about adjustment amounts.

As noted above, standard errors of the sampling distribution of the mean decrease rapidly with increasing sample size when sample size is small. Therefore, where scarcity of closely matched comparables makes the non-random MSE increase rapidly with q, the optimum number of comparable sales is probably usually in the range of 1–10. There is no single answer to the optimal sample size question since error trade-offs vary between subsets of sales. Figure 3 shows an example where minimum MSE is obtained by using 3 comparable sales. This "*buyers make modest mistakes, appraisers' mistakes start small but get bigger due to increasing comparable diversity*" graph was

Figure 3: Optimal Number of Comparables

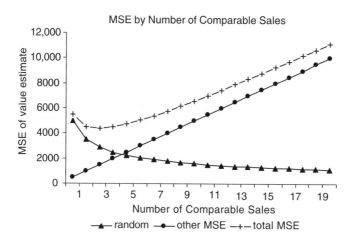

produced by assuming $5000 standard deviation for the observed sale price, and adjustment errors of $500 \times q^{1.5}$. Since both error variances are divided by the square root of q, the adjustment error becomes linear.

Uniform residential appraisal forms widely used in the United States use three comparable sales, implicitly accepting the above error trade-off pattern for typical residential appraisals. The forms, of course, are designed with other factors such as costs of information in mind, so three may not actually minimize MSE in a majority of cases. We believe, however, that this U shaped MSE function with respect to number of sales probably would hold for most sales data.

This reasoning leads to the conclusion that the optimal number of comparables varies depending on the relative sizes of various types of errors. If one has an excellent adjustment model, but little faith in the ability of buyers' to price property accurately, then use of more comparables leads to a more precise value estimate. All the observed sale prices are subject to big random errors due to buyers' and sellers' lack of precision in pricing and this error is reduced by larger sample sizes. On the other hand, if one has little faith in the hedonic model, but more faith that each property has sold for the right price (with little random pricing error), then fewer comparable sales, perhaps only one comparable, will yield the best value estimate. In practice, the situation probably is usually somewhere in between – there are errors in observed prices, in data, and in model specifications – so the optimal number of comparables is generally "a few" with the best number depending upon specific circumstances.

Omitted from the preceding discussion of error variances is the important issue of bias in the adjustments. Expectations of adjustment errors are probably not zero and this bias, like error variance almost certainly increases with sample size. Therefore, the value estimate may tend to drift away from the true value as comparable sales are added to the sample, increasing bias. Omitted variable biases in the four variable hedonic model used in Vandell's 1991 paper may explain why his empirical example's subject price estimate moves downward from $256,000 to $233,000 as the number of comparable sales used to estimate price goes from one to ten. Casual inspection of his data suggests the subject property is most similar to homes that sold for around $240,000–245,000, a result obtained when three or four comparables are used to estimate the price.

6.6.1 Lusht and Pugh's Empirical Results

Lusht and Pugh (1981) examined the question of how widely one should cast the net in choosing comparable sales. From 325 properties sold in 1978, 150 were randomly selected to serve as subject properties (a withheld sample). Those 150 houses were each appraised three times using comparables drawn from first a "traditional neighborhood," second an expanded group of similar neighborhoods, and third the community at large. Mean absolute percentage prediction error results are shown in Table 1.[7]

As one would expect in real data, the patterns are not absolutely regular, but in all cases, the minimum average percentage prediction error occurs with fewer than the maximum number of comparables. Figure 4 sums and averages the three columns of Table 1.

These valuations were performed by a method involving attribute matching for comparable selection, with cost as a basis for adjustment of physical

Table 1: Lusht and Pugh Appraisal % Error versus Number of Comparable Sales

Number of Comparable Sales	One Neighborhood	Similar Neighborhoods	Entire Community
1	15.4	11	19.4
2	8.6	16.2	23.4
3	9.4	8.1	13.9
4	5.3	9.6	16.1
5	6.6	4.7	5
6	11	8	4.3
7	6.3	7.4	10.7

Source: Lusht and Pugh, 1981.

Figure 4: Lusht and Pugh Percent Error in 450 Appraisals by Number of Comparables
Source: Data from Lusht and Pugh, 1981

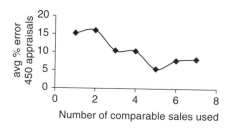

differences, and use of the median comparable's "indicated value" as the final appraised value. With Lusht and Pugh's data set and valuation method, five comparables gave smaller prediction errors (5.4% v 8.1%) than 3 comparables. The arguments presented in this paper suggest that while the details would vary, the pattern shown in the Lusht and Pugh results would probably be typical of sales comparison methods in general, regardless of the details of hedonic price model adjustments and comparable selection.

6.7 Perth Empirical Results

There is little space here for empirical testing so we report only limited results. In any event, our analysis suggests there are no general results to report – the results will vary between samples.

Western Australia uses a Torrens title system, so all real estate sales are registered with a state land titles office. Tens of thousands of sales are included in the data so we begin with a complete population of sales, albeit many with missing data. Five subsets of 1998–1999 sales data were extracted. Coefficients estimated from these subsets of the data or by using clustering methods based on price or other variables are not stable across samples, or even within samples. The results in Table 2 are an excerpt from regressions with 8 predictor variables including land area, house area, bedrooms, bathrooms, number of rooms, a swimming pool dummy, house age, and number of carport/garage spaces. Semi-log versions were estimated, but did not materially improve the results.

This instability of coefficients gives strong evidence for misspecification biases due to omitted variables or measurement errors. This implies a need to fall back on sales comparison for price estimation rather than using regression.

Moreover, standard errors of regression estimates, even in relatively homogeneous submarket subsets of the data, are large. Unless the data set is considerably enriched – an avenue that can be pursued by addition of census

Table 2: Instability of Regression Results Across Samples

Suburb	ADJ R^2	SEE	House Size (*t* statistic)	Bedrooms	Df
All	.54	104900	2043 (.78)	−36400 (−.14)	2339
Como	.56	138300	2135 (.70)	−40730 (−.16)	62
Poor	.78	23400	1116 (1.0)	−11050 (−.12)	34
Rich	.18	152500	1335 (.51)	−36710 (−.20)	129
Ballajura	.87	21900	795 (12.7)	580 (.15)	169

and location variables to the data set – these data do not allow sufficiently precise price estimates by regression methods. Note also that the number of bedrooms variable has the "wrong" i.e. negative, sign, a moot point since bedrooms is not a significant predictor in any of the samples, even one with over 2,000 sales. The model is most successful in the "Ballajura" sample, the most uniform of the data sets, and one where house size happens to have considerable explanatory power. Nevertheless, standard errors still are on the order of 20% of mean house values.

Because the focus here is not on specification, estimation or sample selection issues, but rather the optimum number of comparables and error trade-offs, a simple method was used to test price prediction errors versus number of comparable sales. The four data sets of 1998–1999 sales from "Como", "Rich", "Poor," and "Ballajura" submarkets were each valued repeatedly by averaging the indicated (adjusted) values from a sales comparison using from 1 to *n* comparables found to be "similar enough" to pass through a comparable screening algorithm. This is a common sense approach to disaggregation of data that defines close substitutes (and hence similarity of unknown proxy pricing models revealed by the prices of those comparable sales) based on how people probably search for houses by approximately matching price range, number of bedrooms, and other important house features. This method is essentially an attempt to represent the sales comparison approach as implemented by practicing appraisers. The number of sales that met the attribute matching test for comparability, and hence the number of appraisals for each sale ranged from 0 in a few cases, to as many as 59 sales in these samples. In all, several thousand sales comparison appraisals were estimated for the approximately 400 sales in the four submarkets.

Figure 5 shows an example of aggregate results from using from 1 to the maximum number of available comparables for each of the 42 properties in the Como sample, a total of 518 appraisals. In this set of appraisals, for 10 out of 42 properties the optimum (minimum prediction error) number of comparables was one. In only two out of the 42 subject properties was it the case that the maximum number of comparables led to the smallest prediction error. Therefore, a majority of the sales were valued most precisely by finding the optimum number of comparables along a u-shaped error function.

Figure 5 shows that on average, when each of the 42 sales in the "Como" sample were valued using from one to the maximum number of comparables that fell through the comparable screening algorithm, minimum prediction errors were obtained with three comparable sales. However, in the "Poor" sample minimum errors appear at nine comparables when errors are averaged across the 35 sales in this sample, although four comparables were nearly as good. The larger more uniform Ballajura sample showed slowly declining errors that would generally be expected in a more uniform sample with a less misspecified pricing model with smallest errors at around 20 comparables. With the "Rich" sample, however, one comparable gave the best price prediction in most cases. Therefore, it turns out that these submarkets happen to display the range of possible patterns presented in the simulations above (Figures 1–3).

The error tradeoffs are not a neat or well-behaved function of number of comparables, however, as one would expect due to random variation in small samples. And each subject property has a different pattern. See for example, Figure 6, a plot of the patterns of five individual property price errors as a function of number of comparables from the "Poor" submarket (not averages of errors by number of comparables across the entire sample as in Figure 5). Note that these patterns vary considerably between sales even within a particular

Figure 5: Percent Prediction Error versus Number of Comparables, Perth Example

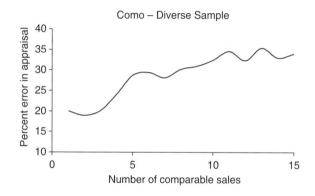

Como – Diverse Sample

Figure 6: Examples of Subject Property Price Prediction Errors

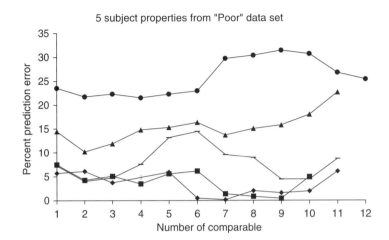

submarket. Some properties can be priced more accurately than others and different numbers of comparable sales yield most precise estimates for different properties. Note however, that all five of the sales in Figure 6 show minimum price prediction errors with fewer than the full number of comparable sales, supporting the idea of a "law of medium numbers" due to error tradeoffs. This example and the average results from the four submarket samples provide additional empirical support for the error tradeoff story.

Each sample one might test would give a different pattern depending on the relative sizes of different sources of errors. Many samples, we believe, would show U shaped relationships between number of comparables and total price prediction error as revealed in these Perth examples.

There is a payoff from seeking the "best" number of comparables, since, for example in the Como data, with the optimum number of comparables, prediction errors averaged 7% of the subject's actual sale price for individual houses. Prediction errors were substantially higher when more or fewer comparables were used. The higher errors in Table 5 come from averaging errors by number of comparables across all sales. Of course, as Figure 6 shows, these patterns are not regular enough to make it easy to determine optimum number of comparables for a particular sale, and random errors play a role in "how many" predict best in particular cases.

6.8 Summary

A long tradition of academic research seeks statistical methods to make real estate appraisal more objective, less open to bias, more precise, more replicable, and to increase productivity by use of information technology. There have been sceptical comments on regression methods along the way (Lessinger, 1969, 1972; Dilmore, 1997), and in practice it has proven difficult to implement hedonic regression models that perform better than traditional appraisal methods. Lentz and Wang (1996) point out the large standard errors of estimate in most regression appraisals due to data limitations and small sample sizes. Some processes may be too disorderly to model without large and unstable errors (Makridakis & Wheelwright, 1989; Gordon, 1991).

This paper implies that we will never be able to estimate property prices very precisely by hedonic regression methods, or any other method due to the nature of reality. Errors will often be large and ill-behaved because pricing processes are messy, diverse, and complex. Furthermore, it is impossible to quantify significant misspecification and measurement errors. The problem is not in the statistics but in the states of nature.

The remedy is not to assume that a particular model is correctly specified regardless of evidence to the contrary, but rather to enrich data sets, disaggregate heterogeneous data into subpopulations, use more sophisticated estimation techniques, and explore subsets of data in search of the most efficient models and sample sizes. A lot of the problems come from data limitations and data can be enriched and better measured. We cannot ask statistical methods to discover more order in the model than exists in the real world, but we can use them to explore pricing processes revealed by the data.

Use of statistics and assessment of sources and distributions of errors can lead to less bias, more precision, and higher productivity for appraisers. Perhaps a realistic hope is that automated methods can provide adequate approximate valuations in a majority of cases, but that for unusual properties or thinly traded markets, traditional case study methods will remain the only option (and remain subject to large and biased errors). There will still be a role for traditional appraisal in finding out what matters to buyers in particular submarkets and measuring these specific characteristics and their interactions for particular houses.

The framework for analysis laid out by Ratcliff, Colwell, Cannaday, and Wu, Vandell and others wherein appraised value is seen as an estimate of the expectation of a random variable offers a theory suitable as a foundation for valuation methods. There is more clarity and precision in representing prices as distributions with outliers, means, and variances than in traditional definitions of market value involving vague and confusing concepts like willing and informed buyers. Processes for deriving estimates of subject property prices from comparables are certainly more defensible and transparent if they use statistics rather than guesses or at least use statistics to inform educated guesses.

There is a bifurcation in methods expressed in equations 4 and 5 between models that are "straight regression" versus those that use sales comparison by adjusting observed sale prices as proxies for subject property prices. So far, most academic research has been along the "straight regression" path. If our discussion of errors is correct, more work is needed along the lines of Colwell, Cannaday, and Wu, Graaskamp, Robbins and Dilmore who have tried to mimic traditional adjustment grid comparable sales methods in more replicable, objective fashion, using computer data bases to improve productivity.

Regression and sales comparison may converge as each improves. The "straight regression" avenue can move towards the sales comparison method by improving the richness of data, particularly by incorporating more spatial and neighborhood variables, by improving specifications through more non-linear and interaction terms, and by using estimation techniques involving spatial autocorrelation, clustering, generalized additive models, or spline regressions. Sales comparison methods can move towards regression methods by relying more on statistical methods in choosing, adjusting, and weighting comparables and by varying the number of comparables used.

The discussion of errors here is oversimplified, no doubt, but the basic idea that the optimal number of comparables involves an error trade-off is probably correct as indicated by our simulations, the Lusht and Pugh data, the Perth examples, and even Vandell's empirical example.[8] The best number of comparables depends upon relative sizes of mean square errors of adjustments versus random errors in observed prices. Industry practice – use of 2–5 comparables – is probably closer to optimum than regression methods where more comparables may not decrease total errors due to sample heterogeneity. It is pleasing to find a theoretical rationale for the market outcome, because one normally expects competitive markets to find a reasonably efficient solution. The fact that competitive markets for appraisals since the 1930s have not found a favorable benefit/cost ratio in requiring more or less than 3 comparables in residential valuations is probably the strongest empirical support for our analysis of error variances tradeoffs.

NOTES

[1] In a sample of 53 student valuations of a home known to be 2100 sq. ft. in area, the measurements fell into a roughly normal curve with outliers more than 20% in error, and a majority falling within 10% of the true value. Appraisers have to make numerous decisions in measuring houses about "what counts" and may differ in their conclusions. Comparing the students to appraisers observed measuring houses, the students spent more time and care to "get it right" (the appraisal was a major assignment) but were less expert than the more experienced appraisers.

[2] In the U.S.A., the total absolute value of adjustments must be less than 25% of the comparable's price and the net value of the adjustments not more than 15% in order to satisfy standards imposed by the secondary mortgage markets. These percentages define when a

comparable is comparable enough. Of course, appraisers have some freedom in deciding the size of adjustments to use.

[3] Sometimes a few events are observed if there are repeat sales of the same property. But strictly speaking, repeat sales come from different distributions of possible prices since the market changes over time.

[4] Another way of saying this is that relationships are not linear. Empirical support for non-linear relationships for at least some variables can be demonstrated in most samples of sales data.

[5] And since prices are generally skewed to the right, the random errors around the observed sale price are probably not normally distributed – which doesn't matter due to the central limit theorem, provided there are sufficient comparable sales to create a normally distributed sampling distribution of the mean.

[6] For simplicity this formulation ignores the variance and covariance of these different types of errors.

[7] Our discussion above has been in terms of MSE (mean square error) while Lusht and Pugh reported MAPE (mean absolute percentage error). Both are summary statistics of error distributions, the difference between the two being that in calculating MSE, individual errors are squared, while the MAPE statistic takes absolute values of errors. Therefore, MSE gives more weight to larger errors. Which is preferable depends on whether large errors have bigger consequences.

[8] Based on his assumptions about model adequacy and lack of measurement errors, Vandell reached a different conclusion – that more comparable sales are always better – but, his empirical example appears to give a more plausible valuation using 3 or 4 comparables than if the maximum number (10) are used.

REFERENCES

Bogart, W. T. and Cromwell, B. A. How Much is a School Worth?, *Journal of Urban Economics*, 2000, 47, 280–305.

Bruce, R. W. and Sundell, D. J. Multiple Regression Analysis: History and Applications in the Appraisal Profession, *Real Estate Appraiser*, 1977 Jan/Feb, 37–44.

Charemza, W. W. and Deadman, D. F. *New Directions in Econometric Practice*, London: Edward Elgar Publishers, 1992.

Cho Man. House Price Dynamics: A survey of Theoretical and Empirical Issues, *Journal of Housing Research*, 1996, 7:2, 145–172.

Colwell, P. F., Cannaday, R. E., and Wu, C. The Analytical Foundations of Adjustment Grid Methods, *Journal of the American Real Estate and Urban Economics Association*, 1983, 11:1, 11–29.

Des Rosiers, F. and Theriault, M. Rental Amenities and the Stability of Hedonic Prices: A Comparative Analysis of Five Market Segments, *The Journal of Real Estate Research*. 1996, 12:1, 17–36.

Dilmore, G. Appraising with Regression Analysis, A Pop Quiz, *Appraisal Journal*, October 1997, 403–404.

Dubin, R., Pace, R. K., and Thibodeau, T. G. Spatial Auto regression Techniques for Real Estate Data, *Journal of Real Estate Literature*, 1999, 7, 79–95.

Ekeland, I. *Mathematics of the Unexpected*, Chicago: University of Chicago Press, 1988.

Epley, D. R. A Note on the Optimal Selection and Weighting of Comparable Properties, *Journal of Real Estate Research*. 1997, 14:2, 175–181.

Fletcher, M., Gallimore, P., and Mangan J. Heteroscedasticity in Hedonic House Price Models, *Journal of Property Research*, 2000, 17:2, 93–108.

Gau, G. W., Lai, T.Y., and Wang, K. Optimal Comparable Selection and Weighting in Real Property Valuation: An Extension, *Journal of the American Real Estate and Urban Economics Association*, 1992, 20:1, 107–123.

Gau, G. W., Lai, T.Y., and Wang, K. A Further Discussion of Optimal Comparable Selection and Weighting, and a Response to Green, *Journal of the American Real Estate and Urban Economics Association*, 1994, 22:4, 655–663.

Gordon, S. *History and Philosophy of the Social Sciences*, London: Routledge, 1991.

Green, R. K. Optimal Comparable Weighting and Selection: A Comment, *Journal of the American Real Estate and Urban Economics Association*, 1994, 22:4, 647–654.

Hendry, D. *Econometrics: Alchemy or Science?*, Oxford Blackwell, 1993.

Isakson, H. R. The Nearest Neighbors Appraisal Technique: An Alternative to the Adjustment Grid Methods, *Journal of the American Real Estate and Urban Economics Association*, 1986, 14:2, 274–286.

Isakson, H. R. The Nearest Neighbors Appraisal Technique Revisited. Presented at the American Real Estate Society Conference, April 2001.

Jackson, T. O. The Effects of Environmental Contamination on Real Estate: A Literature Review, *Journal of Real Estate Literature*, 2001, 9:2, 91–116.

Kang, H. B. and Reichert, A. K. An Empirical Analysis of Hedonic Regression and Grid-Adjustment Techniques in Real Estate Appraisal, *Journal of the American Real Estate and Urban Economics Association*, 1991, 19:1, 70–91.

Kennedy, P. *A Guide to Econometrics, 3rd* Ed., Cambridge: MIT Press, 1993.

Leamer, E. E. Let's Take the Con Out of Econometrics, *American Economic Review*, 1983, 7:1, 31–43.

Lentz, G. H. and Wang, K. Residential Appraisal and the Lending Process: A Survey of Issues, *Journal of Real Estate Research*, 1998, 15:1/2, 11–39.

Lessinger, J. Econometrics and Appraisal, *Appraisal Journal*, October 1969, 501–512.

Lessinger, J. A 'Final' Word on Multiple Regression and Appraisal, *Appraisal Journal*, July 1972, 449–458.

Lusht, K. M. and Pugh, F. A Research Note on the Effects of Changing the Search Area for Comparable Sales, *The Real Estate Appraiser and Analyst*, Winter 1981, 34–36.

Lusht, K. M. Real Estate Valuation and Appraisal (introduction to special edition), *Journal of the American Real Estate and Urban Economics Association*, 1986, 14:2, 175–178.

Makridakis, S. and Wheelwright, S. C. *Forecasting Methods for Management*, 5th edition, New York: John Wiley & Sons, 1989.

Macpherson, D. A. and Sirmans, G. S. Neighborhood Diversity and House-Price Appreciation, *Journal of Real Estate Finance and Economics*, 2001, 22:1, 81–97.

Meese, R. A. and Wallace, N. E. The Construction of Residential Housing Price Indices: A Comparison of Repeat-Sales, Hedonic Regression, and Hybrid Approaches, *Journal of Real Estate Finance and Economics*, 1997, 14, 51–73.

Megbolugbe, I. F. and Johnson, L. Guest Editors' Introduction and Summary (to special issue on residential appraisal and lending), *Journal of Real Estate Research*, 1998, 15:1/2, 1–9.

Morton, T. G. Narrow Versus Wide Stratification of Data in the Development of Regression Appraisal Models, *American Real Estate and Urban Economics Association Journal*, 1976, 4:2, 7–18.

Pace, R. K. Appraisal Using Generalized Additive Models, *Journal of Real Estate Research*, 1998a, 15:1/2, 77–99.

Pace, R. K. Total Grid Estimation, *Journal of Real Estate Research*, 1998b, 15:1/2, 101–114.

Pace, R. K. and Gilley, O. W. Using the Spatial Configuration of Data to Improve Estimation, *Journal of Real Estate Finance and Economics*, 1997, 14, 333–340.

Ratcliff, R. U. *Valuation for Real Estate Decisions*, Santa Cruz, CA: Democrat Press, 1972.

Robbins, M. www.Teauran.com, 2001.

Shultz, S. and King, D. A. The Use of Census Data for Hedonic Price Estimates of Open-Space Amenities and Land Use, *Journal of Real Estate Finance and Economics*, 2001, 22:3, 239–252.

Tashman, L. J., et al. Effect of Regressor Forecast Error on the Variance of Regression Forecasts, *Journal of Forecasting*, 2000, 19, 587–600.

Tchira, A. Comparable Sales Selection – A Computer Approach, *Appraisal Journal*, January 1979, 86–98.

Vandell, K. D. Optimal Comparable Selection and Weighting, *Journal of the American Real Estate and Urban Economics Association*, 1991, 19:2, 213–239.

Watkins, C. Property Valuation and the Structure of Urban Housing Markets, *Journal of Property Investment and Finance*, 1999, 17:2, 157–175.

Weirick, W. N. and Ingram, F. J. Functional Form Choice in Applied Real Estate Analysis, *Appraisal Journal*, January 1990, 57–73.

Whipple, R. T. M. *Property Valuation and Analysis*, North Ryde, NSW: Law Book Company, 1995.

Wolverton, M. L. and Senteza, J. Hedonic Estimates of Regional Constant Quality House Prices, *Journal of Real Estate Research*, 2000, 19:3, 235–253.

Chapter 7

Automated Valuation Models

R. Kelley Pace
*E.J. Ourso College of Business Administration, Louisiana State University, Baton Rouge,
Louisiana*

C.F. Sirmans
Center for Real Estate and Urban Economic Studies, Connecticut

V. Carlos Slawson, Jr.
*E.J. Ourso College of Business Administration, Louisiana State University, Baton Rouge,
Louisiana*

Traditional fee appraisers have welcomed the computer technology of databases, spreadsheets, and word processing. Even further, they have welcomed appraisal software which has reduced the clerical element of writing appraisal reports. However, the basic methods they follow in estimating value have not changed much in some time. In contrast, over the same period, assessors have quietly yet radically changed their valuation technology through application of computer aided mass assessment (CAMA) techniques. These techniques have improved the accuracy of mass appraisals while reducing their cost. As the price of computer power and automated data collection spirals downwards, could the application of CAMA techniques supplant traditional appraisal in other settings?[1]

We examine this question from a number of perspectives. Section 7.1 discusses the problem of appraiser moral hazard, reviews the functions of appraisers, contrasts the accuracy of manual and automated appraisals, examines the market for low-cost appraisal services, and considers a hybrid system of both manual and automated appraisals. Section 7.2 discusses a possible implementation of an automated system. Any implementation must consider how to enter accurately the relevant information into the system and the subsequent processing of such information. Section 7.3 summarizes the key results.

7.1 Traditional Versus Automated Appraisals

This section examines a number of aspects of manual and automated appraisal. Specifically it considers the problems of appraiser incentives, the accuracy of manual and automated appraisals, the costs of appraisal and their effects, and ways of combining manual and automated appraisal.

7.1.1 Appraiser Moral Hazard

In the current housing finance system, primary lenders sell a high proportion of originated loans to the various entities in the secondary mortgage market. Unfortunately, for these entities a number of informational asymmetries and perverse incentives exist among the parties to the loan which create opportunities for moral hazard. First, the seller has the greatest knowledge of the house's characteristics. Second, the buyer has the greatest knowledge of his own financial prospects. Third, the primary lender has a better idea of the quality of the prospective loan than do the secondary market entities. Finally, mortgage bankers, loan officers, and real estate agents have incentives to close the loan. Hence, substantial moral hazard opportunities exist.

The secondary market entities combat these perverse incentives through the use of rigorous criteria, monitoring of loan performance as a function of the originator, and the use of a third party, the appraiser. Ideally, the appraiser independently estimates selling price. However, the appraiser also faces perverse incentives.[2] An appraiser who often provides appraisals for less than the transaction price could expect negative reactions from mortgage bankers, buyers, sellers, and real estate agents. The loss in referrals and subsequent business could reduce the appraiser's income. Insofar as the appraiser often knows the transaction price prior to the appraisal, setting the appraised price to the transaction price plus a small premium constitutes a mini-max strategy.

As evidence of this strategy, Chinloy, Cho, and Megbolugbe (1995) found 80% of the appraisals came in at or slightly above the transaction price. However, Dotzour (1988) found that when appraisers did not have access to the transaction price prior to the appraisal, their estimates were unbiased but with considerably greater dispersion (10% standard deviation). Obviously, appraiser knowledge of the transaction price affects the resulting appraisal. In this sense, an appraiser serves more as an auditor of the transaction than as an independent estimator of value.

7.1.2 Unbundling Appraiser Functions

The problem of appraiser moral hazard coupled with the high cost of manual appraisal suggests a reconsideration of appraiser functions. Historically, appraisers have fulfilled three functions.

First, they gather and serve as a database for local housing transactions. Computerization via databases and MIS have greatly eroded the need for the information gathering function of appraisers. Moreover, the appraiser may redundantly gather many types of information. For example, the listing agent, the assessor, surveyors, and property inspectors jointly collect much of the information appraisers use such as the number of bedrooms, number of bathrooms, living area, and lot size. Private firms such as Experian have begun to specialize in the collection of this type of data (at this point almost all firms repackage assessor data). Effectively, technology has created large economies of scale in data collection and organization.

Second, they provide an estimate of market value. However, given adequate data on the property, the estimation of value can be performed using statistical methods. The continued downward trend in computing costs coupled with progress in statistical methodology could obviate the valuation function of appraisers.

Third, they act as informal property inspectors. They examine the apparent condition of the property as one of the factors in their value estimate. Since appraisers expose themselves to legal liability when documenting the verifiable physical features of the property, they often choose to execute this function carefully. However, they probably do not delve as deep into the structural aspects of the house as a property inspector or engineer.

7.1.3 What Level of Accuracy Should a System Possess?

The level of accuracy needed depends upon the value of the appraisal in reducing fraud and moral hazard in the housing finance system. If professionally employed individuals with substantial assets rarely attempt to defraud the system, the appraisal would not likely decrease the relatively low moral hazard further. Moreover, attempts to defraud the system often vary with macroeconomic conditions. The high inflation of the seventies made housing less affordable using fixed rate loans which led to individuals attempting to bypass the usual standards. Systems which could accurately predict the moral hazard potential of individuals can employ relatively less accurate automated appraisal systems.[3]

If statistical mass appraisal techniques were to supplant traditional fee appraisals, what level of accuracy do these techniques need to provide? The answer to this depends upon the use of the appraisals. However, for housing finance purposes, two potential criteria appear obvious. First, for loan purposes the appraisal should have an error substantially less than the proportion of equity at risk. Ideally, a loan with a 10% downpayment requires a more accurate appraisal than the same house financed with a 25% downpayment. Second, regardless of the accuracy desired, if statistical mass appraisal techniques could match fee appraiser accuracy, this would act as a sufficient condition for using the automated techniques to supplant traditional fee appraisal.

7.1.4 Automated Appraisal Accuracy

Unfortunately, the accuracy of fee appraisals remains difficult to evaluate since appraiser knowledge of the transaction price affects the appraisal. The study of Dotzour (1988), however, provides a rough estimate of their accuracy. Dotzour examined the properties purchased at the appraised price by a corporate relocation firm. The firm resold these properties shortly thereafter. Dotzour computed the percentage difference between the purchase price (appraised value) and the subsequent transactions price. He found appraisers were correct on average with an error standard deviation of about 10%. For normally distributed errors this translates into a mean absolute proportional error of 8% and a median absolute proportional error of 6.8%.[4]

As an alternative accuracy benchmark, computerized automated mass assessment (CAMA) systems estimate the value for the majority of residences in the U.S. for *ad valorem* taxes and these systems have documented performances. Each jurisdiction compiles a database of property records and often uses a turnkey system for the estimation of value and the billing of property owners. Primarily, large and medium sized cities such as Boston,

Chicago, New York City, Salt Lake City, Charleston, and San Antonio use these systems. In addition, various states and provinces such as Arizona, Massachusetts, Saskatchewan, and Vermont employ CAMA systems.

The coefficient of dispersion (COD) is the statistic most frequently used in rating CAMA systems. Equation (1) defines the COD,

$$COD = \frac{\text{mean}\left(\text{abs}\left[\hat{P}/P - \text{median}\left(\hat{P}/P\right)\right]\right)}{\text{median}\left(\hat{P}/P\right)} \tag{1}$$

where P represents the vector of transaction prices and $\hat{P}$ represents the vector of assessed values (division in the formulas is element-wise). The assessment literature refers to $\hat{P}/P$ as the sales ratio. Transforming (1) to express the COD in terms of errors yields (2) and (3).

$$COD = \frac{\text{mean}\left(\text{abs}\left[\left(1 + \left(\hat{P} - P\right)/P\right) - \text{median}\left(1 + \left(\hat{P} - P\right)/P\right)\right]\right)}{\text{median}\left(1 + \left(\hat{P} - P\right)/P\right)} \tag{2}$$

$$COD = \frac{\text{mean}\left(\text{abs}\left[\left(1 + \hat{e}/P\right) - \text{median}\left(1 + \hat{e}/P\right)\right]\right)}{\text{median}\left(1 + \hat{e}/P\right)} \tag{3}$$

The constant 1 will cancel out of the two expressions within the brackets in the numerator of (3) thus yielding (4).

$$COD = \frac{\text{mean}\left(\text{abs}\left[\left(\hat{e}/P\right) - \text{median}\left(\hat{e}/P\right)\right]\right)}{\text{median}\left(1 + \hat{e}/P\right)} \tag{4}$$

If the system uses unbiased statistical estimation and attempts to assess at market value (true of many jurisdictions using CAMA), $E(e)=0$.[5] The median($\hat{e}/P$) will not generally equal 0. However, it will not usually differ from 0 greatly for reasonably accurate, unbiased systems. Hence, one could use (5) as an approximation. Thus, for unbiased CAMA systems the COD will usually lie close to the mean absolute proportional error.

$$COD \cong \text{mean}\left[\text{abs}\left(\hat{e}/P\right)\right] \tag{5}$$

Eckert (1990, p. 534, 540) reports that overall CODs of 15% or less are considered good, that newer, more homogeneous areas can obtain CODs of 10% or less, and that CODs of less than 5% are very rare. Practical CAMA systems can have a COD of less than 10%. Massachusetts, for example, attempts to ensure their system has a COD of less than 10% (Thompson and Gordon (1987, p. 269)). Hence, operational CAMA systems can have COD levels and hence mean absolute proportional errors close to those produced by fee appraisers.

As further examples of possible statistical valuation accuracy, Pace (1998) obtained approximately a 6.6% median absolute proportional ex-sample error from a semiparametric model using the equivalent of 42 variables (442 observations) based upon data from the Memphis MLS. Pace, Barry, Gilley, and Sirmans (forthcoming) obtained an ex-sample median absolute proportional error of 7.4% from a spatial-temporal model using 14 variables (5,243 observations) based upon data from the Baton Rouge MLS. From this, the goal of producing an automated mass appraisal system with about a 6–8% median absolute proportional error seems reasonable.

7.1.5 Potential Markets for Automated Appraisal

The cost of traditional fee appraisals has limited the market for appraisal services. Ideally, owners of mortgages could have the collateral reappraised on a continual basis. This could potentially increase the pricing efficiency of mortgages and mortgage backed securities. In addition, entities with an effective automated appraisal system could sell these services to other financial institutions, marketing research firms, economic consultants, and governments for *ad valorem* tax purposes.[6] Due to the different needs of these clientele, the systems could vary. However, the basic data collection and statistical estimation would stay the same. Already some firms such as Experian have begun marketing real estate data and indices.

In addition, providers of accurate automated appraisal services could underprice traditional appraisers and yet still make profits. For example, the recent home refinancing boom would have been lucrative for sellers of automated appraisals. The speed and presumably lower cost of automated appraisal services seem ideal for refinancings. Alternatively, bundling the automated appraisal with other services could prove effective.

Home equity and home improvement loans tend to have smaller amounts. A traditional fee appraisal cost may prove prohibitive for such small loans. The use of an automated appraisal addresses the need for a low-cost value estimate.

In addition, low-cost value estimates could aid marketing efforts (*e.g.*, identify prospects for home equity loans, insurance policy amount increases, and other financial products).

7.1.6 Integration of Manual and Automated Appraisals

Depending upon the purpose of the appraisal, an automated appraisal system would not necessarily eliminate the need for traditional fee appraisal. An automated system would ideally provide not only a point estimate but also the estimated probability density function (*pdf*) of the price. The system could flag for manual appraisal properties displaying an unusually dispersed *pdf* relative to some set of priors (Bayesian estimation). This would increase the average accuracy of the system. In addition, appraisers would know their estimate would be compared to the automated estimate. This could reduce the problem of appraiser moral hazard or incompetence. Moreover, one can compare appraisers versus an unbiased statistical valuation to discern appraiser bias (see Pace and Gilley (1988)). Having the potential of a human level of review in addition to the computer level of review could also deter borrower moral hazard. Indeed, randomly requiring some small proportion of transactions to undergo manual appraisal could help control the borrower moral hazard problem. Standards for this could resemble those currently in effect for review of manual appraisals on the part of many financial institutions.

7.2 Implementation of an Automated Appraisal System

Any implementation of an automated appraisal system must pay great attention to accurate and relevant data requirements (Section 7.2.1) and the efficient statistical processing of the data (Section 7.2.2).

7.2.1 Data Requirements

7.2.1.1 Potential Independent Variables
A plethora of variables have been used in CAMA systems, repeat sales index construction, and in hedonic pricing studies. In the hedonic pricing literature, Atkinson and Crocker (1987) found 110 distinct variables were used in their survey of 15 hedonic pricing studies. Atkinson and Crocker (1992) employed a data set using 297 structural and neighborhood variables.[7] CAMA systems often employ over 100 variables. In addition, many CAMA systems contain digitized pictures, floorplans, and property layouts. Spatial models add the requirement of locational coordinates. At the other extreme, repeat sales techniques require only the previous sales price.

Many of the variables come from publicly available information sources and have the same structure nationwide. For example, the census and other databases have information on crime, environmental hazards, flood potential, racial composition, and income by different types of spatial aggregations such as census blocks.

Other independent variables may have different definitions which vary by venue. For example, an assessor in one jurisdiction may release extensive and accurate housing data while another may release only number of rooms, bathrooms, and price. Assessors in some jurisdictions may not release any data. Multiple listing services behave similarly.

The variables affecting value fall into at least eight categories: (1) the aggregated publicly available neighborhood data such as crime rates, income levels, and school districts; (2) individual site specific variables such as exposure, slope, and access to utilities; (3) the objectively measured physical variables pertaining to specific houses such as living area, kitchen area and number of bathrooms; (4) the location of the property in latitude, longitude, and elevation; (5) past sales prices of the property and the dates these occurred; (6) subjective variables such as condition, uniqueness, interior layout, attractiveness of the lot, and the degree to which the property matches the others in the neighborhood; (7) market conditions; and (8) conditions of sale.

In any case, the various databases, assessor records, and multiple listing service entries do not provide all the economically relevant information for the most accurate possible prediction of housing prices.[8] This gives rise to the problem of omitted variables.

7.2.1.2 Omitted Variables

For a particular property often only a relatively small number of variables matter. Unfortunately, the key variables vary from property to property. For example, only a small number of houses are owner-built.[9] This will generally have a significant and negative effect on the market value holding constant the usual other variables such as living area, lot area, and number of bathrooms. Similarly, houses situated directly on the water generally sell at premiums. Houses across the street from these sell for lower prices. Houses on the water form a small portion of the overall population of houses, but this variable greatly affects their valuation. In the northern part of the country, a south sloped lot may add greatly to value relative to a north sloped lot. A house on the south side of a ridge may have another house located 100 yards away on the north side of the ridge selling for a much lower price. Each of these variables greatly affects a small number of properties and may yield different effects by region of the country. Cumulatively, unusual variables of one type or another may affect a significant portion of the housing stock. The easy recognition of unique property characteristics (or transaction terms), positive or negative, constitutes one of the strengths of traditional fee appraisers.

The omission of independent variables may or may not have an impact upon prediction. Omitting an independent variable perfectly correlated with another random variable will cause no loss in predictive power. The omission will change the magnitude of the coefficient of the measured random variable, but will not change the prediction. For example, adding the number of rooms as an independent variable will not usually greatly affect prediction if the model already contains living area. In other words, adding multicollinear independent variables to the model does not greatly aid prediction accuracy.

Alternatively, omitting an important independent variable uncorrelated with the included variables will negatively affect prediction accuracy. For example, variables such as aluminum siding, typically sold after the initial production of the house, occur infrequently and probably other variables can not easily predict its presence. If the installation of the aluminum siding occurred subsequent to the previous sale, the past values of the independent variables would not predict its presence and hence the use of repeat sales techniques to difference these away would encounter difficulty with this type of omitted variable. Similarly, one could not use independent variables on the neighboring house to predict the presence of aluminum siding with great accuracy and hence spatial techniques would encounter difficulty as well.

For lenders, the loss from underprediction will likely exceed the corresponding loss from an equivalent overprediction. This stems from the default option embedded in the mortgage security. Hence, omission of variables having a negative impact on value may prove more serious than omission of variables with a positive impact on value. Hence, the worst omitted variables (1) have a material negative impact on valuation; and (2) cannot be predicted by other variables, by spatially separated values of the same variable, or by temporal differencing of the variable (repeat sales). For example, elderly owners often forego maintaining the property during long periods of invalidism which leads to a deterioration of the structure. Such dilapidation may be unique in the neighborhood and may have occurred subsequent to the last sale of the property. Hence, without information on the property condition, hedonic or repeat sales models could greatly overappraise such a house.

7.2.1.3 Data Quality

The resources devoted to maintaining data quality vary greatly across venues. For example, some multiple listing services use agents while others use clerical workers to enter the data. Agents tend to make more mistakes.

Variables such as the number of bathrooms may be measured more precisely than lot size. Age, if it is recorded at all, is often measured imprecisely. Age of the improvements to the house presents even more difficulties.

7.2.1.4 Model Complexity

Two views exist in the literature concerning model complexity (how many variables should the model have and how flexibly should these be specified). One view advocates parsimony while the other advocates including every variable which could affect the value of the property. Various model selection criteria such as the Akaike information criterion (AIC) and Bayesian information criterion (BIC) provide formal (although not necessarily optimal) ways of balancing parsimony versus prediction accuracy (Judge *et al.* 1985, p. 871).

A variety of factors affect this decision. For example, large numbers of observations, such as present in automated appraisal, allow for more complicated specifications while robustness considerations often argue for more parsimonious specifications.[10] More importantly, the economic problem dictates the inclusion of any variables with large pecuniary impact upon price, regardless of whether these pertain to many observations in the sample. For example, a swimming pool could greatly affect the value of the small number of houses with this characteristic. Again, the main interest centers on including characteristics with a large negative impact such as contiguity with an environmental hazard.

Including characteristics such as the presence of a spa would probably not materially affect the quality of predictions from an automated appraisal model. First, arbitrage suggests a spa should not make a large difference in the price of a house since one can obtain it on the home improvement market for a moderate amount (Gilley and Pace (1995) use this in estimation). Only multicollinearity or the correlation of this variable with an important unobservable variable would enable this variable to have a large impact. In the case of multicollinearity, the variable would not affect overall prediction performance (approximately spanned by the existing set of variables). In the case of correlation with an unobservable, one should either attempt to obtain this more directly or specify a better instrument than the single variable.

If the model contains the most common variables such as living area, age, condition, number of bathrooms as well as spatial and temporal variables, it may prove difficult to find many additional variables which simultaneously make both a statistically significant and economically significant impact upon prediction.

However, the collection of a large number of variables can have other uses. For example, it enables the creation of instrumental variables. Such variables could enable the system to recognize idiosyncratic properties and to identify errors in the data collection phase.

7.2.1.5 Data Collection

Insuring the integrity of the data presents a major problem in mass appraisal. If an unscrupulous seller and buyer could affect the data, they could raise the appraised value beyond the market value. For example, the buyer and seller could collude to report a high transaction price, receive a high appraisal with concomitant loan, and as a side transaction the seller would refund the buyer's downpayment. Such a set of transactions effectively create a loan for 100% of the collateral's value.

A number of parties could collect and report the data. For example, the real estate agent, the assessor, the seller, the buyer, the appraiser, or the property inspector could record the data. Of these the appraiser, assessor, and property inspector have the least (but not non-existent) financial interest. However, one could potentially use the input of other parties. For example, it could prove useful to record the opinion of the other parties on the condition, interior layout, and match of the house with the neighborhood.

Incidentally, advances in technology could also reduce the cost of the onsite data collection. For example, digital tape measures make it far easier for a single individual to take interior dimensions. Inexpensive global positioning system (GPS) receivers could make it easy for the data collector to provide the latitude, longitude, and elevation of the property.[11] Portable digital assistants (PDAs) and laptop computers facilitate direct entry of data into an electronic form.[12] For subsequent sales and refinancings, the collector would only need to check the data and update the relevant records in the property database. In such a system it would be important to adopt standards to ensure consistent practices for measuring and recording property data.

To ensure the integrity of the data, the data collector could sign the same type of declaration as in a FIRREA appraisal. This could give rise to "home certification." Indeed, many states already have laws concerning seller disclosure. These also could strengthen the legal penalties for deliberate misentry of data. Ideally, the maximum number of parties should examine the data and attest to its accuracy. The dissemination of the information among the buyer, seller, real estate agent, data collector, and loan officer or mortgage banker should reduce the potential for moral hazard. Additionally, the system should track the identity of all individuals associated with each transaction.

In addition, consideration should be given to waiving only appraisals on properties which were listed on the MLS (some institutions already follow this practice). The involvement of the MLS further reduces the probability of collusion and moral hazard. Preference should be given to data collectors with credentials to act as reputation capital.

Periodically, a screening program could flag data collectors whose data in the aggregate seem unusual relative to the area and to the whole set of collected variables. For example, if in over 50 properties an individual's reported structural condition greatly exceeds the conditions reported by others in the area, a screening program could flag this for further investigation.

The industry has already adopted some of these steps. For example, Freddie Mac's Loan Prospector and Marketability Report (Form 2070) contains many questions concerning the exterior condition of the property and its fit with the neighborhood. The report does not ask for an opinion as to market value or for comparable properties. The form can only be signed by a certified appraiser, although the vast majority of questions asked do not require great expertise.

7.2.2 Statistical Valuation

Naive modeling of the pricing function results in a number of statistically undesirable byproducts which affect the resulting accuracy and applicability. This section examines how one might modify a naive system to reflect the appropriate loss function, the dependent and independent variables functional forms, spatial and temporal error dependence, heteroskedasticity, robustness, nuisance parameters, prior information, multicollinearity, computational issues, and the assessment of predictive accuracy.

7.2.2.1 Loss Functions

From a decision theoretic view, one should begin a statistical problem by defining the relevant loss function. Depending upon the purpose of the appraisal, one may use different loss functions. For example, mortgage investors may face an asymmetric loss function. In valuing the put option of default, an increase in the estimated house price (asset price) relative to the mortgage value (exercise price) has a smaller effect on the value of the option than the corresponding decrease.

From the standpoint of a secondary market agency, too low of an appraisal increases the probability of a losing the profit (opportunity cost) on the purchase of the security (because the reduced loan-to-value ratio could cause the buyers to drop out). Too high of an appraisal increases the probability of an out-of-pocket loss.

Alternatively, if one desires an unbiased estimate of the asset value, one would use a symmetric loss function. Moreover, various statistical estimators use different loss functions. For example, M estimators use a symmetric, but non-squared error loss function.

Fortunately, one can often accommodate different loss functions given an estimate based upon squared error loss. Varian (1975) proposed a LINEX loss function which varied linearly for deviations of one sort and at an exponential rate for opposing variations. Hence, given an estimate based upon squared error loss one could obtain different estimates for the other potentially asymmetric loss functions. Similarly, one can use the results from squared error loss functions to compute relative squared error loss.[13]

Hence, one can divide the problem into two stages: (1) estimate using squared error loss and (2) compute different estimates for the loss functions relevant to each intended use.

7.2.2.2 Dependent Variable Functional Form

Almost certainly the various loss functions will use relative or proportional error since the ratio of the asset price to the exercise price matters as opposed to the absolute level of the asset price. This implies one should use *ln*(price) as opposed to price. Under squared error loss the use of *ln*(price) yields multiplicative and hence proportional errors.

In addition, the logarithmic transformation will (1) often reduce heteroskedasticity; (2) make it easier to obtain stationarity in the spatial or time series settings; and (3) yield more normal errors suited to the use of the squared error loss function.

The transformation can affect accuracy, but pertains only to the internal functioning of the model and not to external reporting. For external reporting, all of the estimates would be transformed back into the original space (*e.g.*, dollars).

7.2.2.3 Functional Form of the Independent Variables

The functional form of the independent variables affects the predictive accuracy of the pricing model. For example, Pace (1998) found the use of the functional form suggested by semiparametric estimation reduced the median absolute proportional error by about 1% in absolute terms (*e.g.*, about $1000 on a $100,000 house). The generalized additive model (GAM) approach followed could be used to (1) specify parametric models; or (2) to automatically allow for functional form. The GAM estimator is (1) guaranteed to converge; (2) automatically estimates functional form; (3) has good efficiency; (4) can accommodate many other adjustments such as robustness, weighting, and spatial-time series differencing since it is computed by iteratively reweighted least squares; and (5) has known asymptotic properties due to its inheritance of the properties of generalized linear models (GLM). Other semiparametric variants exist which also merit consideration (Pace (1995)). Again, the independent variable transformations pertain to the internal functioning of the model and would not typically be communicated to outside parties.

7.2.2.4 Spatial and Temporal Autocorrelation

Unquestionably, the spatial nature of the data has a great effect upon the accuracy of the model. No model can completely specify all the influences on housing prices. By necessity, some variables go unobserved. If these unobserved variables are themselves spatially autocorrelated, the errors will display spatial autocorrelation. By allowing for these, one can dramatically enhance the predictive ability of the model. For example, Can and Megbolugbe (1997) used spatially lagged housing prices to greatly reduce prediction errors. Pace and Gilley (1997) employed spatially lagged errors to reduce the median absolute error by over 46%. Essentially, the use of the spatial estimation techniques acts as low cost insurance against spatially smooth misspecification (Dubin (1988)).

Real estate appraisal techniques such as the adjustment grid estimator make some allowances for this effect (Can and Megbolugbe (1997) and Pace

(1996)). Specifically, the grid estimator can be viewed as a restricted version of a spatial autoregression (Pace and Gilley (1998)). However, modern spatial estimators greatly outperform the traditional adjustment grid estimator.

Not all houses trade simultaneously. Hence, one must allow for temporal variations in housing prices. Errors from estimated housing pricing functions evince both seasonal effects and serial correlation which must be allowed for in estimation.

Traditionally, hedonic pricing models allow for joint spatial and temporal effects through the use of many dummy variables (interactions of temporal and spatial dummies). To completely specify the potential spatial-temporal effects can require huge numbers of dummy variables. For example, if 10 dummy variables suffice to model space at any given year and if one has 10 years of data, this suggests the need for 100 spatial-temporal dummies. As an example of this approach, see Case, Pollakowski, and Wachter (1991) who employed 138 variables in one of their models.

A vastly more parsimonious alternative is to use repeat-sales techniques. Given an index derived from the appreciation rates of houses which have sold more than once, one could estimate the appreciation for a property from the date of the last sale up to the present. Given the past price and the estimated appreciation, one can easily compute an estimated current market value. By examining only repeated measurements (to use the statistical term), one controls for spatial and temporal effects for that particular house. Unfortunately, aggregation of the appreciation rates reintroduces these back into the overall index. The special issue of the *Journal of Real Estate Finance and Economics* (Volume 14, 1997) contained many articles detailing some of the advantages and problems of repeat sales techniques. A more serious problem from an automated appraisal standpoint is the increased variance of the prediction error as the time elapsed from the previous sale becomes large (Goodman and Thibodeau (1998)). Hence, the repeat sales techniques may not work well for houses whose last sale was many years ago. This could limit the applicability of the repeat sales appraisals. Note, one can hybridize the hedonic pricing and repeat sales approaches (*e.g.*, Hill, Knight, and Sirmans (1997)).

Other techniques exist which make parsimonious adjustments for both space and time (see Cressie (1993)). Recently, Pace, Barry, Clapp, and Rodriguez (1998) proposed and estimated a simple spatial-temporal hedonic pricing model. Essentially, they use an autoregressive distributed lag model with spatial, temporal, and spatial-temporal lagged variables. Relative to a traditional hedonic pricing model with dummies for each year, the spatial-temporal model decreased median absolute errors by over 37%, despite using fewer variables.

If the vast preponderance of observations are dispersed over space with little temporal variation, the spatial element should receive the most elaborate modeling. Conversely, if the vast preponderance of observations occur dispersed over time with little spatial variation, the temporal element should receive the most elaborate modeling. Ideally, substantial variation will exist both temporally and spatially, allowing sophisticated estimation of spatial-temporal models.

Insofar as real estate returns appear predictable in the short-run (positively autocorrelated), forecasts for particular properties or regions (*e.g.*, zip codes) will have a ready market. The spatial-temporal model of Pace, Barry, Clapp, and Rodriguez (1998) provides property specific indices. Naturally, a huge literature exists on indices for specific regions and housing forecasts.

Interestingly, traditional appraisal practices and standards allow little scope for temporal adjustments.

7.2.2.5 Heteroskedasticity

Often the variance of the errors varies smoothly across the independent variables and the conditional mean of the model. For example, Goodman and Thibodeau (1995) discuss the age related heteroskedasticity in hedonic models. Spatial heteroskedasticity has received little attention but in reality represents a strong effect (Gilley and Pace (1996)). One should allow for heteroskedasticity because (1) it typically decreases the variability of the predictions thus leading to a reduction in the prediction RMSE; (2) it greatly affects predictive density computations which the system needs; and (3) other techniques such as robustness require homoskedasticity.

7.2.2.6 Robustness, Identification of Idiosyncratic Properties, and Missing Values

Erroneous observations will creep into any database despite all efforts to the contrary. Erroneous observations have the potential to adversely affect the performance of OLS regressions. The areas of regression diagnostics and robust estimation techniques have arisen in response to the undue sensitivity of OLS to outlying observations.

A number of traditional diagnostics based upon the deletion of an observation at a time and the algebra of least squares have been proposed by, among others, Belsley, Kuh, and Welsch (1980) as well as Cook and Weisberg (1982). Haining (1994) has extended these to the spatial context. Unfortunately, traditional diagnostics tend to overwhelm the user with output, and the use of these is something of an art. For a large number of regressions using a large number of observations, the logistics of applying these techniques could prove daunting. Nevertheless, these techniques have a role to play in automated appraisal.

The application of robust techniques such as M estimation represents a somewhat more automatic way of protecting regressions from outlying observations. The use of M estimators and bounded influence function (BIF) estimators can help provide some robustness at a relatively low computational cost (all of these use iteratively reweighted least squares algorithms).[14] Unfortunately, these methods cannot protect least squares against a sufficiently large percentage of outlying observations in terms of the independent variables. The breakdown point of BIF estimators varies inversely with the number of independent variables. Techniques based upon such estimators as the least median of squares (LMS) can protect least squares against a very large percentage of outlying observations.[15] Unfortunately, the computational cost of these methods rises dramatically with the number of observations and variables.

Given the tremendous data an automated system would generate, special purpose algorithms using knowledge of the population of housing and spatial techniques may prove more effective than reliance upon traditional diagnostics or general purpose robust estimators.

With knowledge of the population of housing one could see whether a particular house is outlying in a multivariate sense conditional upon the characteristics of nearby housing.[16] Such a procedure could flag observations for checking the veracity of the data. Provided it seems correct, the estimation procedure could downweight the observation accordingly. In addition, subject properties which seem unusual in their independent variables could be flagged for manual appraisal or judged via tougher criteria than more standard housing since idiosyncratic houses often sell for less than suggested by estimates using a sample of standard housing.

Gibbs sampling can help in imputing missing values as in Knight, Sirmans, Gelfand, and Ghosh (1998). The degree an observation differs from its imputed value also can serve as a way of identifying erroneous observations.

7.2.2.7 Prior Information

Theoretical and practical considerations usually can allow one to at least sign and in some cases bound the coefficient of a particular characteristic. Inequality constrained least squares (or the more computationally intensive Bayesian estimator) can integrate this with the sample information constraints (see Pace and Gilley (1993) and Gilley and Pace (1995)). Alternatively, one can use this information for model assessment in the exploratory phases of model selection (Leamer (1978)).

7.2.2.8 Multicollinearity

Multicollinearity often receives the blame for the sins of other problems. Attention to specification, heteroskedasticity, incorporation of prior information, and the use of spatial autoregression often eliminates the symptoms blamed on multicollinearity.

In particular, spatial statistical techniques that difference observations with their local average of their neighbors can lower the condition number of the design matrix. It introduces more variation and hence information.

Attention to specification such as not placing both the number of rooms and the number of bedrooms in the model can also reduce this form of the identification problem. In other words, specifications should avoid inclusion of functionally related variables. A better specification would use bedroom area, kitchen area, and other area. Continuous variables contain more information than their discrete equivalents and hence ameliorate the multicollinearity problem.

Techniques introducing arbitrary prior information such as ridge regression, stein estimators, and principal components can improve over OLS. However, the high goodness-of-fit of housing data and large sample sizes makes most shrinkage estimators converge to OLS. Principal components does not necessarily improve performance greatly (Judge *et al.* (1985, pp. 909–912)).

7.2.2.9 Computational Issues

The logistics of an effective automated appraisal system necessitates attention to computational issues. For example, the number of characteristics affecting housing and the number of houses sold over time creates a relatively large database.[17]

However, the use of spatial-temporal information in regression comprises the main computational problem. The usual approach to spatial or spatial-temporal statistics involves either an n by n spatial weight matrix or spatial variance-covariance matrix. This alone can create a problem. For example, for 100,000 observations such a matrix would require 40 gigabytes of single precision storage. The storage required makes computing spatial statistics very difficult for large scale applications.

For independently and identically distributed (*iid*) data, one can often avoid such large regressions by randomly sampling observations instead of dealing with a particular population or sub-population. This strategy fails with spatial data since random sampling would increase the average distance among observations thus destroying much of the spatial content which can greatly improve prediction.

To avoid the computational problems associated with large spatial autoregressions, Pace and Barry (1997) proposed (1) only examining the m nearest neighbors (*e.g.*, 15) to each observation and (2) the use of sparse matrices to contain this information. Efficient algorithms exist for obtaining nearest neighbors which require order of $n\log(n)$ computations (Eppstein, Paterson, and Yao (1997, p. 264)). The sparse matrices require $O(nm)$ storage and most sparse matrix computations require time proportional to the storage.

These techniques coupled with the spatial-temporal estimator proposed by Pace, Barry, Clapp, and Rodriguez (1998) enables the use of large sample sizes (70,822 in this paper). Conditional upon discovering the neighbors ($O(n\log(n))$) and computing some products of sparse matrices and n by 1 and n by k matrices ($O(nm(k+1))$), the spatial-temporal estimator reduces to an OLS regression. Ordinary least squares regressions require $O(nk^3)$ computations, where k represents the number of variables (Golub and Van Loan (1989)).

Regressions with large n have become increasingly common in economics and finance. For example, Evans and Ringel (forthcoming) use 10.5 million observations in examining the effect of taxes on tobacco usage with its resultant effect on public health. Hence, with the constant and predictable improvements in storage capacity and computational performance, it becomes possible to calculate regression models using national data.

Several advantages accrue to computing such a global regression model. This allows a top-down approach to the problem. Given a spatial regression for the country, one can examine the issue of housing market integration. A nationally integrated housing market means one model would handle the U.S. while segmented markets would necessitate multiple models for the country. Maintenance costs rise with the number of estimated models. The reduction in the number of observations hurts their potential accuracy especially for rare characteristics. Examination of a global model could suggest ways of partitioning the data to estimate a parsimonious number of smaller models. For example, one model might cover almost all of the Midwest sans Chicago. Previous attempts at examining this question used levels and not spatial differences (Atkinson and Crocker (1992)). Naturally, levels can display nonstationarity over space while differences may not. Some characteristics may evince national integration (*e.g.*, spas) while others may show market segmentation (*e.g.*, land). A global model may perform better in the estimation of rarely occurring nuisance variables (*e.g.*, art deco design). Moreover, large spatial autoregressions suffer less from "edge" effects. One could expand the size of sub-models through the use of varying coefficients over space.[18]

Non-spatial computational considerations include the problems associated with non-linear in the parameters techniques. These create problems not only because of their lack of speed, but because of their frequent failure to converge to the globally optimum estimate. Searching for the globally optimum estimate can greatly increase computational costs. The semiparametric, spatial, heteroskedasticity, and robustness techniques mentioned so far mainly rely upon various forms of linear transformations of variables (differencing and reweighting of observations). The final EGLS or maximum likelihood regression, therefore, employs least squares upon the transformed observations.

7.3 Summary and Conclusions

Traditionally, appraisers have served as keepers of local property information, estimators of value, and as property inspectors. In their role of estimators, appraisers have the ability to sift through the multitude of potential factors to recognize the important determinants of value for a particular property.

Unfortunately, appraisers face perverse incentives. Empirically, they often follow a strategy of modifying their appraisal to yield an estimate very close to the transaction price. Hence, many appraisals may not provide much "value added" relative to their substantial costs.

Insofar as computers can ably store property information and compute accurate appraisals via statistical methods given good data, automated appraisal has an opportunity to assume some of the roles formerly handled by appraisers. However, a purely automated system may work well only for typical housing. Such a system could have difficulty recognizing and appraising problem or unique properties.

From the standpoint of accuracy, an ideal system would hybridize the manual and automated systems. During a visit to the property some party could assess its physical condition, adherence to codes, locational merits, design standardization or uniqueness, conformance to the neighborhood, and unique factors. In addition, this party could collect the various physical data needed by the system such as living area, lot area, and number of bathrooms.

Ideally, the party would (1) answer subjective questions posed in specific terms, and (2) have incentives to accurately provide the data. With these data the automated system could potentially provide a superior estimate of value. This approach would use humans for the subjective, pattern recognition part of the job and use computers for the data management and statistical part of the job.

The property inspection portion of the appraisal has value in and of itself. In the event of foreclosure and subsequent sale of a property, the owners of the mortgage security often must pay to have the property repaired to a certain standard. Properties in poor condition with non-standard designs often take much longer to sell. As problems may exist on the interior and not the exterior of the house, pure "drive by" appraisals would not identify these cases (although these conditions are probably substantially correlated). Knowledge of the property's condition affects the estimate of price and the estimate of time on the market. Hence, this information affects the value of the mortgage security.

Ideally, house-level data can be consistently collected, reported, and integrated with other data sources. Data verification, screening, and management will be an ongoing process.

Given good data, the appraisal becomes a statistical exercise. The errors from naive statistical models do not resemble much the important textbook case of independently and identically distributed normal random variates. The naive models have spatially autocorrelated, heteroskedastic, non-normally distributed errors. The use of spatial-temporal techniques, semiparametric estimators, prior information, and weighted estimation (downweighting outlying observations) can substantially improve the predictive accuracy.

Many ways exist to implement these adjustments. The very strong spatial and temporal nature of the data means any viable system must provide some means for modeling the spatial-temporal dependence. The modeling could use some combination of explicit specification of spatial-temporal error autocorrelation (which subsumes the use of repeat sales) and specification of space and time in the regression model. Due to the irregularity and sparsity of the distribution of data over space and time, reliance solely upon specification of space and time in the regression model will tend to produce over-parameterized models with their associated ills.

The final system should have strong convergence properties and reasonable computational cost since many clients desire a real-time system. Accurate modeling of the prediction and its density would allow the system to optimally flag a portion of properties of uncertain value for manual appraisal. Combining both manual and automated appraisal could reduce errors further.

The industry has already begun to provide and use these automated appraisal products in increasing numbers. For example, Freddie Mac uses automated valuations in conjunction with the Loan Prospector product and provides the Home Value Estimator (with Acxiom/DataQuick). Experian, Case-Shiller-Weiss, Transamerica, MRAC, Chicago Title, and American Title all have products or plan to have products with substantial geographic coverage. A variety of market specific vendors have also launched products. Impressively, Iown and Yahoo provide free reporting of comparable sales for a number of jurisdictions. At this point, to have a functioning product with wide geographical coverage and high "hit-rate" (proportion of properties for which the system can return a prediction) is an accomplishment. As competition increases, standards for accuracy should begin a secular rise.

To provide increased accuracy of valuations while reducing their cost will prove challenging. To compete with automated valuation models, appraisers may need to change the services they provide. As one possible model for the future, the appraiser would become more focused upon examining the property and collecting the data. This role does not completely overlap with the role currently played by property inspectors. First, property inspectors typically represent buyers before the signing of the sales contract while appraisers represent lenders after the signing of the sales contract. Second, property inspectors do not currently have a uniform set of credentials, and thus may have less reputation capital than appraisers. Third, property inspectors may devote more attention to physical aspects of the property which do not greatly affect market value. Despite the current differences, one could imagine these roles converging given the pressure on reducing transactions cost in the industry. If so, the resulting job might come more to resemble the one performed by marine surveyors who primarily examine vessels for structural and other defects and secondarily provide an estimate of value.

ACKNOWLEDGEMENTS

Our thanks to Wayne Archer, Hayden Green, O.W. Gilley, Isaac Megbolugbe, and three anonymous referees for providing valuable criticism. We also gratefully acknowledge the generous research support provided by the University of Alaska, University of Connecticut, and Louisiana State University.

NOTES

[1] We do not make a distinction between assessment, appraisal, valuation, or collateral assessment in the exposition. Various legal and institutional restrictions pertain to appraisals as opposed to the more generic term "valuation." The industry typically uses the term automated valuation model (AVM) to avoid representing this form of value estimate as an appraisal. Also, an appraisal report contains far more information than just a value estimate.

[2] Giving rise to the timeless question, *quis custodiet ipsos custodes*?

[3] This appears to be the practical insight employed by the Freddie Mac Loan Prospector and Collateral Express products. The resulting "collateral assessment" supplants the usual manual appraisal (Freddie Mac (1996)).

[4] Dotzour did not report many details concerning the variability of price in his sample. The approximately zero bias and 10% standard deviation of the appraisers' errors could represent very good or very poor performance depending upon the variability of the prices. As an extreme example, if the appraisers always estimated price at $100,000 and the actual price averaged $100,000 with a 1% standard deviation, the appraisers' estimates would have 0 correlation with the price. This could occur despite a good absolute performance. In addition, to the degree corporate relocation program products and procedures differ from the overall market, the appraisal accuracy may vary relative to other market segments.

[5] Some jurisdictions use CAMA to implement the cost approach. However, most large jurisdictions use CAMA systems based upon market data to calibrate statistical valuation models (Eckert (1990), p. 153).

[6] Eckert and O'Connor (1992) label the application of CAMA techniques to appraise properties for collateral purposes computer-assisted review assurance (CARA).

[7] They did not use all of these variables in the data for their study.

[8] Even if one possessed all the information pertinent to an individual house, the market exhibits some random noise and this sets a limit on the potential accuracy of any appraisal system (manual or automated). Low-cost, reasonably accurate automated valuation models could themselves affect the efficiency of the housing market.

[9] By owner-built we mean actually constructed by the owner's hands as opposed to commissioned by the owner (custom built).

[10] For example, bounded influence estimators have a breakdown point (proportion of arbitrarily bad observations allowed) equal to the reciprocal of the number of independent variables (Rousseeuw and Leroy (1987)).

[11] Geographic information systems do not have perfect accuracy in address matching (geocoding). Direct measurement avoids this problem. Interestingly, many surveyors use specialized GPS systems as part of the survey process and hence could easily report the latitude, longitude, and elevation.

[12] GPS modules exist for both PDAs and laptops which could directly enter the information into an electronic form. Specialized PDAs already exist for assessors.

[13] See Zellner (1988) for references and a discussion.

[14] See Rousseeuw and Leroy (1987) for a discussion of M and BIF estimators.

[15] See Rousseeuw and Leroy (1987) for estimators based upon the LMS.

[16] See Can and Megbolugbe (1997) for an example where conditioning upon the characteristics of nearby housing sufficed for the identification of an erroneous observation. The use of a large number of variables, some redundant, could also help in identifying outlying observations.

[17] For example, suppose one collected information on 75 million homes with 500 fields per home and each field took on average 4 bytes, this would create a database with 150 gigabytes of data. Databases involving terabytes (1000 gigabytes) exist. Augmenting the database with digitized pictures, audio notations, and digital versions of all documentation for each transaction could easily send such a database in the terabyte range. Databases of this size have become feasible. Alternatively, suppose two percent of the 75 million homes sold in a year. Collection of 200 fields of 4 bytes per field on the sold houses would result in a very manageable 1.2 gigabytes for a particular year.

[18] See Casetti (1972), Can (1992), and Hastie and Tibshirani (1993) for ways of allowing coefficients to vary over space.

REFERENCES

Atkinson, Scott E., and Thomas D. Crocker. "A Bayesian Approach to Assessing the Robustness of Hedonic Property Value Studies." *Journal of Applied Econometrics* 2 (1987), pp. 27–45.

Atkinson, Scott E., and Thomas D. Crocker. "The Exchangeability of Hedonic Property Price Studies." *Journal of Regional Science* 32 (1992), pp. 169–183.

Belsley, David. A., Edwin Kuh, and Roy. E. Welsch. *Regression Diagnostics: Identifying Influential Data and Source of Collinearity*. New York: John Wiley, 1980.

Can, Ayse. "Specification and Estimation of Hedonic Housing Price Models." *Regional Science and Urban Economics* 22 (1992), pp. 453–474.

Can, Ayse, and Isaac F. Megbolugbe. "Spatial Dependence and House Price Index Construction," *Journal of Real Estate Finance and Economics*, 14 (1997), pp. 203–222.

Case, Bradford, Henry O. Pollakowski, and Susan M. Wachter. "On Choosing Among House Price Index Methodologies," *AREUEA Journal* 19 (1991), pp. 286–307.

Casetti, E. "Generating Models by the Expansion Method: Applications to Geographical Research." *Geographical Analysis* 4 (1972), pp. 81–91.

Chinloy, Peter, Man Cho, and Isaac F. Megbolugbe. "Appraisals and Real Estate Prices," manuscript, FNMA, 1995.

Cook, R. Dennis, and Sanford Weisberg. *Residuals and Influence in Regression.* New York: Chapman and Hall, 1982.

Cressie, Noel A. C. *Statistics for Spatial Data.* Revised ed. New York: John Wiley, 1993.

Dotzour, Mark G. "Quantifying Estimation Bias in Residential Appraisal." *Journal of Real Estate Research* 3 (1988), pp. 1–12.

Dubin, Robin A. "Estimation of Regression Coefficients in the Presence of Spatially Autocorrelated Error Terms." *Review of Economics and Statistics* 70 (1988), pp. 466–474.

Dubin, Robin A. "Spatial Autocorrelation and Neighborhood Quality." *Regional Science and Urban Economics* 22 (1992), pp. 433–452.

Dubin, Robin, R. Kelley Pace, and Thomas Thibodeau. "Spatial Autoregression Techniques for Real Estate Data," *Journal of Real Estate Literature* 7 (1999), pp. 79–95.

Eckert, Joseph K., and Patrick M. O'Connor. "Computer-Assisted Review Assurance (CARA): A California Case Study." *Property Tax Journal* 11 (1992), pp. 59–80.

Eckert, Joseph K. *Property Appraisal and Assessment Administration,* Chicago: International Association of Assessing Officers, 1990.

Eppstein, D., Paterson, M. S., and F. F. Yao. "On Nearest Neighbor Graphs," *Discrete and Computational Geometry* 17 (1997), pp. 263–282.

Evans, William and Jeanne Ringel. "Can Higher Cigarette Taxes Improve Birth Outcomes?" forthcoming in *Journal of Public Economics.*

Freddie Mac. *Automated Underwriting: Making Mortgage Lending Simpler and Fairer for America's Families,* September 1996.

Gilley, O. W., and R. Kelley Pace. "Improving Hedonic Estimation with an Inequality Restricted Estimator," *Review of Economics and Statistics,* 77 (1995), pp. 609–621.

Gilley, O. W., and R. Kelley Pace. "Spatial Heteroskedasticity," manuscript, University of Alaska, 1996.

Golub, G. H., and C. F. Van Loan. *Matrix Computations,* second edition, John Hopkins, 1989.

Goodman, Allen, and Thomas Thibodeau. "Dwelling Age Heteroskedasticity in Repeat Sales House Price Equations," *Real Estate Economics* 26 (1998), pp. 151–171.

Haining, Robert. "Diagnostics for Regression Modeling in Spatial Econometrics." *Journal of Regional Science* 34 (1994), pp. 325–341.

Hastie, T. J., and Robert Tibshirani. "Varying-Coefficient Models (with Discussion)." *Journal of the Royal Statistical Society, Series B.* 55 (1993), pp. 757–796.

Hill, R. Carter, John Knight, and C. F. Sirmans. "Estimating Capital Asset Prices," *Review of Economics and Statistics,* 79 (1997), pp. 226–233.

Judge, G., W. E. Griffiths, R. C. Hill, H. Lutkepohl, and T.-C. Lee. (1985). *The Theory and Practice of Econometrics* (2nd Ed.), New York: John Wiley.

Knight, John R., C. F. Sirmans, Alan Gelfand, and Sujit Ghosh. "Analyzing Real Estate Data Problems Using the Gibbs Sampler," *Real Estate Economics,* 26 (1998), pp. 469–492.

Leamer, E. *Specification Searches: Ad Hoc Inference with Non-experimental Data,* New York: Wiley, 1978.

Pace, R. Kelley. "Appraisal Using Generalized Additive Models," *Journal of Real Estate Research,* 15, (1998), pp. 77–100.

Pace, R. Kelley. "Relative Efficiencies of the Grid, OLS, and Nearest Neighbor Estimators," *Journal of Real Estate Finance and Economics* 13 (1996), pp. 203–218.

Pace, R. Kelley, and Ronald Barry. "Sparse Spatial Autoregressions," *Statistics and Probability Letters,* 33, (1997), pp. 291–297.

Pace, R. Kelley, Ronald Barry, John Clapp, and M. Rodriguez. "Spatio-Temporal Estimation of Neighborhood Effects," *Journal of Real Estate Finance and Economics,* 17 (1998), pp. 15–33.

Pace, R. Kelley, Ronald Barry, O. W. Gilley, and C. F. Sirmans. "Simple Spatial-temporal Forecasting," *International Journal of Forecasting*, forthcoming.

Pace, R. Kelley, Ronald Barry, and C. F. Sirmans. "Spatial Statistics and Real Estate," *Journal of Real Estate Finance and Economics*, 17 (1998), pp. 5–13.

Pace, R. Kelley, and O. W. Gilley. "Optimally Combining OLS and the Grid Estimator," *Real Estate Economics*, 26 (1998), pp. 331–347.

Pace, R. Kelley, and O. W. Gilley. "Using the Spatial Configuration of the Data to Improve Estimation," *Journal of the Real Estate Finance and Economics*, 14 (1997), pp. 333–340.

Pace, R. Kelley, and O. W. Gilley. "Appraisal Across Jurisdictions Using Bayesian Estimation With Bootstrapped Priors for Secondary Mortgage Market Applications." *Property Tax Journal* 8 (1989), pp. 27–42.

Rousseeuw, Peter J., and Annick M. Leroy. *Robust Regression and Outlier Detection*. New York: John Wiley, 1987.

Tibshirani, Robert. "Neural Networks: A Review from a Statistical Perspective: Comment." *Statistical Science* 9 (1994), pp. 48–49.

Varian, Hal R. "A Bayesian Approach to Real Estate Assessment." In: S.E. Fienberg and Arnold Zellner., Eds., *Studies in Bayesian Econometrics and Statistics in Honor of Leonard J. Savage*. Amsterdam: North-Holland, 1975, pp. 195–208.

Zellner, Arnold. "Bayesian Analysis in Econometrics." *Journal of Econometrics* 37 (1988), pp. 27–50.

Chapter 8

A Note on the Hedonic Model Specification for Income Properties

Bo Söderberg
*Department of Building and Real Estate Economics, Royal Institute of Technology,
Stockholm, Sweden*

8.1 Introduction

8.1.1 Background

The hedonic technique is well established as a tool for analysing the determinants of property prices on the market for single-family housing. The theoretical foundation is solid, including particularly the work by Rosen (1974), and there is a large body of empirical applications. There are fewer papers applying the technique to the investigation of market prices for income property;

Miles, Cole, and Guilkey (1990), Fehribach, Rutherford, and Eakin (1993), Saderion, Smith, and Smith (1994), Colwell, Munneke, and Trefzger (1998).

An important issue in the literature on hedonic estimation with respect to single-family housing, is the choice of functional form for the price equation. A number of critical reviews of the research carried out have pointed out the additive form as being the least suitable; Lessinger (1969), Maclennan (1977). In several papers, the argument is raised that theory does not give any guidance to what the proper functional form should be and that models rather should be evaluated in terms of goodness-of-fit; Halvorsen and Pollakowski (1981). An important argument is that if the hedonic price estimates are to be used in the estimation of the demand for individual property attributes, then one needs second order derivatives of the price function; Rosen (1974).

Almost no similar debate regarding the modelling issues seems to exist with respect to hedonic applications to income property. However, one exception was found; de Silva and Gruenstein (1988). They use different goodness-of-fit estimates as criteria for identifying the best functional form for the price of office buildings.

The Box-Cox transformation technique is often used for testing functional form. It is regarded particularly suitable for this purpose as this general functional form includes the most commonly used model specifications as subsets, including log linear, semi-log linear and trans-log linear models. However, using Box-Cox transformation as a tool for testing functional form is only relevant under the assumption that goodness-of-fit is a reasonable test criterion. Furthermore, there are several other arguments against using the Box-Cox technique; Cassel and Mendelsohn (1985).

8.1.2 Purpose

The purpose of the present study is to compare two standard multiplicative regression model specifications when applied to the study of prices for mixed-use income properties. The first model has basically a log-linear specification. The second model is semi-log linear. The main features of the paper are regressions on a market data sample with the two models and an illustration of differences in terms of the empirical results obtained. The sample consists of income properties centrally located in Stockholm. The regressions are specific to the particular case investigated, but the discussion is partly general.

8.1.3 Organisation

This chapter is organised in the following way. Firstly, some general modelling considerations are discussed and the two models are presented. In the following section, some important institutional aspects of the market under study are briefly described, as well as the data set and the variables. In the following sections, the two price models for mixed-use income properties are estimated and interpreted. The final section concludes the paper. Furthermore, there are three appendices. The first discusses the marginal (hedonic) price in simple multiplicative models. The second discusses the simple relationship between an additive and a semi-log linear model. Descriptive statistics are found in the third appendix.

8.2 General Features of the Models

8.2.1 The Appraisal Formula

According to traditional valuation theory, the value of an investment is determined by the present value of the expected future net returns. The valuation approach is usually reduced to a discounted cash-flow model where the basic variables affecting value are initial net return, expected growth and required rate of return (partly reflecting risk). In traditional valuation methodology, the various cash-flow sources of a particular property (e.g. the revenue from the residential flats, and the revenue from the commercial area of a multi-use real property) are assumed to be independent. Furthermore, their effects on the total value of the property are assumed to be independent. Thus, the contributions to total value from different cash-flow sources, respectively, would be additive, or at least could for practical purposes be regarded additive. This assumption is generally implicit in the application of the income approach; Appraisal Institute (1996).

The income approach in its standard use is not really influenced by financial valuation theories, such as the capital asset pricing model (CAPM) and the arbitrage pricing theory (APT), though some attempts have been made to develop new appraisal methods based upon the financial theories. See Draper and Findlay (1982) and Isakson (1986), for discussions concerning the possible development of valuation techniques based on the CAPM and the APT. Rather, the income approach is a standard application of the net present value technique (NPV). The mathematical and statistical simplicity as well as the straightforward interpretations of the NPV technique are appealing. The traditional income approach (as well as all three approaches in general) is therefore likely to remain in use for some time.

In hedonic applications to single-family residential real estate, the explanatory variables usually include physical attributes of the properties (such as size, age, standard, etc.), cost and income factors (such as subsidies, maintenance costs, etc.), and location attributes (such as social status in the area, commercial and public facilities, local taxes, etc.). The hedonic prices are generally used for the estimation of demand for individual attributes, for price index construction and for various forms of valuation and price prediction.

When applying the hedonic technique to income property, it is less appropriate to perform the study within the framework of consumption theory. The hedonic technique applied to income real estate should rather be used in correspondence with theories of the pricing of investment goods in general, or with established techniques for the appraisal of income property in particular. One way of doing so would be to allow economic attributes, such as for example expected net return, to enter the models as explanatory variables. The regression results can then be interpreted in terms of implicit discounting behaviour of the market actors. In a more traditional approach, the explanatory variables may instead be physical property attributes, in which case it is convenient if the physical attribute variables are chosen so that each attribute represents a well-defined group of income streams, thereby allowing for similar (indirect) interpretations of market discounting.

The present study is based on the assumption that the value of a mixed-use income property with two different uses is determined by two *major* economic attributes: the net income from the residential use and the net income from the commercial use. The two contributions to value are assumed to be additive in principle, i.e. the total value of a real property is supposed to be the sum of two value functions, related to the residential part and the commercial part of the property, respectively:

$$Total\ value = Value\ of\ residential\ part + Value\ of\ commercial\ part$$
$$= f_1(Residential\ return) + f_2(Commercial\ return) \qquad (1)$$

For both these attributes it is assumed that the income streams can be expressed as functions of the rentable areas respectively. These functions may include other property attributes, like the age of the building, the location etc. For the sake of convenience only, we refer to them as *minor* attributes (which does not mean that the economic importance of these variables would be of minor importance). It is assumed that the minor attributes generally enter the price equation within functions that operate on the two major attributes as modifying multipliers. The resulting model will have the following general form:

$$Total\ value = g_1\ (Residential\ space) \cdot h_1\ (Age, \dots)$$
$$+ g_2\ (Commercial\ space) \cdot h_2\ (Age, \dots) \qquad (2)$$

Regression analyses for estimating coefficients in models of this kind, i.e. a combination of additive and multiplicative models, can be carried out in several ways. The equation may occasionally be modelled as strictly additive or strictly multiplicative but still yield regression solutions that approximately have the properties of a combined model. Various forms of variable transformations may then be useful. Furthermore, non-parametric approaches and non-linear regression techniques, easily available in standard packages, may be used. Still, only a handful of standard regression model specifications are in use in empirical research, including particularly linear, log-linear and semi-log linear specifications. This is not surprising, since they are easy to handle and interpret.

8.2.2 The Models

In the present Chapter two different standard multiplicative models are applied. In the first model, the independent variables enter as power functions, i.e. after taking natural logs of both sides of the model the regression equation becomes log-linear (often referred to as a Cobb-Douglas function). In the second model, three of the independent variables enter as exponential functions. Taking natural logs of both sides of the model transforms it into a semi-log linear model.

In the present study, the following four attributes are assumed to affect the property price: residential space, commercial space, age, distance to the city centre. Other variables may also affect property prices. However, in this paper the purpose is to emphasise the modelling effect on these particular variables. In the following section, some arguments are raised for the selection of these explanatory variables, as well as a discussion regarding other variables that possibly may affect prices and how these are handled.

The first model has the following structural form:

$$Value = a_0 \cdot Residential^{a_1} \cdot Commercial^{a_2} \cdot Age^{a_3} \cdot Distance^{a_4} \qquad (3)$$

where $a_0, a_1, ..., a_4$ are unknown constants. The model is similar to those applied in other studies; Yinger (1979), Laakso (1992), Arimah (1997). The Cobb-Douglas function is widely used for the estimation of production output. The analogy to the case of mixed-use income property is not that far-fetched. The "output" would in this case be the total value of the property and the two most important "production factors" would be the two parts of the property that are designed for different uses, the residential space and the commercial space, respectively.

The second model has the structural form

$$Value = b_0 \cdot TotSpace^{b_1} \cdot e^{b_2 \cdot PropCom} \cdot e^{b_3 \cdot Age} \cdot e^{b_4 \cdot Distance} \tag{4}$$

where $b_0, b_1, ..., b_4$ are unknown constants. In this case, the variables *PropCom*, *Age* and *Distance* enter the model as exponential functions. Specified this way, the price effect of these variables decline at a constant rate. Similar models are found in the literature; Saderion, Smith and Smith (1994), McMillen (1996) and Colwell, Munneke and Trefzger (1998).

A short discussion regarding the marginal (hedonic) prices, using these two model specifications, are found in Appendix A.

8.3 Variables and Data

8.3.1 Institutional Aspects and Background

Some institutional aspects of the rental and property markets under study are relevant for the analysis. The first two aspects discussed below have been considered explicitly when specifying the models.

Firstly, the entire rental market for residential flats is subject to a second-generation (or "soft") rent control. In principle, the rent level is tied to age, quality and size of the accommodation. Permitted rent increases are tied to cost increases that pertain to the public housing sector. Svensson (1998) presents further information on the rent setting procedure. Commercial rents are not regulated and are subject to market forces. As a consequence, the hedonic price equations analysed in the present paper allow for different price effects from the residential and commercial space, respectively.

Secondly, Szynkier (1983) reported strong evidence for Stockholm being mono-centric. His models show land values declining with distance from the city centre. As a consequence, the models are mono-centric and account for the possibility that prices decline when the distance to CBD increases.

Furthermore, there are some price affecting institutional issues that have not been considered explicitly in the model. Instead, I control for these issues by excluding all observations where a possible price effect is present.

Firstly, the market under study is subject to interest rate subsidies. The subsidies are substantial. They are paid in cash to the property owner. A complicated administrative system, that would be difficult to model perfectly, determines the size and time-pattern of the subsidies. However, in practice the subsidies are close to proportional to the residential space of the property and decline almost linearly over the first 15–18 years of the property's life.

Hendershott and Turner (1999) present further information on the subsidy system. As a consequence, all observations where the property was subject to subsidies were excluded from the sample.

Secondly, some of the buildings in the market are on leased land. In the case of leasehold properties, the owner of the land is formally the municipality, and the lessee pays an annual fee to the owner, corresponding to an assumed land rent. Except for the lease payment, leasehold properties are generally regarded as perfect substitutes for freehold properties. It is reasonable to expect that the lease payments cause leasehold properties to be traded at prices that are systematically lower than are those of freeholds. As a consequence, all observations that are leasehold were excluded from the sample.

8.3.2 Data

The original data source is the official Real Property Sales Price Data Base. Attribute variables were taken from the official Property Assessment Register.

From these records, observations referring to income properties, centrally located in downtown Stockholm, that were traded during a three year time period, 1992–1994, were collected. These years were selected as the market for income property was regarded as stable and free from cyclical effects and trends. Multiple sales in the original data file were deleted as well as observations where variable values necessary to the analyses were missing. The original sample contained 352 observations.

The properties in the sample are mixed-use with rental space for residential use as well as for commercial use. However, the residential space dominates in all properties in the sample. The location of the properties in the sample is shown in Figure 5 in Appendix C. The observations are distributed rather evenly over the inner city, however with some concentration to the eastern part, and with no observations in the very centre (CBD). The eastern part has traditionally been regarded the most attractive residential area, but the entire inner city is considered highly attractive for residential purpose. The less attractive areas of Stockholm, as well as the decayed ones are all found outside the inner city. Consequently, we may regard the observations as all representing a homogenous concentric zone of attractive residential locations surrounding the CBD. Thus, there is an element of homogeneity among the properties in the sample as they are all rather similar in terms of size, age, use, and geographic sub-market location. Most naturally, the study area has attracted high-income residents.

As previously stated, all observations in the database where the property was leasehold were deleted, as well as all observations where the property was subject to interest rate subsidies. In addition, three observations were deleted as the rent variables were missing. The number of observations in the reduced sample is $n = 282$.

8.3.3 Variables

The variable definitions are given in Table 1. Descriptive statistics are given in Table 7 in Appendix C. The dependent variable, the market selling price, is expressed in real terms using the official consumer price index (CPI) as deflator.

The possible price effects of distance to CBD and the age of the building are controlled for within the regression. These two variables remain the only *minor* attributes of the models investigated. In both models, the two *major* attributes are the ones related to the two different uses, residential and commercial, respectively. In the first model, the major attributes are the net rentable space (in square metres) devoted to residential and commercial use respectively. In the second model, the major attributes are the proportion commercial space and the total space.

The assessment authority determines for assessment purposes the effective age of each property, which represents its condition, considering relative obsolescence as well as age. The variable *Age* is that relative to effective age. The *Distance* measure represents distance as the crow flies. The distances to each property are obtained from the geodetic co-ordinate system for the country, which establishes the central point for each property. We use distance from the very city centre (defined as the square "Sergels torg") as distance measure.

Table 1: Variable Definitions

Y	*Price*	Transaction price, real (thousands of SEK).
X_1	*Residential*	Residential rental space (m^2).
X_2	*Commercial**	Commercial rental space (m^2).
X_3	*TotSpace*	Total space (m^2). $X_3 = X_1 + X_2$
X_4	*PropCom*	Proportion commercial space (%). $X_4 = X_2/X_3$
X_5	*Age*	Effective age of the building (years).
X_6	*Distance*	Distance to city centre (m).
Q_j	*Quarter*	Eleven dummy variables representing quarters of the time period, $j = 2, \ldots 12$, leaving the first quarter as the reference. $Q_j = 1$ for quarter when transaction occurs, otherwise $Q_j = 0$.

*Observed values of 0 were changed to 1, in order to make it possible to compute the logarithm for each value.

Two dummy variables were initially included to control for the possible effect of the buyer being a bank and a co-operative, respectively. None of these variables were significant, and they were not considered in the regressions reported here.

The dummy variables $Q_2, \ldots, Q_{12}$ represent quarter two to twelve of the three year time period, thus the first quarter becomes the base group. These variables are included to control for possible market fluctuations during the period under study. The time dummies were expected to be insignificant, and largely they were. However, in both models the variable Q_2 had a highly significant positive effect. The straightforward interpretation is that the price level was higher during this quarter than during the other quarters of the time period studied.

Though the result with respect to the time dummies should in principle be reported, they are not. The emphasis in the paper is on the price effect of the four explanatory variables reported. Other aspects are suppressed to simplify the presentation of the results.

8.4 Regressions

8.4.1 The Regression Models

Using the variable definitions in Table 1, expression (3) becomes

$$Y = a_0 \cdot X_1^{a_1} \cdot X_2^{a_2} \cdot X_5^{a_3} \cdot X_6^{a_4} \cdot w \tag{5}$$

The error factor w is assumed to be independent, identically distributed following a log-normal distribution with mean value 1 and constant variance. It is also assumed to be independent of the explanatory variables. After taking natural logarithms of both sides of expression (5), the model is transformed into a log-linear expression

$$\ln Y = \ln a_0 + a_1 \cdot \ln X_1 + a_2 \cdot \ln X_2 + a_3 \cdot \ln X_5 + a_4 \cdot \ln X_6 + \ln w \tag{6}$$

The coefficients $a_0, \ldots, a_4$, are to be estimated. Similarly, expression (4) becomes

$$Y = b_0 \cdot X_3^{b_1} \cdot e^{b_2 \cdot X_4} \cdot e^{b_3 \cdot X_5} \cdot e^{b_4 \cdot X_6} \cdot w \tag{7}$$

which is transformed into the semi-log linear model

$$\ln Y = \ln b_0 + b_1 \cdot \ln X_3 + b_2 \cdot X_4 + b_3 \cdot X_5 + b_4 \cdot X_6 + \ln w \tag{8}$$

where w is a log-normal error, and the coefficients $b_0, \ldots, b_4$, are to be estimated. The equations (6) and (8) are estimated with OLS using the computer program EViews.

8.4.2 Results

The regression results are largely as expected. They are summarised in Table 2; model I is an estimate of equation (6), model II is an estimate of equation (8). On the whole, the results with respect to the two models appear similar. Both equations are highly significant and in both equations the variables used explain some 68 percent of the observed variation in the log of the selling price. With one exception, all property attribute variables were significant, with the expected sign and estimated parameters that appear reasonable.

The variable *PropCom* in model II is not significant. The magnitude of the coefficients for *Age* and *Distance* are much smaller in model II, than in model I. The variable having the greatest impact on the estimated price in the models are *Residential* and *TotSpace*, respectively. The parameter values are very close to one, for both these variables. Interestingly enough it is slightly higher than one for *TotSpace*. This would indicate something of a returns-to-scale phenomenon.

Residual analyses were carried out to check for possible assumption violations. The results for both regressions are similar. A histogram of the residuals and a p-p plot indicated only slight deviations from normality and a

Table 2: Regression Analysis on Real Price for Mixed-Use Income Properties. Dependent Variable is Natural Log of Selling Price, ln(*Y*). *t*-statistics in Parentheses

Variable	Explanation	Model I Expression (6)	Model II Expression (8)
	Constant	4.823 (8.1)*	1.968 (5.2)*
$\ln X_1$	*Residential*	0.988 (19.7)*	
$\ln X_2$	*Commercial*	0.033 (3.6)*	
$\ln X_5$	*Age*	−0.139 (−2.3)*	
$\ln X_6$	*Distance*	−0.349 (−5.5)*	
$\ln X_3$	*TotSpace*		1.021 (21.0)*
X_4	*PropCom*		−0.08900 (−0.3)
X_5	*Age*		−0.00405 (−2.8)*
X_6	*Distance*		−0.00017 (−5.4)*
R^2		0.684	0.686
Adj. R^2		0.666	0.669
S.E. of regression		0.309	0.308
F-statistic		38.4	38.9
Prob(*F*-statistic)		0.000	0.000
No. of observations, *n*		282	282

* Coefficient is significant at the 5 percent level.

Kolmogorv-Smirnov test did not reject the null hypothesis of normality. A case-wise residual plot with the observations in time order and a plot of the residuals against the predicted dependent variable showed no evidence of heteroscedasticity. The residuals from the two regressions are highly correlated, the coefficient being 0.981, which indicates that the two models have very similar predictive properties within the sample. For illustrative purposes the residuals from both regressions are plotted against the variable *Distance* in Figure 4 in Appendix C.

It is reasonable to expect that omitted micro-location attributes have had an effect upon the property prices. It is therefore reasonable to assume that there might be a spatial autocorrelation between the residuals in both regressions. Plotting residuals can not be trusted to reveal such patterns. To properly handle spatial dependence, the regression model should include an autoregressive component that allows controlling for the possible effect on each independent variable from other closely located observations. In practice, specially designed software packages are needed.

In the present study, the models were not estimated within a spatial regression framework. However, a test for spatial residual autocorrelation was carried out. The test applied was suggested by Anselin, Bera, Florax and Yoon (1996, p. 12). The null hypothesis of no spatial autocorrelation was rejected for both equations. Thus, the two models are likely to be affected by spatial autocorrelation. Therefore the parameter estimates may be slightly biased, and possibly the over-all fit is affected. However, this does not affect the over-all purpose and conclusion of the present study, and therefore the models are not re-estimated.

With the regression solutions entered in expression (5) and (7), respectively, we obtain the following prediction models for the dependent variable:

$$\hat{Y} = e^{4.82} \cdot X_1^{0.99} \cdot X_2^{0.03} \cdot X_5^{-0.14} \cdot X_6^{-0.35} \tag{9}$$

$$\hat{Y} = e^{1.97} \cdot X_3^{1.02} \cdot e^{-0.0890 \cdot X_4} \cdot e^{-0.0041 \cdot X_5} \cdot e^{-0.00017 \cdot X_6} \tag{10}$$

8.4.3 Applying the Prediction Models to a Particular Property

The effect of the independent variables in the two models is illustrated by applying the estimation formulae (9) and (10) to a hypothetical "average observation" with variable values equal to the sample averages. The variable values are found in Table 3.

The predicted price for the "average observation" using equation (9) then becomes:

$$\hat{Y} = e^{4.82} \cdot 1{,}659^{0.99} \cdot 147^{0.03} \cdot 53^{-0.14} \cdot 2{,}055^{-0.35}$$
$$= 124.3 \cdot 1{,}512 \cdot 1.12 \cdot 0.58 \cdot 0.07 = 8{,}920 \tag{11}$$

Table 3: Sample Average of Variable Values

Variables	Explanation	Values
Y	*Price*	10,212 KSEK
X_1	*Residential*	1,659 m^2
X_2	*Commercial*	147 m^2
X_3	*TotSpace*	1,806 m^2
X_4	*PropCom*	0.081
X_5	*Age*	53 years
X_6	*Distance*	2,055 m

The deviation from the average transaction price, i.e., 10,200 KSEK, is of some significance, but not dramatic. We now interpret the result for each factor separately using approximate figures. Then, in the case of a new property located in the very centre of the city, the predicted price is basically 124,000 SEK/m^2 of residential space times the residential space in m^2 (however with a slight reduction that increases with increasing residential space, usually interpreted as diminishing marginal value). There is a slight price adjustment upwards as there is some commercial space that renders some extra value to the property (in this case the price increases by 12%). The factor accounting for accrued depreciation during 53 years is 0.42, i.e. in this case only 58% of the value of a new property remains. Finally, there is a substantial price adjustment due to distance, i.e. the price for a property located 2 kilometre from the centre is only 7% of the price for a similar property situated in the very central part of the city.

The predicted price for the "average observation" using equation (10) becomes:

$$\hat{Y} = e^{1.97} \cdot 1{,}806^{1.02} \cdot e^{-0.0890 \cdot 0.081} \cdot e^{-0.0041 \cdot 53.4} \cdot e^{-0.00017 \cdot 2{,}055}$$
$$= 7.2 \cdot 2{,}119 \cdot 0.99 \cdot 0.81 \cdot 0.71 = 8{,}580 \tag{12}$$

The predicted price is slightly lower than when applying the first model. The interesting interpretations, however, are to be made with respect to each factor separately. The effect of the individual variables is indeed different between the two models. In particular, this is true regarding the intercept and the distance effect.

Had the property been new (however without subsidies) and located in the very centre of the city, the predicted price would basically have been 7,200 SEK per square metre (of total space), with a slight premium that increases with increasing residential space, i.e., an increasing marginal value. There is a slight (in this case negligible) price adjustment downward that is greater the higher the percentage commercial space. The factor accounting for accrued depreciation during 53 years is 0.19, i.e. in this case 81% of the value of a new property remains. Finally, there is a moderate price adjustment due to location, i.e., the price at the distance 2 kilometre is 71% of the price in the very central part of the city, all else being equal.

8.4.4 The Effect of Age and Distance

The effect of *Age* differs between the two models. The remaining value of a property with a 53-year-old building is 58% and 81% when modelled as a power function and an exponential function, respectively. Both values fall within an interval of what seems empirically possible. The power function has a steeper decline for low values of the independent variable, but as the *degree* of decline depends inversely on the value of the independent variable, the depreciation effect levels out for properties with older buildings. The depreciation effect as estimated by the two regression models studied is illustrated by (a) in Figure 1.

Considering the power function, the interesting part of the depreciation curve is the age-interval from zero up to approximately 20, where the curve declines rather steeply. However, this part of the curve is entirely an out-of-sample phenomenon. In the sample, the variable *Age* takes on values in the interval 19–66. Consequently, the shape of the depreciation curve in the interval 0–19 has not been affected by observations in that interval.

The effect of *Distance* differs more dramatically between the two models. The price effect of a location some 2 km away from the CBD, was found to be 7% and 71%, respectively, depending on the way in which the variable *Distance* is modelled. The distance effect as estimated by the two regression models studied is illustrated by (b) in Figure 1.

Figure 1: Comparison of the effect of *Age* (a) and *Distance* (b) on Price/m² in Two Models. "Power Function" refers to the Effect According to Expression (9), i.e. the Log-Linear Model; "Exponential Function" refers to the Effect according to Expression (10), i.e. the Semi-Log Linear Model

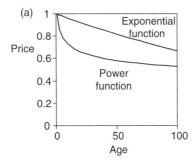
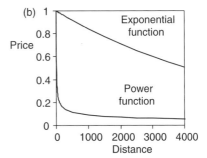

In most empirical studies of the price gradient with respect to distance, the distance effect is found to be small, in some cases not even detectable. Regarding the particular market under study, practical experience would also point towards the distance effect being moderate. We can therefore be confident that a distance effect according to the power function illustrated by (b) in Figure 1 is unrealistic. The explanation to the result is the following.

The distance effect in the power function case is extremely dramatic close to the CBD, whereas the curve flattens out some 500 metres from CBD. However, no observations in the sample are located in the interval where the distance gradient is the steepest. Thus, the distance parameter is determined by the distance effect where the slope is small. The absolute effect of the distance variable therefore has to be considered in combination with the constant factor of the model. In the case of the log-linear model, the distance effect close to CBD is unrealistic, and so is the constant effect. However, in the distance interval where the observations of the sample are located the effects approximately average out. Consequently, the model would make strange predictions in the interval 0–594 (i.e., a small area with a radius of some six hundred metres surrounding the very centre of the city).

8.4.5 The Effect of Proportion of Commercial Space

The price effect of the proportion of commercial space in the two models is a bit more difficult to illustrate. We learn from model II that the effect of proportion commercial space is slightly negative, however not significantly different from zero. The result indicates that the market values residential space and commercial space are approximately equal. This may seem odd, taking into account the discussion on partial rent control above. However, we have to remember that all properties in the sample are dominated by residential use. Thus, the small shares of commercial space may partly be devoted to inferior non-residential use. The dependent variable is in this model insensitive to changes in the proportion commercial space. The multiplicative effect goes from 1 to 0.91 when the variable *PropCom* increases from 0 to 1.

In model I, the hedonic price for commercial space (at the sample mean) is lower than that of residential space, thus allowing for the same interpretation as in the case of model II. The hedonic price for commercial space is also found to be very sensitive to the variation in commercial space.

As the commercial space enters the model with its absolute value, and as the value of the coefficient is very low, it ensures that the predicted price increasing effect of the total commercial part of a property reaches not more than some 0–40%. The model effect is also independent of the percentage of commercial space in the property, i.e., it is independent of the relative importance to value of the commercial part. Therefore the model would work poorly as a predictor for properties with a large commercial space, independent of the size of the residential space in those properties.

The sensitivity of the log-linear model will be illustrated in the following. Firstly, both sides of expression (9) are divided by the total space of the property.

$$\hat{Y}/(X_1 + X_2) = \frac{e^{4.82} \cdot X_1^{0.99} \cdot X_2^{0.03} \cdot X_5^{-0.14} \cdot X_6^{-0.35}}{X_1 + X_2}$$

$$= \frac{X_1}{(X_1 + X_2)} \cdot e^{4.82} \cdot X_1^{-0.01} \cdot X_2^{0.03} \cdot X_5^{-0.14} \cdot X_6^{-0.35}$$

(13)

Thus, the model is transformed into an expression where price per square metre is the product of six factors. The first factor on the right hand side can take on values between 0 and 1 and the second is a constant. The remaining factors take on strictly positive values, each one of them on a rather narrow interval that is far from including zero. Thus, the predicted price per square metre becomes very sensitive to changes in the first factor, but not so sensitive to changes in the other factors. To further illustrate this, a sensitivity analysis is conducted. It is interesting to apply this sensitivity analysis to values that define the range of a potential population within which the model may be used for out-of-sample predictions. Therefore, I have subjectively chosen "assumed extreme values" for each one of the variables X_1, X_2, X_5 and X_6. The extreme values are found in Table 4, together with the corresponding maximum and minimum values in the sample.

For each factor of the right-hand side of expression (13), the multiplicative effect on the dependent variable is computed for the assumed extreme values. Furthermore, the quotient between the so computed extreme multiplicative effects is given. The latter is an indication of how sensitive the dependent variable is to changes in the independent variables within the range defined by the assumed extreme values. The sensitivity analysis is presented in Table 5.

Table 4: Extreme Values for Four Independent Variables used in Expression (13)

Variable	Assumed extreme values		Minimum value in sample	Maximum value in sample
	Low	High		
X_1	500	4,000	525	3,510
X_2	1	1,000	1	965
X_5	1	100	19	66
X_6	1	4,000	594	3,868

Table 5: Sensitivity Analysis Applied to the Dependent Variable in Expression (13)

Right-hand side factors of expression (13)	Computed extreme (multiplicative) effect on dependent variable		Quotient: Maximum effect Minimum effect
	Minimum effect	Maximum effect	
$X_1^{-0.012}$	0.91	0.93	1.02
$X_2^{0.033}$	1	1.26	1.26
$X_5^{-0.139}$	0.53	1	1.90
$X_6^{-0.349}$	0.06	1	18.08
$e^{4.823} \cdot X_1^{-0.012} \cdot X_2^{0.033} \cdot X_5^{-0.139} \cdot X_6^{-0.349}$	3.60	145.70	40.47
$X_1/(X_1 + X_2)$	0.00025	0.6667	2,666.67

The minimum and maximum multiplicative effects for the different factors of the right, hand side of expression (13), as well as the quotient between the maximum and the minimum effect for each factor, are estimated using the assumed extreme values in Table 4.

Figure 2: Price/m^2 according to Expression (13) as a Function of the Proportion Commercial Space. The Variables *Age* and *Distance* are Held at their Sample Averages

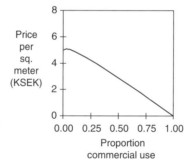

From Table 5 we conclude that the predicted price per square metre is extremely sensitive to changes in the proportion commercial space. The formula can easily produce price per square metre predictions that are completely unrealistic, particularly in out-of-sample predictions.

The model's sensitivity to the proportion commercial space is illustrated graphically in Figure 2. The graph is derived using expression (13) in the following way. The variables X_1 and X_2 are allowed to vary, but their sum is kept constant, $X_1 + X_2 = 2,000$. The other independent variables are kept constant at their sample averages (i.e., $X_5 = 53$ and $X_6 = 2,055$).

The function found in Figure 2 shows how the predicted price per square metre depends on the composition of the property, with respect to the mix of residential and commercial uses when the total space is 2,000 m². A similar pattern will be found for every set of values of the independent variables other than X_1 and X_2, when the latter two are allowed to vary but with a constant sum. Consequently, the model is not a stable predictor of property prices. However, the instability will not necessarily be obvious as long the percentage of commercial space varies little within the regression sample, within the prediction sample as well as between these two samples.

In Appendix B some issues with respect to the modelling of the price for mixed-use properties are further discussed.

8.6 Discussion

The hedonic technique may be used for estimating marginal (hedonic) prices for property attributes, but also for estimating price prediction (valuation) models. Different aspects may be important in the two different uses. When using the technique for valuation purposes, the goodness-of-fit criterion is relevant. However, it is also necessary to evaluate the models according to the price effect of each explanatory variable; each variable, including the constant factor, has to have a realistic total effect on the dependent variable, individually as well as jointly. The constant is usually of little importance in traditional hedonic analyses, but not so in appraisal applications. Furthermore, valuation models should be evaluated in terms of how stable they are for prediction purposes, in out-of-sample applications.

In several studies, theory is said to give no guidance as to what the appropriate hedonic functional form should be when applied to composite consumption goods. In the case of income property, the argument may be softened. The appraisal techniques based on ordinary NPV computations may be of some guidance when specifying the hedonic model. In an appendix to this paper, a short discussion is provided regarding the interpretability of a multiplicative model in terms of a simple additive relationship.

In the above application of the hedonic technique to a sample of income properties, two popular multiplicative models were investigated. The models performed equally in terms of goodness-of-fit. The coefficients were with few exceptions significant when expected to be so. The coefficient estimates appeared realistic. When examining some aspects in detail we found that the log-linear model produced coefficients that were unrealistic or would possibly cause unstable out-of-sample-range predictions.

The example illustrates the advantage of modelling the variables *Age* and *Distance* so that the rate of price decline due to these variables is a constant fraction of the dependent variable. In the log-linear model the rate of distance effect depends heavily on the variable *Distance* itself, making this specification potentially less suitable in certain situations.

APPENDIX A

The Marginal (Hedonic) Price Effect in Multiplicative Models

The variables W and Z represent the power function and the exponential function respectively in the following example:

$$Y = a_0 \cdot W^{a_1} \cdot e^{a_2 Z} \cdot f_i(\circ) \tag{14}$$

Naturally, independent variables affect the dependent variable differently depending on how they are specified in the model.

First, qualitative independent variables are considered, i.e., variables indicating the presence or absence of a characteristic. These are similar to ordinary dummy variable that in additive models take the values 0 or 1. When the models follow expression (14), the dummy variables can be of two different kinds. Power form dummies, like W, must have the value 1 when the variable does not effect the dependent variable and a constant value c in the cases where the effect is present, where $c \begin{Bmatrix} >0 \\ \neq 1 \end{Bmatrix}$. Exponential form dummies, like Z, should have the value 0 when the variable does not affect the dependent variable and a constant value d in the case where the effect is present, $d \neq 0$.

Variable W can only take the values 1 and c (usually $c=2$), and variable Z can only take the values 0 and d (usually $d=1$). Expressions (15) and (16) give the relative effect on variable Y, in expression (14), caused by a value switch in the dummy variables W and Z respectively.

$$\frac{Y(W=c) - Y(W=1)}{Y(W=1)} = \frac{Y(W=c)}{Y(W=1)} - 1 = c^{a_1} - 1 \tag{15}$$

$$\frac{Y(Z=d) - Y(Z=0)}{Y(Z=0)} = \frac{Y(Z=d)}{Y(Z=0)} - 1 = e^{a_2 \cdot d} - 1 \tag{16}$$

The hedonic price for an attribute, i.e. the marginal price for the attribute, is the first order derivative of the price equation with respect to that particular attribute variable. In multiplicative models of the kinds discussed here there are two possibilities, depending on whether the independent variable in question enters as an exponential or power function. We now assume that expression (14) represents a rather general form of a multiplicative price equation, where a_0, a_1 and a_2 are constants to be estimated, Y is the price observed, W and Z are two of the independent variables and $f(\circ)$ represents the rest of the independent variables. In this case the variables W and Z are assumed not to be dummy variables.

Expressions (17) and (18) give the hedonic prices for the attributes W and Z respectively, i.e., the partial derivatives of the dependent variable with respect to the independent variables.

$$\frac{\partial Y}{\partial W} = a_0 \cdot a_1 \cdot W^{a_1-1} \cdot e^{a_2 Z} \cdot f(\circ) = \frac{a_1}{W} \cdot Y, \tag{17}$$

$$\frac{\partial Y}{\partial Z} = a_0 \cdot W^{a_1} \cdot a_2 \cdot e^{a_2 Z} \cdot f(\circ) = a_2 \cdot Y. \tag{18}$$

As a consequence, the hedonic value of a variable that enters the model as a power function is a constant fraction of the dependent variable divided by the independent variable itself, i.e., the price elasticity is constant. The hedonic value of a variable that enters the model as an exponential function is a constant fraction of the value of the dependent variable.

This insight makes it obvious that the (empirical) nature of the independent variables has to be thoroughly considered when the functional form of the hedonic model is designed. In particular, the range of observed values for each independent variable has to be considered.

APPENDIX B

A Simple Transformation of the Additive Price Model

This section discusses the simple relationship between a semi-log linear and an additive specification for modelling the price for mixed-use properties.

For the purpose of discussing the relevance of the model specification, the following variables will be used:

V_T Total value of the property
V_C Value of the commercial part of the property
V_R Value of the residential part of the property
P_T Price/m^2 of the property
P_C Price/m^2 of the commercial part of the property
P_R Price/m^2 of the residential part of the property
S_T Total space of the property
S_C Commercial space
S_R Residential space
R_C Proportion commercial space

We assume that P_C and P_R are market determined constants, and that there are no other attributes affecting the total value than those listed above.

Thereby, the expression (2) above can be reduced to:

$$V_T = P_T \cdot S_T = V_C + V_R = P_C \cdot S_C + P_R \cdot S_R \tag{19}$$

This expression can be rearranged in the following way:

$$V_T = P_R \cdot (S_R + S_C) + (P_C \cdot S_C - P_R \cdot S_C) = P_R \cdot (S_R + S_C) + S_C \cdot (P_C - P_R)$$

$$= P_R \cdot (S_R + S_C) \cdot \left(1 + \frac{S_C}{(S_R + S_C)} \cdot \frac{(P_C - P_R)}{P_R} \right)$$

$$= (P_R \cdot S_T) \cdot \left(1 + R_C \cdot \frac{(P_C - P_R)}{P_R} \right)$$

This can be simplified as:

$$V_T = (P_R \cdot S_T) \cdot (1 + R_C \cdot (q - 1)) \tag{20}$$

where q is the proportional relation between residential and commercial price per square metre, $q = P_C/P_R$.

As the variable R_C only can have values between 0 and 1, the second factor in expression (20) is a linear function of R_C that takes on values in the interval $[1,q]$. If this factor is substituted by an exponential function we get an expression that is purely multiplicative:

$$V_T = (P_R \cdot S_T) \cdot e^{R_C \cdot \ln(q)} \tag{21}$$

By entering $\ln(q)$ in the exponent, we have assured that the second factor in expression (21) takes on values in the same interval as the second factor in expression (20). This non-linear substitution deviates from the linear relationship. However, as long as the value of q is rather low, the exponential substitutions' deviation from linearity is negligible. Some values for the maximum relative deviation, as a function of q, are given in Table 6. The two expressions are presented graphically for $q = 3$ in Figure 3.

Table 6 should be read in the following way. Assume the price per square metre of commercial space is twice as high the price per square metre of residential space, then a multiplicative model, expression (21), may model a truly additive market price, expression (19), without deviating more than 6.2 percent from the true value of a property.

Table 6: Approximate Values for the Maximum Relative Difference Between a Linear Function and its Exponential Substitution on a Limited Interval

q	$\max\limits_{R_C \in [0,1]} \left[\dfrac{(1 + R_C \cdot (q - 1))}{e^{R_C \cdot \ln(q)}} - 1 \right]$
1	0.0%
2	6.2%
3	16.0%
4	26.4%
5	36.7%
10	85.7%

Figure 3: Price/m² as a Function of Proportion Commercial Space According to Expression (19), Linear, and Expression (21), Exponential. The Price for Commercial Space is Assumed to be Three Times that of Residential Space ($q = 3$)

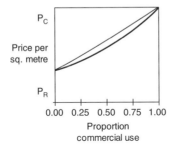

APPENDIX C

Descriptives

Table 7: Descriptive Statistics

Variable	Explanation	Mean	Maximum	Minimum	Standard dev.
Y	*Price*	10212.26	56213.79	1178.31	6472.94
X_1	*Residential*	1659.12	3510.00	525.00	628.60
X_2	*Commercial*	147.09	965.00	0.00	164.05
X_3	*TotSpace*	1806.21	3964.00	525.00	702.92

Table 7: (*Continued*)

Variable	Explanation	Mean	Maximum	Minimum	Standard dev.
X_4	*PropCom*	0.08	0.47*	0.00	0.07
X_5	*Age*	53.41	66.00	19.00	13.24
X_6	*Distance*	2054.87	3867.69	594.42	650.63
Q_2	*Quarter 2*	0.09	1.00	0.00	0.29
Q_3	*Quarter 3*	0.04	1.00	0.00	0.20
Q_4	*Quarter 4*	0.10	1.00	0.00	0.30
Q_5	*Quarter 5*	0.10	1.00	0.00	0.30
Q_6	*Quarter 6*	0.10	1.00	0.00	0.29
Q_7	*Quarter 7*	0.04	1.00	0.00	0.20
Q_8	*Quarter 8*	0.11	1.00	0.00	0.32
Q_9	*Quarter 9*	0.12	1.00	0.00	0.32
Q_{10}	*Quarter 10*	0.11	1.00	0.00	0.31
Q_{11}	*Quarter 11*	0.07	1.00	0.00	0.25
Q_{12}	*Quarter 12*	0.07	1.00	0.00	0.26
Y/X_3	*Price per square metre*	5.57	18.19	2.14	2.09

*The observations in the sample are classified by the assessment authority as mixed-use properties with mainly residential rental space.

Figure 4: Regression Residuals from Model I (a) and Model II (b) Plotted against *Distance*

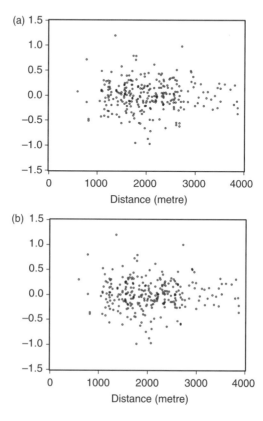

Figure 5: The Inner City of Stockholm, Including the Study Area. Black Dots Indicate the Location of Properties in the Sample

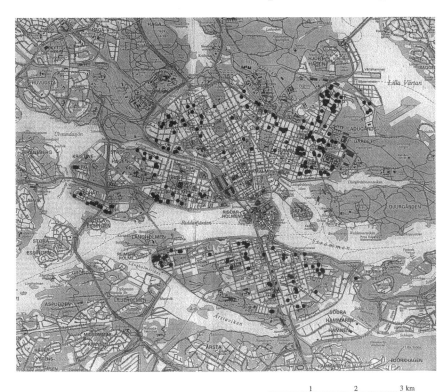

REFERENCES

Anselin, L., Bera, A. K., Florax, R., and Yoon, M. J. (1996) Simple Diagnostic Tests for Spatial Dependence, *Regional Science and Urban Economics*, 26, 77–104.

Appraisal Institute (1996) *The Appraisal of Real Estate*, Chicago, Ill: Appraisal Institute.

Arimah, B. C. (1997) The Determinants of Housing Tenure Choice in Ibadan, Nigeria, *Urban Studies*, 34, 105–124.

Cassel, E. and Mendelsohn, R. (1985) The Choice of Functional Form for Hedonic Price Equations: Comment, *Journal of Urban Economics*, 18, 135–142.

Colwell, P. F., Munneke, H. J., and Trefzger, J. W. (1998) Chicago's Office Market: Price Indices, Location and Time, *Real Estate Economics*, 26, 83–106.

de Silva, H. and Gruenstein, J. M. L. (1988) Hedonic Index Estimation for Commercial Buildings: Assessors and Economists and the Parallel Search for the Optimal Functional Form, *Working Paper* 88–154, IBER, University of California, Berkeley.

Draper, D. W. and Findlay, M. C. (1982) Capital Asset Pricing and Real Estate Valuation, *Journal of the American Real Estate and Urban Economics Association*, 10, 152–183.

Fehribach, F. A., Rutherford, R. C., and Eakin, M. E. (1993) An Analysis of the Determinants of Industrial Property Valuation, *Journal of Real Estate Research*, 8, 365–376.

Halvorsen, R. and Pollakowski, H. O. (1981) Choice of Functional Form for Hedonic Price Equations, *Journal of Urban Economics*, 10, 37–49.

Hendershott, P. H. and Turner, B. (1999) Estimating constant-quality capitalization rates and capitalization effects of below market financing, *Journal of Property Research*, 16, 109–122.

Isakson, H. R. (1986) The Accuracy of Arbitrage Pricing Versus Hedonic Pricing Valuation Methodologies in Computer-Assisted Mass Appraisal Systems, *Property Tax Journal*, 5, 97–109.

Laakso, S. (1992) Public Transport Investment and Residential Property Values in Helsinki, *Scandinavian Housing and Planning Research*, 9, 217–229.

Lessinger, J. (1969) Econometrics and Appraisal, *Appraisal Journal*, 37, 501–512.

Maclennan, D. (1977) Some Thoughts on the Nature and Purpose of House Price Studies, *Urban Studies*, 14, 59–71.

McMillen, D. P. (1996) One Hundred Fifty Years of Land Values in Chicago: A Nonparametric Approach, *Journal of Urban Economics*, 40, 100–124.

Miles, M., Cole, R., and Guilkey, D. (1990) A Different Look at Commercial Real Estate Returns, *AREUEA Journal*, 18, 403–430.

Rosen, S. (1974) Hedonic Prices and Implicit Markets: Product Differentiation in Pure Competition, *Journal of Political Economy*, 82, 34–55.

Saderion, Z., Smith, B., and Smith, C. (1994) An Integrated Approach to the Evaluation of Commercial Real Estate, *Journal of Real Estate Research*, 9, 151–167.

Svensson, K. A. S. (1998) Neither Market nor Command Economy: Swedish Negotiative Rent Setting in Practice, *Scandinavian Housing and Planning Research*, 15, 79–94.

Szynkier, S. (1983) *Taxerade markvärden i Stockholm 1933–1981* (*Assessed land values in Stockholm 1933–1981*), Department of Real Estate Economics (Memorandum 5:17), Royal Institute of Technology, Stockholm.

Yinger, J. (1979) Estimating the Relationship Between Location and the Price of Housing, *Journal of Regional Science*, 19, 271–289.

Chapter 9

Neural Network vs. Hedonic Price Model: Appraisal of High-Density Condominiums

K.C. Wong
Department of Real Estate and Construction, University of Hong Kong, Hong Kong

Albert T.P. So
Intelligent Building Research Center, City University of Hong Kong, Hong Kong

Y.C. Hung
Department of Real Estate and Construction, University of Hong Kong, Hong Kong

9.1 Introduction

In Hong Kong, high-density condominiums are routinely appraised by practitioners using the traditional comparative method. They collect a vast volume of transaction records, selecting suitable comparables from their data bank and then apply their professional judgment to adjust for any differences on factors such as view, orientation, area, floor height and market situation etc.

This comparative method relies on the expertise of the appraiser, and may sometimes be rather arbitrary; especially when there are very few comparables in the market. Researchers are recently looking for alternatives to the traditional approach.

After Rosen's (1974) work on hedonic prices, hedonic regressions have been widely used to study the contribution of the various characteristics to the price of housing, which is one of the clearest examples of a composite good. Goodman (1978) wrote on hedonic prices and indices; Linneman (1980) on empirical results of the hedonic price function; Butler (1982) on hedonic indices; Spitzer (1982) on the Box-Cox (1964) estimation, Follain and Jimenez (1985) on applications to developing countries; Megbolugbe (1989) on Nigeria; Mok, Chan and Cho (1995) on Hong Kong private housing.

On the other hand, neural network did not catch the attention of researchers in real estate until early nineties. Applications include Evans, James, and Collins (1991) on residential appraisal in UK; Borst (1992) on US real estate; Do and Grudnitski (1992) on comparison of neural network to multiple regression model for US properties; Tay and Ho (1992) on mass appraisal of condominiums in Singapore; Worzala, Lenk and Silva (1995) on further comparisons to regression models using US houses data.

The purpose of this paper is to compare the prediction performance of neural networks to hedonic price models. Data from a high-density residential development in Hong Kong is chosen for analysis. This is because a high concentration of brand new condominiums, sold at about the same time, would allow a strong focus on a few specific housing attributes affecting prices.

9.2 The Data Set

Kingswood Villas is a massive comprehensive residential located at Tin Shui Wai, a newly developed area at the northwestern end of the Territory of Hong Kong. A total floor area of 0.95 million square meters was built on this 80 hectares site. There are totally 58 residential towers, 32 stories high on average, and was constructed in 7 phases. On each floor of the towers, there are 8 flats, all of which are very standardized in layout, and is about 70 square meters.

For the simplicity of analysis, only prices of first time sales by the developer from 1992 to 1995 are used in this analysis. These are all actual transactions. Prices are deflated by a quarterly GDP deflator published by the Hong Kong Government.

216 residential flats are selected as the training data set. The 216 samples distribute over three phases:

- Towers 2, 7, 11 of Phase 1, Locwood Court;
- Towers 1, 5, 6 of Phase 2, Shewood Court; and
- Towers 1, 6, 14 of Phase 7, Kenwood Court.

Then, three floors were further selected from each of these towers. In both sets of data, all of the eight flats in each floor were selected in order to obtain as many flats with different orientation, floor area and interior layout.

The testing data set consists of 35 condominiums distributed in three phases as in those of the training data set.

9.3 Selection of Housing Attributes

In general, housing attributes can be defined as the characteristics of a flat that affect its price. In this study, these attributes are chosen according to the norms in appraisal practices, and defined as follows:

In Exhibit 1, twelve relevant housing attributes are selected and classified as structural, location, and neighborhood variables. Compared to another study of condominium prices in Hong Kong (Mok, Chan and Cho (1995)), these twelve attributes are quite different because the data sets are all within the same large-scale development. Within the same development, factors like distance to the CBD, building age, availability of schools, etc would be the same. The following attributes are chosen primarily to reflect the prevailing practices in the market in appraising similar types of condominiums.

The gross floor area of a flat directly determines the quantity of living space. It is clear that the more living space a flat contains, the higher the total price of the flat. This does not, however, imply that the *price per square footage* is necessarily higher. It is true that developers generally reserve better views and orientations for larger units, this does not imply that, after eliminating other effects such as view by means of a hedonic equation, the 'pure' effect of space to unitary price be positive. This is because the units with better views may sometimes become too large to be affordable.

Bathrooms-to-bedrooms ratio is a measure to quantify the adequacy of bathroom. Its inadequacy would strongly affect the lives of residents and considered undesirable. In Kingswood Villas, there are three different bathrooms-to-bedrooms ratios: 1/3, 1/2 and 2/3.

The effect of floor height on selling price is significant in Hong Kong, where densities are high. Flats at higher floor would be less affected by street condition. In addition to other attributes of view, a higher floor would provide

Exhibit 1: Housing Attributes

Variable	Definition	Unit of Measurement
Structural	• (GFA) – Gross floor area • (BATH-R) – Bathrooms-to-bedrooms ratio	• square feet • ratio of numbers
Location	• (FLOOR-H) – Floor Height • (BR-ORIEN) – Master-bedroom orientation • (SR-ORIEN) – Sitting room orientation • (EXP-V) – Total exposed view • (BLDG-V) – Building view • (GAR-V) – Garden view • (GRA-V) – Graveyard view • (TRAN-D) – Distance to public transport • (SHOP-D) – Distance to shopping center	• number of storey • degrees: angle of main window view from the axis pointing north • degrees: ditto • degrees: maximum angle of view unobstructed within 50 meters • direct distance of the nearest building seen from the sitting room in meters • degrees • degrees • meters • meters
Neighborhood	• (PHOUSE-D) – Distance from public housing	• meters
Dependent Variable	• (USP) – Unit selling price	HKD per square feet (approx. 1.38 USD per square meter)

better quality of air. Besides, the orientation would have a strong influence to the 'Feng-Shui' of a flat. The general belief of the Chinese is that premises facing south are the best. In this paper, the orientation of a flat was measured for two locations: the sitting room and the master bedroom. Both directions were measured from the line perpendicular to the center of the largest window of rooms. There are also beliefs that high voltage wires may affect 'Feng-Shiu', and hence on prices. In Kingswood Villas, high voltage cables are underground, and are therefore not considered as a factor affecting price.

The total exposed view is defined as one not obstructed by any obstacle within 50 meters. Again, this angle of view is measured from the center of the largest window of the sitting room. It is commonplace in Hong Kong that the sitting room of a high-density condominium faces another building, or even another sitting room of the flat next door. Privacy is therefore affected. It is therefore logical to deduce that a larger angle of total exposed view would contribute positively to selling price.

The view from a property substantially affects its value. Views of the sea are most popular. A commanding view of the surrounding landscape can sometimes compensate for other adversities. Conversely, a poor view can produce a value penalty. The views being selected as housing attributes here includes garden view, building view and graveyard view. Sea view and a good mountain view is not available in Kingswood Villas. Instead, the development is located along the periphery of the Tin Shui Wai Park, and there are also landscaped playground, ponds and recreational facilities such as tennis court within the development. Therefore, most residential flats would possess a garden view.

It would be very rare for a flat of a comprehensive residential estate in Hong Kong that it has no building view from the window of its sitting room. Although people generally accept it as being one of the result of the dense population of Hong Kong, a building view which is too close would normally reduce property value. In this paper, the direct distance of the nearest building, which can be seen from the window of the sitting room, is selected as one of the housing attributes.

There had been rumor of potential construction a graveyard nearby during the early sales of Kingswood Villas. Although it was only formally confirmed at October, 1994 by publication in the Government Gazette, a professional appraiser would consider the likelihood of any obstruction to the view in the near future. In the sales brochure of Laiwood Court, the developer also includes the proposed location of the graveyard as one of the information on the map, it shows that the developer also considers it as one of the factor that can affect selling price. It is believed that a view of Graveyard would definitely reduce the value of a residential flat.

The convenience of public mass transportation in Hong Kong makes it the most popular means of commuting. Since Kingswood Villas locates at quite a remote area from CBD, it requires very effective means of public transportation. Buses going to different parts of the city center; and the Light Railway Transit (LRT), which links Kingswood Villas to Tuen Mun, where there is direct-to-Central ferry service, are considered to be the two most important commuting means. Therefore, the summation of distance from both the LRT and bus station is selected as an attribute to housing price.

A large shopping center with a well tenant mix provides wide range of products and services. It creates great convenience to residents and thus enhances property value. The negative effect, on the other hand, is that a condominium too close to the shopping center would suffer more from noise, neon lights, or even trespassers. In Kingswood Villas, the shopping center in Phase 1 is the largest and most convenient. The distance from it is taken into account.

The desirability of a neighborhood is affected by physical and social factors of typical residences. Public housing is chosen for this case, because people often consider low-income people as inferior neighbors, since they tend to invest less in exterior maintenance and have a lesser sense of responsibility to the neighborhood environment. Moreover, public housing is always

Exhibit 2: Descriptive Statistics of the Data Sets

Housing Attributes	Unit of Measurement	Maximum	Minimum	Mean	Standard Deviation
USP	HKD per square foot	2241	1303	1755	216
GFA	Square feet	824	576	704	84
BATH-R	Ratio	1	0.33	0.46	0.14
FLOOR-H	Number	38	3	19	12
BR-ORIEN	Degrees	335	0	184	103
SR-ORIEN	Degrees	335	0	167	104
EXP-V	Degrees	112	60	91	16
GAR-V	Degrees	110	0	48	43
BLDG-V	Degrees	170	0	49	42
GRA-V	Degrees	25	0	2	6
TRAN-D	Meters	1710	210	844	518
SHOP-D	Meters	1370	40	534	511
PHOUSE-D	Meters	420	0	71	107

associated with high crime rate and nuisance. The distance from two nearby public housing estates, Tin Yiu Estate and Tin Shui Estate, is measured as the last housing attribute.

Exhibit 2 summarizes the descriptive statistics of the housing attributes in the data set.

The same sets of data are used for both hedonic and neural network analyses, except that these figures are normalized before being fed to the neural network computer program. The program used in this study is specially written in PASCAL for this purpose, and is not a a software available in the market. The method of normalization is as follows.

The values of all data are normalized to a decimal value between 0 to 1, using the minimum and maximum values of the respective attribute. For example, if the Unit Selling Price (USP) of a particular unit is HKD1500 per square foot, then the normalized value of this variable is:

$$\frac{1500 - (\text{the minimum USP})}{\text{maximum USP} - \text{minimum USP}} = \frac{1500 - 1303}{2241 - 1303} = 0.2100 \qquad (1)$$

9.4 The Hedonic Price Model

In general, the housing attributes are classified into three groups: location traits (L) such as access to economic and social facilities; structural traits (S)

such as area or floor height of the residential unit; and neighborhood traits (N) such as quality of the neighborhood.

Therefore the selling price, P, can be constructed as a function of L, S, N.

$$P = f(L, S, N) \tag{2}$$

Following Linneman (1981), Spitzer (1982), and Megbolugbe (1989), the Box-Cox (1964) technique was used to search for the best specification of the hedonic equation when the theory is ambiguous about the function form. It can been seen as a systematic mean for choosing an optimal functional form.

First, if we assume a linear relationship between selling price and housing attributes, then we may write:

$$P = f(L, S, N) = \beta_0 + \sum \beta_1 L + \sum \beta_2 S + \sum \beta_3 N + \varepsilon \tag{3}$$

where

β_0 is the constant term;
β_1 the regression coefficient of the location attribute L;
β_2 the regression coefficient of the structural attribute S;
β_3 the regression coefficient of the neighborhood attribute N; and
ε a stochastic or error term.

β_1, β_2 and β_3 are the partial derivatives of P with respective to L, S, and N, and can therefore be interpreted as 'implicit prices', or marginal trait appraisals, of the attributes.

Consider Box-Cox transformation of the variables on both sides of equation (3) gives:

$$P^* = \beta_0 + \sum \beta_1 L^* + \sum \beta_2 S^* + \sum \beta_3 N^* + \varepsilon \tag{4}$$

where

$P^* = (P^{\lambda_1} - 1)/\lambda_1$
$L^* = (L^{\lambda_2} - 1)/\lambda_2$
$S^* = (S^{\lambda_3} - 1)/\lambda_3$
$N^* = (N^{\lambda_4} - 1)/\lambda_4$ for $\lambda_i \neq 0$

In the analysis of housing markets, the focus should be mainly on the specification of the dependent variable, P, rather than the independent variables, L, S and N (Linneman, 1980). Therefore, the Box-Cox transformation technique on the dependent variable side only would be suitable for the above hedonic function. In this case, the response P is transformed but not the regression function $f(L, S, N)$.

As a result, in this paper, two alternative specifications of the hedonic equation will be applied. They are firstly, the linear model (when all $\lambda = 1$); and secondly the Box-Cox transformation on dependent variable P (when λ_2, λ_3, λ_4 are equal to 1 and an optimal, λ_1, is found using the Maximum Likelihood Estimate, MLE, method).

Consider the first linear specification. When $\lambda_1, \lambda_2, \lambda_3 = 1$, equation (4) becomes:

$$P = \beta_0 + \sum \beta_1 L + \sum \beta_2 S + \sum \beta_3 N + \varepsilon. \tag{5}$$

Meanwhile, under the second specification of Box-Cox transformation on dependent variable, P, when $\lambda_2, \lambda_3, \lambda_4 = 1$, equation (4) becomes:

$$(P^{\lambda_1} - 1)/\lambda_1 = \beta_0 + \sum \beta_1 L + \sum \beta_2 S + \sum \beta_3 N + \varepsilon \tag{6}$$

where an optimal λ_1 is to be estimated with the MLE method.

9.5 Results of the Hedonic Price Model

The results of the hedonic price model are summarized in Exhibit 3. It should be noted that the coefficients of the two specifications are not directly comparable because of different functional forms. Their signs, relative magnitude and t-statistics, however, are consistent and comparable.

In Exhibit 3, the signs of the regression coefficients are generally expected except for: the negative signs of GFA (gross floor area) and BATH-R (bathrooms-to-bedrooms) ratio; and the a positive one for SHOP-D (shopping distance). These observations indicate that home purchasers prefer smaller flats with fewer bathrooms, and would not consider long shopping distance as a disadvantage.

Kingswood Villas is very remote from city center. Most purchasers are first time buyers of properties and they have a tight budget. They are willing to sacrifice some convenience in transport, but resist paying for floor area they do not need, nor for an additional bathroom.

The shopping center is within walking distance (534 meters on average) from our data set of flats in the development. It seems that the negative effects of being close the shopping center: noise, lights, etc., are significant, though the magnitude of the coefficient is not large.

As indicated by the magnitude of the coefficients, the floor height and garden view of a residential unit are most influential positive attributes. On the

Exhibit 3: Result of Hedonic price regression

Variables	Coefficients & (*t*-Values)	
	Linear: $\lambda = 1$	Box-cox: $\lambda_1 = 2.31$
Intercept	1,751.2724 *(19.3354)	3,044.2432 *(8.4193)
GFA	−0.0551(−0.4316)	−0.2783 (−0.5459)
BATH-R	−90.8278 (−1.1838)	−387.0604 (−1.2637)
FLOOR-H	6.8064* (8.4946)	28.6787 *(8.9656)
BR-ORIEN	−0.1894** (−1.8401)	−0.6821 **(−1.6599)
SR-ORIEN	−0.2595 *(−2.5030)	−1.2169 *(−2.9401)
EXP-V	0.0904 (0.1375)	1.2752 (0.4858)
GAR-V	1.7375 *(7.5383)	6.9809 *(7.5869)
BLDG-V	−0.3623 (−1.4962)	−1.3607 (−1.4074)
GRA-V	−9.9115 *(−5.9217)	−42.2991 *(−6.3304)
TRAN-D	−0.3449 *(−5.7240)	−1.1598 *(−4.8215)
SHOP-D	0.7988 *(10.0225)	3.4661 *(10.8943)
PHOUSE-D	−0.2917 **(−1.7637)	−1.8036 *(−2.7321)
R square	0.6474	0.6682

Observations: 216; * 99% significant; ** 90% significant.
Notes: For the sake of a same order comparison, the coefficients of Box-Cox model are values divided by 10,000 (e.g. coefficient of GFA = −2783/10,000 = −0.2783).

other hand, high bathroom ratios (coefficient of −90.8) and large graveyard views (−9.9) contribute nearly most of the price penalty.

The *t*-statistics show good significance for most of the attributes. Both the linear and Box-Cox specification give a high *R* square value: 0.65 and 0.67. The Box-Cox specification performs slightly better in correlation.

9.6 Artificial Neural Network

Wasserman (1989) stated that the artificial neuron was designed to mimic the first-order characteristics of the biological neuron. The basic processing unit of a neural network is the artificial counterpart of a neuron in the brain. Exhibit 4 shows the components of a typical artificial neuron, with typical summation and threshold functions. Each processing unit accepts a number of inputs from other units and sends output to some other units after the process of iteration.

In this figure, X_i is an input to the processing unit, which may be from an external source, or from outputs of other processing units; W_i are weights indicating the degree of influence of the input value on the processing unit; U is a summation function, usually the weighted sum of the input; and f is a threshold value where the neuron is activated to determine an output.

Exhibit 4: The Components of a Typical Processing Unit

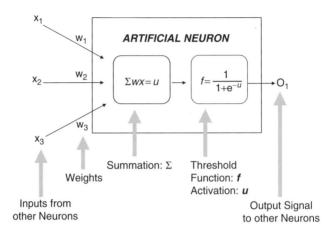

Exhibit 5: The architecture of the neural network for residential property valuation: a three layer feed-forward network with supervised learning and supported by back-propagation

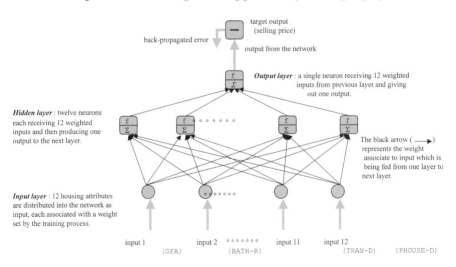

Typical mathematical functions used are as follows:

$$U = \sum W_i X_i \tag{7}$$

and

$$f = 1/(1 + e^{-u}) \tag{8}$$

To handle complex problems, hidden neuron layers must be incorporated. A normal neural network consists of a number of consecutive layers: the input layer, one or more hidden layers and the outer layer. The major problem of a multi-layer neural network is its training algorithm, which is extremely computationally intensive. One very common method of training is the back-propagation method. This method is used to construct our neural network for residential property appraisal. The artificial neural network program being adopted is specially design for this experiment. It is a feed-forward architecture with supervised training algorithm, with multi-layers (3 layers) network using back-propagation to measure its errors. Exhibit 5 gives a clear picture of its structure.

9.7 Results

In this application, the neural network being tested consisted of 12 inputs, which describe the properties, one output neuron, and the selling price of the property. When learning had been achieved, the network was tested on data which had not been included in the training data sets.

Four different tests with different network parameters have been carried on the same testing data set. Firstly, three different tests of 32K, 84K and 250K iterations had been done on the network with 12 hidden nodes while other network parameters were kept unchanged. Here, one iteration means training the ANN with the 216 sets of training data one time. 32K iterations mean that the ANN is trained 32,000 times, and so on. Then the fourth test was carried out using 6 hidden nodes and being trained up to 32K iterations. The results of these four different tests, together with those from the two hedonic models, are shown in Appendix 1.

In order to compare the accuracy of predictions offered by alternative methods, results in Appendix 1 is summarized in Exhibit 6 and 7 below:

There are a few important observations from these results.

Firstly, ignoring the 32K/6 model for the time being, all the first five models (2 hedonic, 3 neural) give mean prediction errors within 7% to 8%.

Exhibit 6: Average & Standard Deviation of the Prediction Error

Methods	Minimum Error	Maximum Error	Mean Error	Standard Deviation of Error
Linear	$0.40 (0.02%)	$532.20 (35.68%)	$130.75 (7.72%)	$134.54 (8.92%)
Box-Cox	$1.04 (0.07%)	$493.80 (33.11%)	$136.94 (8.00%)	$132.66 (8.56%)
32 K	$2.79 (0.15%)	$326.16 (19.92%)	$128.19 (7.20%)	$89.64 (5.03%)
84 K	$12.33 (0.69%)	$367.22 (19.71%)	$134.02 (7.57%)	$89.27 (5.13%)
250 K	$20.79 (1.10%)	$321.97 (17.15%)	$133.60 (7.48%)	$90.77 (4.94%)
32 K/6	$5.73 (0.32%)	$761.17 (49.86%)	$219.33 (13.07%)	$201.34 (13.54%)

Exhibit 7: Prediction Performances of Hedonic vs. Neural Network Models

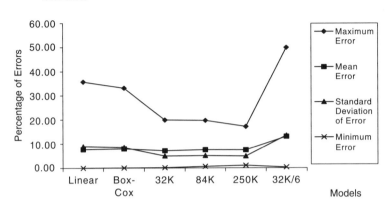

However, the neural networks, however, give notably smaller standard deviations in the errors, around 5%, compared to 8% to 9% from the hedonic methods. Moreover, the maximum errors of the predictions by the hedonic methods are between 33% to 36%. They almost double those of the neural methods.

This means that both hedonic and neural methods give predictions within reasonable limits of 7% to 8%, but the hedonic methods give larger variances in predictions, and hence a higher risk of getting a bigger error in any single prediction. In this sense, the neural network method co-relates price and housing attributes better: not only to minimize errors on the average, but also their variances. This is supported by the Suykens, Vendewelle and De Moor's view (1996, pp. 23–26) that a multi-layer feed-forward neural network with one or more hidden layers is sufficient in order to approximate any continuous non-linear function arbitrarily well on a compact interval, provided sufficient hidden neurons are available.

Secondly, comparing the two hedonic models, Linear and Box-Cox, neither of them performs significantly better than the other does. The linear model gives a very slightly smaller (by 0.3%) mean error, but also a 2% higher standard deviation in prediction.

Thirdly, as we increase the number of iterations from 32 K to 84 K, the accuracy in predictions increases from 7.2% to 7.53%,. This may be accounted for by the possible existence of a local minimum point. To confirm, the network was then trained up to 250 K, 350 K, 450 K and 520 K. The mean error drops from 7.53% to 7.23%, as we increased from 84 K to 520 K. The last result of 7.23% derived at 520 K was close to that of 7.2% at 32 K. This indicates the potential existence of a global minimum if we train the data set even further, and 32 K could be a local minimum point. The observation of an increasing prediction error with the number of iterations may also be explained by the argument of "over-fitting" – a decrease in accuracy as the number of training is increased beyond its optimal level.

Fourthly, we have also tested the results against a smaller number of hidden nodes: reducing from 12 nodes to 6 nodes for the 32 K iterations. Exhibit 7 shows a significant increases, for about 2 to 3 times, in mean, maximum, as well as standard deviation of prediction errors. It is therefore observed that the increase in number of hidden nodes could improve the performance of the network significantly. This is demonstrated in Exhibits 8 and 9. However, further increase in the number of nodes beyond 12 seems not desirable in this project. The reasons are threefold: Firstly, Increasing the number of hidden nodes increases computation time significantly. Secondly, Too many hidden units would over-load the network in memorizing the training examples, instead of focusing on the extraction of general features that will allow it to handle cases it has not seen during training (See Falman (1988)). Thirdly, according to Kolmogorov's Theorem, the number of hidden layers should not be more than $2n+1$, n being the number of inputs. With 12 housing attributes, this maximum number of hidden layers should be $2 \times 12 + 1 = 25$ in our case. Having 25 hidden nodes, however, seems superfluous as we are mapping 12 attributes to only one, instead of many, appraisal function. The accuracy of predictions has also justified the use of 12 hidden nodes.

Exhibit 8: Tendency of network with 6 hidden nodes (32 K)

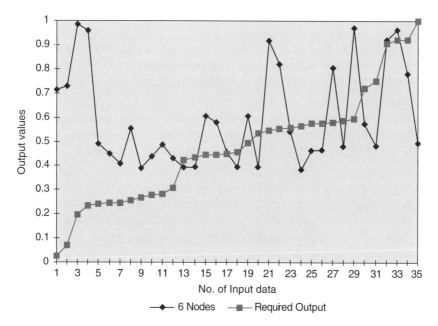

Exhibit 9: Tendency of network with 12 hidden nodes (32 K)

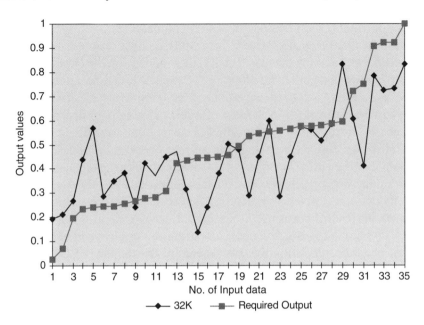

9.8 Conclusion and Further Research

Neither method, hedonic or neural, has shown absolute advantage over the other. They average accuracy in prediction are similar, but the neural network performs better in terms of smaller standard deviations of prediction errors, hence avoiding large maximum error on individual jobs of appraisal.

Both hedonic and neural network methods have their own limitations. Unlike neural networks, hedonic models require prior knowledge of the appraisal function, as well as assumptions of co-relations amongst input variables. The proper choice of these relationships would affect the results significantly.

On the other hand, predictions of neural networks fluctuate, and its performance is quite dependent on the architecture chosen for the network. Increasing the number of hidden nodes, for instance, enable the network to represent more complex appraisal functions, but this increases the learning time greatly. In response to the problem of long computation hours, a powerful computer is therefore required. Moreover, neural network suffers another problem of not attaining a global optimal function, but just a local one. Further training iterations can be applied, and the number of hidden nodes can be also varied to see if better results are obtained. This requires further empirical testing.

Coefficients of inputs variable offered by hedonic regressions represents the implicit prices of individual housing attributes. Neural networks, on the other hand, do not provide such references directly. The contribution of each housing attribute to the estimation of the selling price are related by weights at the output and hidden layers. Unfortunately, these weights are not directly comparable to regression coefficients as they form a 12×12 matrix, inter-relating one another. Alternatively, contributions of individual housing attributes can be assessed by repetitive tests using a notional property, during which a single attributes is varied over the desired range while the remainder are fixed. This kind of sensitivity analysis is achievable by further research, but is much more complicated process than hedonic regressions.

There are also limitations in our research. Apart from the physical attributes of the property, there are so many other factors affecting property prices. Factors like political, economic factors, speculation and pricing and marketing strategy are just impossible to be quantified and added into the research. Considering this limitation, neural network is potentially a more suitable method, as it would follow the overall trend of property price, without quantifying such factors of trend. This is particularly useful for predicting prices in the second market, where condominiums are not sold at nearly the same time, unlike the first hand market in the case of our research. The neural network could become a suitable alternative to the traditional regression analysis of property prices. Result of this research have proved its reliability and potential.

Commercial neural network software are available in the market, some are easy to use. It is a black-box technique, which does not require any knowledge on the working principle of the network. It is particularly suitable for the layman in the property field such as individual investors or home purchasers. They can ask the network for an un-biased judgement, yet as good as one given by professionals.

Both hedonic price models and neural networks require adequate training data. It is therefore essential to develop a training data bank on different types of properties, and update them at regular intervals. As statutory bodies have a large database for tax purposes, they are immediate candidates for such applications.

REFERENCES

Appraisal Institute, Appraising Residential Properties, Chicago, 1992.

Azoff, E. M. Reducing error in Neural Network Time Series Forecasting, *Neural Computing and Applications*, Vol 1, 1993, pp. 204–247.

Bajic, V. The Effect of a New Subway Line on Housing Prices in Metropolitan Toronto,

Bajic, V. An Analysis of the demand for housing attributes. *Applied Economics*, 16, 1984, pp. 597–610.

Ball, M. J. Recent empirical work on the determinants of relative house price, *Urban studies*, 10, 1973, pp. 213–231.

Borst, R. A. Artificial Neural Networks: The Next Modeling/Cligration Technology for the Assessment Community, *Artificial Neural Networks*, 1992, 69–94.

Box, G. E. P. and Cox, D. R. An Analysis of Transformation, *Journal of Royal Statistic Society*, B26, 1964, pp. 211–243.

Butler, V. Richard. The specification of Hedonic Indexes for Urban Housing, *Land Economics*, 1982, pp. 97–108.

Caroll, J. Raymond. Transformation and Weighting in Regression, New York: Chapman Hall, 1992.

Chester, Michael. Neural Networks – A Tutorial, Englerwood Cliffs, N.J.: PTR Prentice Hall, 1993.

Dewees, D. N. The effect of subway improvement on residential property values in Toronto, *Journal of Urban Economics*, 3, No. 4, 1976, pp. 357–369.

Dhrymes, J. Phoebus, Price and quality changes in consumer capital goods, Price indexes and quality change, Zvi Griliches. Cambridge, Mass.: Harvard University Press.

Do, Q. and Grudnitski G. A neural network approach to residential property appraisal, *Real Estate Appraiser*, December, 1992, pp. 38–45.

Dubin, A. Robin, and Chein-Sing Sung. Specification of Hedonic Regression: Non-nested Tests on Measures of Neighborhood Quality, *Journal of Urban Economics*, 27, 1990, pp. 97–111.

Edmonds, Radcliffe G. Jr. Some Evidence on the Inter-temporal Stability of Hedonic Price Functions, *Land Economics*, 61, No. 4 Nov 1985, pp. 445–451.

Evans, A., James, H., and Collins, A. Artificial Neural Networks: An Application to Residential Valuation in the UK, *Journal of Property Valuation and Investment*, 1991, 11:2, 195–204.

Falman, S. E. *Faster-learning Variations on Back-Propagation: An Empirical Study*, Proceedings of the 1988 Connections Models Summer School, Morgan Kaufmann Publishing. CA 944403, P41.

Follain, James R., and Jimenez, Emmamuel. The Demand for Housing Characteristics in Developing Countries, *Urban Studies* 22, 1985, 421–432.

Goodman, Allen C. Hedonic prices, Price Indices and Housing Market, Journal of *Urban Economics*, 5, 1978, pp. 471–484.

Goodman, A. Hedonic prices, Price indices and housing markets, *Journal of Urban Economics*, 5, 1978, pp. 471–484.

Goodwin, S. Measuring the value of housing Quality, *J. Reg. Sci.*, 17, 1977, pp. 107–115.

Grether, D. M. and Mieszkowski, Peter. Determinants of Real Estate Values, *Journal of Urban Economics* 1, Apr. 1974, pp. 127–145.

Hawlwy, D. D., Johnson, J. D., and Raina, D. Artificial Neural Systems: A New Tool for financial Decision-Making, *Financial Analysts Journal*, Nov/Dec 1990, p. 63. J. Reg. Sci., 17, 1977, pp. 107–115.

Jurik, Mark. Consumer's Guide to Neural Network Software, *Futures*, Vol. XXII, No. 8, July 1993, pp. 36–42.

Kain, Joun F, and Quigley, John M. Measuring the value of Housing Quality, Journal of the American Statistical Association, 65, June 1970, pp. 532–48.

Kirrmann, H. Neural computing: The new gold rush in informatics, *IEEE Microworld*, June 1989.

Lapham, V. Do blacks pay more for housing? *Journal of Political Economics*, 79, 1971, pp. 1244–1257.

Linneman, Peter Some Empirical Results on the Nature of the Hedonic Price Function for the Urban housing Market, *Journal of Urban Economics*, 8, 1980,

Lisboa, P. G. J. Neural Network: Current Applications, London: Chapman & Hall, 1992.

Mackmin, David, The valuation and Sale of Residential Property, London and New York: Routliedge, 1994.

Mebolugbe, Isaac F. A Hedonic Index Model: The Housing Market of Jos, Nigeria, *Urban Studies*, 26, 1989, pp. 486–494.

Mok, H. M. K., Chan, P. P. K., and Cho, Y. S. A Hedonic Price Model for Private Properties In Hong Kong, *Journal of Real Estate Finance and Economics*, 10, 1995, pp. 37–48.

Palmquist, Raymond B. Estimating the Demand for the Characteristics of Housing *The Review of Economics and Statistics*, XXX, pp. 394–404.

Phillips, John L. Jr. How to think about Statistics, New York: W. H. Freeman and Company, 1988, pp. 34–55., and pp. 47–68.

Rational Research Council Highway Research Board, Moving Behavior and Residential Choice, Washington, D.C. The Board, 1969.

Rojas, R. Neural Networks – A Systematic Introduction, USA: Springer, 1991.

Rosen, Sherwin. Hedonic Prices and Implicit Markets: Product differentiation in Pure competition, *Journal of Political Economy*, 82, Jan./Feb. 1974,

Spitzer, J. J. A Premier on Box-Cox Estimation, The Review of Economics and Statistics 64, 1982, 307–313.

Straszaeim, M. R. An Econometric Analysis of the Urban Housing Markets, Columbia, New York 1975.

Suykens, J. A. K., Vandewalle, J. P. L., and De Moor, B. L. R. *Artificial Neural Networks for Modelling and Control of Non-Linear Systems*, Kluwer Academic Publishers, Boston, 1996, pp. 23–26.

Swales, George S. Jr. and Yoon, Young. Applying Artificial Neural Networks to Investment Analysis. *Financial Analysts Journal*, Vol. 48, No. 5, Sep/Oct 1992. Urban Studies, XXX, pp. 147–158.

Tay, D. P. H. and Ho, D. K. K. Artificial intelligence and the mass appraisal of residential apartments, *Journal of Property Valuation and Investment*, 1991/92, Vol. 10, No. 2, pp. 525–540.

Terry, V. G. and Julian, D. III. Real Estate Valuation, U.S.A. John Wiley & Sons, 1991.

Wasserman, Philip D., Neural computing: Theory and Practice, USA: Von Nostrand Reinhold, 1989.

Worzala E., Lenk M., and Silva A. An exploration of neural networks and its application to real estate valuation, *The Journal of Real Estate Research*, Vol. 10, No. 2, 1995, pp. 185–201.

Zurada, M. Jecek Introduction to Artificial Neural Systems, USA: West Publishing Company, 1992.

APPENDIX 1: Prediction Results of Hedonic Models and Neural Networks

Testing Data Set				Required Output		Error In Prediction Absolute Value					
Location				Hedonic $psf	Neural Network	Hedonic in $psf		Neural Network			
Ph	blk	flr	flat			Linear	Box-C	32K	84K	250K	32K/6
1	6	4	A	1540.602	0.2466	23.627	1.036	0.1045	0.1045	0.0368	0.1607
1	6	6	B	1538.354	0.2443	56.159	40.983	0.0411	0.0411	0.0618	0.2065
1	6	8	C	1560.445	0.2672	103.17	89.342	0.0254	0.0254	0.0513	0.1214
1	6	10	D	1574.244	0.2816	93.903	80.987	0.09	0.09	0.0397	0.2057
1	6	12	E	1571.602	0.2788	0.655	23.516	0.1432	0.1432	0.174	0.1595
1	6	14	F	1600.429	0.3088	13.556	33.41	0.141	0.141	0.1731	0.1236
1	6	16	G	1536.612	0.2425	39.073	81.463	0.3252	0.3252	0.2801	0.2467
1	6	18	H	1548.576	0.2549	55.707	99.185	0.1267	0.1267	0.1588	0.2978
1	14	13	A	1858.111	0.5765	107.89	95.664	0.0029	0.0029	0.066	0.111
1	14	15	B	1870.027	0.5889	105.61	93.099	0.0047	0.0047	0.071	0.1105
1	14	17	C	1846.444	0.5644	190.02	188.86	0.116	0.116	0.1021	0.1812
1	14	19	D	1858.292	0.5767	239.73	234.88	0.0145	0.0145	0.0217	0.1107
1	14	21	E	1721.639	0.4347	0.396	9.073	0.139	0.139	0.1268	0.0423
1	14	23	F	1737.652	0.4514	7.687	17.969	0.0841	0.0841	0.0977	0.0059
1	14	25	G	1779.962	0.4953	8.975	17.226	0.016	0.016	0.079	0.1089
1	14	27	H	1818.489	0.5353	17.5	13.18	0.2513	0.2513	0.2157	0.1419
2	3	3	A	1730.866	0.4443	20.121	17.074	0.3074	0.3074	0.2569	0.1609
2	3	6	B	1731.027	0.4445	57.051	55.856	0.2026	0.2026	0.1436	0.1365
2	3	9	C	1711.971	0.4247	7.988	14.69	0.0485	0.0485	0.0361	0.032
2	3	12	D	1743.95	0.4579	13.024	17.333	0.0434	0.0434	0.0412	0.065
2	3	15	F	1838.312	0.5559	243.2	250.94	0.2742	0.2742	0.3256	0.0166
2	3	17	G	1997.654	0.7215	83.592	98.699	0.1165	0.1165	0.0917	0.1502
2	3	19	H	2026.319	0.7513	168.4	174.46	0.3389	0.3389	0.3212	0.2682
7	2	5	A	1861.954	0.5805	252.09	291.73	0.0629	0.0629	0.0477	0.2279
7	2	7	B	1835.188	0.5527	197.88	232.78	0.0447	0.0447	0.0938	0.2705
7	2	13	C	1827.811	0.545	36.339	10.401	0.0958	0.0958	0.2871	0.3716
7	2	15	D	1877.156	0.5963	54.397	17.063	0.2377	0.2377	0.3346	0.3739
7	2	19	E	2175.298	0.906	163.08	209.29	0.1207	0.1207	0.0473	0.0148
7	2	27	F	2190.385	0.9217	137.87	188.33	0.1976	0.1976	0.0619	0.0411
7	2	29	G	2190.7	0.922	156.35	206.47	0.1892	0.1892	0.2043	0.1416
7	2	31	H	2265.746	1	239.5	287.59	0.1679	0.1679	0.2503	0.5067
7	10	3	A	1327.209	0.0249	338.27	332.3	0.1685	0.1685	0.1673	0.6877
7	10	9	B	1369.661	0.069	336.88	334.43	0.1425	0.1425	0.1162	0.6599
7	10	31	G	1491.577	0.1957	532.2	493.8	0.0712	0.0712	0.1024	0.7908
7	10	33	H	1527.639	0.2332	474.42	439.69	0.2056	0.2056	0.1739	0.7251

III

APPRAISING CONTAMINATED PROPERTY

Chapter 10

Comparative Studies of United States, United Kingdom and New Zealand Appraisal Practice: Valuing Contaminated Commercial Real Estate

William N. Kinnard, Jr.
University of Connecticut, President, Real Estate Counseling Group of Connecticut, USA

Elaine M. Worzala
Department of Finance & Real Estate, Colorado State University, Colorado, USA

Sandy G. Bond
Property Studies Department, Curtin University of Technology, WA, Australia

Paul J. Kennedy
Henderson Real Estate Strategy, United Kingdom

10.1 Introduction: Background to the Research Problem

The late 1980s and early 1990s saw the development of official govern-mental concern about merging risks of ownership and threats to the investment value of sites affected by contamination. These concerns were prompted by the earlier discovery of negative impacts on property values associated with a number of high-profile sites around the world: Love Canal, New York and Times Beach, Missouri in the United States; Lekkerkerk in the Netherlands; and Seveso in Italy, for example. Owners of both residential and commercial/industrial properties in or near these sites suffered substantial financial losses as a result of on-site and nearby contamination that was identified.

Concerns about contaminated property valuation issues were reinforced with the introduction of national legislation governing the environment. For example, the 1986 Superfund Amendment and Reauthorization Act (SARA), which amended the original Comprehensive Environmental Response Compensation and Liability Act (CERCLA), in the United States (US); the 1991 Resource Management Act (RMA) in New Zealand (NZ); and the 1995 Environment Act in the United Kingdom (UK). Together, these statutes and the regulations that have accompanied them have brought contaminated land issues forcibly to the attention of appraisers (labeled "valuers" in the UK and NZ), highlighting the need to take both contamination and "stigma" into account in property valuation assignments.

Uncertainty exists as to the levels and durations of whatever negative impact contamination will likely have on property values. This is due mainly to the difficulty in determining the existence and extent of contamination on or near a site, the likely duration and cost of remediation of any such contamination, and the lack of clarity within much of the legislation concerning legal liability and responsibility for remediation of on-site contamination.

In this arena of uncertainty about the market impacts of the risks associated with both on-site and nearby off-site contamination on property value, a portion of the valuation profession is confronted with the daunting task of both identifying and measuring whatever impact may exist. It is recognized that appraisers do not typically have the requisite skills to determine the existence and extent of on-site (or nearby off-site) contamination, or to estimate the cost of conducting an appropriate program of remediation. Nevertheless, it is inappropriate for all appraisers simply to avoid assignments to value property known or suspected to be impacted by contamination. Such impacts must be incorporated into their estimates of property value.

The objective of this chapter is to present and compare results from parallel surveys of appraisers conducted in the US, UK and NZ, which identify the valuation procedures and techniques used when valuing contaminated or contamination-impacted property. Such comparisons should provide insights into the extent to which proposals to standardize procedures to value contaminated or "stigmatized" properties are reasonable and feasible.

10.2 Summary Literature Review

A rich and growing body of literature in English has emerged in the US, the UK and NZ (and in Australia and Canada as well) which recommends and illustrates appropriate procedures and techniques to follow in valuing property which has on-site contamination, or is proximate to sources of known or suspected contamination. Nearly all the books and articles published on the subject of valuing real property impacted by on-site or nearby contamination focus on what is "proper" valuation methodology. The illustrative examples found in most publications and papers are general and frequently hypothetical, to illustrate the points being made. To date, little hard market information is provided, either in case studies or in tabulations of market behavior. One exception is the Mundy-McLean article (1998) that compares the results of several alternative independent valuation measures.

Much is known about the attitudes and behavior of lenders and investors toward contaminated properties. See, for example Adams & Mundy (1993); Bond, Kinnard, Worzala & Kapplin (1998); Kinnard & Worzala (1996); Mundy (1995); Richards (1997a); Wilson & Alarcon (1997); and Worzala & Kinnard (1997). Yet relatively little has been published on the practices of appraisers in valuing real property impacted by either on-site or off-site contamination. In the UK such studies have been undertaken and reported, by Kennedy (1997); Lizieri (1996); Richards (1995, 1997b); and Syms (1994, 1995, 1996a). Only Bond (1998) and Kinnard & Worzala (1998, 1999) studies, which are incorporated in this paper, have provided findings for NZ and the US, respectively.

The focus of this paper is three-fold. First, we present a comparative analysis of how appraisers go about estimating the impacts on the value of real property from on-site contamination, from proximity to off-site contamination, and from post-remediation "stigma" in the US, the UK and NZ. The similarities, the differences and the apparent reasons for those differences are presented.

Second, the extent to which reported practices of appraisers adhere to or differ from the procedures and techniques recommended in published articles and in papers presented at conferences of both academic and professional valuation societies is identified and analyzed.

Finally, there is an underlying theme in the published literature on the valuation of contaminated property (particularly in the UK) that there should be one appropriate, recommended valuation procedure that is followed consistently by practicing appraisers. To that end, the Guidelines provided by professional valuation societies in the US, the UK and New Zealand are considered in the context of the comparative findings from the parallel surveys by the authors, which identify the practices of appraisers of contaminated property.

10.2.1 Guidelines from Professional Societies

One stated reason for studying the practices of appraisers, and for analyzing valuation procedures that are available for appraising individual contaminated properties, is the concern that non-standard procedures, techniques and data sources may lead to inconsistent results among valuations produced for similarly contaminated properties under similar market conditions. In particular, Bond and Kennedy (1998) stress the need to standardize valuation techniques and procedures. Further, Richards (1995, 1997a,b) presents a recurring theme of the importance and desirability of developing "best practice" standards for the valuation of contaminated property, as well as the identification and measurement of "stigma".

It appears that the desire for greater consistency in valuation practice may be hindered by the limited scope of Guidelines from professional societies. These offer little beyond admonitions to perform competently, acquire technical assistance and expertise from others where necessary, and report fully on what has been done. Generally speaking, the Guidelines produced by the leading property valuation societies in five English-speaking countries[1] offer little substantive direction, few or no details on how the existence of contamination is best treated, and only limited illustrative materials to provide guidance to their members.

For the US and Canada in particular, the International Association of Assessing Officers (IAAO) published a *Standard on the Valuation of Property Affected by Environmental Contamination* in 1992. This 20-page document does provide some detail, some illustrations and some examples. However, it is internally inconsistent on whether the total amount of cost to remediate or the *present value* of that cost should be deducted from unimpaired market value as of the valuation date. Also in 1992, the Appraisal Standards Board of The Appraisal Foundation in Washington, DC issued a non-binding Advisory Opinion (AO-9) which mirrored the Appraisal Institute *Guide Note 8 (1992)* but with even less detail.

However, a task group has been established by the Appraisal Institute in the US to develop standards for determining the acceptability of applications of statistical and market survey techniques to the valuation of real property. In March 2000, the task group issued an exposure draft of a Proposed USPAP Statement on Appraisal Standards. Their stated objective is "to insure that any application of statistical or market survey technique (including hedonic modeling and contingent valuation) to the appraisal of real property is in conformance with the requirements of the modifications to Rule 702[2]

(Federal Rules of Evidence)", p. 2. This is an attempt to obtain consistency and standards in application so that the results will be acceptable as evidence of value in court settings. Until such statements are formalized and accepted, it will be for the courts to decide the acceptability, or otherwise, of the methods used for identifying and measuring the impact of environmental risks and stigma on market value.

In the US, the Courts are the arbiters of what is acceptable or non-acceptable practice. For example, the *Inmar Associates, Inc v. Borough of Carlstadt et al.* decision of the New Jersey Tax Court (112 N.J. 593; 549 A.2d 38: 1988) has received widespread recognition and acceptance. This is indicated in Ferruggia (1991). Its impact has extended beyond the US to Canada. Milligan (1995) quotes the *Inmar* Court to the effect that:

> "One thing is certain: the methodology for resolving the question [i.e., how to handle 'cost to remediate'] is not simply to deduct the cost of cleanup from a putative value of the property." (p. 19)

The difficulty in the US is that there are 50 separate state court systems, plus the Federal court system, plus various quasi-independent systems such as Federal Bankruptcy Court. Moreover, state courts, in particular, tend to differentiate among standards for adjudicating property tax valuation appeals, eminent domain (expropriation) cases, civil damage suits, and regulatory agency claims, when identifying what is "proper" (i.e., "admissible") procedure. The plethora of court-imposed "standards" has generally led to more diversity and inconsistency than would be the case if US appraisers relied primarily on the essays, case studies and illustrative examples contained in the professional and academic literature cited below.[3]

Guidance statements for the UK, NZ and Australia are likewise lacking in specific constructive recommendations. In the UK, for example, guidance from the RICS (1993, 1995) on the valuation of contaminated land has been restricted to information about the ranges of potential impacts on value, as well as the characteristic contaminants and remediation options. A similar statement has been produced by the New Zealand Property Institute (1995), based primarily upon the first guidance note produced by the RICS in 1993.

The Australian Property Institute (2000) outlines four main approaches to the valuation of contaminated land. These are: unaffected valuation basis; affected valuation basis; environmental balance sheet approach (the unaffected value less all costs associated with remedying the contamination: e.g., site investigations and environmental "stigma"); and comparative approach. However, the statement does not include detailed information about how (or when) these suggested approaches should be used. Appraisers are therefore required to interpret the requirements of each method.

Although the information and comments contained within each country's guidance statement are of some value, the lack of a recommended methodology has contributed to inconsistencies among techniques used in practice (Kennedy 1997). These inconsistencies are reflected in the survey results presented in this chapter.

10.2.2 Contaminated Property Valuation Literature

10.2.2.1 US Journals and Papers

The US literature on the effects of on-site contamination on the value of real property dates from approximately 1984, when the Campanella article (1984) appeared in *The Appraisal Journal*. Thereafter, only a handful of articles and papers appeared before 1991: e.g., Mundy (1988); Patchin (1988) and Kinnard (1989). It was Patchin (1988) who first publicly introduced the concept of "stigma" to the valuation of properties with on-site contamination.

In that 1988 article, Patchin also noted a dearth of "comparable sales" of contaminated properties. Indeed, he reported that "Corporate real estate personnel ... were practically unanimous in voicing the opinion that a seriously contaminated property will not sell at any price. More than one respondent stated the old adage 'Don't buy trouble'." (p. 9) Patchin goes on to report: "The first thing I concluded from the series of interviews was that seriously contaminated properties are generally unmarketable." (p. 9) Thus, the importance of marketability, especially when market value is to be estimated, was recognized and introduced.

Patchin also indicated, "lenders are understandably wary of contaminated properties ... There is virtually no chance of obtaining mortgage financing for a seriously contaminated property." (p. 11) This finding was reinforced by Mundy (1988) in his survey of institutional lenders. He found that they generally reported aversion to and avoidance of lending on properties either known or suspected to be contaminated.

Finally, Patchin (1988) identified the causes of market-value reduction experienced by contaminated properties as falling under three broad categories:

1. Cost of cleanup [now "remediation"]
2. Liability to the public
3. Stigma after cleanup [now "post-remediation stigma"]

In discussing "stigma after cleanup", Patchin observed, "a physical cleanup does not usually eliminate the value loss resulting from stigma ... The result is that even a cleaned-up property may suffer from reduced marketability." (p. 12)

Reiterating the virtual lack of market sales transactions data for individual contaminated properties, Patchin concludes that "a valuation tool that utilizes all of these [foregoing] factors is the capitalization rate, (which) is dependent on three major factors: (1) equity yield rate; (2) mortgage terms available; and (3) anticipated future appreciation or depreciation." (p. 13)

The US valuation literature of 1990–1992 (Appraisal Institute 1992; Kinnard 1992; Mundy 1992b,c; Patchin 1992) emphasized the necessity to use the framework of income capitalization to identify the *deductions* from unimpaired market value (i.e., market value as if non-contaminated), in order to estimate the market value of a contaminated property. That approach persists to the present (2000), with only a few exceptions. The general framework that is identified is to estimate unimpaired value ("as if non-contaminated") of a property, and then to deduct the following elements:

- Present value of the estimated cost to remediate (typically obtained from environmental engineers or technicians);
- Present value of the difference between expected revenues as if unimpaired and expected revenues as if impaired, stemming from a combination of reductions in occupancy and rent;
- Present value of increased operating expenses, including (but not restricted to): (1) increased insurance; (2) increased interest on debt; and (3) monitoring costs anticipated after remediation;
- Present value of holding costs: (1) insurance; (2) property taxes; and (3) repairs and maintenance.

Present value is calculated as a function of the anticipated duration of the remediation period, plus the marketing period (for sale or rental) forecast when remediation is completed. Over that period of time, the discount rate (or, sometimes, the capitalization rate) that is applied is adjusted upward to reflect the perception of increased risk associated with the existence or suspicion of on-site contamination. This increased discount rate for anticipated income is further increased by the likelihood of having to pay higher interest on debt (assuming debt financing is available at all) or relying on a higher proportion of equity investment, with its requirement of a higher rate of return. Anticipated *losses* or necessary *expenses*, on the other hand, are discounted at an applicable (and lower) "safe rate."

A further deduction is made for post-remediation "stigma." It is subtracted from the figure that remains after deducting the present value of the sum of estimated costs to remediate, estimated revenue reductions and estimated increased operating expenses and holding costs from the unimpaired value estimate. Initially, stigma was often reflected in further increases in the risk rates applied to the reduced income stream. In recent years, more sales transaction information in the US has been available from several sources. This is used to indicate the percentage difference between the sales price of a reme- diated property with "closure" from a regulatory body (or indemnification from a creditworthy seller) and the estimated unimpaired market value of the property, as of the same date. Thus, market sales transactions data have become sufficiently numerous and available[4] in the US (and, reportedly, Canada) for direct market evidence to be utilized in estimating post-remediation "stigma" (see, e.g., Bell 1996). Appraisers in the UK and NZ do not have market sales data available at this level, however. (See, for example, Jackson 2000; Mundy 1993; Simms et al. 1997; and Wilson 1997.)

There is growing evidence in the US that supports the use of sales of similarly contaminated properties following completion of remediation (with and without indemnification and/or "closure"). Nevertheless, most US authors still recommend increasing the discount rate (or capitalization rate) for the identification and measurement of post-remediation "stigma." This procedure is intended to recognize and account for the increased risk associ- ated with marketing a property that is known to have been contaminated. As the volume of available sales transactions data increases and becomes gener- ally known, however, it is anticipated that more "objective" sales evidence will be the major source of identifying and measuring post-remediation "stigma" in the US.

Nevertheless, alternative methods of identifying and quantifying "stigma" continue to be suggested. Weber (1996, 1998) utilizes Monte Carlo tech- niques to develop a probability estimate of post-remediation "stigma." Alternative approaches to identifying and measuring "stigma" have also been suggested by Mundy & McLean (1998); Roddewig (1996, 1997); and Elliot- Jones (1994, 1995, 1998). However, all but Mundy & McLean (1998) employ market sales transactions data of remediated properties (with and without indemnification), or seek to identify the appropriate surcharge for additional risk associated with "stigma." Except for Weber and Mundy & McLean, US authors generally follow the same path as most of those in the UK, by developing a subjectively identified increment for "stigma risk". These efforts are tempered by increasing market-wide knowledge of the growing body of market sales transactions data.

In situations (common in the UK) where market sales and market rental information relating to contaminated properties is not available, some authors (academics and practitioners alike) recommend the use of opinion survey research. The great majority of these UK surveys (similar to those of Richards 1995, 1997a,b and Syms (1994, 1996a,b)) have focused primarily on the atti- tudes and perceptions of "professionals" in real estate markets: lenders, bro- kers, and appraisers. In the US, most opinion survey research involving potential buyers or tenants (or sometimes sellers) has addressed "stigma" from proximity impacts, which is discussed in Kinnard (1997).

10.2.2.2 UK Journals and Papers

With the exception of Goldsmith (1980), the UK literature on the valuation of contaminated properties and the identification and measurement of "stigma" is quite recent. The great majority was published in 1995 and later. These include the works of Dixon (1995), Kennedy (1997) (and with Bond 1998), Lizieri (1996), Richards (1995, 1996, 1997a,b) and Syms (1994, 1995, 1996a,b).

Dixon (1995), Richards (1997a,b) and Syms (1996a) all agree that experience in the US provides valuable lessons for appraisers of contaminated properties in the UK. The US studies often indicate what *not* to do or to try, as well as what to do or try – and the reasons why. Following that precept, and recognizing that market sales transactions data are considerably less widely available to appraisers in the UK, they generally agree that some variant of the income capitalization approach must be applied in the valuation of contaminated commercial properties.

Dixon (1995), while questioning the use of "value as if clean" (i.e., unimpaired value) as the starting point, nevertheless agrees that the "cost to correct" (i.e., "remediation costs") should be deducted from "value as if clean." It is not clear, however, whether the recommendation is to deduct total "cost to correct" or its present value. The survey results of Richards (1995) generally agree: "The most appropriate valuation method was found to be a 'cost to correct' whereby the costs of remediation are deducted from an unimpaired value figure. Correspondingly, the discounted cash flow technique (DCF) was found to be the most appropriate method to produce a calculation of worth of a property." (p. v)

Richards also agrees with Patchin (1991a) that "It is also essential to consider the use of "stigma" within valuations and calculations of worth." (p. vi) Richards accepts Patchin's definition of "stigma" as "the value impact of environmentally-related uncertainty." Richards cautions, however, that "It must be remembered that this is a highly subjective adjustment to make and should therefore always be conducted with extreme caution." (p. vi) Further, open market value (OMV)[5] continues to dominate as the most appropriate valuation base for UK appraisers in many instances. However, the "existing use value (EUV) may produce a more realistic measure of value or worth, in the case of, for example, contaminated industrial operations." (p. vi)

Richards' conclusions, which carry over to his Ph.D. thesis (1997b), are presented in the Executive Summary (pp. vi–vii):

1. Valuers need some form of environmental education, so that they might better appreciate when the value of a property may be affected by contamination, and when they should seek further advice from environmental consultants or experts.

2. The "cost to correct" approach provides a logical and realistic valuation basis, and helps establish "best market practice." (In the US, "cost to correct" has been supplanted by "cost to remediate", in recognition of the demonstrated fact that the contamination may never be fully "corrected" or "cured.")

3. When "stigma" must be accounted for within valuations or calculations of contaminated land, either by adjusting the yield figure ("discount rate" in the US) or by making an end deduction or allowance, "it must be remembered that any such adjustment will be inherently subjective." (p. vi)

4. There is a great need for improvement to the guidance available to valuers for the valuation of contaminated properties.

5. A market-wide database, containing details of transactions that have involved contamination, "could significantly reduce the subjectivity of adjustments made in respect of 'stigma'." (p. vii)

Kennedy (1997) and Syms (1995, 1996a,b) concur that such a market-wide database would be extremely useful to appraisers analyzing contaminated properties. They also agree that there must be a value adjustment to reflect environmental "stigma." Nevertheless, Syms criticizes the yield adjustment procedure for measuring environmental "stigma" as excessively subjective. In its place, he suggests quantifying a capital value adjustment [which would, of course, require support from market evidence: sales and/or opinion surveys].

Syms' proposed model involves identifying factors that influence the perceptions of financial risks held by potential purchasers on a scale, which would assist in quantifying environmental "stigma." This is akin to the procedures suggested by Chalmers (1996), Mundy (1992a,b,c) and Patchin (1991b, 1992) in the US.

All the UK authors whose work is reported above appear to agree that the use of so-called "simplistic methods of valuation" for contaminated properties may well be justified pragmatically because of the severe limitations on the availability of market data (especially sales data) for contaminated properties. Additionally, there appears to be considerable agreement about proper methodology and procedure. After accounting for the differences in market data availability between the two market areas, the framework of valuation analysis considered "best practice" in the UK is strikingly similar to that advocated by many authors in the US.

10.2.2.3 Canadian and New Zealand Journals and Papers

There is relatively little market-specific analysis in the Canadian or New Zealand literature to distinguish either from that of the UK and the US. See, for example, Bond (1998) and Dybvig (1992). By inference, one can reasonably conclude that there are no major distinctions that differentiate the views of authors and researchers in Canada or New Zealand. The structural limitations on the ready availability of market sales transactions data (and market rental transactions data as well) that exist in the UK appear not to impact either the Canadian or the NZ market. Rather, the small size of the NZ market appears to be the limiting factor.

10.2.2.4 Market and Neighborhood Proximity Impact Studies: Stigma Identification and Measurement

There is another extensive body of articles and papers that deal with identifying and quantifying any negative impact on the market prices of residential properties that are proximate to, and/or with an unobstructed view of, some source of alleged hazard to human health and safety. These proximity impact studies address "hazards" to the value of the allegedly impacted residential properties themselves. They do this by focusing on "stigma" that reflects locational obsolescence associated with off-site, but nearby and/or visible contamination.

None of the representative proximity impact studies cited in the selected references include the valuation or appraisal of an individual residential (or commercial) property or even demonstrate how to do so in the context of "stigma". Instead, they focus on the measurement, on a market-wide basis, of one facet of accrued depreciation: locational obsolescence. (See Guntermann 1995; Reichert 1992, 1997, 1999; Smolen et al. 1992; Thayer et al. 1992.)

The same lack of application to individual property valuation or appraisal is apparent in the studies cited in the extensive bibliography contained in Kinnard (1998). These include Bryant and Epley (1998); Delaney and Timmons (1992); Roulac (1993). Still others are presentations of suggested methodology (Manning 1992; McLean & Mundy 1998), similar in intent and focus to those articles and papers cited earlier in this paper as "Methodological Essays."[6]

10.3 Surveys of Practice: The US, The UK, and NZ

This section of this chapter outlines the methodology of the surveys of US, UK and NZ practice. The survey of UK practice was undertaken in late 1996. The NZ and US studies were both conducted in 1998, using adaptations of the survey vehicle developed and used in the UK. The contents of the survey forms may be inferred from the topics covered in the summaries of results provided in Appendix Tables 1, 2 and 3.

10.3.1 Objectives of the Survey

The primary aim of each study was to identify the approaches used by appraisers when providing advice or producing valuations that reflect the impact of on-site (or nearby off-site) contamination on the value of real property. A secondary objective was to identify the extent to which respondent appraisers employed the valuation methods and techniques recommended in the literature (and guidelines) appropriate to their respective national market environments. Based on those findings, the final objective was to conclude whether it is feasible to identify and recommend appropriate techniques to be used for this type of valuation.

10.3.1.1 The Survey Samples

Although there is potential for all appraisers to be given assignments to value a parcel of vacant land or an improved property affected by contamination, it is likely that only a fraction of them will actually become involved in such work. The latter experienced "sub-group" are more likely to respond to a survey investigating valuation methods for valuing sites affected by contamination. Given the large number of appraisers in each of the three countries (the US [and Canada], the UK and NZ), a targeted approach of contacting appraisers known to work on contaminated properties was used.

To enhance the validity of comparative findings between the studies, a similar survey was used in all three countries. For the New Zealand and US surveys a simplified and shortened version of the eighteen-page UK survey instrument was adopted. These questionnaires were further adapted for relevancy to their particular market.

Each survey included questions to determine the respondent's professional background and level of experience, as well as the valuation techniques and information sources he or she used to identify and value individual parcels of real property affected by contamination. Questions were also included to ascertain how respondents account for the possible effects of on-site and off-site contamination, and of post-remediation "stigma," on each valuation variable (i.e., its quantification and integration into estimates of value). Similarly, the sources of information used to determine those effects were sought.

10.3.1.2 The Survey Responses

Kennedy (1997) developed a lengthy and detailed questionnaire that was circulated to 100 potential respondents in the UK selected from a variety of recommendations and sources. An overall usable response rate of 54% was achieved after two follow-up reminders.

The NZ surveys were administered by mail in December 1997 to the fifteen NZ appraisers who replied to a call for participation (which was sent to all 2000 NZPI members, approximately half of whom held practicing certificates). This poor response was probably indicative of the relative lack of experience of NZ appraisers with valuing contaminated property. Seven responses were received. This represented an overall response rate of 47% after a single follow-up reminder.

In June 1998, Kinnard and Worzala (1998) administered a mail questionnaire survey to a targeted, pre-selected group of 208 appraisers in the US and Canada. The target group consisted of 192 appraisers in the US and 16 in Canada. After 5 questionnaires were returned as undeliverable and 9 were returned blank, a total of 194 potential responses remained (183 from the US and 11 from Canada). From this group, 90 usable responses were received. Of the usable responses, 85 were from the US and 5 from Canada. Because of the small number from Canada, all 90 responses were analyzed as a single group. The response rate was over 45%.

10.4 Comparison of Survey Responses: US, UK, and NZ

10.4.1 Introduction

This section presents a summary of the major findings that emerged from the analysis of the three surveys. In the interest of brevity, only a limited amount of data is cited directly. In Appendix Tables 1, 2 and 3, responses to those questions that were contained in all three countries' surveys relating specifically to how appraisers value contaminated property, and how they identify and measure the risk and uncertainty that constitutes "stigma", are compared. Those responses are summarized in the following text.

10.4.2 Professional Background and Level of Experience

The first few questions identified each respondent's professional background and level of experience. The results indicate that respondents in the UK are concentrated in urban areas. Just under half (48%) came from London, 15% came from four towns outside London and the remaining 37% came from 20 regional towns. As a group, these respondents had more than 15 years of general practical experience. Nearly all (96%) were qualified (i.e., professionally designated) and 76% had been qualified for more than five years.

In terms of experience with calculations of market value involving individual sites affected by contamination, slightly over half (56%) of the UK respondents were responsible for between 1 and 25 of such calculations for the one year period (1995); 11% for between 26 and 50; and 4% for over 100.

However, more than a quarter (30%) had not conducted or supervised any valuations of contaminated property.

In NZ, surprisingly, while respondents were geographically spread, one from each community (4 from the North Island and 3 from the South Island), none were from major urban areas. All respondents were qualified registered appraisers (Associate Member designation), with the great majority (85%) having been so for more than five years. All respondents had carried out at least 1–25 valuations of property where contamination was an issue within the last five years.

In the US (and Canada), responses came from 29 states (and 3 Provinces). The most frequent states of origin were California and New Jersey, with 8 responses each. All but two of the US respondents were licensed or certified in one or more states. Sixty-five (76%) of respondents held the MAI designation, followed by 44 CREs, 15 SRAs (some of whom were dually designated as MAIs), 10 ASAs and 4 AACIs (Canada). Over half the respondents (52%) reported more than 10 years' experience in appraising individual contaminated properties. Also, 39% indicated they had over 10 years' experience in identifying and measuring "stigma".

10.4.3 Types of Contaminated Sites and Properties Valued

Respondents were asked to identify types of properties affected by contamination on which they had provided advice or appraisals. A number of land uses were specified in each country. In the UK, for example, 10 (18%) had valued former landfill sites and 17% former gasworks. In New Zealand, land uses specified included: timber treatment sites (57%); tannery sites (14%); and former landfill sites (14%). Similarly, in the US the examples were wide-ranging, with over 75% of the respondents indicating that vacant industrial land, improved industrial properties, vacant commercial land and improved commercial properties were all "frequently appraised."

10.4.4 Valuation Methods Employed

The UK survey listed a capital-based method and three income-based methods (income; profits and residual)[7] whereas the New Zealand and US surveys did not differentiate among the income-based methods and so listed only two valuation approaches: sales comparison and income capitalization.[8] The income capitalization approach was further sub-categorized between the discounted cash flow technique and direct capitalization.

In each country over half the respondents reported using more than one valuation method or technique for each contaminated property assignment. This may be interpreted in two ways: the methods employed may differ according to site type; or some respondents may use more than one method in a single assignment. Although such a combined approach is common in US texts (and practice), and recommended practice in NZ, the UK literature generally recommends valuations produced by a single method only.

It is notable that most respondents in the US (80%) reported that they used the sales comparison approach whenever required data were available. This is in contrast to both the UK (0%) and the NZ (29%) responses. Moreover, comments made by US respondents indicated that the required data were generally available, which probably explains the higher rate of use (in their opinion) compared to the other two countries. Many respondents also indicated that they supplement the findings based on a sales comparison approach with opinion-based survey research, preferably interviews with buyers and lenders.

The use of a full DCF approach in appraisals also varied widely by country. In the UK, only 4 (7%) respondents indicated that they used full DCF techniques. In NZ, 29% reported using full DCF approaches but only between 5% and 25% of the time. In contrast, 64% of US respondents reported that they used DCF models (although not always). These results confirm expectations that income-based methods of limited technical sophistication are used to value sites affected by contamination in the UK and NZ. The US respondents appear to use more advanced techniques more regularly.

10.4.5 Incorporating Remediation Costs into Value Estimates

Over half of the NZ (57%) and US (60%) respondents deduct the present value of anticipated remediation costs from unimpaired value (i.e., value as if non-contaminated). In contrast, only 24% of UK respondents do so. At the same time, a large minority (43% UK; 43% NZ; 52% US) use a capital deduction (of the total cost, not its present value). The popularity of the latter relatively simplistic approach represents a source of some concern, as it necessarily produces a lower value than if the present value of those costs were deducted. Further, the deduction of total (non-discounted) cost has become disfavored by state courts in the US. This was noted earlier in the discussion of the Inmar decision in New Jersey.

An additional source of concern in the UK is the fact that 20% of those respondents claim to use a yield rate adjustment to reflect contamination costs, although only 7% report the use of a "full DCF approach". This approach is criticized by several texts, even in the UK. In contrast, none of the

NZ and US respondents report using the simplistic technique of adjusting a discount or yield rate to account for the present value impact of contamination costs. In this regard, results produced by the NZ and US surveys suggest more supportable techniques are used than those noted in the UK survey.

10.4.6 Information Sources for Estimating Environmental Risks and Uncertainties

Typically, information and data limitations were used to justify the use of simplistic approaches to quantify perceived risks and uncertainties ("stigma") caused by contamination in all three countries. Seventy percent of US respondents, 66% of UK respondents, and 50% of NZ respondents typically use comparable evidence from non-contaminated sites or improved properties in locations similar to that of the subject property to quantify the value adjustment required for perceived financial risks ("stigma"). Assuming the non-contaminated sales properties are truly competitive or "comparable" with a subject property that has been remediated, the difference may be used as a measure of post-remediation "stigma." Similarity in location is not necessarily sufficient to make a property a "comparable" for the subject property.

Over half of the US (59%) and UK (53%) respondents and 83% of NZ respondents use evidence from sites similar in contamination type but not location. Three quarters or more of the NZ (83%) and US (75%) respondents but only 38% of the UK respondents use evidence from sites similar in both location and type of contamination (when available). As stated earlier, the availability of such data is likely to be restricted.

Only 6% of the UK respondents and 17% of the NZ respondents specified the use of some form of cash flow risk analysis. This may reflect limitations in the quantitative valuation methods used by the majority of respondents in those two surveys. On the other hand, 43% of US respondents reported using DCF analysis to identify and measure the impact of perceived environmental risk. This reinforces the finding that more sophisticated analytical methods are employed more widely in the US.

At the same time, over half of the US (55%) and NZ (57%) respondents also relied primarily or heavily on their own experience. This high degree of subjectivity was apparently offset, at least partially, by the simultaneous use of other information sources specified. Few respondents mentioned the published literature in academic or professional journals as a useful or important source of guidance or information on how best to approach the valuation of a contaminated or "stigmatized" property. This was the case despite the robust (and growing) body of pertinent articles and papers cited in the selected references, and discussed earlier in this chapter.

10.4.7 Incorporating Environmental Risks and Uncertainties into Value Estimates

The preferred method, reported by respondents in both the UK (84%) and NZ (83%), in developing value estimates that identify and measure perceived financial and investment risks ("stigma") associated with on-site contamination at a property was to adjust the discount rate upward. In the US 61% report employing such an adjustment. US respondents also indicated that they regularly make adjustments in one or more components of the income capitalization approach in order to reflect the increased perceived risks of purchasing or investing in contaminated properties. Most commonly, US respondents indicated that they increased the capitalization rate (67%), while 58% reduced rental income.

Whenever possible, US respondents rely on sales transactions information to identify the percentage reduction in unimpaired market value that is attributable to post-remediation "stigma". Generally, US respondents appear to prefer using such a capital value reduction (76%, as opposed to 44% in the UK and 33% in NZ).

The much heavier reliance on DCF modeling and analysis in the US and NZ is reflected in Appendix Table 3, where 58% of the respondents in the US and 50% in NZ specify use of a cash flow adjustment (i.e., a reduction in or omission of anticipated cash flows in specified years, most commonly during the remediation period). Only 9% of the UK respondents indicated that such a cash flow adjustment would be incorporated into their analysis.

As with the use of comparable sales transactions data to develop measures of "stigma", the selection of methods to incorporate perceived environmental risks and uncertainties into value estimates appears to depend heavily on the quantity and quality of information available concerning financial and investment risks. The predominance of the upward yield adjustment approach in the UK and NZ appears to confirm the limited availability of sales transaction data in these countries, as well as the simple, straightforward approaches to individual property valuations. Further, these data limitations also necessitate the reliance on subjective judgments reported by respondents.

Responses from US and (to a lesser degree) NZ appraisers indicate greater reliance on market evidence, not only of sales transactions but also of income variations associated with on-site contamination at a property. These results also explain the greater reliance on DCF analysis, particularly in the US.

10.4.8 Comments by Respondents

Only the US-Canadian and UK respondents took advantage of the opportunity to comment on any aspect of the valuation of individual properties affected by contamination. Space was provided for such comments in the final section of the questionnaire in all three surveys. The issue most frequently raised by US respondents was the need for more and better market sales transactions data to support their estimates of "stigma". In the UK, the importance of market and investor perceptions in the assessment of perceived financial risks was highlighted, as were the problems associated with market information limitations. As these limitations increase in number and magnitude, the reliance on the appraiser's judgment (i.e., subjective expert assessment of likely market and investor risk perceptions) also increases.

The comments of several US respondents also indicated that a property would be non-marketable, and therefore have a market value of zero, if the present value of the cost to remediate exceeded estimated unimpaired market value.

10.5 Summary

Although many of the respondents to the surveys of valuation practice in the UK and (especially) NZ had limited practical experience in the valuation of sites affected by contamination, all reported and asserted a particular interest in the subject area. The response rate to the NZ survey was disappointing, although not surprising, given the suspected small number of appraisers in NZ with experience in valuing contaminated property. Because of this, however, broad generalizations about practice in that country cannot be made.

The approaches adopted by UK appraisers have been characterized as "typically simplistic."[9] Most value estimates are underpinned by limited market data and quantitative analysis. In addition, the survey results suggest that some appraisers may ignore certain value effects of contamination (e.g., time effects). Further, little emphasis is given to the analysis of perceived financial risks.

US (and Canadian) appraisers are rather more experienced in the valuation of contaminated properties than are their counterparts in the UK and NZ. Moreover, they believe that sufficient market data are frequently available to enable them to base their estimates of individual property value "as if contaminated" on sales transactions, rentals, and market-derived discount rates (and capitalization rates). They are also remarkably self-confident about their skills and abilities to estimate the market value of contaminated properties competently and convincingly.

At the same time, US (and Canadian) appraisers are prone to rely more heavily on licensed professional environmental engineers and technicians for estimates of both cost to remediate and the duration and magnitude of the remediation process, than are those in the UK and NZ.

A wide range of methods is reported to be employed by US and Canadian appraisers. Differences of opinion about how best to employ those methods are evident. Comments made throughout the questionnaire responses, indicate strongly that few US or Canadian appraisers experienced in the valuation of individual contaminated properties believe that there is (or, indeed, should be) a single, standardized approach that is universally appropriate. As a result, none is recommended. Because of their strong belief in the efficacy of real estate markets, US respondents in particular typically made it clear that they apply whatever method(s) or procedure(s) can be applied by using whatever market data (sales, rentals, rates) are available to them in each particular assignment.

This is in contrast to the research findings of Kennedy (1997) that variations in methods used, in the UK at least, may have substantial impacts on estimates of property value. It is uncertain, however, whether these impacts are a function of the different methods employed, or of the limitations on availability of market data about comparable sales or rental transactions. Either factor, and certainly both in combination, would limit the reliability of market value estimates. As noted previously in this paper, the US (and Canadian) respondents generally believe that sufficient market data on sales transactions, rentals, and both discount and capitalization rates, are available for effective use both in estimating the market value of individual contaminated properties and in measuring post-remediation "stigma". Nevertheless, those same US appraisers also want more and better market data. In this respect, they agree with their counterparts in the UK and NZ.

The greater awareness of "stigma" by the US (and Canadian) respondents, compared to that of those in the UK and NZ surveys, was reflected in their numerous comments. They highlighted the identification and measurement of "stigma" most frequently as an issue requiring further investigation. These concerns addressed both proximity "stigma" and post-remediation "stigma."

Respondents in all three surveys believe strongly that some variant of the income capitalization approach is necessary to identify and measure the deductions from unimpaired market value that are appropriate and necessary to estimate market value "as is" for a contaminated property. Both increased discount rates (and capitalization rates) and reduced cash flows are used whenever they can be supported by market evidence and analysis. Moreover, whenever data on sales transactions for similarly contaminated properties are available, those data are relied on to identify both appropriate deductions from unimpaired market value and any post-remediation "stigma", in order to estimate market value "as is" (i.e., "as contaminated").

The diversity of data availability from market to market tends to argue against a single "preferred" valuation method to date, although refinement of recommended techniques over time is likely to reduce spreads between value estimates of a contaminated property "as is" that are based on different valuation procedures and techniques. Further research is warranted to test the reliability of the market value estimates of individual contaminated properties derived by appraisers in each country. Such studies would help to determine whether using different approaches based on more market sales data (as is the case in the US) or whether applying standardized approaches, especially in the absence of sufficient data on market sales transactions (as in the UK), provides more reliable estimates of value.

Meanwhile, one important contribution of this paper is that it reports what individual valuation practitioners do, attempt to do, or consider doing when they appraise a single property with on-site contamination, or with off-site contamination nearby. Their infrequent reliance on the results of proximity-impact or view-impact studies (their own or those conducted by others) indicates the need for better dissemination of market impact study findings. Similarly, few cited published studies of post-remediation "stigma" as sources on which they relied. More regular publication of such findings in professional appraisal/valuation journals is recommended as an important first step. This should be supplemented with more systematic cross-referencing of articles from professional and academic journals, and papers presented at meetings of academic and professional practitioner societies.

NOTES

[1] See Appraisal Institute (AI) in the US (1991), International Association of Assessing Officers (IAAO) in the US and Canada (1992), Royal Institution of Chartered Surveyors (RICS) in the UK (1995, 1997), New Zealand Property Institute (NZPI) (1995), and Australian Property Institute (API) (1994).

[2] The suggested Rule 702, Testimony by Experts, states the circumstances under which "an expert by knowledge, skill, experience, training, or education" can testify and includes, "(1) the testimony is based upon sufficient facts or data, (2) the testimony is the product of reliable principles and methods, and (3) the witness has applied the principles and methods reliably to the facts of the case", (Proposed Amendments to the Federal Rules of Evidence, December 6, 1999, p. 17).

[3] See Jaconetty (2000) for a detailed discussion of conflicting decisions that have been issued by State Supreme Courts and Courts of Appeal over the decade of the 1990s.

[4] In this context, "sufficient numerous" means perhaps 15–20 verifiable and quantifiable sales of remediated properties of all types (vacant land; improved residential, commercial and industrial) with all types of contaminants, throughout the United States in any given year.

[5] In US terms this would be equivalent to market value as if unimpaired.

[6] Without application of the results to the valuation of individual properties, proximity impact studies are not "mass appraisals" according to the definitions promulgated by the International Association of Assessing Officers. See IAAO 1990, 1996, 1997.

[7] See Bond & Kennedy (1998), p. 11 and 23; and Richards (1997b), p. 94–104. The three income-based "methods" account for the effect of increased risk from on-site contamination on property value through either (1) an increase in the capitalization rate, (2) a decrease

in forecast net operating income, based on anticipations of diminished revenues, and/or (3) an increase in the yield rate (discount rate). Richards (1997b) in particular ascribes these alternative methods to the initial work of Patchin (1988), Mundy (1992a,b), and Chalmers & Jackson (1996).

[8] The US-Canadian and NZ respondents did not distinguish between Direct Capitalization and Discounted Cash Flow modeling as different income capitalization "methods." Rather, both are included under the "income approach" label. This is consistent with the standard appraisal texts in the US (and Canada).

[9] Bond & Kennedy (1998), p. 13.

REFERENCES

Adams, V. and Mundy, B. "Attitudes and Polices of Lending Institutions Toward Environmental Impairment," *Environmental Watch*, 1(4): 1–4, Winter 1993.

Australian Property Institute, *Guideline to the Valuation of Contaminated Land*, 2000

Appraisal Institute, "Guide Note 8: The Consideration of Hazardous Substances in the Appraisal Process," *Standards of Professional Appraisal Practice of the Appraisal Institute*. Chicago, IL: The Appraisal Institute, February 1999 (Effective January 28, 1994), pp. D-1 through D-2.

Appraisal Institute, *Measuring the Effects of Hazardous Materials Contamination on Real Estate Value: Techniques and Applications*. Papers and proceedings of the 1991 Appraisal Institute Symposium, Philadelphia, PA. William N. Kinnard, Jr., Editor. Chicago, IL: The Appraisal Institute, 1992.

Bell, R., "Ten Standard Classifications of Detrimental Conditions," *Right of Way*, 43(4): 28–29, July/August 1996.

Bond, S., *The Appraisal of Contaminated Land in New Zealand Practice*. Fourteenth American Real Estate Society Conference in conjunction with the International Real Estate Society. Monterey, California, April 15–18, 1998.

Bond, S. and Kennedy, P. *The Valuation of Contaminated Land: NZ and UK Practice Compared*. Joint conference of the European Real Estate Society and American Real Estate and Urban Economics Association. Maastricht, The Netherlands, June 1998.

Bond, S., Kinnard, W. N. Jr., Worzala, E., and Kapplin, S. "Market Participants' Reactions Toward Contaminated Property in New Zealand and the USA," *Journal of Property Valuation & Investment*, 16(3): 251–272, 1998.

Bryant, J. and D. Epley, "Cancerphobia: Electromagnetic Fields and Their Impact on Residential Values," *Journal of Real Estate Research*, 12(1): 115–129, 1998.

Campanella, J., "Valuing Partial Losses in Contamination Cases," *The Appraisal Journal*, 52(2): 301–304, April 1984.

Chalmers, J. and T. Jackson, "Risk Factors in the Appraisal of Contaminated Property," *The Appraisal Journal*, 64(1): 44–68, January 1996.

Delaney, C. and D. Timmons, "High Voltage Power Lines: Do They Affect Residential Property Value?", *Journal of Real Estate Research*, 7(3): 315–330, 1992.

Dixon, T., *Lessons from America: Appraisal and Lender Liability Issues in Contaminated Real Estate*. Reading, England: The College of Estate Management, 1995.

Dybvig, L., *Contaminated Real Estate: Implications for Real Estate Appraisers*, Appraisal Institute of Canada, 1992.

Elliot-Jones, M., "Part II: Valuation of Post-Cleanup Property – The Economic Basis for Stigma Damages," *Bureau of National Affairs Toxics Law Reporter*, December 16, 1994.

Elliot-Jones, M., *Bixby Ranch: Some Observations on Plaintiffs Expert's Appraisal of Post-Clean-Up 'Stigma'*, San Francisco, CA: Foster Associates, 1995.

Elliot-Jones, M., *Markets for Contaminated Properties*, San Francisco, CA: Bala Research, Inc., 1998.

Ferruggia, F., "Valuation of Contaminated Property: New Jersey's *Inmar* Decision," *Assessment Digest*, 13(2): 2–6, March/April 1991.

Goldsmith, D., *Reclamation of Contaminated Land – Some Consideration of Land Values*. Paper presented at Reclamation of Contaminated Land, Society of Chemical Industry, London, 1980.

Guntermann, K. "Sanitary Landfills, Stigma and Industrial Land Value," *Journal of Real Estate Research*, 10(5): 531–542, 1995.

Jackson, T. O., "The Effects of Previous Environmental Contamination on Industrial Real Estate Prices," *Valuation 2000 Papers and Proceedings*. Chicago, IL: Valuation 2000 Alliance, 2000, pp. 59–69.

Jaconetty, T. M., "Property Tax Trends: Approaches to Valuation of Contaminated Property," *Journal of Property Tax Management*, 84–88, Spring 2000.

International Association of Assessing Officers, *Standard on the Valuation of Property Affected by Environmental Contamination*, Chicago, IL, 1992.

Kennedy, P., *Investment Valuation of Contaminated Land and UK Practice: A Study with Special Reference to Former Gasworks*. Unpublished Ph.D. Thesis. The Nottingham Trent University, England, 1997.

Kinnard, W. N., Jr., "Analyzing the Stigma Effect of Proximity to Hazardous Materials Sites," *Environment Watch*, 2(4): 1–4, 1989.

Kinnard, W. N., Jr., "Measuring the Effects of Contamination on Property Values," *Environmental Watch*, 4(4): 1, 3–4, 1992.

Kinnard, W. N., Jr., *Stigma and Property Values: A Summary and Review of Research and Literature*. Paper presented at Appraisal Institute Symposium, Washington, DC, June 1997.

Kinnard, W. N., Jr. and Worzala, E. *Evolving Attitudes and Policies of Institutional Investors and Lenders Toward On-Site and Nearby Property Contamination*. The Cutting Edge Conference, Bristol: RICS, 1996.

Kinnard, W. N., Jr. and Worzala, E. *The Valuation of Contaminated Properties and Associated Stigma: A Comparative Review of Practice and Thought in the US, the UK and New Zealand*. The Cutting Edge Conference, Leicester: RICS, 1998.

Kinnard, W. N., Jr. and Worzala, E. "How North American Appraisers Value Contaminated Property and Associated Stigma", *The Appraisal Journal*, 67(3): 269–279, July 1999.

Lizieri, C., Palmer, S., Charlton M., and Finlay, L., *Valuation Methodology and Environmental Legislation: A Study of the UK Commercial Property Industry*. The Cutting Edge Conference, Bristol: RICS, 1996.

Manning, C. "Managing Environmental Risk and Investment Opportunities to Maximize Shareholder Wealth," *Journal of Real Estate Research*, 7(3): 351–359, 1992.

McLean, D. and B. Mundy, "The Addition of Contingent Valuation and Conjoint Analysis to the Required Body of Knowledge for Estimation of Environmental Damages to Real Property," *Journal of Real Estate Practice and Education*, 1(1): 1–19, 1998.

Milligan, P., "Contaminated Land or Toxic Real Estate: Lessons from Ontario," *Journal of Property Tax Management*, 16(3): 1–24, Winter 1995.

Mundy, B., "Stigma and Value," *The Appraisal Journal*, 60(1): 7–14, January 1992a.

Mundy, B., "The Impact of Hazardous Materials on Property Value," *The Appraisal Journal*, 60(2): 155–162, April 1992b.

Mundy, B., "The Impact of Hazardous and Toxic Materials on Property Value: Revisited," *The Appraisal Journal*, 60(4): 463–471, October 1992c.

Mundy, B., "Contamination, Fear, and Industrial Property Transactions," *SIOR Professional Report*, Washington, DC: Society of Industrial and Office Realtors, 52(3): 17–19, May–June 1993.

Mundy, B., "Environmentally Impaired Property and the SIOR," *SIOR Professional Report*, 54(2): 17–20, Spring 1995.

Mundy, B. and D. McLean, "Using the Contingent Value Approach for Natural Resource and Environmental Damage Applications," *The Appraisal Journal*, 66(3): 290–297, July 1998.

New Zealand Property Institute, "New Zealand Institute of Valuers Guidance Note 3: The Valuation of Contaminated Land – An Overview and Bibliography," *New Zealand Valuers' Technical Handbook*, January 1995.

Patchin, P., "Valuation of Contaminated Properties," *The Appraisal Journal*, 56(1): 7–16, January 1988.

Patchin, P., "Contaminated Properties – Stigma Revisited," *The Appraisal Journal*, 59(2): 167–173, April 1991a.

Patchin, P., "The Valuation of Contaminated Properties," *Real Estate Issues*, 16(2): 50–54, Fall/Winter 1991b.

Patchin, P., "Valuing Contaminated Properties: Case Studies," *Measuring the Effects of Hazardous Materials Contamination on Real Estate Values: Techniques and Applications*, Chicago, IL: The Appraisal Institute, 1992.

Reichert, A., "Impact of a Toxic Waste Superfund Site on Property Values," *The Appraisal Journal*, LXV(4): 381–392, October 1997.

Reichert, A., "The Persistence of Contamination Effects: A Superfund Site Revisited," *The Appraisal Journal*, LXVII(2): 125–135, April 1999.

Reichert, A., M. Small and S. Mohanty, "The Impact of Landfills on Residential Property Values," *The Journal of Real Estate Research*, 7(3): 297–314, 1992.

Richards, T., *A Changing Landscape: The Valuation of Contaminated Land and Property*. Reading, England: The College of Estate Management, 1995.

Richards, T., "Valuing Contaminated Land and Property: Theory and Practice," *Journal of Property Valuation and Investment*, 14(4): 6–17, 1996.

Richards, T., *Is It Worth the Risk? The Impact of Environmental Risk on Property Investment Valuation*. Reading, England: The College of Estate Management, 1997a.

Richards, T., *An Analysis of the Impact of Contamination and Stigma on the Valuation of Commercial Property Investments*. Unpublished Ph.D. Thesis. The University of Reading, England, 1997b.

Roddewig, R., "Stigma, Environmental Risk and Property Value: 10 Critical Inquiries," *The Appraisal Journal*, 64(4): 375–387, October 1996.

Roddewig, R., "Using the Cost of Environmental Insurance to Measure Contaminated Property Stigma," *The Appraisal Journal*, 65(3): 304–308, July 1997.

Roulac, S., "Environmental Due Diligence Information Requirements and Decision Criteria," *Journal of Real Estate Research*, 8(1): 139–148, 1993.

Royal Institution of Chartered Surveyors (RICS), "Valuation Guidance Note 11 (VGN 11): Environmental Factors Contamination and Valuation," in RICS *Manual of Guidance Notes*, Third Edition, RICS, London, 1993.

Royal Institution of Chartered Surveyors (RICS), *Land Contamination Guidance for Chartered Surveyors*, London, England: RICS, 1995.

Simons, R., W. Bowen and A. Sementelli, "The Effect of Underground Storage Tanks on Residential Property Values at Cuyahoga County, OH," *Journal of Real Estate Research*, 14(1/2): 29–42, 1997.

Smolen, G.E., G. Moore and L. Conway, "Economic Effects of Hazardous Chemicals and Proposed Radioactive Waste Landfills on Surrounding Real Estate Values," *Journal of Real Estate Research*, 7(3): 283–296, 1992.

Syms, P., *The Post-Remediation Values of Contaminated Land*. ISVA Half-Day Seminar, United Kingdom: ISVA, 1994.

Syms, P., *Environmental Impairment: An Approach to Valuation*. The Cutting Edge Conference, England: RICS, 1995.

Syms, P., *Perceptions of Risk in the Appraisal of Contaminated Real Estate*. Working Paper, School of Urban and Regional Studies, Sheffield Hallam University, Sheffield, UK, 1996a.

Syms, P., *Environmental Impairment: Further Developments in an Approach to Valuation*. The Cutting Edge Conference, Bristol, England: RICS, 1996b.

Thayer, M., H. Albers and M. Rahmatian, "The Benefits of Reducing Exposure to Waste Disposal Sites, A Hedonic Housing Value Approach," *The Journal of Real Estate Research*, 7(3): 265–282, 1992.

Weber, B., *Stigma-Unquantified Risk?* The Cutting Edge Conference, Bristol, England, 1996.

Weber, B., "Stigma: Quantifying Murphy's Law," *Urban Land*, 57(6): 12, 106, June 1998.

Wilson, A., "Emerging Approaches to Impaired Property Valuation," *The Appraisal Journal*, 64(2): 155–170, April 1996.

Wilson, A. and A. Alarcon, "Lender Attitudes Toward Source and Non-Source Impaired Property Mortgages," *The Appraisal Journal*, 65(4): 396–400, October 1997.

Worzala, E. and W. N. Kinnard, Jr., "Investor and Lender Reactions to Alternative Sources of Contamination," *Real Estate Issues*, 22(2): 42–48, August 1997.

APPENDIX

Table 1: Methods of Valuing Contaminated Property

	Percent "Yes"[1]		
	U.S.	U.K.	New Zealand
Value as if non-contaminated with a disclaimer:	54%	–	–
Less total cost to remediate	52%	43%	57%
Less P.W. cost to remediate	35%	24%	43%
Less P.W. cost to remediate and stigma	66%	–	57%
Value as contaminated	85%	–	29%
Decline Assignment	0%	0%	0%
Sales Comparison Approach	80%	0%	29%
Income Capitalization Approach	80%	100%	100%
Adjustments:			
Reduced Rental Income	61%	80%	33%
Increased Vacancy Rate	49%	–	–
Increased Capitalization Rate	70%	–	–
Increased Discount Rate	66%	80%	83%
Increased Debt Interest Rate	38%	–	–
Reduced Loan-to-Value Ratio	42%	–	–
Reduced Amortization Period	30%	–	–
Increased Equity Yield Rate	50%	–	–
Increased Equity Dividend Rate	41%	–	–
Discounted Cash Flow Model	64%	9%	29%

[1] Total number of "Yes" responses divided by total "Yes" plus total "No"
– Question was not included in indicated survey.

Table 2: Causes and Measures of Temporary Interruptions in NOI

	Percent "Yes"[1]		
	U.S.	U.K.	New Zealand
Causes			
Phase I Investigation	32%	–	57%
Phase II Investigation	41%	–	–
Remediation Activity	85%	–	43%
Monitoring Activity	42%	–	29%
Litigation, Regulatory Orders	68%	–	14%
Post-remediation Marketing			
Leasing	50%	–	–
Sales	53%	–	–

Table 2: *(Continued)*

	Percent "Yes"[1]		
	U.S.	U.K.	New Zealand
Measures			
No Adjustment	8%	5%	0%
Reduced/Zero NOI in DCF Model	77%	9%	60%
Increase Discount Rate	43%	67%	80%
Increase Capitalization Rate	45%	–	0%

[1] Total number of "Yes" responses divided by total "Yes" plus total "No"
– Question was not included in indicated survey.

Table 3: Handling of Environmental Risks/Uncertainties (Stigma)

	Percent "Yes"[1]		
	U.S.	U.K.	New Zealand
Information Sources			
Experience	55%	69%	57%
Comparable Sales/Lease Evidence for:			
Non-contaminated, similar location	69%	66%	50%
Contaminated, similar location but not contaminants	49%	33%	14%
Contaminated, similar contaminants but not location	58%	53%	83%
Contaminated, similar location and contaminants	73%	38%	83%
Cash Flow Risk Analysis	42%	21%	57%
Phase I Reports	41%	–	29%
Phase II Reports	51%	–	–
Basis for Stigma Identification & Measurement			
Ignore	2%	5%	14%
Experience	50%	69%	83%
Market Sales Data	85%	–	29%
Buyer/Seller/Broker Opinion	51%	–	–
How to Adjust for Stigma			
Increase Yield (Discount) Rate	61%	84%	83%
Increase Capitalization Rate	67%	–	0%
Reduce Cash Flow Estimates	58%	9%	50%
Capital Value Reduction	76%	44%	33%

[1] Total number of "Yes" responses divided by total "Yes" plus total "No"
– Question was not included in indicated survey.

Chapter 11

Hedonic Modeling in Real Estate Appraisal: The Case of Environmental Damages Assessment

Alan K. Reichert
Professor of Finance, College of Business, Cleveland State University

11.1 Introduction

The literature regarding the use of hedonic pricing models in the real estate appraisal field is quite extensive (Freeman, 1979; Epple, 1987; Palmquist, 1992). While empirical studies using hedonic regression date back to the 1960's, in 1974 Rosen published the seminal article regarding the theory which underlies hedonic pricing models.[1] Over the years hedonic modeling has been applied to estimating the value of a wide range of economic and social amenities such as the value of nearby golf courses, properties with ocean views, and the impact of resort communities (Do and Grudnitski, 1995;

Spahr and Sunderman, 1999; Rush and Bruggink, 2000) and dis-amenities such as proximity to landfills and environmental pollution (Harrison and Rubinfield, 1978; Li and Brown, 1980; Reichert, 1991).

During the past several decades growing concern over environmental pollution and its damaging economic and physiological impacts has lead to a growing number of studies where hedonic appraisal models have been employed to determine the impact of pollution and the degree of pollution-related stigma. For example, as early as 1980 Quigley analyzed the relationship between airport noise and property values, while Harrison and Rubinfield (1978) and Chattopadhyay (1999) examined the impact of air quality on housing values. Havlicek and Davies (1971), Reichert, Small, and Mohanty (1992), and Nelson, Genereux, and Genereux (1992) studied the impact of sanitary landfills on nearby property values, while Swartzman, Croke, and Swible (1985), Dunn (1986), Smith and Desvousges (1986), Clarke and Nieves (1991), Kohlhase (1991), Smolen (1991), Greenberg and Hughes (1992), Ketkar (1992), and Reichert (1997 & 1999) examined the effects of a variety of hazardous waste sites. Recently Simons, Bowen, and Sementelli (1997) examined the impact of underground gasoline storage tank leaks, while Gamble and Downing (1982), Kinnard and Geckler (1991), Miller (1992), and Kinnard, Mitchell, Beron, and Webb (1991) analyzed the likely effects of radioactive releases on property values.

Research Objectives   These and other related studies generally use some form of regression-based hedonic model and report a wide range of damage or stigma estimates when studying the same or similar classes of environmental problems. The objective of this paper is to identify a number of important issues researchers need to address to ensure accurate and reliable results. Critical issues include model design, statistical considerations such as reliability and predictive accuracy, plus issues involving data quality and related measurement issues. In addition, the paper addresses a number of specific concerns which have been raised concerning the application and interpretation of hedonic regression results. It should be noted that this paper is not designed to be a comprehensive treatment of both the basic and advance elements of regression analysis, although where relevant the reader is referred to some excellent statistics texts at both the introductory and advance level. Instead the topics covered and their level of coverage are designed to fill a void in the applied hedonic modeling literature in the context of real estate appraisal and environmental impact assessment.

Empirical research is often messy in the sense that attempting to correct a given statistical issue such as highly collinear variables in a model by deleting one variable may introduce another equally difficult statistical problem, such as omitted variable bias. From a practical point-of-view, data collection is expensive and time consuming. Furthermore, the required data may not exist and a proxy measure must be substituted. Erroneous data or poor proxies introduce an "errors in variables" problem. In the final analysis, the researcher needs to examine and carefully weigh the trade-offs and select the model which provides the most logical solution to the problem at hand. Unfortunately there is no magical model which will be optimal in every situation, but a careful examination of the key issues and tests of the robustness of the findings will hopeful ensure reasonable if not ideal results. The objective of this paper is provide the reader with some helpful guidelines which will lead to more accurate and reliable statistical results. While the data in this paper focuses on residential real estate values and a number of examples relate to estimation of the negative influence of contamination upon such prices, many of the concepts described can be applied outside of the real estate and environmental assessment fields.

Section 11.2 discusses modeling and research design issues such as the appropriate selection of variables, sample size considerations, the impact of model misspecification, and the use of appropriate control samples. Section 11.3 discusses various statistical and data issues which include the effects and interaction of multicollinearity and heteroscedasticity, differences in the design and quality of commercially available real estate data bases, and the reliability of geocoding measurement techniques. Section 11.4 analyzes a number of issues such as the correct interpretation of regression coefficients, the temporal stability of the coefficients, the correct use of confidence intervals, and the handling of insignificant variables. Section 11.5 summarizes the main findings of the paper. As mentioned above, each of these issues will be analyzed and discussed in the context of a data base employed in several environmental studies.[2]

11.2 Model Design Issues

Modeling issues include the appropriate selection of variables, sample size considerations, the use of appropriate control areas, and the impact of model misspecification.

11.2.1 Variable Selection Priority

The data on the following list of variables were collected from two Multiple Listing Services (MLS) which covered the Uniontown area for the period January 1977–November 1996. These variables are common to most statistical real estate appraisal models and have been structured in a conventional manner.[3]

1. Selling price (continuous variable)
2. Age of property at time of sale (continuous variable measured in years)

3. Square feet of living space (continuous variable)
4. Presence of a fireplace (categorical or binary "dummy" variable measured as 1 or 0)
5. Presence of central air conditioning   "   "   "   "   "
6. Presence of a partial or full basement   "   "   "   "   "
7. Presence of an in ground swimming pool   "   "   "   "   "
8. Total number of full plus half baths
9. Number of bedrooms
10. New house (categorical or binary "dummy" variable measured as 1 or 0)
11. Lot size in square feet (continuous variable)
12. Size of garage in square feet (continuous variable)
13. Style of house (set of categorical or binary "dummy" variables, with one variable for each housing style; where the total number of variables is one less than the total number of housing styles)
14. Location of property on a high or medium traffic road (categorical or binary "dummy" variable measured as 1 or 0)
15. High school district (categorical or binary "dummy" variable measured as 1 or 0; where one variable is sufficient to represent the two local school districts)
16. Presence of city versus well-water (categorical or binary "dummy" variable measured as 1 or 0)
17. Year of sale (set of 20 binary "dummy" variables measured as 1 or 0, with one variable representing each year from 1977 to 1996)
18. Seasonality (set of four binary "dummy" variables measured as 1 or 0, with one variable representing each of the four seasons or calender quarters).
19. "Trend" represents a continuous variable time variable which counts the days starting with January 1, 1977 = 1 through November, 1996.

11.2.1.1 Functional Form

Three basic functional forms are considered in this study: linear, log-linear, and exponential. As discussed by Berry and Feldman (1985) it is useful to make a distinction between linearity and additivity in hedonic models. A model is linear if the marginal impact on change in an independent variable (X_1) on the dependent variable (Y) is constant regardless of the value of the independent variable being considered. On the other hand, additivity assumes that the constant partial effect discussed above is independent for changes in all the other independent variables in the model. Thus, equation (1) is both linear and additive. If the partial effect of a change in X_1 on Y is impacted by the value of the other variables then the model is said to be non-additive or interactive. Thus, in a nonadditive or interactive model, the partial effect of X_1 on Y varies with the level of the other independent variables. Thus $Y = \beta_0 + \beta_1 XZ$ is a nonadditive or interactive model.

At the same time it is often possible to transform a nonlinear (or nonadditive) model into a linear (or additive) one. For example, in the simplest case if $Y = \beta_0 + \beta_1 X^2$ one can define Z to equal X^2 and redefine the model such that $Y = \beta_0 + \beta_1 Z$. In the first specification the model is non- linear in terms of the variables but linear in terms of the parameters. In the example above, a log transformation can be use to linearize the model such that $\ln(Y) = \beta_0 + \beta_1 \ln(X) + \beta_2 \ln(Y)$. Most of the models discussed in this paper fall into this category and hence can be appropriately estimated using ordinary least squares regression. These models are classified as *intrinsically* linear and are the most likely used form employed in hedonic modeling. Models which are non-linear in both the variables and the parameters need to be estimated using a maximum likelihood procedure such as Box-Cox. (See Halvorsen and Pollakowski, 1981, Cropper, Deck, and McConnell, 1988, Kang and Reichert, 1987, and Murphy, 1989 for an in-depth discussion of alternative functional forms). Mathematically, the most commonly used functional forms are:

Linear model:

$$P = \beta_0 + \beta_1 X_1 + \beta_2 X_2 + \cdots + \beta_n X_n + \beta_{n+1} D_1 + \cdots + \beta_{n+m} D_m \quad (1)$$

where,

P is selling price,

X represents a vector of "n" continuous housing characteristics, such as square footage of living space, age, lot size, time, etc.

D represents a vector of "m" discrete housing characteristics such as style, air conditioning, etc.

Non-linear model:

$$\ln P = \beta_0 + \beta_1 \ln X_1 + \beta_2 \ln X_2 + \cdots + \beta_n \ln X_n$$
$$+ \beta_{n+1} D_1 + \cdots + \beta_{n+m+1} D_m \quad (2)$$

Exponential Models:

(a) $$\ln P = \beta_0 + \beta_1 X_1 + \beta_2 X_2 + \cdots + \beta_n X_n + \beta_{n+1} D_1 + \cdots$$
$$+ \beta_{n+m+1} D_m \quad (3)$$

(b) $$P = \beta_0 + \beta_1 \ln X_1 + \beta_2 \ln X_2 + \cdots + \beta_n \ln X_n + \beta_{n+1} D_1 + \cdots$$
$$+ \beta_{n+m+1} D_m \quad (4)$$

The log-linear model specified above (equation 2) is estimated using a forward stepwise regression procedure where a variable's minimum F-value to

Figure 1: Contribution to R^2
Source: Author's database

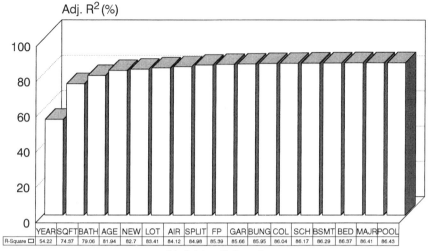

R-Square □	YEAR	SQFT	BATH	AGE	NEW	LOT	AIR	SPLIT	FP	GAR	BUNG	COL	SCH	BSMT	BED	MAJR	POOL
	54.22	74.37	79.06	81.94	82.7	83.41	84.12	84.98	85.39	85.66	85.95	86.04	86.17	86.29	86.37	86.41	86.43

Variables Entered

Discrete Time Variables

enter the model is 0.15, Figure 1 indicates the order in which the variables are entered into the model. The variables, in order of importance are: year-of-sale, square footage, number of baths, age, new home, lot size, air condition-ing, split-level style, fire place, garage, bungalow style, colonial style, school district, basement, number of bedrooms, major road, and pool. (The remain-ing variables failed to enter the model). As each variable enters, the following graphs indicate the impact upon the model's adjusted R^2, standard error of the estimate (S.E.E.), regression coefficient on square footage, and in-sample prediction accuracy (both level and percentage change.)

The definition of R^2 or the coefficient of determination is: $1 - (SSR/SST)$, where SSR is the residual sum-of-squares and SST is the total sum-of-squares associated with the regression. On a more intuitive level, R^2 represents the proportion of the total sample variation explained by the regression. The equation for the "adjusted" R^2 is $1 - (1 - R^2)(n-1)/(n-k)$, where "n" and "k" are the sample size and number of coefficients being estimated, respectively. (Note that "k" is the number of independent variables plus the intercept.) When comparing regression models estimated with different numbers of independent variables and different samples sizes the adjusted R^2 is more appropriate than R^2 since it adjusts for the degrees-of-freedom required in the estimation process. When estimating a multiple regression model with "k" independent variables, each of the estimated regression coefficients reduces the degrees-of-freedom available to estimate the remaining $k-1$ coefficients. For any given model and data sample, the adjusted R^2 is always smaller than R^2 although the difference diminishes rapidly as sample size increases. Thus for large samples with a considerable number of degrees of freedom the difference between the two statistics is negligible. But when small samples are used to estimate a large number of regression coefficients, the difference can be significant. In fact it is possible to have a positive R^2 and a negative adjusted R^2. On the other hand, when adding variables to a given model it is possible that the adjusted R^2 could decline if the estimated R^2 remains about the same. This would occur when we add a variable which has little or no relationship to the dependent variable. In most empirical work the adjusted R^2 is reported. To simplify the exposition, all references to R^2 in this paper can be interpreted as the adjusted R^2.

Given that the data set spans a 20 year time period it is not surprising that year-of-sale is the first variable to enter the model and alone explains over half (54%) of the variation in the sales prices. The next most important variable is square footage which increases adjusted R^2 by approximately 20%. Adding number of baths increases adjusted R^2 by 5%, while age contributes 3%. The remaining variables contribute less than 1% each. While adjusted R^2 continuously increases, for all practical purposes it converges on a value of about 87%. In Figure 2, the standard error of the estimate decreases rapidly at first

Figure 2: Std. Error of Regression
Source: Author's database

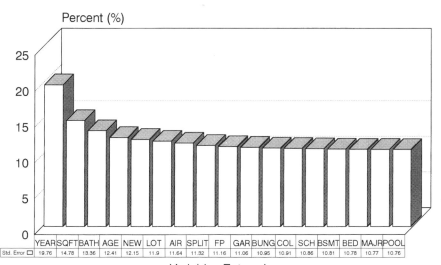

Variables Entered

Discrete Time Variables

Figure 3: Coefficient on LSQFT
Source: Author's database

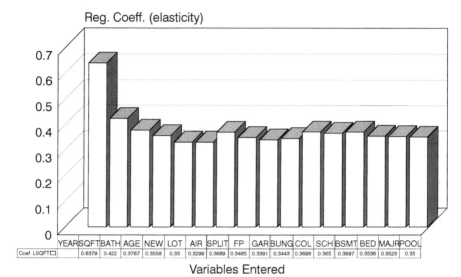

Discrete Time Variables

Figure 4: Prediction Accuracy
Source: Author's database

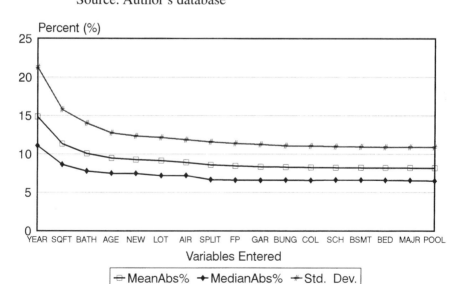

In-sample prediction results

Figure 5: Percentage Change
Source: Author's database

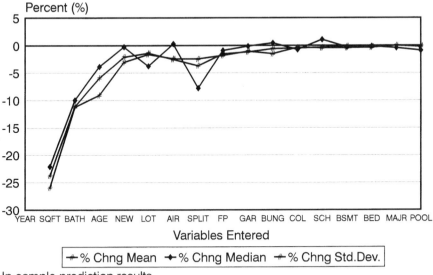

Variables Entered

| ✦% Chng Mean ✦% Chng Median ✦% Chng Std.Dev. |

In-sample prediction results

and then converges on a value of about 10.75%. The regression coefficient on square footage decreases rapidly as other variables are added and converges on a value of approximately 0.35 (Figure 3). Note that the coefficient actually increases when two style variables are entered into the model (split level and colonial). Split level and colonial style are the two least expensive type of housing styles to build for a given square foot of living space. The introduction of the number of bedrooms provides a downward adjustment on square footage. As seen in Figure 4, prediction accuracy as measured by the median absolute percentage error decreases by half from approximately 11.5% to 6.25%. The importance of modeling housing style (especially split level) is also demonstrated by a noticeable decline in the error rate. Figure 5 illustrates the improvement in the accuracy of the model as it charts the percentage change in the mean and median prediction error rates and the standard deviation of the errors. (Note that a negative change represents an improvement in the accuracy of the model.)

11.2.1.2 Conclusion

While the precise order or ranking may vary from one market to another, in general the most important variables in a cross-sectional hedonic real estate model appear to be: square footage, either bedrooms or baths (generally not both), and age of property. Furthermore, in a time series analysis one would generally expect time to play a significant role in determining market prices. This in not to say that other factors such as style, lot size, and location are not important. In fact, in most hedonic models they would be statistically significant. The fact that they appear to make a relatively small contribution to adjusted R^2 can be misleading, since the improvement in adjusted R^2, although small in absolute terms, is generally statistically significant. A better way to view their contribution is the percentage reduction in unexplained variation $(1-R^2)$. These small-incremental adjusted R^2 variables serve to "refine" and improve the precision of the estimated coefficients on the high-incremental adjusted R^2 variables. In all cases the researcher should of course test for excessive levels of multicollinearity.

11.2.2 Sample Size Effects

Two distinct approaches are employed to determine the effect of sample size on the hedonic models using the Uniontown data.

11.2.2.1 Incremental Sampling Approach

The entire Uniontown data set (1977–'96) was randomly divided into ten samples of approximately 250 home sales. The horizontal axis on each chart (Figures 6–13) indicates the regression results using a 5% sample (approximately 125 transactions). The 10% percent sample includes the observations contained in the 5% sample and randomly adds an additional 5% of sales. The 20% sample includes the previous 10% sample, plus an additional 10%. The remaining samples are constructed in the same manner. Thus, the relative magnitude of the difference in the composition of the samples declines markedly as sample size increases. For example, half of the sales in the 10% sample are unique compared to the sales in the 5% sample, while only 10% of the sales in the 100% "sample" are unique compared to the 90% sample.

The set of independent variables employed in each of the regressions are the same and include variables typically found in hedonic housing models. These variables include: time trend(ln), sqft(ln), age(ln), lotsize(ln), baths, bedrooms, central air, new, style (bisplit, bungalow, colonial), basement, fireplace, garage, school, plus an autoregressive error term AR(1) to adjust for autocorrelation. The regression results generated by each sample are compared in terms of: Adjusted R^2, Standard Deviation of Prediction Errors, S.E.E, Mean and Median Absolute Percentage Errors, F-ratio, Number of Significant Variables, Average Significance Level on All Variables, and the Regression Coefficient on LSQFT (natural log of square feet of living space).

11.2.2.2 **Mutually Exclusive Sampling Approach**

Using this approach the Uniontown data is divided into five mutually exclusive samples of 5% (n = 126), 10% (n = 260), 15% (n = 370), 20% (n = 491) and 25% (n = 588). The use of mutually exclusive samples eliminates the increasingly severe "overlap" issue discussed above when using the incremental sampling approach. This generates only five samples compared to 11 using the incremental approach.

1. Statistical Findings: Incremental Sampling Approach

Adjusted R^2 Comparison: (Figure 6) Sample size appears to have little or no effect on adjusted R^2, as adjusted R^2 randomly fluctuates between 79.4% and 81.5% The correlation coefficient between adjusted R^2 and "n" is $-.133$ (prob. = 0.70).

Std Deviation of Prediction Errors: (Figure 7) Standard deviation of prediction errors shows a decline between the 5% and 10% samples (15.49% to 13.99%) and then stabilizes around 15.0% for the larger samples. The correlation coefficient between the standard deviation of the prediction errors and "n" is: 0.44 (prob. = 0.17).

S.E.E. Comparison: (Figure 8) Standard Error of the Estimate for the regression declines noticeably between the 5% and 10% samples (from 13.65% down to 12.64%) and then remains relatively constant for larger sample sizes. The correlation coefficient between SEE and "n" is: .037 (prob. = 0.91).

Median Absolute % Error: (Figure 9) The median absolute % error appears to be positively related to sample size beginning with a 40% random sample, where the median error consistently increases from 9.7% to 10.53%. The correlation coefficient between the median absolute % error and "n" is: .35 (prob. = 0.026).

Mean Absolute % Error: (Figure 9) The mean absolute % error appears to be positively related to sample size beginning with the 10% sample, where the % error increases from 11.31% to 12.16%. The correlation coefficient between the mean absolute % error and "n" is: .667 (prob. = 0.026).

F-ratio: (Figure 10) The equation for the F-ratio, which tests the hypothesis that all the regression coefficients are equal to zero, is as follows:

$$F = \frac{R^2}{1 - R^2} \times \frac{T - k}{k - 1}$$

The F-ratio has $k-1$ degrees of freedom in the denominator and $T-k$ degrees of freedom in the numerator, where k is the number of regressor variables and T is the total sample size. If one holds R^2 constant an increase in sample size will automatically generate a proportional increase in the F-ratio.

Figure 6: Adjusted R²
Source: Author's database

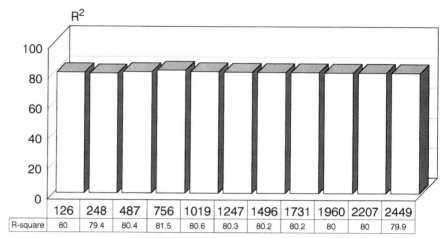

Figure 7: Std. Dev. Of Errors
Source: Author's database

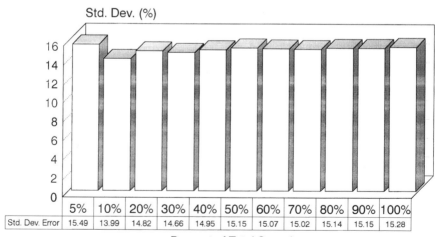

Figure 8: S.E.E. of Regression
Source: Author's database

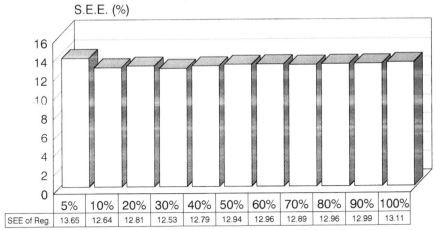

S.E.E. (%)

	5%	10%	20%	30%	40%	50%	60%	70%	80%	90%	100%
SEE of Reg.	13.65	12.64	12.81	12.53	12.79	12.94	12.96	12.89	12.96	12.99	13.11

Percent of Total Sample

☐SEE of Reg.

Figure 9: Median & Mean Absolute % Error
Source: Author's database

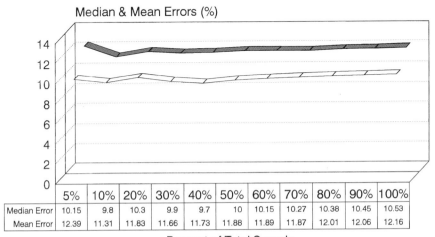

Median & Mean Errors (%)

	5%	10%	20%	30%	40%	50%	60%	70%	80%	90%	100%
Median Error	10.15	9.8	10.3	9.9	9.7	10	10.15	10.27	10.38	10.45	10.53
Mean Error	12.39	11.31	11.83	11.66	11.73	11.88	11.89	11.87	12.01	12.06	12.16

Percent of Total Sample

☐Median Error ■Mean Error

Figure 10: Equation F-ratio
Source: Author's database

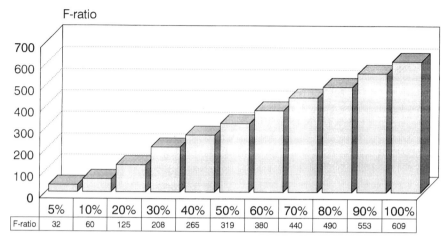

Figure 11: Number of Significant Variables
Source: Author's database

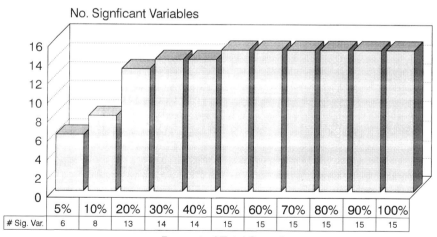

Figure 12: Average Sign. Level on All Variables
Source: Author's database

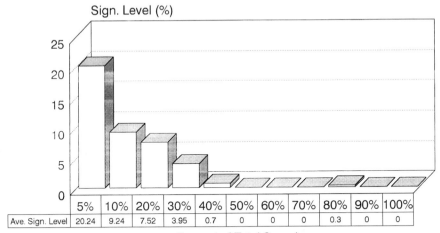

Sign. Level (%)

	5%	10%	20%	30%	40%	50%	60%	70%	80%	90%	100%
Ave. Sign. Level	20.24	9.24	7.52	3.95	0.7	0	0	0	0.3	0	0

Percent of Total Sample

☐ Ave. Sign. Level

Figure 13: Regress. Coefficient on LSQFT
Source: Author's database

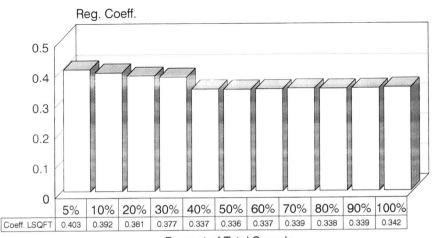

Reg. Coeff.

	5%	10%	20%	30%	40%	50%	60%	70%	80%	90%	100%
Coeff. LSQFT	0.403	0.392	0.381	0.377	0.337	0.336	0.337	0.339	0.338	0.339	0.342

Percent of Total Sample

☐ Coeff. LSQFT

Thus, one should not read too much into the close correlation between sample size and the F-ratio which equals: 0.999 (prob. = 0.000).

Number of Significant Variables: (Figure 11) The number of significant variables increases rapidly at first and reaches its maximum at a sample size of 50% (A maximum of 15 variables are available to enter the equation). The largest improvement is between a 5% and 20% sample (n = 126 to n = 487) where the number of significant variables increases from 6 to 13. The correlation coefficient between the number of significant variables and "n" is: 0.772 (prob. = 0.005).

Average Significance Level of All Independent Variables: (Figure 12) The average significance level of all the independent variables behaves in an inverse but similar fashion to the number of significant variables, with the majority of the reduction in the P-value reached at a sample size of 20–30% (n = 487−756). Note that a reduction in P-values represents an *increase* in the level of statistical significance associated with the statistical test. The correlation coefficient between the average significance level and "n" is: −0.781 (prob. = 0.005)

Size of Regression Coefficient on LSQFT: (Figure 13) The size of the regression coefficient on LSQFT declines moderately between the 5% and the 30% sample (from .403 to .377) and remains relatively constant thereafter. The correlation coefficient between the size of the regression coefficient on LSQFT and "n" is: −0.835 (prob. = 0.001)

2. Statistical Findings: Mutually Exclusive Sampling Approach (Given the similarity of the results with the incremental sampling approach the results are not depicted in graphic form).

Adjusted R^2 Comparison: Sample size appears to have no effect on adjusted R^2, as adjusted R^2 randomly fluctuates between 79.3% – 83.8% Correlation coefficient: −.248 (prob. = 0.69).

Std Deviation of Prediction Errors: Standard deviation of prediction errors show a decline between the 5% and 10% samples (15.49% to 13.99%) and then begins to rise again for the larger 20% and 25% samples. Correlation coefficient: −.134 (prob. = 0.83).

S.E.E. Comparison: Standard Error of the Estimate for the regression declines noticeably between the 5% and 15% samples (from 13.65% down to 11.8%) and then begins to rise for the 20% and 25% samples. Correlation coefficient: −.233 (prob. = 0.71).

Median Absolute % Error: The median absolute % error appears to be quite stable with the exception of the 10% sample where the median error equals 8.84% compared to approximately 10% for the remaining samples. Correlation coefficient: .22 (prob. = 0.73).

Mean Absolute % Error: The mean absolute % error declines between the 5% and 10% samples (from .1239 to .1096) and then begins to rise for the

20% and 25% samples (approximately, 11.83). Correlation coefficient: −.11 (prob. = 0.86).

F-ratio: As mentioned before the equation for the F-ratio which tests the hypothesis that all the regression coefficients are equal to zero. Correlation coefficient: .969 (prob. = 0.007).

Number of Significant Variables: The number of significant variables increases rapidly between the 5% and 10% samples (from 6 to 10) and slower thereafter but fails to reach its theoretical maximum with a 25% sample. (A maximum of 15 variables are available to enter the equation). Correlation coefficient: 0.98 (prob. = 0.004).

Average Significance Level of All Independent Variables: The average significance level of all the independent variables behaves in an inverse but similar fashion to the number of significant variables, with the majority of the reduction in the P-value reached at a sample size of 20%. As mentioned before, a reduction in P-values represents an *increase* in the level of statistical significance associated with the statistical test. Correlation coefficient: −0.99 (prob. = 0.001).

Size of Regression Coefficient on LSQFT: The size of the regression coefficient on LSQFT appears to be quite unstable but declines moderately as sample size is increased from 5% to 25%. Correlation coefficient: −0.681 (prob. = 0.21).

11.2.2.2 Conclusions

As a bare minimum one should employ at least ten data points for each regression coefficient estimated. Ideally the number of observations per coefficient should be closer to 30. Given that the hedonic real estate models typically employ approximately 15 independent variables, plus the intercept, this would require a minimum sample of approximately 160 observations, or ideally, 480 observations. The empirical results discussed above seem to bear this out. The results for the 5% sample (n = 126), while not completely out of line, appear to be unstable compared to larger samples. When sample size reaches approximately 450–500 much of this instability disappears. For example, the maximum number of significant variables is attained at this sample size and the regression coefficient on the most important variable in the model (LSQFT) stabilizes. Furthermore, there appears to be little benefit from increasing sample size much beyond 500.

11.2.3 Importance of Control Sample Selection

The selection of an appropriate statistical control sample can have a significant impact upon the estimation results of an hedonic model. A control sample or area serves as the bench mark against which the price behavior of houses in the subject area are compared. A control group is used to account for various broad macro factors, such as changes in interest rates and income levels, which affect housing prices in general. By comparing the subject area to the control area, the effects of these general factors are eliminated. In the context of environmental impact studies, to serve as an effective control area the region should be located sufficiently far from the environmental problem to be unaffected and should contain housing of the same price range, age, style, and comparable appreciation rates found throughout the subject area *prior* to the public awareness of the environmental situation. Housing trends in the subject and control areas will possibly differ once the environmental problem is recognized and internalized by the market.

Properties in the control area used in the initial Uniontown study lie up-grade to the West of the Uniontown toxic landfill at a distance of 8,000 feet or more (Control Area 1). Table 1 provides basic descriptive statistics on several key factors such as age, size, and style for properties located in both the subject and control areas between 1977 and 1987 (the beginning of the public's recognition of a major environmental problem). An alternative control area (Control Area 2) is also included for comparison purposes.

One difficult issue was how to treat an area called Williamsburg Estates, which lies in the middle of the Control Area 1. All the houses in this area were built after 1987, while little new building took place in the subject area after 1987. Houses in Williamsburg were considerably larger and more expensive that those in the subject area. On the other hand, an area just south of the IEL was scheduled to be developed with large houses similar to Williamsburg but was never developed because of the environmental problems which had surfaced by 1988. Thus, absent the IEL, the two areas would likely have developed along similar lines. Table 2 represents damages using (a) the Control Area 1 with and without Williamsburg included, (b) Control Area 2, (c) a combination of the Control Area 1 (without Williamsburg) plus the Control Area 2, and (d) the entire area which includes an area not included in any of the two controls.

As indicated in Table 2, while the parameters of each model were quite similar in terms of goodness-of-fit, error rates, etc. aggregate damages fluctuated between a low of $8.5 million using Control Area 2 to a high of $14.2 million using Control Area 1 with Williamsburg included. Excluding Williamsburg from Control Area 1 reduces damages to $11.5 million. Using the entire area as a control generated damages of $10.8 million.

11.2.3.1 Conclusion

The careful selection of a reliable and effective control is critical to an accurate assessment of environment damages. The key issue is to ensure that the major difference affecting the housing market in the subject and control areas relates to the environmental concern. If other unrelated factors have

**Table 1: Summary Statistics: Subject Area vs. Control Area 1
(1977–1987)***

Characteristic	Mean	Subject Area Min.	Max.	Std. Dev.
Price	68243	23000	155000	16350
Sqft	1688	660	3200	342
Lotsize	23484	6956	174350	13262
Year Built	1973	1907	1987	–

Style:	(%)	Bedrooms	(%)	Baths	(%)
Ranch	25.9	One	0.1	1.0	10.8
Colonial	33.2	Two	2.9	1.5	20.4
Bisplit	38.6	Three	53.7	2.0	24.0
Other	2.3	Four	41.3	2.5	42.0
		Five	1.8	3.0+	2.8

Characteristic	Mean	Control Area Min.	Max.	Std. Dev.
Price	65793	34000	118000	12547
Sqft	1660	1040	2600	280
Lotsize	20397	10440	54400	6859
Year Built	1977	1962	1987	–

Style	(%)	Bedrooms	(%)	Baths	(%)
Ranch	21.3	One	0.0	1.0	0.0
Colonial	27.0	Two	0.7	1.5	22.3
Bisplit	48.6	Three	70.3	2.0	29.1
Other	0.8	Four	27.7	2.5	33.4
		Five	1.3	3.0+	3.0

*Prior to Williamsburg Estates being built.
Source: Author's database.

developed or changed in either the control or the subject area (e.g., airport development or expansion, increased auto and truck traffic at a given location, etc.) then their potential influence must be incorporated into the model. In my view it is better to carefully define the control area than to include the entire set of transactions in some broad area which serves as a generic control. While this places the burden of proof on the researcher to defend why a specific control area was selected, it should reduce the need to model a wide range of potentially disruptive and extraneous factors whose influence often changes over time. Generic control areas which cover a large city and its many suburbs are particularly vulnerable to extraneous influences.

Table 2: Control Samples 1 and 2 Hedonic Model Comparisons (Fixed Effects – Discrete Time-Space Specification Equally Weighted Annual Impacts)

	Control 1		Control 2	Controls 1&2	Entire Area
	(w/o Wilm)	(w/Wilm)		(w/o Wilm)	(w/Wilm)
Summary Statistic:					
N	1537	1583	1603	2112	2449
Adj. R^2	0.870	0.875	0.866	0.871	0.871
Std. Error Est.	0.105	0.106	0.104	0.102	0.105
D-W	2.00	1.94	1.97	2.03	2.00
Loglikelihood	1354	1365	1421	1891	2111
F-statistics	83.6	90.4	84.6	115.6	134.6
Mean Abs. % Error	7.7%	7.9%	7.6%	7.6%	7.8%
Median Abs. % Error	6.0%	6.4%	6.0%	5.9%	6.2%
Min. % Error	−89.1%	−87.1%	−84.4%	−90.1%	−89.6%
Max.% Error	31.0%	31.0%	31.5%	31.7%	33.3%
Std. Dev. % Error	10.2%	10.4%	10.2%	10.0%	10.4%
Estimate Impact by Distance Ring:					
Ring #1 (0–2,250 ft.)	−14.6%	−16.3%	−12. 0%	−13 8%	−14 0%
Ring #2 (2,250–4,500 ft.)	−7.3%	−9.0%	−5.4%	−6.4%	−6.5%
Ring #3 (4,500–6,750 ft.)	−5.8%	−7.6%	−4.0%	−5.1%	−5.4%
Total Damages	$11.5 M.	$14.2 M.	$8.5 M.	$10.3 M.	$10.8 M.

Source: Author's database.

11.2.4 Model Misspecification: The Case of Over-Modeling and Multicollinearity

The implications of model misspecification can be illustrated by examining an alternative model, labeled Model 2, which divides the subject area into three distance rings and includes both intercept and time-slope shift variables to capture changes in the housing market in each ring. This is a reasonable approach except that a common error is to include the same type of intercept and time-slope shift variables for the entire subject area, in addition to each of the distance rings. Modeling the entire subject by itself following this procedure would be reasonable but modeling it using both individual distance rings and the entire area simultaneously is not. The subject area is effectively "double counted" in Model 2 which introduces a good deal of multicollinearity since the effect of the IEL is being attributed to both the entire subject area and three sub-regions which collectively define the subject area. This type of over-specification is bound to dilute any observed impacts. In fact this procedure estimated maximum damages to be in the range of only $2 million using Control Area 2, compared to $8.5 million using Model 1 with the same control area.

The following results illustrate the impact coefficients estimated using the mis-specified Model 2 and a "corrected" Model 2 which excludes the *subject area* intercept and time-slope shift variables, leaving only the ring or distance-related variables. Using the 1977–96 data, Model 2 generates a statistically significant intercept shift for only ring #1, −11.1%. This compares with the Model 1 results where damages were found in the first three rings out to a distance of 6,750'. When Model 2 is specified correctly (i.e., the full subject area variables excluded) the "corrected" Model 2 exhibits a negative and statistically significant impact for *all* three rings which are roughly in line with the estimates generated using Model 1. Specifically, the following impacts are reported using Model 1, Model 2, and the corrected Model 2. (Note that the negative impact coefficients decline as distance from the landfill increases. That is, properties located closer the landfill suffered a larger negative impact. This is sometime referred to as locational obsolescence in the appraisal field.)

Ring	Model 1	Model 2	Corrected Model 2
1	−14.6%***	−11.1%**	−17.1%***
2	−7.3***	−4.6	−10.3**
3	−5.8***	−1.3	−7.2*

*** Statistically significant at the 1% level.
 ** Statistically significant at the 5% level.
  * Statitically significant at the 10% level.

11.2.4.1 Conclusion

Model misspecification, such as over-modeling introduces severe multi-collinearity into the model that can lead to major errors in damage estimates and an erroneous identification of the potential geographic extent of damages.

11.3 Data and Statistical Issues

11.3.1 Comparison of Alternative Data Sets

The purpose of this section is to evaluate three alternative data bases. The Uniontown analysis was based upon data provided by both the Canton and Akron Multiple Listing Service (MLS). This information going back to 1977 was keyed into a computer from monthly and annual "sold" books.

MLS – MLS data has both advantages and disadvantages. The major advantage is its accuracy since it is in the sellers best interest to make sure that nothing important is missing from the listing which would make the property attractive to a potential buyer. Furthermore, while most MLS organizations do not guarantee the accuracy of the data, they have a strong legal/professional obligation to present the property as fairly as possible. It is true that sellers and their brokers will want to present the property in its best light so there might be a small across-the-board favorable bias in the data. Another major advantage is that by listing and selling through the MLS, the property is given widespread market exposure and can easily be compared to other properties offered for sale. Thus, MLS prices should represent a reasonably accurate depiction of true market conditions. (Compare this to a property which transfers through an estate to family member at a favorable price or a property sold in a distress situation such as a bank foreclosure or a sheriff sale.)

MLS data disadvantages include the fact that not all residential sales go through MLS. For example, houses sold by their owners and certain new houses sold by builders (both spec and custom houses) may not be listed in the MLS. (Overall approximately 70–75% of all Uniontown properties were sold through either the Akron and Canton MLS.) In addition, certain MLSs will not provide square footage of living space due the potential legal liability, which is not the case in Canton or Akron. In this event, square footage must be estimated based upon foundation size or by summing individual room sizes and making an adjustment for hall and entrance ways (usually an additional 25%). Finally, as of now the MLS data is not publicly available and one needs to work through a member broker/appraiser, or possibly the MLS Board, to obtain the data.

METROSCAN – An alternative source of data would be the county auditor's or tax assessor's data base, which includes certain property characteristics as well as sales price history. TransAmerica's Information Management Services provides data for approximately 150 counties in the following states: Arizona, California, Colorado, Florida, Georgia, Minnesota, Missouri, North Carolina, Nevada, Ohio, Oregon, Pennsylvania, and Washington.

PACE – Ameristate is a regional company which provides data for numerous counties in Ohio and Michigan (PACE was recently acquired by METROSCAN). The data for a given county generally goes back 5 to 10 years. For example, the PACE data for Uniontown goes back 11 years while the METROSCAN data extends back only 5 years. (In certain counties METROSCAN also has data back 10+ years but for new counties they usually begin with the last 5 years.) Both companies provide updated data. METROSCAN provides a monthly CR-ROM update while PACE provided a quarterly CD-ROM update with daily or weekly on-line updates. It is pretty straightforward to download the data from either data source into an EXCEL file, but prior to use in a statistical program a substantial amount of edit and reformatting is required. The PACE software also included a considerable amount of demographic data and mapping software along with the property's physical characteristics and sales history. In terms of sales history, each property had only one unique listing but this listing included the most recent sales price as well as the previous sale price and sale date (METROSCAN) or the previous two sales in the case of the PACE data.

11.3.1.1 Data Limitations

A limitation of both the commercial databases is the way they treat style of home, at least for Stark county (were Uniontown is located). Both generally follow the assessors definition of the house as either a one, 1.5, or two-story home. Thus, the METROSCAN data treats a bi/multi-level similar to a ranch. The PACE data attempts to identify these multi-level styles but it is not clear how accurate or comprehensive this effort is. Another limitation in the METROSCAN data for Stark county relates to garage size. Little information was provided regarding square footage. Furthermore, a variable called "type of deed" can often be used to identify arm-length transactions. The MET-ROSCAN data for Stark county did not have this variable so one would find a large four bedroom house selling for $20,000, which probably indicates a transfer value used for estate tax purposes. By screening for outliers it was possible to identify these unusual non-market transactions which can greatly influence regression results which are quite sensitive to outliers. For example, using the METROSCAN data the untrimmed regression model produced an adjusted R^2 of only 14.3%, compared to 77.2% for the trimmed data.

TransAmerica indicated that about 70% of their counties have a "type of deed" variable. For the PACE data a significant number of properties (roughly 10%) were missing lot size as measured by either square feet or number of acres. One interesting variable that METROSCAN includes is property condition. They record condition as either average, good, or excellent. Using average as the base condition, one regression model found that houses in excellent condition on average sold for 14% more that average condition houses, while houses in good condition sold for 8.5% more that the average home. Both regression coefficients were statistically significant.

11.3.1.2 Modeling using Different Data Sets

In order to fairly compare all three data bases a common or standardized regression model was used which included the most important variables present in all three data bases. These include square feet of living space, age, number of bedrooms and baths, lot size, number of stories (or home style), presence of a fireplace, and a time trend variable, where January 1, 1991 = 0. (For this comparison the data set begins in 1991 since that is the earliest data available from METROSCAN. Thus, while the MLS data includes a total of 2,450 observations between 1977 and 1996, only 660 MLS transactions occurred after 1990.) The data does not include garage size because very limited information regarding the garage was available from METROSCAN. On the other hand, all the houses in the PACE data base had a basement so this variable was excluded since one can not include a variable with zero variance into a regression model. Thus, the standardized model is not intended to be the best or optimal model for each data base but is designed to capture the most important factors common across all three data sources. Table 3 summarizes the regression and prediction accuracy results.

The regression coefficients on only two variables, trend and fireplace were essentially identical. For the remaining variables the coefficients tended to fluctuate in a systematic manner. For example, the regression coefficients on square foot of living space for the MLS and the PACE data were reasonably comparable (0.411 vs. 0.360). On the other hand, the coefficient on square footage for the METROSCAN data was considerably smaller (0.237). At the same time, the size of the regression coefficients on the number of baths and bedrooms using the METROSCAN data was considerably larger than for the other two data sets. Considerable variation was reported in the value of the coefficients on "style", which was undoubtedly due to the wide variation in the way the variables are defined and the number of categories available. In terms of goodness-of-fit the adjusted R^2 for the MLS and METROSCAN models were virtually identical (71.7% vs. 71.5%), while the comparable value for the PACE model was moderately lower (64.6%). A similar trend was noticed for each model's F-ratio.

The standard error of the estimate (S.E.E) was substantially lower for the MLS data (0.1215) compared to 0.1413 for METROSCAN and 0.1499 for PACE. In terms of prediction accuracy, the MLS data generated the lowest mean (9.33%), median (7.30%), and maximum (102%) absolute percentage errors. The METROSCAN data generated the next lowest set of error rates (with the exception of the maximum error). The METROSCAN median absolute percentage error rate was 7.76%, or 6.4% larger in relative terms than the comparable MLS rate. On the other hand, the PACE median error of 8.21% was 12.5% larger. While not as reliable a measure, the difference in relative mean error rates was roughly twice as large, with METROSCAN's mean average error of 10.61% being 13.7% larger than the MLS mean error rate. The PACE mean error of 11.07% was 18.6% greater than the comparable MLS mean error.

11.3.1.3 MLS Sub-Analysis

The following discussion breaks the MLS data into two sub-groups: 1,517 observations from the Canton MLS and 933 observations from the Akron

Table 3: Regression Results Using Alternative Database (t-Values in Parenthesis)

Variable	MLS	METROSCAN	PACE
Constant	7.561	8.66	8.07
	(29.4)	(33.7)	(24.2)
Lsqft	0.411	0.237	0.360
	(11.6)	(7.2)	(8.5)
Lage	−0.081	−0.141	−0.138
	(11.2)	(15.4)	(11.5)
Baths	0.018	0.088	0.054
	(6.5)	(6.9)	(3.6)
Bedrooms	0.018	0.052	0.024
	(1.7)	(4.3)	(1.6)
Llotsqft	0.027	0.040	0.020
	(2.3)	(3.0)	(1.0)
Bungalow	−0.089	–	o
	(4.1)		
CapeCod	–	0.021	−0.063
		(0.9)	(1.9)
Bislpit	−0.093	–	−0.056
	(6.78)		(3.1)
Colonial	−0.031	0.026	−0.012
	(2.02)	(1.8)	(0.6)
Frpl	0.050	0.061	0.050
	(3.56)	(4.2)	(2.7)
Ltrend	0.097	0.105	0.113
	(19.2)	(16.2)	(14.8)
Goodness-of-Fit Statistics:			
N	660	658	558
Adj. R^2	71.7%	71.5%	64.6%
F-ratio	168	183	103
S.E.E.	.1215	.1413	.1499
Prediction Accuracy (In-sample)			
Median Absolute			
% Error	7.30	7.76	8.21
Mean Absolute			
% Error	9.33	10.61	11.07
Maximum Absolute			
% Error	101.7	127.9	123.3

Source: Author's database.

MLS. T-tests of the mean differences among the two groups found statistically significant differences for virtually all the variables, although in most cases the actual differences were quite small. For example, the mean value for property age was 10.98 years vs. 10.62 years for Canton and Akron, respectively. The mean values for square footage was 1,665 vs. 1,700. For distance from the landfill, the mean values were 7,810 vs. 8,747 feet. For lot size the respective mean values were 25,362 and 24,580 square feet. For year-of-sale the average values were 1984.2 versus 1985.5. Estimating separate models for both groups of data generated essentially identical prediction results. Adding the MLS designation as an additional explanatory variable in a pooled model using all the MLS data generated virtually identical prediction results, although the MLS designation variable proved to be statistically significant.

11.3.1.4 Conclusions

The following conclusions are based upon a detailed comparison of the data for one county. For other areas around the country the results may differ depending upon the comprehensiveness and quality of the data collected at the local level. Beyond correcting for obvious errors, neither of the two commercial data bases (PACE and METROSCAN) make a determined effort to verify the accuracy of the public record data. The analysis indicates that hedonic models based upon carefully screened data drawn from public records are sufficiently reliable to make valid statistical judgements. Information regarding the most important factors in an hedonic model such as price, sales date, basement, square footage of living space, number of beds and baths, age, and lot size are generally quite accurate. Information regarding certain amenities such as style, garage size, fireplaces, central air conditioning is considerably less reliable. Furthermore, pooling data from several nearby MLS appears to be appropriate.

11.3.2 The Effectiveness of Geocoding in Hedonic Pricing Models

Most commercial real estate data bases such as METROSCAN and mapping software such as MAP INFO and MAPTITUDE geocode properties to facilitate locating and mapping housing transactions. Geocoding is the assignment of unique locational parameters to a property. The most widely used parameters are latitude and longitude. The geocoding information is produced by the U.S. Census Bureau and made available to users in what is called a TIGER file which is updated periodically. To assign latitude and longitude coordinates to a given property the latitude and longitude of two major intersections which lie on either side of the subject property is determined by either aerial photos and/or using a GPS (satellite global positioning system). For example, if there are 20 properties located between two street intersections (10 on each side of the street) and if the intersections are determined to be 1,000 feet apart, then each property is assumed to be of equal size and linear interpolation is used to position individual properties. Thus each property is assumed to have 100' frontage. Using this method a unique latitude and longitude coordinate is assigned to each property. Note that the latitude and longitude coordinates are being estimated and hence involves some degree of error.

The research question is whether or not geocoding is sufficiently accurate to generate reliable results when conducting either a macro-level or micro-level hedonic housing price study. I consider the Uniontown IEL study to be a macro-level hedonic study since it covers thousands of properties located over 5–6 square miles. I consider an under ground storage tank study which has potential effects limited to only a few city blocks to be a micro-level study (For example, see Simons, Bowen, and Sementelli, 1997). To examine these issues I have geocoded the Uniontown data and have compared the results with the hand-measurement technique initially employed in analyzing the Uniontown market. It should be pointed out that the hand-measurement approach also involves a certain degree of human skill and the potential for random measurement error. In addition, I have selected several commercial properties (gas stations) in the Cleveland area and examine the accuracy of geocoding-based measurement techniques relative to hand-calculated distance measures using detailed parcel maps which indicate the actual property dimensions.

11.3.2.1 Uniontown Results

The MAPTITUDE software successfully assigned a latitude and longitude coordinate to each property in the Uniontown data base. Using the Pythagorean theorem, the Euclidean distance from the center of the landfill (latitude = N40.9688333° and longitude = W81.405067°) to each property was calculated. (While this procedures ignores the curvature of the earth, for distances of only a few miles this would make very little difference). On the other hand, the fact that the IEL is essentially a square area of about 30 acres introduces another issue. Using geocoding, distance is generally measured to the *center* of a given point of interest (e.g., a contaminated landfill), while the hand-measuring approach used in the Uniontown study calculates distance to the *closest edge* of the landfill. The center of the landfill is approximately 600' from the middle of each side of the landfill, so the distance calculation procedure adds 600' to the hand-measured distance values. (This procedure is admittedly crude in the sense that while it would be reasonably accurate for most properties, those few houses which lie in a direct line off the northwest

Figure 14: Untrimmed Data Plot of Derror
Source: Author's database

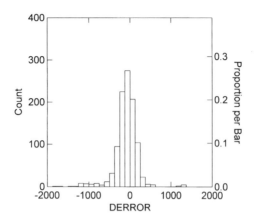

Figure 15: Untrimmed Data Plot of ADerror
Source: Author's database

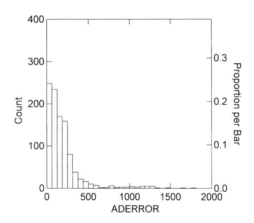

and southwest corners of the landfill would find that their adjusted hand-measured distances are understated by perhaps as much as 200 feet.)

With these caveats in mind, Figures 14 and 15 depict the difference in the two distance measures for the 1,028 observations in the subject area. DERROR is the signed difference in the two measurements (hand measurement less geocoded estimate), while ADERROR is the absolute value of the differences. The average DERROR is −90′, which indicates that geocoding on average over-estimates distance by approximately 90 feet, although the differences ranged from an under-estimate of 1,303′ to an over-estimate of 1,798′, with a standard deviation of 281′. On the other hand, the average

Figure 16: Plot of Residuals against Predicted Values
Source: Author's database

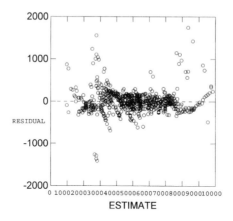

Figure 17: Trimmed Data Plot of Derror
Source: Author's database

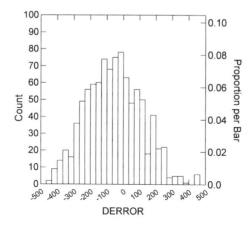

absolute difference is 193′, with a standard deviation of 224′. A simple regression of the geocoded distance measured against the hand-measured value indicates a significant intercept value of 736′, with a t-value of 33.1. The correlation coefficient between the two measures is 0.989. The residuals when plotted in Figure 16 reveal the tendency for the geocoded values to exceed the hand-measured values. The plot of the absolute difference errors indicates that a few large errors (>450′) may be skewing the results.

To adjust for the influence of outliers, Figures 17 and 18 illustrate the comparable results when the 72 absolute error values in excess of 450′ are dropped. The average DERROR is now −57′ which indicates that geocoding

Figure 18: Trimmed Data Plot of ADerror
　　　Source: Author's database

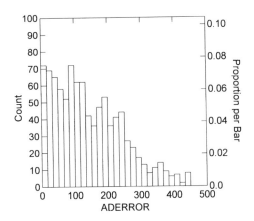

on average still over estimates distance by approximately 57′, although the constrained differences now range from an under estimate of 442′ to an over estimate of 445′, with a standard deviation of 167′. The average absolute difference is 143′, with a standard deviation of 102′. A simple regression of the geocoded distance measure on the hand-measured value reported indicates a significant intercept value of 719′ with a t-value of 51.3 and a correlation coefficient between the two measures of 1.0.

Further analysis of the measurement errors reveals that a major portion of the large errors (i.e., >450′) can be explained by the fact that the property is located on a street which has a significant bend or curve in it. In certain cases these properties were located on streets which were circular. These would make it difficult to geocode using linear interpolation techniques. On the other hand, several large errors (i.e., 493′–1,168′) were found on a major straight east-west road.

The next step was to recalculate IEL damages using the geocoded distance measures. As indicated in Table 4, the percentage impacts by ring are almost identical when compared with the impacts generated using the hand-measured distance values. The only major difference is in ring # 4 where geocoding generated a negative impact of −2.26%, compared to essentially no impact using the hand-measured approach. On the other hand, geocoding generated $1.2 million less in aggregate damages. The reduced level of damages was approximately $2.2 million for the first two rings, primarily due to the smaller number of properties assigned to these rings (The number of observations in the first and second rings decreases by 81 and 76, respectively.) On the other hand, geocoding generated approximately $1 million additional damages in rings 3 and 4, where the number of properties assigned

**Table 4: Damages Estimates Made Using both Hand
Measured and Geocoded Distance Estimates**

	Distance Hand-Measured	Distance Geocoded
Ring #1	−14.58%	−14.31%
	n = 223	142
$ damages	$3,892,058	$2,377,487
Ring #2	−7.26%	−7.37%
	n = 505	429
$ damages	$4,502,250	$3,860,511
Ring #3	−5.80%	−5.57%
	n = 484	572
$damages	$3,142,975	$3,656,507
Ring #4	+0.002%	−2.26%
	n = 69	160
$damages	−$20,750	$398,070
Total Damages	$11,516,533	$10,292,575

Source: Author's database.

to these rings increased by 88 and 91, respectively. Thus, it appears that the method of distance measurement has little effect upon the estimated impact coefficients, while aggregate damages have been reduced by about ten percent due to "incorrect" ring assignment. The fact that geocoding tends to bias ring assignments upward is consistent with the above mentioned finding that, on average, geocoding tends to over-estimate distance from the landfill.

11.3.2.2 Micro-level Analysis

Three properties containing corner lot gasoline stations were selected in Highland Heights, Ohio, a residential suburb of Cleveland. These stations are located on the following roads: Wilson Mills, Bishop, and Richmond. Using Metroscan, the surrounding parcel maps were printed. Metroscan allows one to request a radius and/or a proximity search based upon geocoding. The number of property parcels identified as being within 500' of each location is as follows: Wilson Mills (22) Bishop (18) Richmond (10). Using parcel maps which provide actual lot dimensions plus the results of on-site visits, the following accuracy rates presented in Table 5 were achieved.

Thus, the computerized radius search correctly identified 28 parcels and made a total of 40 type I and type II errors (29+11). If one excludes the parcels incorrectly included in the radius search and only focuses on properties actually located within 500', the percent of correctly classified parcels is slightly less than 50% (28/57).

Table 5: Micro-Level Analysis Classification Accuracy Rates

Selection Results	Wilson Mills	Bishop	Richmond	Total
Properties which were:				
a. correctly identified	16	10	2	28
b. missed (type II)*	9	13	7	29
c. incorrectly included (type I)	1	6	4	11
Number of quadrants examined	4	3	2	9

* The null hypothesis for the type I and II errors is that the parcel selected is *not* within 5009 feet of the subject property.
Source: Author's database.

11.3.2.3 GPS vs. MAPTITUDE Results

Comparing the latitude and longitude estimates generated using a hand-held GPS and MAPTITUDE the following errors were observed. MAPTITUDE placed the Richmond property 83′ north and 101′ feet east of the GPS position. MAPTITUDE placed the Wilson Mills property 49′ north and 21′ feet east of the GPS position. The GPS readings were averaged over 10–20 minute periods. GPS results for the Bishop Rd. property proved to be unreliable due to interference from a large number of nearby electrical transmission lines. (Note that recent improvements in the GPS system made after this analysis was conducted may have increased the overall accuracy.)

11.3.2.4 Conclusions

The evidence suggests that geocoding is *not* sufficiently accurate or reliable to be used in micro-level hedonic pricing studies where the market is defined over a small distance, such as 500′–1000′. On the other hand, geocoding can be effectively used in larger macro-level studies. But even here the researcher needs to carefully examine the geocoded data for outliers and situations where streets are not amenable to linear interpolation (e.g. circles and curved streets). Distance estimates using a hand-held a GPS instrument appears to be reasonably accurate and a technique whose accuracy should improve over time.

11.3.3 Interaction of Multicollinearity and Sample Size

In a previous section, the impact of sample size on hedonic regression results was examined (Section 11.2 – part 11.2.2). The results are summarized as follows: For the smallest 5% sample (n = 126) the regression results appear unstable compared to larger samples. When sample size reaches approximately 450–500 much of this instability disappears. Furthermore, there appears to be little benefit for increasing sample size much beyond 500. The purpose of this section is to examine how multicollinearity changes as sample size increases.

11.3.3.1 Multicollinearity

Multicollinearity refers to the condition where the independent variables in a regression are correlated to some degree with one another. As pointed out by Berry and Feldmand (1985) multicollinearity is a problem associated with data samples rather than a condition in the overall population. That is, while observations in the population have characteristics which may be orthogonal (uncorrelated) a more or less random sample will contain observations which are non-orthogonal. In a controlled experimental environment such as in a chemistry or physics lab the researcher would select only observations, or conduct experiments, which are independent (orthogonal). But when dealing with actual data samples in the economics and social science field the researcher is often forced to take what is available. If the correlation among two or more independent variables is perfect, a unique solution to the regression equation is not feasible. As long as the correlation among the regressor variables is less than one, a unique solution will be generated which yields BLUE (best linear unbiased) regression coefficients. On the other hand, while the OLS estimates will have "minimum variance" for estimators of the same class, these variances, while minimized, may no longer be small. For a more detailed discussion of various types of multicollinearity and other related issues see Moore and Reichert (1984) and Reichert and Moore (1986).

Multicollinearity tends to inflate the size of the variance of the regression coefficients, making the estimated coefficients less reliable, but still unbiased. When severe multicollinearity is present it is difficult to identify the effect of a given independent variable on the dependent variable. Hence, it can have a major impact on the significance tests on individual regression coefficients[4]. If the purpose of the regression model is simply to predict the value of the dependent variable then as long as the pattern of multicollinearity does not change through time it will have little impact on the model's prediction accuracy. On the other hand, if the purpose is primarily explanatory (versus predictive) then multicollinearity can be a significant problem. Multicollinearity tends to be more severe in smaller samples, hence expanding the sample (if possible) may be one way of reducing the influence of a few highly correlated observations. (Note that expanding the sample is not guaranteed to reduce the degree of multicollinearity since the ultimate impact depends upon the nature and degree of independence of the additional data being added.)

11.3.3.2 Measuring Multicollinearity

There are two common measures of the degree of multicollinearity: (1) the variance inflation index (VIF) which is based upon the adjusted R^2 generated when one independent variable is regressed against the remaining independent variables in the regression equation. The equation for VIF is $1/(1-\text{adjusted } R^2)$. As a rule of thumb, if the VIF is larger than 10.0 (i.e., adjusted $R^2 > 0.90$) then multicollinearity is a concern, and (2) the Condition Index developed by Belsley, Kuhn, and Welsh. The Condition Indices are the square roots of the ratios of the largest eignevalue in a scaled $X'X$ matrix to each successive eigenvalue.[5] The Variance Proportions are the proportions of the total variance of the estimates accounted for by each principal component associated with each eignevalue. An index larger than 30, along with at least two variance proportions larger than 50% suggests that multicollinearity is "moderate to strong". The program use to measure multicollinearity (SYSTAT) calculates the Tolerance Ratio instead of the VIF for each independent variable. The tolerance ratio is equal to the inverse of the VIF (i.e., $1-\text{adjusted } R^2$). Thus, if a variable has a VIF in excess of 10, it's tolerance ratio is less than 0.10. Two alternative sampling approaches where employed in the sample size analysis. The multicollinearity statistics are presented for both approaches but the major focus of the discussion of the findings will use the overlapping sampling approach.

11.3.3.3 Overlapping Sampling Approach

As discussed previously, the entire Uniontown data set (1977–96) was randomly divided into ten samples of approximately 250 house sales. The 10% percent sample includes the observations contained in the 5% sample but randomly adds an additional 5% of sales. The 20% sample includes the previous 10% sample plus an additional 10%. The remaining samples are constructed in the same manner. Thus, the relative magnitude of the difference in the composition of the samples declines markedly as sample size increases. The set of independent variables employed in each of the regressions are the same and include variables typically found in hedonic housing models. These variables include: trend(ln), sqft(ln), age(ln), lotsize(ln), baths, bedrooms, central air, new, style (bi/split, bungalow, colonial), basement, fireplace, garage, and school.

11.3.3.4 Mutually Exclusive Sampling Approach

Using this approach the Uniontown data is divided into five mutually exclusive random samples of 5% (n = 126), 10% (n = 260), 15% (n = 370), 20% (n = 491) and 25% (n = 588). The use of mutually exclusive samples eliminates the increasingly severe "overlap" issue discussed above when using the incremental sampling approach.

11.3.3.5 Statistical Results

Figure 19 summarizes the maximum Condition Index produced for each sample size. While the values are much larger than 30, ranging from 242 to 287, in no case are two or more variance proportions greater than 0.50. The variance proportion associated with square footage is consistently above 0.90 but no other variable has a variance proportion close to 0.50. Hence, as measured by the Condition Index, multicollinearity appears not to be a major concern. Not surprisingly the value of the Condition Index is largest for the two smaller samples (5% and 10%). Figure 20 summarizes the impact of sample size on the average tolerance ratio for each independent variable. As discussed above, a smaller ratio indicates an increasing degree of mult collinearity, with a value of less than 0.10 an indication of significant multicollinearity As can be seen from Figure 20 the tolerance ratio tends to rise as sample size increases but in no case is the ratio near 0.10. Once again multicollinearity appears not to be a major concern.

In Table 6, sections A–K, a series of model parameters are related to the various tolerance values by a simple linear regression equation. The predictive power of the model is measures by adjusted R^2 (regression H), the accuracy of the model is measured by the mean and median absolute percentage errors (regressions F and G), and reliability of the model is measured the standard error of the estimate (regression A). Regression theory would suggest that multicollinearity would have little or no impact upon predictive

Figure 19: Maximum Condition Index
Source: Author's database

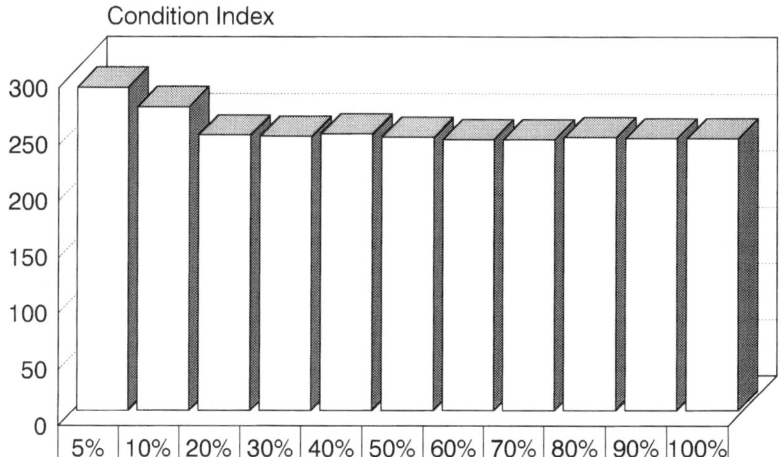

	5%	10%	20%	30%	40%	50%	60%	70%	80%	90%	100%
Cond. Index☐	287	270	245	244	246	243	241	241	243	242	242

Percent of Total Sample

Figure 20: Average Tolerance Ratio
        Source: Author's database

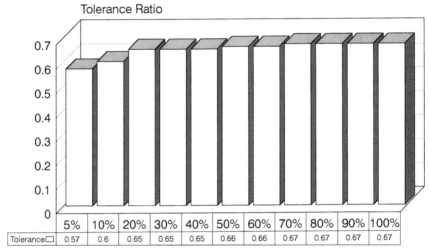

Tolerance Ratio

Tolerance□	5%	10%	20%	30%	40%	50%	60%	70%	80%	90%	100%
	0.57	0.6	0.65	0.65	0.65	0.66	0.66	0.67	0.67	0.67	0.67

Percent of Total Sample

Tolerance = 1/VIF

accuracy or reliability. This is in fact what is observed since the regression coefficients on the average tolerance ratio in regressions A, F, G, and H are all statistically insignificant.

The hypothesis testing ability of the regression is measured by: (1) the average significance level for all independent variables (regression C), (2) the regression coefficient on log of square footage (regression D), and (3) the number of significant variables (regression E). In all three cases the regression coefficients on the average tolerance ratio are statistically significant and have the correct sign. For example, one would expect the average P-value to decrease (or the average level of statistical significant to increase) as the tolerance ratio increases do to a reduction in multicollinearity. This is what is reflected in regression C, where the coefficient on the tolerance ratio is -184.7, with a significance level of 0.0. Furthermore, the number of significant variables is directly related to the tolerance ratio as can be seen in regression E, where the regression coefficient is 95.6 with a significance level of 0.0. To ensure that the significant impacts are not driven by some other factor(s) related to sample size, regressions I–K repeat the analysis but include sample size as an explanatory variable. The inclusion of sample size has no impact upon the level of significance associated with the tolerance ratio discussed above.

Table 6: The Effects of Multicolinnearity in Hedonic Pricing Models

---

A) Regression of See on Average Tolerance Ratio

Dep Var: See   N: 11   Multiple R: 0.380   Squared Multiple R: 0.144
Adjusted Squared Multiple R: .049   Standard Error of Estimate: 0.003

Variable	Coefficient	Std Error	Std Coef	Tolerance	T	P(2 Tail)
Constant	0.152	0.018	0.000	–	8.392	0.000
Toler	−0.034	0.028	−0.380	1.000	−1.232	0.249

Analysis of Variance

Source	Sum-of-squares	Df	Mean-square	F-ratio	P
Regression	0.000	1	0.000	1.517	0.249
Residual	0.000	9	0.000		

B) Regression of Maximum Condition Index on Average Tolerance Ratio

Dep Var: Cond   N: 11   Multiple R: 0.983   Squared Multiple R: 0.966
Adjusted Squared Multiple R: .962   Standard Error of Estimate: 2.935

Variable	Coefficient	Std Error	Std Coef	Tolerance	T	P(2 Tail)
Constant	541.911	18.455	0.000	–	29.365	0.000
Toler	−451.969	28.478	−0.983	1.000	−15.871	0.000

Analysis of Variance

Source	Sum-of-squares	Df	Mean-square	F-ratio	P
Regression	2169.041	1	2169.041	251.875	0.000
Residual	77.504	9	8.612		

C) Regression of Average Significance Level of Independent Variables on Tolerance Ratio

Dep Var: Avesign   N: 11   Multiple R: 0.942   Squared Multiple R: 0.888
Adjusted Squared Multiple R: .875   Standard Error of Estimate: 2.253

Variable	Coefficient	Std Error	Std Coef	Tolerance	T	P(2 Tail)
Constant	123.341	14.171	0.000	–	8.704	0.000
Toler	−184.664	21.868	−0.942	1.000	−8.444	0.000

Analysis of Variance

Source	Sum-of-squares	Df	Mean-square	F-ratio	P
Regression	362.087	1	362.087	71.309	0.000
Residual	45.699	9	5.078		

D) Regression of Reg. Coeff. on Lsqft on Average Tolerance Ratio

Dep Var: Lsqft   N: 11   Multiple R: 0.855   Squared Multiple R: 0.730
Adjusted Squared Multiple R: .701   Standard Error of Estimate: 0.014

Variable	Coefficient	Std Error	Std Coef	Tolerance	T	P(2 Tail)
Constant	0.799	0.090	0.000	–	8.908	0.000
Toler	−0.683	0.138	−0.855	1.000	−4.939	0.001

Analysis of Variance

Source	Sum-of-squares	Df	Mean-square	F-ratio	P
Regression	0.005	1	0.005	24.391	0.001
Residual	0.002	9	0.000		

Table 6: (*Continued*)

E) Regression of Number of Significant Variables on The Average Tolerance Ratio
Dep Var: Nosign   N: 11   Multiple R: 0.987   Squared Multiple R: 0.975
Adjusted Squared Multiple R: .972   Standard Error of Estimate: 0.530

Variable	Coefficient	Std Error	Std Coef	Tolerance	T	P(2 Tail)
Constant	−48.719	3.331	0.000	–	−14.627	0.000
Toler	95.834	5.140	0.997	1.000	19.605	0.000

Analysis of Variance

Source	Sum-of-squares	Df	Mean-square	F-ratio	P
Regression	97.112	97.112	346.164	0.000	
Residual	2.525	9			

F) Regression of Median Absolute Percentage Error on Average Tolerance Ratio
Dep Var. Media   N: 11   Multiple R: 0.414   Squared Multiple R: 0.171
Adjusted Squared Multiple R: .079   Standard Error of Estimate: 0.260

Variable	Coefficient	Std Error	Std Coef	Tolerance	T	P(2 Tail)
Constant	7.920	1.635	0.000	–	4.844	0.001
Toler	3.442	2.523	0.414	1.000	1.364	0.206

Analysis of Variance

Source	Sum-of-squares	Df	Mean-square	F-ratio	P
Regression	0.126	1	0.126	1.861	0.206
Residual	0.608	9	0.068		

G) Regression of Mean Absolute Percentage Error on Average Tolerance Ratio
Dep Var. Mean   N: 11   Multiple R: 0.003   Squared Multiple R: 0.000
Adjusted Squared Multiple R: .000   Standard Error of Estimate: 0.295

Variable	Coefficient	Std Error	Std Coef	Tolerance	T	P(2 Tail)
Constant	11.908	1.857	0.000	–	6.411	0.000
Toler	−0.028	2.866	−0.003	1.000	−0.010	0.992

Analysis of Variance

Source	Sum-of-squares	Df	Mean-square	F-ratio	P
Regression	0.000	1	0.000	0.000	0.992
Residual	0.785	9	0.087		

H) Regression of R-squared on Average Tolerance Ratio
Dep Var R2   N: 11   Multiple R: 0.257   Squared Multiple R: 0.066
Adjusted Squared Multiple R: .000   Standard Error of Estimate: 0.533

Variable	Coefficient	Std Error	Std Coef	Tolerance	T	P(2 Tail)
Constant	77.556	3.355	0.000	–	23.119	0.000
Toler	4.127	5.177	0.257	1.000	0.797	0.446

Analysis of Variance

Source	Sum-of-squares	Df	Mean-square	F-ratio	P
Regression	0.181	1	0.181	0.635	0.446
Residual	2.561	9	0.285		

I) Regression of Average Significance Level on Both Tolerance Ratio and Sample Size

Dep Var: Avesign   N: 11   Multiple R: 0.943   Squared Multiple R: 0.889

Adjusted Squared Multiple R: .861   Standard Error of Estimate: 2.384

Variable	Coefficient	Std Error	Std Coef	Tolerance	T	P(2 Tail)
Constant	119.550	23.710	0.000	–	5.042	0.001
Toler	−176.176	39.030	−0.909	0.351	−4.565	0.002
Size	−0.008	0.039	−0.041	0.351	−0.206	0.642

Analysis of Variance

Source	Sum-of-squares	Df	Mean-square	F-ratio	P
Regression	362.329	2	161.164	31.663	0.000
Residual	45.457	8	5.662		

J) Regression of Number of Significant Variables on Both Tolerance Ratio and Sample Size

Dep Var: Nosign   N: 11   Multiple R: 0.968   Squared Multiple R: 0.977

Adjusted Squared Multiple R: .971   Standard Error of Estimate: 0.534

Variable	Coefficient	Std Error	Std Coef	Tolerance	T	P(2 Tail)
Constant	−52.534	5.310	0.000	–	−9.694	0.000
Toler	102.162	8.741	1.055	0.351	11.668	0.000
Size	−0.008	0.009	−0.084	0.351	−0.927	0.361

Analysis of Variance

Source	Sum-of-squares	Df	Mean-square	F-ratio	P
Regression	97.357	2	48.678	170.819	0.000
Residual	2.280	8	0.265		

K) Regression of Coefficient on Square Footage on Both Tolerance Ratio and Sample Size

Dep Var: Lsqft   N: 11   Multiple R: 0.886   Squared Multiple R: 0.785

Adjusted Squared Multiple R: .731   Standard Error of Estimate: 0.014

Variable	Coefficient	Std Error	Std Coef	Tolerance	T	P(2 Tail)
Constant	0.651	0.134	0.000	–	4.642	0.001
Toler	−0.430	0.221	−0.538	0.351	−1.943	0.088
Size	−0.000	0.000	−0.394	0.351	−1.423	0.192

Analysis of Variance

Source	Sum-of-squares	Df	Mean-square	F-ratio	P
Regression	0.005	2	0.003	14.599	0.002
Residual	0.001	8	0.000		

Source: Author's Database.

11.3.3.6 Conclusions

The statistical results substantiate the fact that multicollinearity has little impact upon a regression model's ability to forecast or predict but can affect significance tests on individual regression coefficients. In terms of the Uniontown data the level of multicollinearity appears to be not very severe.

11.3.4 Comparisons of t-Values versus Functional Form in the Presence of Heteroscedasticity

Hedonic models can be specified as linear or non-linear in the parameters. Most hedonic models are specified as either a semi-log or double-log transformation of both the dependent variable and/or selected continuous independent variables. In certain cases the precise functional form is determined by the data using a Box-Cox or Box-Tidwell exponential transformation on either the left side and/or right-side of the equation. The following analysis was motivated by the work of Spitzer (1982) and others which indicates that the use of the Box-Cox estimation procedures can inflate estimated t-values by very large factors (e.g., several thousand times) in the presence of heteroscedasticity.[6] In simple terms, heteroscedastic represents a violation of the assumptions of OLS which, among other things, assumes that the variance of the error term is constant. In economic analysis the variance of the error terms often increase over time. For example, in hedonic housing models the errors might logically increase when predicting the value of larger houses, or if the housing market is inflating rapidly the estimation errors may be larger for more recent higher priced sales. This is an example of positive heteroscedasticity which would understate the standard errors of the regression coefficients, leading to an upward bias in their associated t-statistics. (Negative heteroscedastic would do just of opposite. Note that heteroscedasticity, positive or negative, has no impact upon the estimated regression coefficients See Berry and Feldman, 1985, for further details).

Judge et al. (1985) discuss the use of Box-Cox in the presence of heteroscedasticity. They conclude that in the presence of heteroscedasticity, the estimated functional form parameter lambda in the Box-Cox model will be biased in the direction required to transform the dependent variable to be more homoscedastic. Furthermore, using iterative OLS procedures to compute the maximum likelihood estimate of lambda as well at the regression coefficients, generates a downward-biased estimate of the variance-covariance matrix. Thus, OLS will understate the true variances associated with the regression coefficients and hence over-state their t-values. In a paper by Blackley, Follain, and Ondrich (1984) they estimate the range of inflated t-value to be anywhere from 0% to 600% for two hedonic land value models.

A similar comparison and results are presented by Green (1999) when estimating a money demand function. As discussed in the various papers referenced above, the real issue is not estimating a double-log or semi-log model but using iterative OLS estimation procedures to find the maximum likelihood estimates of both the data transformation parameter (lambda) and the regression coefficients.

11.3.4.1 Functional Form and the Box-Cox Transformation

The Box-Cox model is a flexible estimation procedure which allows one to fit the functional form to a given data set. The linear, semi-log, and double-logs models are special cases of the general Box-Cox model where the right hand lambda and the left side lambda have the following values:

Functional Form	Right-side Lambda	Left-side Lambda
1. Linear model	1	1
2. Semi-log model (Log of dependent variable)	1	0
3. Semi-log model (Log of independent variables)	0	1
4. Log-linear (double-log model)	0	0

11.3.4.2 Uniontown Results

A typical hedonic price model using the four functional forms discussed above was estimated using the Uniontown data. The results are shown in Table 7 for each functional form with and without a correction for heteroscedasticity.

Impact of Functional Form and Heteroscedasticity – As mentioned above, the potential upward bias in t-values reflects the use of iterative OLS procedures in the maximum likelihood estimation of the Box-Cox model. Models such as those estimated by Reichert for Uniontown involve a non-linear transformation of the data to which OLS is applied. As can be seen from the table above, the actual functional form has very little impact upon the average t-value. (The only noteworthy difference relates to the semi-log model which takes the log of the continuous independent variables: models C and G. In both cases, the adjusted R^2 and the average t-values are noticeably *lower*.) On the other hand, while the impact is not dramatic, the average t-value declines when the estimation process includes a correction for heteroscedasticity. This is consistent with the discussion presented above which indicates that positive heteroscedasticity generates an upward bias in the estimated t-values; hence, a correction for heteroscedasticity should reduce the average estimated

Table 7: Functional Form and Heteroscedastic Correction

	R-square	Average t-Value*
Panel A. No correction for heteroscedasticity:		
Model A – Linear Model	.808	11.0
Model B – Semi-log Model	.840	12.7
(Log of *dependent* variable)		
Model C – Semi-log Model	.748	9.4
(Log of *independent* variables)		
Model D – Double-log Model	.797	11.3
Panel B. With heteroscedasticity correction:		
Model E – Linear Model	.809	9.6
Model F – Semi-log Model	.841	11.5
(Log of *dependent* variable)		
Model G – Semi-log Model	.748	8.8
(Log of *independent* variables)		
Model H – Double-log Model	.797	10.6
Panel C. Box-Cox Solution With heteroscedasticity correction:		
Model I – Double-log Model	.810	10.8
(Optimal left and right side lambda = 0.4)		
Model J – Semi-log Model	.812	7.9
(Log of *dependent* variable. Optimal left side lambda = 0.8)		
Model K – Semi-log Model	.808	9.4
(Log of *independent* variables. Optimal right side lambda = 1.0)		

* The average excludes the t-values for the intercept and the autoregressive term: AR(1).
Source: Author's database.

t-value, which is what we observe in Uniontown (the percentage reduction ranges from 7% to 13%).[7]

11.3.4.3 Box-Cox Transformation

In Figures 21–23, the approximate optimal lambda value for each of the four functional forms with the heteroscedastic correction are estimated. Lambda takes on eleven different values starting with 0.0000001 (essentially zero), 0.1, 0.2, 0.3, 0.4 ... 0.5, up to 1.0. The lambda value which maximizes the likelihood function is considered to be close to optimal. The optimal lambda for the double-log model is approximately 0.4, the lambda for the dependent variable semi-log function is 0.8, and the lambda for the independent variable semi-log function is 1.0 (Note that in the latter case the optimal solution is in fact the linear model). A comparison of the average t-values once again indicates no significant variance inflation effect as suggested by the literature.

Figure 21: Likelihood Ratios vs. Lamda (Left and Right Side)
Source: Author's database

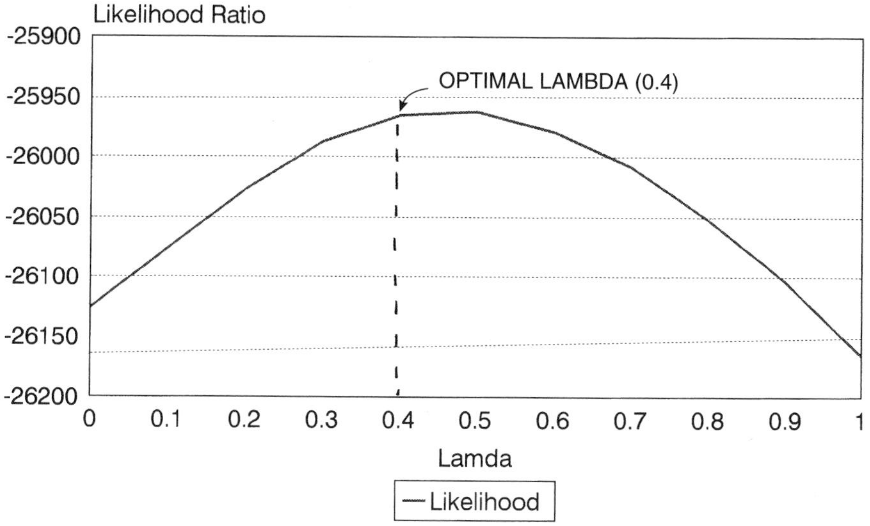

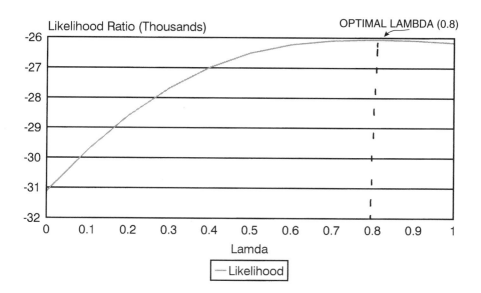

Figure 22: Likelihood Ratios vs. Lamda (Left Side only)
Source: Author's database

11.3.4.4 Conclusions

While Green points out that once lambda is determined ... "it sometimes treated as if it were a known value in the least squares results. But, lambda is an estimate of an unknown parameter. It is not hard to show that the least squares

Figure 23: Likelihood Ratios vs. Lamda (Right Side only)

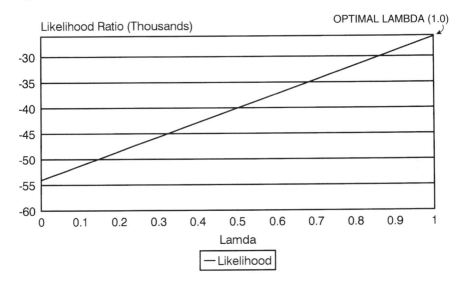

standard errors will always underestimate the correct asymptotic errors." While this may be true in theory, given the results presented above one is led to conclude, at least for the types of residential hedonic modeling employed in Uniontown, that reasonable non-linear transformations of the data do not severely inflate the estimated t-values when compared to the untransformed linear model. And in the case of iterative Box-Cox estimation procedures of the types discussed above, the t-values once again appear to be stable. Greene reports the standard errors in his money demand equation. The errors on his interest rate variable are also quite stable, although the standard errors on his income variable were significantly impacted. Thus, the bias appears to be selective in that certain variables are impacted while others in the same model are not. On the other hand, the presence of positive heteroscedasticity will inflate the standard errors associated with OLS estimation. But as mentioned by Berry and Feldman (1985, p. 78) … "unless heteroscedasticity is "marked", significance tests are virtually unaffected"…. Thus the degree of heteroscedasticity must be severe to produce a major distortion in the results. And for both Uniontown and Cuyahoga county, the degree of heteroscedasticity is relatively mild, producing a noticeable but not dramatic impact.

To summarize:

1) Appropriate transformations of the data prior to OLS estimation yields stable standard errors.
2) The use of the Box-Cox transformation using an iterative search procedure to find the optimal lambda also yields stable standard errors.
3) OLS estimation in the presence of moderate positive heteroscedasticity generates downward-biased standard errors and, hence, inflated t-values.

11.3.5 The Accuracy of Hedonic Models

Multiple regression is often used in mass appraisal applications where one needs to determine the market value of hundreds, or possibly thousands of parcels, in a heavily populated taxing jurisdiction. On the other hand, individual appraisals are generally done when valuing one or a small number of properties. The individual appraiser may often be more accurate since he/she can take additional information into consideration which may not be available in an MLS or tax assessors database. On the other hand, hedonic models such as employed in the Uniontown analysis have a median absolute error rate of 6–7%, which is well within the 10–15% range suggested for appraisers. At the same time, the regression approach may produce a relatively small number of large errors in the 30–40% range. It seems likely that if one conducted an individual appraisal on each of several thousand properties, that a number of appraisals would also have errors substantially in excess of 10%–15%.

To illustrate, Table 8 reports the results of using the Uniontown data to predict housing prices using both an "in-sample" and a "holdout" prediction sample approach. The "in-sample" approach uses the entire database to estimate the hedonic regression coefficients and then uses these coefficients to predict housing prices in five mutually exclusive randomly selected sub-samples. In the "holdout" approach the coefficients are estimated using in the entire Uniontown data set minus the observations in a given holdout sample. The regression results are then used to predict the value of each property in the holdout sample. The prediction results are then averaged across the five holdout samples. As expected, the in-sample results are slightly superior given that the coefficients which are used to predict property values were generated using the identical set of properties used to test the accuracy of these coefficients. This "in-sample" prediction bias is well known and typically ranges from 3 to 5% for real estate prediction models. (In the Uniontown case the bias is 5.7% for the mean absolute error and 3.1% for the median absolute error). Thus, the holdout results are more appropriate and indicate an average adjusted R^2 of 87.0%, an average mean absolute error of 8.1%, and a median absolute error of 6.3%. The average standard deviation of the error terms (i.e., the average SEE) is 10.8%, with maximum errors of -62.5% and $+36.8\%$.[8]

11.3.6 Additional Modeling Issues

Various researchers such as Wilson (1998), Stack and Jacobsen (1998), and Dilmore and Stauffer (1999) argue that hedonic modeling is insufficiently accurate or reliable to be used to accurately assess environmental damages. While their concerns have been raised in the context of estimating environmental damages the issues raised apply to a much wider range of valuation applications,

Table 8: In-Sample vs. Holdiout Sample Accuracy Results*

	N=	Adj. R^2 (%)	Mean Abs. (% Error)	Median Abs. (% Error)	Minimum (% Error)	Maximum (% Error)	Std.Dev. (% Error)
Sample 1							
In-sample	487	87.1	7.70	6.12	−89.5	30.6	10.7
Holdout	487	87.4	8.24	6.33	−113.2	31.9	11.7
Sample 2							
In-sample	532	87.1	7.23	5.62	−63.4	28.1	9.8
Holdout	532	86.7	7.71	5.85	−66.1	41.3	10.5
Sample 3							
In-sample	510	87.1	6.96	5.48	−38.7	28.1	9.1
Holdout	510	86.6	7.41	5.69	−37.5	41.4	9.8
Sample 4							
In-sample	478	87.1	8.00	6.52	−45.5	33.3	10.5
Holdout	478	87.5	8.37	6.60	−45.6	33.7	11.0
Sample 5							
In-sample	489	87.1	8.17	6.87	−49.0	31.7	10.5
Holdout	489	87.0	8.63	7.13	−50.1	35.8	11.1
Mean							
In-sample	499	87.1	7.61	6.12	−57.2	30.4	10.1
Holdout	499	87.0	8.07	6.32	−62.5	36.8	10.8
Difference (In-sample less holdout)	0	0.06	−0.46	−0.20	5.28	−6.46	−0.71
% Difference (In-sample less holdout)	0	0.07	−5.70	−3.13	−8.45	−17.54	−6.56

* In-sample results use the entire database to forecast individual housing prices, while the holdout results exclude the holdout sample from the estimation sample.
Source: Author's database.

which include the full range of regression studies and not just hedonic regression models. For this reason it is important to examine a number of the issues which have recently been raised. These include the appropriate interpretation of the regression coefficients, the size of the regression coefficient relative to their standard errors, and the stability of the coefficients over time.

11.3.6.1 Interpreting the Regression Coefficients

These researchers such as Wilson (1998) point out that hedonic models often report regression coefficients which are illogical in terms of sign or size undermining or invalidating the hedonic modeling approach. The specific concern is that if one has independent comparative estimates on the expected size of certain regression coefficients (e.g., the marginal value of a fireplace estimated using a regression model versus the cost to build a fireplace) and these estimates diverge, this reduces the researchers confidence in the remaining regression coefficients, where one may not have comparative estimates.

For example, assume the regression coefficient in an hedonic price model estimates the marginal value of a given property feature (e.g., swimming pool) to be substantially different that its production or replacement cost. As mentioned previously, the regression coefficients in an hedonic price model measures the marginal contribution of a variety of factors to market value over a given sample period of time, which may or may not reflect production costs. While the cost of adding certain features may increase overtime due to inflation and rising building costs, the market may decide to place less value on the amenity. For example, in some localities given the expense of maintenance, safety issues, and limited seasonal use of an in-ground swimming pool, its marginal value may be significantly lower than the current cost of adding a pool. In Uniontown a total of 81 properties with an average market value of $84,000 had an in-ground pool. Estimating the marginal contribution of a pool to selling price using an hedonic regression model generated an estimate of approximately 4.6%. Thus the marginal contribution of an in-ground pool to typical property's entire value is approximately $3,865, which is substantially below the cost of constructing a pool. Furthermore, it is well known among REALTORS and builders that adding unique and costly amenities to a home often does not increase the total value of the home by an equal amount. While it is true that in a reasonably competitive market the marginal cost of production and marginal value will bare some relationship to price, the relationship is often not perfect. Thus, a variety of factors need to be considered when testing the relevance of regression coefficients.

Furthermore, to adequately evaluate a coefficient we need to examine the entire model and the other remaining coefficients. Simply analyzing a single coefficient may be misleading since the coefficient needs to be viewed in a meaningful context. This is not to say that some hedonic models may not have been poorly specified. Not all models (or data sets for that matter) are created equal. For example, as demonstrated in Section I (D), an hedonic model can be *over-specified*. To illustrate, one often sees hedonic real estate models which include all the following size-related variables: total square feet of living space, total rooms, number of bedrooms, and number of bath rooms. According to the concerns stated above, if one of the coefficients on any of these variables seems to be too small or too large, or perhaps has the wrong sign, one should then question the validity of the entire hedonic modeling approach. Assume, for example that the regression coefficient on total rooms is negative and statistically insignificant. An insignificant coefficient implies that size had no impact on value. One might be tempted to question how an increase in size might have no impact on property values. As mentioned before, the presence of severe multicollinearity tends to inflate the standard errors of the estimated regression coefficients, producing a downward bias in their associated t-values. In this case, it could be appropriate to question the need to model house size in four different ways in the same model. The model has been "over-specified" in this regard.

Multicollinearity aside, conceptually it is entirely possible to have the coefficient on a variable such as total rooms to be negative and statistically significant. A naive interpretation would suggest that rooms are "bad" since they reduce the value of the home. At first glance this may seem illogical but one can make the case that after holding total square footage, number of bedrooms and baths all constant, an increase in the total number of rooms may indicate that a home is being divided into more and smaller rooms which, given the current trend towards larger rooms, may reduce the total value of the house. In effect, the negative coefficient on total rooms measures a "chopped-up effect".

In addition to "over-specification" one must be careful to correctly state and interpret what a given variable is intended to measure or what might be called the "proxy effect". In an early study Cho and Reichert (1980) attempted to account for older properties which may have been renovated, and specifically to include a variable for a remodeled kitchen which is an expensive undertaking The data base used in the study had no variable to designate a remodeled kitchen but it did indicate the presence of a built-in dishwasher. This variable was included as a proxy for a remodeled kitchen reasoning that an older house, which now has a built-in dishwasher, more than likely has a remodeled kitchen. The resulting hedonic model estimated a sizeable regression coefficient of approximately $7,500 for the dishwasher variable. To correctly interpret the regression coefficient one needs to recognize that the build-in dishwasher is a proxy for a remodeled kitchen and not the value of the dishwasher itself. Spending $7,500 (or $20,000 adjusted for inflation) to remodel a kitchen does not seem unrealistic but attributing that value to a dishwasher is. Thus, the researcher needs to carefully define and label each variable to prevent any possible misinterpretation. That is, the researcher should be make quite clear what a proxy variable is designed to proxy.

11.3.6.2 Temporal Stability of Regression Coefficients

Some researchers such as Dilmore and Stauffer (1999) are concerned about the temporal variability associated with certain coefficients. For example, some criticize hedonic models when the value of a regression coefficient on a certain variable changes dramatically over time. It is presumed that the value of the regression coefficient should remain relatively constant overtime.

The variation in the regression coefficient can often be explained by changes in the business cycle, where shifts in home buyer preferences are expected to change in a logical way. Some conclude that this "instability" is a reflection of the unreliable nature of the hedonic modeling approach, while just the opposite appears to be true. That is, the hedonic approach is able to objectively quantify changing economic conditions and housing preferences.

11.3.6.3 Large Confidence Intervals

In many cases researchers should not only report the significance level associated with a regression coefficient but also report appropriate confidence intervals. Failure to calculate confidence intervals in certain cases can be misleading. While it seems clear that when performing the standard t-test, one is actually constructing a confidence interval and observing whether or not the null hypothesis is captured by the confidence interval. In addition to testing the null hypothesis one may also be concerned with the size of interval itself.

We usually establish a confidence interval using the following equation:

$$\beta (\pm) t^*(\sigma)$$

Where t represents the desired confidence level and σ is the standard deviation of the regression coefficient β. The same applies to setting up a confidence interval around a forecasted property value. Assume using regression we estimate the value of a home to be $100,000 with a standard error of the price estimate of $7,500. Thus, if p = $100,000 and σ = $7,500, and we want a 95% confidence interval around our predicted price estimate, the interval is approximately: $85,000 − $115,00 [$100,000 ± (1.96*$7,500)]. At first glance, this seemingly wide range may seem trivial but it is import to remember that each of the possible values from $85,000 − $115,000 are not equally likely. The closer the value is to $100,000 the more confident we are in our estimate, and the single mostly likely value is in fact $100,000. Furthermore, let's assume that we want some reasonable percent of the observations to fall within 12% of the parameter estimate (roughly the mid-point of the suggest performance range suggested for professional appraisers. Note: the appraisal standard does *not* require all values to fall within a 10 to 15% range, just the average). Using the above information, we would achieve the desired degree of precision (± 12%) with slightly less than a 90% confidence level.

It may be useful to develop confidence internals associated with environmental damages for specific property owners. In the typical damage assessment model the researcher use hedonic regression to both estimate the likely impact on a certain class of property owners (e.g., those within 0.50 mile of the contamination site) and to predict the market value of property with and without the presence of contamination. In this case there are two potential sources of error, one associated with the size of the environmental impact and the other associated with the market value of the property. Once again, assume that the researcher has estimated an hedonic model with a standard error of the estimate of $7,500 and an *estimated* environmental impact coefficient of 15%, with its own standard deviation of 5% (i.e., a calculated t-value of 3.0). The impact coefficient is then used to determine damages. Assume that we have a home that is worth $100,000 without an adverse environmental impact and worth only $85,000 with a negative effect. Now furthermore let's assume that our hedonic model, for what ever reason, makes a forecast which is either too low or too large. Since only a few errors (5%) would be more than two standard errors away from the mean, lets assume the confidence range is within ± 1.0 standard deviation. In this case, errors this large or larger will happen about 30% of the time. This suggests a low value of $92,500 and a high value of $107,500. Now assume that the *true* impact coefficient is also within one standard deviation of 15%, i.e., 10 to 20%. The hypothetical model estimates losses to be $15,000, but it is realistic to assume that losses could be as low as $9,250 (0.10 × $92,500) and as high as $21,500 (0.20 × $107,500). Thus, based upon our assumptions, in a reasonable *worst* case scenario the homeowner could possibly be under-compensated by $6,500 or over-compensated by $5,750 ($15,000−$21,500 and $15,000–$9,250, respectively). Thus, it might be helpful to know that the range of likely damages is $9,250 to $21,500, but once again the mostly likely damage estimate remains $15,000.

11.3.6.4 Insignificant Variables

Hedonic real estate models often contain insignificant variables. In this case the researcher has the option to include or delete the insignificant variables. Some elect to drop insignificant variables to simplify the model. On the other hand, if valuation theory suggests that the variables belong in the equation then it may be appropriate to retain them, especially if the sample is sufficiently large such that the corresponding reduction in degrees-of-freedom is not a constraint. If repeated estimates consistently find that the variables are not significant then perhaps the theory is wrong. If we consistently delete all insignificant variables, we will never have evidence to support a new theory or refute old ones. Furthermore, insignificant variables in a model can be useful in the following way. Assume that proximity to an underground leaking gas tank is shown to have a negative impact upon surrounding housing values. This finding will be viewed as being more reliable if the model incorporates variables such as the volume of train, auto, truck traffic, airport noise, etc. That is, if the model carefully tests and controls for either the presence of, or changes in, various non-environmental related influences, one can more confidently and correctly interpret the estimated environmental impact coefficients. Some of these factors may turn out not to be statistically significant, while others will be significant. I would argue that both sets of variables provide valuable information to the researcher and hence should remain in the model.

As discussed above, the standard error of the regression estimate is related but still quite distinct from the standard deviation associated with a regression coefficient. Both have their own unique confidence interval and interpretation. Mixing the two concepts is not appropriate. Some researchers argue that the contribution of the individual environmental impact variable to the overall explanatory power of the model is often quite low and that in many cases dropping the variable has little impact on the model's overall adjusted R^2. The variable logically belongs in the model in the sense that the environmental problem is of sufficient magnitude that it could, at least potentially, have a meaningful impact upon housing values. If the impact variable is correlated with other variables in the model, then dropping the variable generates an omitted variable problem. Omitted variables will likely cause the other variables in the model to inappropriately compensate and biased regression coefficients will be produced. The result of these "adjustments" made by the remaining coefficients may be reflected in little or no change in the explanatory power of the model (adjusted R^2). In other words, the included variables which are correlated with the excluded impact variable end up "speaking" for the excluded variables in the model. Secondly, if the impact effect is relatively small and invariant to the size of the dependent variable (such as would be generated by using a dummy variable specification), adding or subtracting a fixed amount to the intercept term may have a relatively small impact on adjusted R^2. Thirdly, assume that adding the impact variable to the equation only increases the resulting adjusted R^2 from 0.80 to 0.81. While this represents a relatively small increase in the level of the overall explanatory power of the model, the improvement or increase in adjusted R^2 may still be statistically significant. More importantly, it represents an appreciable 5% reduction in the *unexplained* variation in the dependent variable (from 20% to 19%).

11.4 Summary of Conclusions

11.4.1 Model Design Issues

While the precise ranking may vary slightly from one market to another, in general the most important variables in an hedonic model appear to be: time, square footage, either bedrooms or baths (generally not both), and age. This in not to say that other factors such as style, lot size, and location are not important. A good way to view their contribution is the percentage reduction in unexplained variation ($1-$ adjusted R^2). These small-incremental adjusted

R^2 variables serve to "refine" and improve the precision of the estimated coefficients on the high-incremental adjusted R^2 variables. In terms of sample size, ideally the number of observations per coefficient should be close to 30. Given that the hedonic real estate models typically employ approximately 15 independent variables (plus the intercept) this would require a minimum sample of approximately 480 observations. The empirical results for Uniontown seem to bear this out. Furthermore, there appears to be little benefit for increasing sample size much beyond 500.

The careful selection of a reliable and effective control is critical to an accurate assessment of environment damages. The key issue is to ensure that the major difference affecting the housing market in the subject and control areas relates to the environmental concern. It is generally better to carefully define the control area than to include the entire set of transactions in some broad generic control area, such as a large city, since it would reduce the need to model a wide range of potentially disruptive and extraneous factors whose influence often changes over time. Furthermore, model misspecification, such as "over-modeling" the data can lead to major errors in damage estimates and an erroneous identification of the potential geographic extent of damages.

11.4.2 Data and Statistical Issues

Hedonic models based upon carefully screened data drawn from public records are reliable enough to make valid statistical judgements. Information regarding the most important factors in an hedonic model such as price, sales date, square footage, etc. are generally reasonably accurate. Information regarding certain characteristics, such as style and the presence of fireplaces and central air conditioning is considerably less reliable. In terms of geographic location, the evidence suggests that geocoding is not sufficiently accurate to be used in micro-level hedonic pricing studies where the market is defined over a small distance, such as $500'-1000'$. On the other hand, geocoding can be effectively used in larger macro-level studies. But even here the researcher needs to carefully examine the geocoded data for outliers and situations where streets are not amenable to linear interpolation.

The statistical results substantiate the fact that multicollinearity has little pact upon a regression model's ability to forecast or predict but can impact significance tests on individual regression coefficients. Careful selection of the appropriate functional form and subsequent transformation of the data prior to OLS estimation generally yields stable standard errors. In addition to standard natural log transformations, the use of Box-Cox transformations using an iterative search procedure to find the optimal lambdas also yields stable standard errors. Hedonic models which are appropriately designed and estimated using a comprehensive set of carefully screened data can generate median absolute percentage errors of 6–7% which are competitive with the maximum error rates achieved by appraisers and tax assessors.

11.4.3 Interpreting Statistical Results

Once the model is carefully designed and appropriately estimated the researcher must interpret the results properly. For example, a simple comparison between the estimated value of a statistically significant regression coefficient and an alternative value measure, such as cost-to-construct, is frequently not appropriate since the value of hedonic regression coefficients may change over time as consumer preferences change and general market conditions fluctuate. Furthermore, in addition to presenting the results of significance tests on the size of the estimated regression coefficients it may be useful to calculate a confidence interval around the predicted price or individual regression coefficient, fully recognizing that values within the confidence interval are not equally likely. Whether insignificant coefficients should be deleted from a regression model should be left up to the researcher since the decision should be consistent with the initial research objectives. In any event it would be helpful and appropriate to disclose any variables where were initially included and subsequently deleted.

NOTES

[1] Hedonic modeling and hedonic regressions refer to estimating the statistical relationship between the physical characteristics of some object, such as an automobile or residential property, and another other variable which is often market value or price. If the dependent variable is in fact price then, as discussed by Rosen, the hedonic model generally represents a single-equation reduced-form model of housing market equilibrium and associated regression coefficients or model parameters present the implicit marginal contribution of each physical characteristic to the over all value of the object. For a more detailed discussion of hedonic modeling see Rosen (1974), White, Sumka, and Erekson (1979), Muray (1984), Palmquist (1984), Horowirz (1985), Diamond and Smith (1985), McConnel and Phipps (1987), and Michaels and Smith (1990). An alternative approach to hedonic models which involves estimation of a system of structural equations which represent supply and demand conditions. For more details on this approach Mayo (1981), Mendelsohn (1984 & 1985), and Reichert (1991).

[2] The data was collected from Uniontown, Ohio which is a community with a population of approximately 10,000 located in the northeast portion of the state. The 30 acre landfill known as the Industrial Excess Landfill (IEL) is located approximately one mile south of the center of Uniontown in close proximity to a large number of residential properties and a few commercial establishments. From 1966 to when it was ordered closed in 1980, the

facility operated as both a municipal and industrial landfill. The landfill accepted a variety of household trash and commercial liquids (latex and organic solvents), sludge, and various solid wastes. The liquid wastes were dumped directly into a large lagoon or mixed with solid wastes. It later became apparent that toxic waste had begun to contaminate the ground water which was a major concern to homeowners who were on well-water at the time. In addition, significant accumulations of explosive methane gas were discovered in basements near the landfill. During 1984 the IEL was placed upon the EPA's Superfund list and in 1989 a class-action suit was filed on behalf of approximately 1,600 property owners.

[3] The use of categorical, indicator, or "dummy" variables in regression has been widely discussed. (See Netter, Wasserman, and Kutner, 1985, for an excellent discussion of the issues regarding proper specification and interpretation of dummy variables). A common error in hedonic appraisal models is to take an essentially continuous variable and arbitrarily subdivide it into distinct groups or value ranges. This results in an unnecessary loss of information and potential model misspecification. Another common mistake is to form an interaction term by taking the product of two dummy variables, or the product of a dummy variables times a continuous variable, and then not including both of the individual variables along with the interaction term in the model. Once again this represents model misspecification and often leads to an incorrect interpretation of the results.

[4] Note that multicollinearity among several variables in the model does not necessarily impact the estimated coefficients of all the predictor variables in the model. In particular, if X_2 and X_3 are highly correlated but X_1 is not correlated with either X_2 and X_3, then the coefficient on X_1 will not be impacted.

[5] Multicollinearity measures such as the Condition Index are based upon a spectral decomposition of the $X'X$ matrix which identifies: 1) the presence of multicollinearity by one or more characteristic roots being "small" in value, and 2) the type of the linear dependance involved (predictive versus non-predictive dependancy). When two or more variance proportions are large (e.g., >0.50) it suggests that the degree of multicollinearity is adversely impacting the precision (standard error) of the estimated regression coefficients.

[6] For a more in-depth and theoretical discussion of Box-Cox type transformations see Spitzer (1982 & 1984), Seaks and Layson (1982), and Judge, Griffith, Hill, Putkepohl, and Lee (1985)

[7] Similar results were obtained when estimating an hedonic model for Cuyahoga county in Ohio. Using 11,897 observations a typical hedonic model was estimated with and without White's correction for heteroscedasticity. Without this correction the standard errors are somewhat inflated. For example, the uncorrected and corrected standard errors for the four most significant variables are as follows: log of square feet (21.2 vs. 17.8), log of age (27.7 vs. 26.7), number of baths (13.9 vs. 11.6), and garage (23.3 vs. 16.6)].

[8] This is certainly not a perfect forecast but it compares favorably to what an appraiser might do. While most appraisers try do a conscientious job, significant differences in estimates may occur. Cleveland Tomorrow, an economic growth organization, conducted a study during the mid-1990's where a number of local appraisers were asked to estimate the market value of the same urban property. The appraisers selected their own comparables and made their own assumptions regard the likelihood of continue economic development and public housing assistance in the area. For the same property, the individual appraisals came back with a range of $45,000–$80,000. Even when using a well constructed hedonic model, large errors may be observed when forecasting the value of highly unique properties. At the same time, it seems likely that even professional appraisers could have trouble appraising the same unique properties. For example, in a 1998 study of lake front properties in Pioneer, Ohio an hedonic regression model was used to estimate property values. The model predicted the most expensive property on the lake to be worth $242,000, while a

local appraiser independently estimated its market value to be $240,000–250,000. The homeowner listed the house for $350,000, and sold it for $325,000.

REFERENCES

Berry, W. and Feldman, S. *Multiple Regression in Practice*, Sage Publications, Inc., paper #50, 1985.

Blackley, Paul, James Follain, and Jan Ondrich. Box-Cox Estimation of Hedonic Models: How Serious is the Iterative OLS Variance Bias, *Review of Economics and Statistics*, 1984, 66: 2, 348–353.

Brown, I. and Rosen, H. On the Estimation of Structural Hedonic Price Models, *Econometrica*, 1982, 50: 3, 765–768.

Burgess, I and Harmon, O. Specification Tests in Hedonic Models. *Journal of Real Estate Finance and Economics*, 1991, 4, 375–393.

Chattopadhyay, S. Estimating the Demand for Air Quality: New Evidence Based on the Chicago Housing Market. *Land Economics*, 1999, 75: 1, 22–38.

Chichilnisky, G. and Heal, G. Managing Unknown Risks. *Journal of Portfolio Management*, 1998, 24: 4, 85–91.

Cho, Chien-Ching and Alan Reichert. A Statistical Approach to Real Estate Appraisal: An Analysis of the Fort Wayne Market. Indiana Business Review, April, 1980, 9–16.

Clarke, D. E. and Nieves, L. A. An Interregional Hedonic Analysis of Noxious Facility Impacts On Locational Wages and Property Values, paper presented at the 38th annual meeting of the Regional Science Association, 1991, New Orleans, Louisiana.

Cropper, M., Deck, L., and McConnell, K. On the choice of Functional Form for Hedonic Price Functions. *The Review of Economics and Statistics*, 1988, 70: 4, 668–675.

Dezube, D. Living in a Disaster Area, *Mortgage Banking*, 1994, 54: 9, 28–35.

Diamond, D. B. and Smith, B. A. Simultaneity in the market for housing characteristics, *Journal of Urban Economics*, 1985, 17, 280–292.

Dilmore, G. and Stauffer, T. On the Economic Insignificance of Statistical Significance in Post-Daubert Hedonic Pricing Models, paper presented at the annual meeting of the American Real Estate Society, 1998, Monterey, California

Do, A. and Grudnitski, G. Golf Courses and Residential House Prices: An Empirical Examination, *Journal of Real Estate Finance and Economics*, 1995, 10, 261–270.

Dunn M. B. Property Values and Potentially Hazardous Production Facilities: A Case Study of the Kanawha Valley, West Virginia, unpublished Ph.D. Dissertation, Florida State University, 1986, Tallahassee, Florida.

Epple, D. Hedonic Prices and Implicit Markets: Estimating Demand and Supply Functions for Differentiated Products, *Journal of Political Economy*, 1987, 95: 1, 59–80.

Freeman, A. M. Hedonic prices, property values and measuring environmental benefits, *Scandinavia Journal of Economics*, 1979, 81, 154–173.

Follain, I. and Jimenez, E. Estimating the Demand for Housing Characteristics: A Survey and Critique, *Regional Science and Urban Economics*, 1985, 15, 77–107.

Gamble, H. and Downing, R. Effects of Nuclear Power Plants on Residential Property Values, *Journal of Regional Science*, 1982, 22, 457–478.

Green, William. *Econometric Analysis*, 4th Prentice Hall, 1999.

Greenberg M. and Hughes, J. The Impact of Hazardous Waste Superfund Sites on Property Value and Land Use: Tax Assessors Appraisal, *The Appraisal Journal*, January, 1992, 42–51.

Harrison, D. Jr. and Rubinfield, D. L. Hedonic housing prices and the demand for clean air, Journal of Environmental Economics and Management, 1978, 5, 81–102.

Halvorsen, I. L. and Pollakowski, H. Choice of Functional Form for Hedonic Price Equations, *Journal of Urban Economics*, 1981, 10, 7–49.

Havlicek, J., Richardson, R., and Davies, L. Measuring the Impacts of Solid Waste Disposal Site Location on Property Values, *American Agricultural Economics Association*, 1971, 53: 5, 869.

Kang, Han-Bin and Alan Reichert, An Empirical Analysis of Hedonic Regression and Grid-Adjustment Techniques in Real Estate Appraisal, *American Real Estate and Urban Economics Association Journal*, 1991, 19: 1, 70–91.

Kang, Han-Bin and Alan Reichert. An Evaluation of Alternative Estimation Techniques and Functional Forms in Developing Statistical Appraisal *Models, Journal of Real Estate Research*, 1987, 2: 1, 1–29.

Ketkar, K. Hazardous Waste Site and Property Values in the state of New Jersey. *Applied Economics*, 1992, 24, 647–659.

Kinnard, W. and Geckler, M. B. The Effects on Residential Real Estate Prices From Proximity to Properties Contaminated with Radioactive Materials, *Real Estate Issues*, 1991, 16: 2, Fall/Winter.

Kinnard, W., Mitchell, G. Beron, and Webb, J. Market Reaction to an Announced Release of Radioactive Materials: The Impact on Assessable Value, *Property Tax Journal*, 1991, 10: 3, 283–297.

Kohlhase, Janet. The Impact of Toxic Waste Sites On Housing Values, *Journal of Urban Economics*, 1991, 30: 1, 1–26.

Judge, George, W. E. Griffith, R. Carter Hill, Helmut Lutkepohl, and Tsoung-Chao Lee, *The Theory and Practice of Econometrics*, John Wiley and Sons, Inc., 1985.

Li, M. and Brown, H. Micro-Neighborhood Externalities and Hedonic Housing Prices, *Land Economics*, 1980, 56, 125–141.

Mayo, S. Theory and Estimation in the Economics of Housing Demand, *Journal of Urban Economics*, 1981, 10, 95–116.

McConnel, K and Phipps, T. Identification of Preference Parameters in Hedonic Models: Consumer Demands with Nonlinear Budgets, *Journal of Urban Economics*, 1987, 22, 35–52.

Mendelsohn, R. Estimating the Structural Equations of Implicit Markets and Household Production Functions, *The Review of Economics and Statistics*, 1984, 66, 673–677.

Mendelsohn, R. Identifying Structural Equations with Single Market Data *The Review of Economics and Statistics*, 1985, 67, 525–529.

Michaels R.G. and Smith, V. K. Market Segmentation and Valuing Amenities with Hedonic Models: The Case of Hazardous Waste Sites, *Journal of Urban Economics*, 1990, 28, 223–242.

Miller, Norman. A Geographic Information System Based Approach to the Effects of Nuclear Processing Plants on Surrounding Property Values: The Case of the Fernald Settlement Study", unpublished paper, University of Cincinnati, College of Business, 1992.

Moore, James and Alan Reichert. Analyzing the Temporal Stability of Appraisal Model Coefficients: An Application of Ridge Regression Techniques, *The American Real Estate and Urban Economics Association Journal*, 1984, 12: 1, 50–71.

Mundy and William. Stigma and Value, *The Appraisal Journal*, 1992, 60, 1.

Murdoch, J., Singh, H. and Thayer, M. The Impact of Natural Hazards on Housing Values: The Loma Prieta Earthquake, *The American Real Estate and Urban Economics Association Journal*, 1993, 21: 2, 167–184.

Murphy, Lloyd. Determining the Appropriate Equation in Multiple Regression Analysis, *Appraisal Journal*, October, 1989, 498–516.

Murray, M. Mythical Demands and Mythical Supplies for Proper Estimation of Rosen's Hedonic Price Model, *Journal of Urban Economics*, 1984, 14, 327–337.

Nelson, A., Genereux, J., and Genereux, M. House Price Effects of Landfills, *Land Economics*, 1992, 68: 4, 359–365.

Nelson, J. Three Mile Island and Residential Property Values: Empirical Analysis and Policy Implications, *Land Economics*, 1981, 57: 3, 363–372.

Nelson, J. Residential Choice, Hedonic Prices and the Demand for Urban Air Quality, *Journal of Urban Economics*, 1978, 5, 357–369.

Neter, Wasserman, and Kutner. Applied Linear Statistical Models (2nd Edition) Richard Irwin, Inc., Homewood, Illinois, 1985.

Palmquist, I. Estimating the Demand for the Characteristics of Housing, *The Review of Economics and Statistics*, 1984, 66, 394–404.

Palmquist, I. Valuing Localized Externalities, *Journal of Urban Economics*, 1992, 31, 59–68.

Pedrozo, N. Essays on Market Efficiency in Real Estate, Dissertation Abstract, *Journal of Real Estate Literature*, 1998, 6, 1.

Quigley J. Airports and Property Values: A Survey of Recent Evidence, *Journal of Transport Economics and Policy*, 1980, 14, 37–52.

Reichert, Alan. Evidence on the Persistence and Robustness of Contamination Effects The Case of a Super Fund Site Revisited, *Appraisal Journal*, 1999, 65: 4, 126–135.

Reichert, Alan. The Impact of a Toxic Waste Super Fund Site On Property Values, *The Appraisal Journal*, 1997, 67: 2, 381–392.

Reichert, Alan Michael Small, and Sunil Mohanty. The Impact of Landfills Upon Residential Property Values, *Journal of Real Estate Research*, 1992, 7: 3, 297–314.

Reichert, Alan. The Impact of Interest Rates, Income, and Employment upon Regional Housing Prices, *Journal of Real Estate Finance and Economics*, 1990, 3: 4, 373–391.

Reichert, Alan and James Moore. Using Latent Root Regression to Identifying Non-predictive Collinearity in Statistical Appraisal Models, *American Real Estate and Urban Economic Journal*, 1986, 14: 1, 136–152.

Seaks, T. and Layson, S. Box-Cox Estimation with Standard Econometric Problems, *Review of Economics and Statistics*, 1983, 65: 1, 160–164.

Smith, V. K. and Desvousges, W. H. The Value of Avoiding a LULU: Hazardous Waste Disposal Sites, *Review of Economics and Statistics*, 1986, 68, 293–299.

Spitzer, John. A Primer on Box-Cox Estimation, *Review of Economics and Statistics*, 1982, 64: 2, 307–313.

Spitzer, John. Variance Estimates in Models with the Box-Cox Transformation Implications for Estimation and Hypothesis Testing, *Review of Economics and Statistics*, 1985, 66: 4, 645–652.

Swartzman, D., Croke, K., and Swible, S. Reducing Aversion to Living Near Hazardous Waste Facilities through Compensation and Risk Reduction, *Journal of Environmental Management*, 1985, 20, 43–50.

Rosen, S. Hedonic Prices and Implicit Markets: Product Differentiation in Pure Competition, *Journal of Political Economy*, 1974, 82, 4–55.

Rush, R. and Bruggink, T. The Value of Ocean Proximity on Barrier Island Houses, *The Appraisal Journal*, 2000, 68: 2, 142–150.

Schultze, W., McClelland, G., Doane, M., Balistreri, E., and Boyce, R., Hurd, B., and Simenauer, R. An Evaluation of Preferences for Superfund Site Cleanup: A Preliminary Assessment, Volume 1, Office of Policy, Planning, and Evaluation, U.S. Environmental Protection Agency, Washington, D.C., March, 1995.

Smolen,G., Moore, G., and Conway, L. Hazardous Waste Landfill Impacts on Local Property Values, *Real Estate Appraiser*, 1992, 58: 1, 4–11.

Simons R., Bowen W., and Sementelli, A. The Effect of Underground Storage Tanks on Residential Property Values in Cuyahoga County, Ohio, *Journal of Real Estate Research*, 1997, 4, 29–42.

Spahr, R. and Sunderman, M. Valuation of Property Surrounding a Resort Community, *Journal of Real Estate Research*, 1999, 17, 227–243.

Stack W. and Jacobsen, T. Hedonic Models of Diminished Property Values: Proof that Procrustes Lives, *Analysis and Perspective*, Bureau of National Affairs, 13: 11, 374–381.

Wilson, Albert. The Scientific Validity of Hedonic Modeling, presented at Mealey's Underground Storage Litigation conference, 1998.

Witte, A., Sumka, H., and Erekson, H. An Estimate of a Structural Hedonic Price Model of the Housing Market: An Application of Rosen's Theory of Implicit Markets, *Econometrica*, 47: 5, 1151–1173.

Zivot, Startz and Nelson. Valid Confidence Interval and Inference in the Presence of Weak Instruments. *International Economic Review*, 1998, 1119–1144.

Chapter 12

Do Market Perceptions Affect Market Prices?
A Case Study of a Remediated Contaminated Site

Sandy, G. Bond
Department of Property, Faculty of Architecture, Property, Planning & Fine Arts
University of Auckland, Auckland, New Zealand

"Stigma",[1] in relation to remediated contaminated land, is the price (value) reduction required to compensate investors for perceived financial risks[2] and uncertainties[3] associated with remediated contaminated property. Uncertainties relate to negative intangible factors such as: the inability to effect a total "cure";[4] the possibility of failure of the remediation method; the possibility of changes in legislation or remediation standards; difficulty in obtaining financing, or simply, a fear of the unknown. Post-remediation "stigma" equates to the difference in value between a remediated contaminated site and a comparable "clean" site with no history of contamination.[5]

This paper summarizes the results from two studies conducted in parallel to determine the existence of stigma associated with a site's soil contamination history. Firstly, a hedonic pricing model was employed to analyze prices of post-remediated vacant residential land along the Swan River, in Perth Western Australia (WA), from 1992 to 1998. Secondly, a survey was used to study the attitudes and reactions of actual residential property owners toward living on a previously contaminated site. The studies helped to determine firstly, if market perceptions about post-remediated contaminated sites are reflected in market prices of such land (i.e. if stigma exists) and secondly, if opinion surveys can be used as a proxy for market sales data and analysis. The studies can be employed in tandem to check on their credibility and reliability as tools to explain and measure stigma.

The results from both studies were consistent and indicate that while an area's contamination history may impact negatively on property prices, the stigma-based price decreases can be compensated by positive influences on price from desirable features evidenced within the case study neighborhood. These features include river views, river and beach access, proximity to public transport, and cycle-walking pathways.

12.1 Introduction

Environmental activism commenced in the US in the 1960's and organizations were established as vehicles to effect change. These groups were instrumental in helping shape the environmental legislative agenda in the US with the first law being signed in 1970, the National Environmental Policy Act, which created the present Environmental Protection Agency. Partially in response to a number of high profile contaminated sites where property owners suffered substantial financial losses the Comprehensive Environmental Response, Compensation, and Liability Act (CERCLA) was passed in 1980. This gave the EPA considerably more power to protect the environment and enforce clean up standards. It also established joint and several "strict" financial liability of previous and current owners of contaminated property for both clean up (now termed "remediation") and damages established in court by injured parties. Such damages now include compensation for "stigma". Other industrialized nations have subsequently followed suit by introducing similar environmental legislation.

These statutes have highlighted the need for property appraisers to take both contamination and "stigma" into account in their appraisals. However, uncertainty exists as to the possible magnitude and duration of impacts on property value arising from land contamination. This chapter presents and compares two complementary methods available to determine the existence of "stigma" associated with remediated contaminated property.

12.2 Brief Literature Review

12.2.1 Background

Much of the literature dealing with the issues of contaminated land focuses on reported, perceived or expected difficulties in obtaining financing and associated impacts on value. Those that relate to appraisal methodology focus mostly on commercial property and what is "proper" valuation methodology. Others document the practices of appraisers[6] (e.g., Lizieri et al. (1995), Dixon (1995), Richards (1995a,b, 1997), Syms (1994, 1995, 1996), Kennedy (1997), Bond & Kennedy (1998), and Kinnard & Worzala (1998, 1999)).

The concept of environmental "stigma", while first emerging in the appraisal literature in the late 1980's (see for example, Kinnard, 1989, 1990; Mundy, 1988, 1989, and Patchin, 1991, 1992), has been difficult to quantify, with some appraisers ignoring it all together. For example, only a few of the appraisers surveyed in the UK by Dixon (1995), Richards (1995) and Kennedy (1997) use an adjustment for environmental stigma. However, their adjustments tend to be subjective (a yield rate adjustment or capital value deduction) justified as a pragmatic approach on the basis of information limitations. Syms (1996) criticizes such an approach and suggests an alternative methodology. He believes that understanding the risk perceptions of property market participants is necessary to facilitate the construction of a valuation model for contaminated land that will enable stigma to be assessed. This is consistent with the work of Mundy in the US.

12.2.2 Alternative Valuation Methodologies

12.2.2.1 The "Syms" Model

Syms associates the term "stigma"[7] with risk perception – the perception of risk is what causes the stigma effect – and defines it as:

> That part of any diminution in value attributable to the existence of land contamination, whether treated or not, which exceeds the costs attributable to (a) the remediation of the subject property, (b) the prevention of future contamination, (c) any known penalties or civil liabilities, (d) insurance and (e) future monitoring. (Syms, 1997, p. 179.)

To assess stigma Syms uses two approaches. The first approach uses the results from a case study approach advocated by Patchin (1994). In Patchin's study the allowance for stigma at properties for which values had to be deter-mined was based on estimates of stigma determined at comparable case study sites,[8] i.e., properties that had either sold at reduced figures or where agreed transactions had failed due to contamination. The stigma estimates at the case study sites were derived from determining the unimpaired value of the sites and deducting the impaired value and the costs of remediation. The unim-paired value was derived from either a purchase agreement that had failed due to the discovery of contamination, a previous sale, or an appraisal. From only eight case studies Patchin postulated that the stigma impact was between 21% and 69% of the unimpaired value of the properties.

This approach (using stigma estimates derived at comparable sites) has been criticized by some commentators (e.g., Dixon (1995) and Richards (1996)) due to the unique site-specific nature of contamination and hence, lack of compa-rability between sites. Yet the lack of contaminated land sales evidence in the UK means that such an analysis to derive a base range of stigma impact is not possible in that country. It is for this reason, while recognizing the problems associated with adopting US-based information for application in the UK, that Syms adopts the figures derived in the Patchin study.[9] However the problems with adopting limited and dated US-based data remain. The results from such a study that are based on limited findings from a study that occurred in a different time period, in a different country where purchasers may perceive hazards differently, are very likely non-transferable.

Syms' second approach to stigma assessment overcomes some of these problems and is less reliant on both comparable evidence (to overcome the problem of data availability indicated above) and the results from one approach (or arbitrary yield adjustments that are used by many UK valuers). It incorpo-rates the results from the first approach with findings from a number of risk perception studies that are based on the work of Slovic (1992). He suggests a risk assessment model that utilizes five sets of data:

1. Observed stigma effects (from Patchin's US-based study).
2. Perceptions as to the relative levels of risk associated with different industrial activities (derived from postal surveys of both valuation and non-valuation experts – Phase 1).
3. The assessed risk of the subject site before remediation (from interview surveys of valuers – Phase 2).
4. The perceived impact on value from alternative methods of remediation and the expected end use of the site (from the postal surveys of both valuation and non-valuation experts – Phase 1).
5. The estimated assessment of risk after treatment and redevelopment of the site (from postal surveys of both valuation and non-valuation experts – Phase 3).

The stigma effect range from the Patchin (1994) study sets the baseline for the impact of stigma on property value, while the second data set listed above enables stigma values to be identified for a range of activities. Data sets three through five link the survey results to actual properties that are to be valued, by obtaining "value adjusters" which are aggregated and divided by four to give a mean value adjustment (the stigma effect to be applied as a percentage reduction to value). However, given that each "value adjuster" relates to either the use of the site, the different stages of the redevelopment process, or the treatment method, the logic behind averaging such figures is questionable, particularly where the stigma-adjustment factors vary widely.

12.2.2.2 Contingent Valuation Approach

Chalmers and Roehr (1993), like Syms, recognize the importance of knowing how perceptions towards contaminated land affect property value, including those arising from stigma. They suggest the use of contingent valuation (CV). This involves the use of formal surveys of knowledgeable market participants to determine their willingness to accept compensation for reductions in environmental amenities. However, the use of the contingent valuation (CV) approach, particularly when assessing damages to contaminated property, has been cautioned (see for example, the comments of the U.S. National Oceanic and Atmospheric Administration (NOAA), Federal Register, January 15, 1993) due to limitations including the requirement of a high response rate, careful questionnaire design and administration, and appropriate validation checks. Thus, Chalmers and Roehr also suggest the use of regression (within an hedonic pricing framework), the results of which can be used to verify the opinion survey results. This method is valid, however, only where large quantities of sales transaction data and complete data files on all relevant variables are available to allow meaningful analysis.

McLean & Mundy (1998), as well as recommending the use of contingent valuation for the estimation of environmental damages to property also suggest two other survey-based techniques: conjoint analysis and perceived diminution (a qualitative survey with similarities to a CV survey). They suggest the use of these complementary techniques in recognition of the limited historical or recent sales data that often faces appraisers valuing contaminated property for damage assessment purposes. Further, they suggest that when potential buyers are unaware of, or not fully knowledgeable about, the nature and extent of contamination the sales data may not fully reflect damages. In these instances the usefulness of the traditional valuation approaches is limited and each of the three survey techniques presented provides an alternative.

To justify the use of the CV approach (described above) McLean & Mundy (1998) argue that the acknowledged limitations of the approach can be overcome if the guidelines recommended by the Blue Ribbon Panel appointed by the NOAA, (Federal Register, January 15, 1993) are followed. Caution is still warranted in the application of CV, however. For example, the NOAA panel conclusion that "hypothetical markets tend to overstate willingness to pay for private as well as public goods. The same bias must be expected to occur in CV market studies" (Federal Register, January 15, 1993, 4610) appears to be substantiated from recent papers on the application of CV.[10]

While contingent valuation has been applied, with degrees of success, to real estate problems, including the assessment of damages to contaminated property for over twenty-five years[11] evidence of the application of conjoint analysis to real estate problems is limited. Yet conjoint analysis appears to have potential in the field of property valuation.

12.2.2.3 Conjoint Analysis

In introducing the conjoint analysis method McLean and Mundy refer to the description provided by the NOAA Final Rule (Federal Register, January 5, 1996), as follows:

> Conjoint analysis is a survey procedure that is used to derive the values of particular attributes of goods or services. Information is collected about individuals' choices between different goods that vary in terms of their attributes or service levels. With this information, it is possible to derive values for each particular attribute or service. If price is included as an attribute in the choice scenarios, values can be derived in terms of dollars, which can be used with the valuation approach.

McLean and Mundy (1998) provide an illustration of how conjoint analysis can be applied in practice. Further, they present it as a complementary approach to the traditional valuation approaches for estimating damages to real property arising from contamination but one that overcomes the limitations of the traditional valuation approaches for estimating those damages.

12.2.3 Tests of Opinion Survey Reliability as a Proxy for Market Sales Evidence

To test whether the results of opinion survey and contingent valuation can be used as a substitute or proxy for actual market sales transactions Kinnard et al. (1994) compared the results from each survey with the those of the market sales analysis of two case studies in the US. The overall results indicate that opinions of respondents not necessarily involved in buying in areas claimed to be affected by proximity to a source of hazard to human health and safety are not a reliable or suitable substitute for market sales transactions data in identifying and measuring the impact on sales prices of residential properties. The opinions are much more negative than the reflections of actual market behavior of individual buyers.

To address this discrepancy Kinnard et al. (1994) recommend the use of both forms of evidence (market prices and market opinion) in tandem to check on their "probity and credibility". Further, in response to the difference in behavior one might observe when comparing the market sales data (current residents) to opinion survey results (commonly from those who are not necessarily prospective purchasers in the impact area under study), they suggest that a study of *ex post* opinion surveys of *actual* buyers would produce useful results.

While the results from opinion surveys do not necessarily reflect actual market behavior, information limitations in the UK (as in NZ, Bond and Kennedy (1998)) prevent the verification of opinion survey results and hinder the use of more sophisticated methods for stigma assessment. At least in the US, from results of the Kinnard & Worzala (1999) study, it appears that market sales data are becoming sufficiently numerous and available for direct market evidence to be utilized in estimating post-remediation "stigma".

The study reported here adopted the Kinnard et al. (1994) recommendations and measures the effects of stigma on post-remediated residential sites using both *ex post* opinion surveys of *actual buyers* of affected sites and market sales analysis in tandem. Comparing the results from each study served to determine whether the results from the opinion surveys can serve as a proxy for actual market sales data and analysis. Due to the problems associated with the Syms' approach and CV (outlined above) a generalist survey was adopted initially.[12]

The literature dealing specifically with the measurement of the impact of environmental hazards on *residential* sale prices (including proximity to transmission lines, landfill sites and ground water contamination) indicates the popularity of hedonic pricing models, as developed by Rosen (1974) and Freeman (1979). Accordingly, this approach was adopted for the current study. The more recent studies, including those by Dotzour (1997); Simons & Sementelli (1997); Reichert (1997), focus on *proximity* to an environmental hazard and demonstrate that this reduces residential house prices by varying amounts depending on distance from the hazard.[13] There are very few published studies, however, which use hedonic housing models to measure the impact of "stigma" on post-remediated residential sites (see Dale et al., 1999). The results from the study reported here serves to redress this deficiency.

12.3 Research Methodology

12.3.1 Part I: Market Study

As in the previous residential house price studies reported above, the standard hedonic methodology developed by Rosen (1974) and Freeman (1979) was used to quantify the effect of a site's contamination history on the post-remediated prices. Control variables used in the model to account for the property attributes were taken from other well-tested models reported in the literature and from appraisal theory.

12.3.1.1 Model Specification
The basic model used to analyze the impact on sale price of a post-remediated site is as follows:

$$P_i = f(X_{1,i}, X_{2,i}, \ldots, X_{n,i})$$

where

P_i = property price at the ith location
$X_{1,i}$–$X_{n,i}$ = individual characteristics of each sold property (e.g., lot size, view, sales date, post-remediated site, etc.)

The more recent hedonic pricing studies[14] that demonstrate the effects of proximity to an environmental hazard use different functional forms to represent the relationship between price and various property characteristics. In hedonic housing models the linear and log-linear models are most popular. The linear model implies constant partial effects between house prices and housing characteristics, while the log-linear model allows for non-linear price effects and is shown in the following equation:

$$LnP_i = b_0 + b_1 X_{1,i} + b_2 X_{2,i} + b_3 X_{3,i} + \cdots + b_n X_{n+1}$$
$$+ a_o D_0 + \cdots + a_m D_m + e_0$$

In the above model the dependent variable LnP_i being the natural logarithm of sales price, and b_1 to b_n, and a_o to a_m are the model parameters to be estimated, i.e., the implicit unit prices for increments in the property characteristics (X_1 to X_n – the continuous characteristics such as site size, and D_o to D_m – the categorical (dummy) variables such as river views). Sometimes the natural logarithm of size is also used. The parameters are estimated by regressing property sales on the property characteristics. The null hypothesis states that the effect of being located on a post-remediated site does not explain any variation in property sales price.

The models tested in this study included the linear and log-linear forms, as well as both of these forms with the different transformations of the variable *Area*, including square root, and log. The following statistics and checks were used to help select the most appropriate model: the coefficients have the expected signs as suggested by theory or practice; the adjusted coefficient of determination (adjusted R^2); the standard error of the regression equation; the AIC[15] and SBC[16] statistics; *t*-test of significance of the coefficients and F-statistic to determine the statistical significance of the regression. Finally, the models were checked to determine if the assumptions underlying them were met. Based on these model selection criteria the model selected to complete the analysis was a semi-logarithmic form.

12.3.1.2 The Data

Part of the selection process for finding an appropriate case study area was to find one where there was a sufficient number of post-remediated property sales for analysis to provide statistically reliable and valid results. Rocky Bay Estate in Perth, WA met this criterion, with 78 sales recorded from 1992–1998. Further, as many of the sales occurred at auction, they represented true "market" prices, unaffected by a real estate agents' price-setting criteria that can often confound the open-market price-setting mechanism by biasing potential purchasers' own estimates of value.[17]

Similarly, vacant land sales in control areas, not affected by a contamination history, were required for analysis. Due to the multitude of factors that combine to determine a neighborhood's character (e.g. proximity to the Swan River, recreational facilities provided, standard of housing, proximity to amenities, etc.) and the difficulty in allowing for these separately, sales that are located in areas with comparable neighborhood characteristics to the subject area were preferred.

Four areas were identified that contained many, but not necessarily all, of the neighborhood characteristics observed in the subject area. For example, one area was close to the Swan River but had no view of it. Generally, all areas had a similar standard of housing and with similar facilities and amenities nearby to that of the subject area found and include:

- Mosman Park: 70 sales from 1996 to 1998
- North Bank: 34 sales from 1995 to 1998
- Richmond Racecourse: 117 sales from 1994 to 1998
- Ascot Waters: 110 sales from 1996 to 1998.

Table 1: Comparison of Areas

Feature	Rocky Bay	Mosman Park	North Bank	Race-course	Ascot Waters
Views	Panoramic river	Limited river	River	None	Limited river & city
Proximity to River	Adjoining	1 km	Adjoining	1 km	200 m
Proximity to Fremantle	5 km	6 km	2.5 km	2 km	27 km
Proximity to Perth CBD	13 km	12 km	15.5 km	17 km	8 km
Amenities	Cycle-walk path, river-access, playground	None	Walk path, hotel, and shops	None	Island reserve, park, and marina
Standard of housing	High	High	Medium-high	Medium	Medium

Table 1 above compares the control areas with the case study area.

Case Study Area – Rocky Bay Estate

The case study area comprises some 8 hectares of prime riverfront land located in North Fremantle. Riverfront property is traditionally the most valuable in Perth. Since Federation much of it has been occupied by the Federal or State governments, which have intermittently released land for private residential development. In the case of the subject site, Land Corp was the developer, an independent government agency.

In 1990–92, the former State Engineering Works[18] site was redeveloped as a high-class, single-family residential suburb, known as Rocky Bay Estate, containing approximately 110 fully serviced sites ranging in size from 249 to 880 m². The subdivision also includes areas of public open space, in addition to a 9 m wide strip of general open space comprising a cycle-walking path between the site and the top of the cliff adjacent to the Swan River. Located above the river it provides panoramic views over the river, to Preston Point and East Fremantle in the south. It is conveniently located within walking distance of Leighton Beach, easy commuting distance (5–10 minutes) of both Fremantle and Mosman Park and within 15 km of Perth's CBD.

History of the Site[19]

The site was originally part of a limestone hill that dropped steeply to the Swan River. In the late 1800's and early 1900's the Public Works Department quarried limestone from the site. In 1908, operations at the State Engineering Works (SEW) started. They involved mostly the manufacture of harvesters and ploughs and later, metal fabrication. The SEW were finally closed down in 1987.

Contamination

The bulky by-product pyrites cinders from the sulfuric acid production plant on the adjoining site were used for general filling of the SEW site. Further, a foundry operated as part of the SEW. During the earlier years it had coal-fed furnaces. Foundry clinker consisting of general wastes from the foundry operation, and coal residues, were generally distributed over the site.

Site testing

Results from groundwater testing indicated excessive levels of nitrate and salinity. Arsenic and cyanide were at the upper limits of safe standards for domestic supply.[20] Results from soil tests indicated that the site's waste materials had heavy metal values many times greater than established recommended concentrations in soils set by Australian authorities for various land uses. These wastes were found to be leaching into the sands beneath and resulted in the elevated levels of selected heavy metals found in the ground waters.

Site clean up

Site clean up[21] was completed in November 1990. This involved relocating 47,000 m^3 of visually contaminated materials (pyrites-clinkers, building rubble) off-site to the landfill in Henderson. The additional 15,000 m^3 of contaminated sands beneath these wastes were relocated on-site to the base of the limestone hillock on the northwestern section of the site, well away from the river. It is understood that the relocated sand will be covered with 5 meters of clean soil when the final stage of the development is completed.[22] The entire site was covered with clean fill, to a depth of 1.5 meters.

Control area descriptions

Mosman Park   This small sub-division of 114 sites ranging in size from approximately 350–750 m^2, is located northeast of Rocky Bay Estate. The land rises gently from the main access road with homes built on the upper sites receiving restricted views south over the Swan River and East Fremantle. Housing is in the medium to high price bracket for Perth.

North Bank   The site occupies a prominent location on the north side of, and adjoining, the Swan River, between the Stirling Highway and Queen Victoria bridges. These bridges act as key gateways to Fremantle. The development comprises mostly high-density housing: duplex, apartment blocks, and townhouses. Only two streets have single-family sites. A walkway has been developed along the foreshore reserve. While Stirling Highway, Queen

Victoria Street and their bridges provide easy access for residents to Fremantle, these busy thoroughfares create substantial traffic noise.

Richmond Racecourse   Richmond Racecourse, as the name implies, was previously used as a horse racecourse (trotting club). According to the East Fremantle Shire no contamination existed on the site that they are aware of. The subdivision has been designed around a park. Located a kilometer away from the Swan River and on generally level topography. No river or ocean views are obtained. Most of the homes are moderately priced single-story homes of Neo-Federation style design.

Ascot Waters   This subdivision comprising approximately 14 hectares, situated to the east of Perth city, was originally used for a clay works with the remainder of the land comprising a swamp. A rubbish tip adjoining the site has subsequently been remediated to Department of Environmental Protection standards and is now designated as an island reserve, separated from the main development by waterways and linked by narrow road causeways.

The subdivision is located in the City of Belmont, on an inverted "U" shape bend of the Swan River. As such, the site is bound on three sides by the river with many of the sites receiving water views. It is in an area zoned predominantly industrial and commercial with Ascot Raceway located opposite, disused kilns, and the Great Eastern Highway immediately to the south. Substantial amenities have been developed and include a 16-hectare island reserve, lagoon, boating marina and parks. However, the area is disadvantaged by the distance to convenience stores and shopping facilities, with none located nearby.

12.3.1.3 Multiple Regression Analysis Procedure

Data specifics

The dependent variable is the vacant land sale price (in Australian dollars) sold between 1992 and 1998. The data set includes 409 property sales obtained from the Valuer General's Office (VGO) and Land Corp. The data set includes independent variables that correspond to property attributes known and suspected to influence price. All land sales properties were individually inspected as part of data collection or verification on many of the independent variables.

To take account of price movement in the sales analyzed, dummy variables were used. Each sale was coded to the year in which it occurred. The base year that each such dummy variable is compared to was set at 1992, the first year sales occurred at Rocky Bay Estate. A positive coefficient on a year dummy variable indicates a price increase over the 1992 base year, with a negative coefficient indicating a price decrease since that year. In a log-linear model, that coefficient approximates the percentage difference from the base year.

The other variables included in the regression include river views (*View*), contamination history (*Contamination*), adjoining a park (*Park*), additional amenities provided (*Amenities*), land area (*Area* in m^2), and locations 1 to 3 (*Location 1* to *Location 3*). Land quality is depicted by land area and zero-one dichotomous variables for the presence of a river view, a park, and additional amenities. The zero-one dichotomous variable, location, is a proxy for neighborhood quality and is based primarily upon the quality of the housing, accessibility to amenities including public transport, schools, recreational facilities etc., within each location. *Location 1* includes Rocky Bay Estate, Mosman Park, and North Bank, *Location 2* comprises Richmond Racecourse and *Location 3* includes the Ascot Waters sales. These "locations" were identified from the location similarities between Rocky Bay Estate, Mosman Park and North Bank as indicated from Chow tests (they are not statistically significantly different) and from a sales price analysis of each location. The environmental indicator is the zero-one dichotomous variable for the presence of previous contamination on the site. The variable descriptions are listed in Table 2 below.

Table 3, in Appendix I, shows the descriptive statistics for the 409 sales. The average sale price was $178,494,[23] with an average land area of 420 m^2.

Table 2: Variable Descriptions

Variable	Definition	Units
Sale price[1]	Sale price of vacant land	$A
Sale date (SD1 to SD5)[2]	Year in which the sale occurred (1994 to 1998)	0/1
Views	River views	0/1
Contamination	Contamination history	0/1
Park	Adjoining a park	0/1
Amenities[3]	Additional amenities provided	0/1
Area	Land area	m^2
Location 1 to 3	1 = Rocky Bay Estates, Mosman Park, and North Bank, 2 = Richmond Racecourse, 3 = Ascot Waters	0/1

[1] Sales price is the dependent variable.

[2] The base year was 1992, the year the first of the Rocky Bay Estate sites were auctioned. Note that the other location sales did not commence until 1994.

[3] All sales in Rocky Bay Estate, North Bank and Ascot Waters are coded as "Amenities" as all are located next to the Swan River and have additional amenities compared to the other locations. For example: Rocky Bay Estate and North Bank have a park and a riverfront cycle-walking path. Ascot Waters has a central park and boating marina. The difference in additional amenities found within each of these areas was not specifically addressed.

12.3.1.4 Empirical Results

Model selection criteria

The model of choice is one that best represents the relationships between the variables and has a small variance and unbiased parameters. Various models were tested and the results are described in the next two sections. The following statistics were used to help select the most appropriate model: the adjusted coefficient of determination (adjusted R^2); the standard error of the regression equation; the AIC[24] and SBC[25] statistics; *t*-test of significance of the coefficients and *F*-statistic.

Tests

1. *Variable and Model Significance: The Linear Model*

The linear model results are illustrated first for interpretive ease. Results from the testing of different functional forms are described in the next section. The linear model results are summarized in Table 4, in Appendix I. Four regressions are illustrated. As the coefficient for park proximity (*"Park"*) was shown to be only marginally significant at the 5% level the first two regressions look at the impact of the variable *Park* on the model by excluding it in one and including it in the other. The final two regressions show the impact of *River View* on the variable *Contamination*.

For the first two linear models shown in Table 4, the variables are listed in order of significance from highest to lowest. The *F*-statistic (140 and 129 respectively) shows that the estimated relationship in each model is statistically significant at the 95% confidence level and that at least one of the coefficients of the independent variables within each model is not zero. Based on the model selection test statistics AIC, and SBC, the regression that excludes the variable *Park* is marginally superior to the regression that includes it (AIC and SBC are minimized for the former model). For this reason, the model excluding *Park* was selected for analysis and is discussed next.

The coefficient of determination (R^2) indicates that approximately 79% of the variation in sale price is explained by the variation in the independent variable set. All variable coefficients had the expected signs. The most significant variables were *Location 3, View, Area*, and *Amenities. Contamination* and *Location 2* were the least significant variables in the regression.

View, Area, Amenities and *Sale Dates* (when compared to the base year 1992) all have a positive influence on price. Both *Locations 2 and 3* are shown to be inferior to *Location 1* selling, on average, for $54,219 and $180,087 respectively, less than properties in *Location 1*. These large differences are not surprising given that *Location 3* sites are in an area away from amenities and surrounded by industrial land uses and *Location 2* is more distant from the Swan River and in an area of lower priced properties compared to *Location 1*.

View increases price by $98,671 and reflects the desirability of a river view and scarcity of sites that obtain these. *Area* increases prices by $291 per square meter. A site with *Amenities* sells for $140,203 more than one without these and again reflects what people are willing to pay for access to such facilities and the prestige-factor of living in an area exclusive enough to provide these. A site with *Contamination* has a negative influence on price, reducing price by $78,767.

As not all properties with contamination have a view, it is conceivable that prices of properties with a view are less sensitive to previous contamination than those without a view. This premise was tested by sorting the data by *View* and running separate regressions on the prices of property with, and without, a view, (refer Table 4, Appendix I). As expected, prices of properties with a view are less sensitive to previous contamination. The coefficient on the *Contamination* variable became insignificant and was only $-27,427$. However, for properties without a view the coefficient of $-74,988$ on the *Contamination* variable was significant. This is a significant finding as it implies that a river view somehow compensates for the contamination history of a property.

The regression coefficients on the yearly dummy variables measure the annual rate of price appreciation across the entire sample in relation to the base year, 1992. The coefficient of $124,688 for *SD1* (1994) indicates that prices increased at a greater rate than in the other subsequent years. The coefficient of $89,303 for *SD2* (1995) indicates a price decrease from 1994. Coefficients for *SD3–SD5* show that prices increased each year but not to the degree of the initial increase evidenced in 1994.

To confirm these results market price trend data for land in the Perth Metropolitan area was obtained from the Valuer General's Office. This indicates that prices increased on average by 17.6% per annum from mid 1992 to late 1994 but rapidly slowed to 5% in 1995 thus confirming the direction (but not magnitude) of the above results. In 1996 and 1997 market activity became subdued with growth of only 5% over the two years confirming again the above regression results. However, this market price trend data relates to the entire Perth Metropolitan area and not to the particular locations of interest, the case study and control areas.

To consider price trends within each specific location sale prices within each were analyzed separately using the linear regression model.[26] Again, this generally confirmed the above regression results. For example, prices for land in Rocky Bay Estate increased from mid 1992 to late 1994 by 49%, on average. According to the developers, Land Corp, the first stage sections were "slow to move", whereas the second stage sections sold rapidly. It is hypothesized that the cause of this phenomenon was due to the stigma from the contamination history of the site. At the time of the first auction the subdivision had only recently being remediated and this was likely to be fresh in the minds of the purchasers. But as the development proceeded and the time period from initial remediation extended it is likely that the stigma effect reduced as buyers apparently discounted the history of the site and the subsequent remediation. The higher prices of the second stage property sales provide evidence of a reduction in stigma over time. However, due to limited data within each time period the effect of time on stigma could not be tested.

The property appraisal profession commonly checks how well their valuations predict market behavior by comparing the difference between their valuation estimate of a property (an estimate of the hypothetical sale price of the property) and the sale price of that property. This validation approach assumes, however, that actual sale prices are always "correct". The appraisal profession (and appraisal courts[27]) seek to achieve a value range ("margin of error") of between 10 and 15% for valuations of the same property (Crosby, 2000).

To check the prediction accuracy of the MRA model a similar approach can be used. A confidence interval is calculated using the following formula: Predicted sale price (mean) $\pm$ $t^*(\sigma)$, where t represents the t-value for the desired confidence level at the number of degrees of freedom of the model, and σ is the standard error of the estimate.

Using a 90% confidence interval this formula suggests that if many random samples of the same size were selected from the same population and interval estimates constructed for each sample then 90% of all those intervals would contain the true parameter. The width of the interval estimate is a measure of the reliability of the predicted sale price (Hill et al. 1997). The appraisal-court determined acceptable "margin of error" would require that $t^*(\sigma)$ fall within the 10–15% range.

For the linear model shown above with 12 degrees of freedom and using a 90% confidence interval the value range would be: \$178,494 $\pm$ (1.782* \$43,773), or \$178,494 $\pm$ \$78,003. This represents an error of 43.7% of the mean sale price and falls well outside the appraisal professions "margin of error" of between 10 and 15% for valuations. The comparison of these prediction margins is not entirely fair as multiple regression analysis is generally used in mass appraisal applications where the market value of hundreds or possibly thousands of properties are assessed commonly for tax purposes whereas individual valuations are generally undertaken on one or a small number of properties. In the latter instance much more additional information is usually available to the appraiser for consideration. For example, they usually conduct a full inspection of the property to be valued and have often fully inspected the sales-comparison properties as well. Such detailed inspections are not possible when valuing hundreds or thousands of properties at once and so a lesser degree of accuracy for mass appraised properties would not be unexpected.[28]

Multicollinearity appeared to pose a problem. Some high correlations were found between the sale dates as would be expected. *Amenities* and *Contamination* are highly negatively correlated as would be expected (contaminated sites are a subset of sites with additional amenities). *Amenities* is also highly correlated with *Location 3*. This neighborhood is a subset of the *Amenities* sites and in fact has the most amenities of all the *Amenities* coded areas (this is a very industrialized area and there are more amenities to compensate – a marina; island reserve, park etc.).

2. *Functional Forms*

As predicted hedonic prices can vary significantly across different functional forms. Various commonly used functional forms were examined to determine the model specification that best describes the relationship between price and the independent variables and to test the stability of the hedonic price on *Contamination*.

Also, to test the belief that the relationship between *Price* and *Area* is not a linear function of *Price* the variable *Area* was transformed to reflect the correct relationship. Several transformations were tested including: linear of *price and* square root of *Area*; linear of *price* and log of *Area*; log of *Price* and linear of *Area*; log *Price* and log *Area*; and log *Price* and square root of *Area*. All dummy variables remained in their linear form in each model.

The variable coefficient for *Contamination* was very consistent between the models where the *log of price* was the dependent variable. In these models price is reduced, on average, by 30%[29] for properties that have a history of contamination. Similar consistency was shown for the models where the linear of price was the dependent variable. Of these models price is reduced, on average, by $82,195 for properties that have a history of contamination.

Based on the model selection test statistics AIC, and SBC, it was found that the best result was obtained from using the *log of Price* and log of *Area*, and the linear form of all the dummy variables. Taking the log of an independent variable implies diminishing marginal benefits. For example, an extra $50 \, m^2$ of land area on a 550 m^2 site would be worth less than the previous $50 \, m^2$. The log–log model shows the percent change in price for a one-percent change in the independent variable, while all other independent variables are held constant.

In the semi-logarithmic equation the interpretation of the dummy variable coefficients involves the use of the formula: $100(e^{b_n} - 1)$, where b_n is the dummy variable coefficient (Halvorsen & Palmquist, 1980). This formula derives the percentage effect on price of the presence of the factor represented by the dummy variable and is advocated over the alternative, and commonly misused, formula of $100 * (b_n)$.

Finally, it is believed that the location of a site may have an impact on the effect river view has on price. For example, in a more prestigious location the effect of river view on price is believed to be greater. To test this belief the interaction variable "*Location * View*" was included in the model.

The most appropriate models in terms of the selection criteria outlined above are summarized in Tables 5 and 6 in Appendix II. Table 5 shows the model excluding the interaction term, and Table 6 includes this term. Comparing the AIC and SBC statistics for the two models in Tables 5 and 6 respectively indicate that the latter model is an improvement over the former. Thus, the final model selected is in Table 6. In both tables the variables are listed in order of significance from highest to lowest. The F-statistic for each model (201 and 194 respectively) shows that the estimated relationship in each model is statistically significant at the 95% confidence level and that at least one of the coefficients of the independent variables within each model is not zero. General explanations of the results are similar to those for the linear model with only the magnitude of the effect of the independent variables on price indicated below. The model excluding the interaction term is discussed first.

The coefficient of determination (R^2) indicates that approximately 85% of the variation in sale price is explained by the variation in the independent variable set. All variable coefficients had the expected signs. Tests for normality, heteroskedasicity, and multicollinearity generally indicate that the model is adequately specified and that the data are not severely ill conditioned (heteroskedasicity and mulitcollinearity were diminished when the data were transformed). This model is a significant improvement over the linear form.

The regression coefficient on *Location 3* is -0.834 and indicates that properties in that location sell for 57% less, on average, than those in *Location 1*. The regression coefficient on the *log of Area* is 0.752, which indicates that, on average, a 10% increase in land area will generate a 7.52% increase in price. The coefficient of 0.374 for *View* indicates that the presence of a river view adds 45% to the price of a property.[30]

The regression coefficient on *Amenities* of 0.576 has a higher statistical significance than the variable *Contamination* and indicates that *Amenities* add 78% to the sales price of a property. The regression coefficient on *Contamination* of -0.362 shows that a site with a history of contamination reduces price by 30.4%. As these two variables are correlated it would appear that the negative impact of being located on a site with a history of contamination is compensated by being located in an area near the Swan River with additional amenities.

As for the linear regression model results, the coefficients on the yearly dummy variables in relation to the base year, 1992, show the rapid appreciation during 1992–1994 (properties in 1994 (*SD1*) sold for 92% more than properties that sold in 1992), the slowdown from 1995 to 1997 (*SD2–SD4*), and the rapid appreciation again in 1998 (*SD5*).

The results from the regression, including the interactive term (Table 6), indicates that the effect of river view on price is only statistically significantly different in one of the locations. Again, as for the previous regression in Table 5, all variable coefficients had the expected signs and tests for normality, heteroskedasicity, and multicollinearity generally indicate that the model is adequately specified and that the data are not severely ill conditioned. The coefficient of determination (R^2) of 87% indicates that the regression has a high level of explanatory power.

The coefficients of the interaction terms were not highly significant indicating that the degree of estimation is not very precise. The three most precisely estimated variables in that model are *Location 3*, the log of *Area* and *Sale Date 1*, with t-test statistics over 15.

The *Location 2*View* variable was significant which indicates that *Location 2* (Richmond Racecourse) prices are more sensitive to river views than either *Location 1* (the constant), or *Location 3*. The coefficient on *Location 2*View* indicates that properties with a view in *Location 2* sell, on average, for 9.9% less than properties in *Location 1* with a view. The coefficient for *Location 3*View* was not statistically significant. However, *Location 3*View* was only marginally insignificant at the 10% level with a t-test of -1.639 and a *p*-value of 10.2%. These properties sell for 61.8% less than properties in *Location 1* with a view.

The negative interactive variable indicates that the effect of a river view on price for properties in *Location 2* (and *Location 3*) is much less than the effect this variable has on property prices in *Location 1*. This may be because there is only 7 out of 117, or 6% of sales in *Location 2* that have a view, and those with a view have only a glimpse of the ocean. Likewise, those properties in *Location 3* that have a view (only 14 out of 110 or 12.7% of sales) have only a view of the man-made waterway. *Location 1* has more properties with views (34 out of 182, or 19%), and the views received are generally unobstructed views of the Swan River. The results are therefore what would be expected given the quality of river (or water) views at each location.

The regression coefficient on *Location 3* is -0.814 and indicates that properties in that location sell for 55.7% less, on average, than those in *Location 1*. Properties in *Location 2* sell for 24.5% less than those in *Location 1*. The regression coefficient on log of *Area* is 0.684, which indicates that, on average, a 10% increase in *Area* will generate a 6.84% increase in price. A river *View* adds 58.9% to the price of a property.

The coefficient on *Sale Date 1* (1994) of 0.657 indicates that properties in *Sale Date 1* sell, on average, for 92.9% more than those in 1992, the base sale date year. Properties with *Sale Date 2* (1995) to *Sale Date 5*(1998) sell for 67.4%, 74.4%, 75.2% and 97.6%, respectively, more than those in 1992.

The regression coefficient on *Amenities* indicates that additional amenities add 75.6% to the sales price of a property. A site with a history of contamination reduces price by 29%. As these two variables are correlated it would appear that the negative impact of being located on a site with a history of contamination is compensated by being located in an area near the Swan River with additional amenities.

As for the previous models discussed, the coefficients on the yearly dummy variables in relation to the base year, 1992, show the rapid appreciation during 1992–1994, the slowdown from 1995–1997 (*SD2–SD4*), and the rapid appreciation again in 1998 (*SD5*).

3. *Test of Predictive Accuracy*

The coefficient of determination (R^2) of 87.3% for the selected model would be considered high in comparison with the amount of explanation obtained in similar hedonic house studies reported in the literature.[31] This indicates that the regression explains, on average, 87.3% of the variation in sale price.

Using an approach similar to that used by appraisers to predict valuation accuracy (outlined previously), and for illustrative purposes, the accuracy of the selected model (Table 6) was tested on two randomly selected sales from Rocky Bay Estate, one with a river view and one without, as follows:

1. Lot 48 Keel Place, of 451 m² with no river views sold 1995 for $232,000
Log of *Price* = 7.291 + 0.684(log of 451 m²) − 0.346(*Contamination*)
              + 0.563(*Amenities*) + 0.515(*SD2*) = 12.203
Price = $199,435
Error: $232,000−199,435 = $32,565 or 14.04%

2. Lot 68 Foundry Court, 556 m² with river views sold 1994 for $490,000
Log of *Price* = 7.291 + 0.684(log of 556 m²) − 0.346(*Contamination*)
              + 0.563(*Amenities*) + 0.463(*View*) + 0.657(*SD1*) = 12.9514
Price = $421,429
Error: $490,000−421,429 = $68,571 or 13.99%

The error in price predicted by the model for these two properties ranges from 13.99 to 14.04% and is within the appraisal-court determined range of between 10 and 15% for valuations of the same property, discussed above.

The more formal approach to check the prediction accuracy of the MRA model uses the formula shown above, as follows:

$$\text{Predicted estimate (mean log of sale price)} \pm t^*(\sigma)$$

Using a 90% confidence interval for the selected model with 14 degrees of freedom the price range would be calculated as follows:

$$11.98 \pm (1.761 * 0.1646), \text{ or } 11.98 \pm 0.2899$$

The anti-logs are then derived with the following result:

Mean sale price: $159,532, and Price range: $119,389 to $213,173
$$= \$159,532 \pm \$46,892$$

This represents an error of 29.4% of the mean sale price and falls well outside the appraisal profession's "margin of error" of between 10–15% for valuations. This degree of accuracy also does not conform to the prediction accuracy of approximately 14% derived above from the two randomly selected sales. Note that the 29.4% error was calculated from the model's prediction of sale prices for the entire sample in the database, yet only those properties in the case study area are of particular interest in this research. The predictive reliability results from the random sample of two properties from Rocky Bay Estate suggests that the model performs better at predicting sale prices in that location than it does at predicting prices of properties in the entire sample.

Again, as mentioned earlier, comparison of these prediction margins with the appraisal professions determined 10–15% range is not entirely pertinent as multiple regression analysis is generally used in mass appraisal applications and not for valuing one or a small number of properties where additional information is usually available to the appraiser. The level of error indicated by the model is considered quite acceptable, especially for the purposes of prediction. Further, by comparing and correlating these results with those from the conjoint study the range of estimation can be narrowed, thus increasing the precision of price prediction (valuation estimation).

12.3.2 Part Two: Opinion Survey

As another tool to determine the magnitude of property value impacts arising from investors' perceptions towards post-remediated contaminated land, a survey of residential purchasers of affected sites was undertaken in 1999. The methodology used followed the lines of similar research carried out by Priestley and Ignelzi (1989) who have established a sound standardized methodology for assessing environmental impacts in residential communities using postal surveys.

In-depth interviews were held with a small number of property owners of the affected sites within the Case Study Area to identify the issues and to determine the attributes considered important in their purchasing behavior. This information also helped in the development and wording of the questionnaire. The preliminary questionnaire was pilot tested on a small sample of respondents from the Case Study Area to determine the understandability of the questions, their relevance, and the length of time to complete the instrument.

The questionnaire contained 50 individual response items. Questions related to overall neighborhood environmental desirability, knowledge about the site's contamination history and sources of this information, attitudes towards different types of contamination sources, importance of river views, concerns about specific contamination land issues, and factors affecting their purchasing decisions.

The survey was posted to all residents (60) living in the case study area using uniquely coded questionnaires. Collection was by freepost mail. Reminder letters were sent to improve the response rate. Of the 60 questionnaires mailed out 33 were returned, 29 of which were usable. This indicates a response rate of 55% (48% usable).

12.3.2.1 The Results

This section presents a summary of the major findings that emerged from the analysis. Tables are presented in Appendix III. To keep this section brief, only a limited amount of data is cited directly.

The overall finding in this study is that while nearly three quarters (72.4%) of respondents knew about the contamination history of Rocky Bay Estate prior to purchasing their sites, over half (55.2%) were not told about it by either the vendor or their selling agents. Under current environmental legislation (the Environmental Protection Act 1986) a vendor is not required to inform purchasers about a site's contamination history where the site has been remediated. However, under the Real Estate Business Agency Act 1978, Code of Conduct Section 101, real estate agents must disclose information about a property, if known, particularly if such information could materially effect the decision to purchase. While it is suggested here that a site's contamination history could be claimed to be a material factor in a land purchasing decision, this has not yet been tested in court.

Despite an agent's responsibility to inform purchasers of pertinent property information, the majority of residents (91.7%) that did not know about the site's history prior to purchasing their sites (27.6% of all respondents), indicated that even if they had known, would still have purchased anyway. The results indicate that the site's contamination history did not greatly influence respondents' decision to buy in Rocky Bay Estate or the price they were willing to pay for their sites.

It appears that the desirability of the location overcomes any concerns residents may have about the site's history. For example, nearly all respondents are owner-occupiers and rate the neighborhood as somewhat, or much more, desirable than other neighborhoods in North Fremantle and Mosman Park due to the beach and river access and the close proximity to public transport.[32] Further, the fact that the site has been remediated appears to abrogate any concerns residents may have about the site's history, with no respondents seeking indemnities, and few believing provision of such would alter their concerns.

A question was included to determine if residents would react differently to various types of contaminants. In terms of attitudes towards purchasing previously contaminated sites, those least likely to be invested in are remediated sites known to have been contaminated with radioactive materials, asbestos and toxic chemicals. Other sites avoided, in decreasing magnitude of negative reaction include heavy metals,[33] volatile chemicals, and petroleum products with underground storage tanks receiving the least adverse reaction.

As many of the Rocky Bay Estate residents are located within 50 meters of the Minim Cove remediated site where contaminants are buried on-site in a containment cell, a similar question was included to determine residents' perceptions to living near various sources of contamination, including a site that has been remediated. To prevent the responses to this question being influenced by the probing questions about specific remediated sites this option was provided last, in the list of options.

Responses indicate that properties within 50 meters of various sources of contamination most likely to be avoided (in decreasing magnitude of negative reaction) are: an oil refinery, a chemical plant, a high-traffic street, high voltage transmission lines, and waste treatment plants. Other sites avoided include an industrial landfill, a remediated site (contaminants contained on-site), and a defense site, with a non-toxic landfill having the least negative response.

While the remediated site (contaminants contained on-site) was one of the least avoided, still as many as 41.4% of respondents would either not, or probably not, invest in a property within 50 meters of such a site. This response was surprising given that many of the respondents either live this close or within 400 meters of a remediated site where the contaminants are contained on-site. To explain this response it is hypothesized that they are either not aware they live so close to such a site or they consider they live far enough away from the site for it not to be of concern to them. It may be reasonably assumed that had their reaction been much stronger, they would not have purchased next to the Minim Cove Remediated site.

River views appear to override concerns residents may have about a site's contamination history with nearly 70% responding they would prefer a view even if it were from a site with a history of contamination than no view and no contamination history. Living within 300 meters of the river did not have the same compensating influence with over 85% of respondents preferring a site with no contamination history than one with such a history but that is close to the river.

Few respondents had concerns about the possibility of the remediation technique failing, that not all of the contamination was removed or that the government-imposed safe "clean" standards may change and effectively render the site "unclean" by the new standards. Most frequently recorded factors that influenced respondent's decision to purchase in Rocky Bay Estates include river access, proximity to Fremantle, cycle path nearby, price and river view.

When asked about the effect the contamination history of the site had on their purchasing decision, 36% responded that they did not know about the contamination history of the site. This was in excess of the 28% who responded to a similar question earlier in the questionnaire. The reason for this discrepancy is unclear, although it is possible that some respondents misunderstood the question and read it as meaning they did not know the effect that the contamination history of the site would have on price. The remainder of the respondents had either mild reservations about buying the property or it did not influence their decision to buy one way or another.

Similar responses were obtained when respondents were asked about the effect the contamination history of the site had on the price they were prepared to pay for their property, compared to that of a similar property that is unaffected by contamination. Of the 63% that did have knowledge about the site's history, none of them had strong reactions, either positive or negative, toward purchasing their sites or the price they were willing to pay for them. Over a third of these respondents (or 22% of all respondents) responded that they would pay "a little less" for their site, while 59% (or 37% of all respondents) indicated it did not influence the price they were prepared to pay.

All responses were separated into two groups: those that had knowledge of the contamination history of the site (72% of respondents) and those that did not (28%). Comparing the results from the Mann-Whitney tests between the two groups indicated significantly different responses to the following variables:

• The contamination history of the site affected their home purchase decision.
• The contamination history of the site affected the price they were willing to pay for their property.

This confirmed expectations that those that knew about the contamination history to the site might react differently to the purchase of their site's than those that did not know. It was expected that such knowledge would cause purchasers to pay less for their property. The results indicate that of those that knew about the site's contamination history (i.e. 72%), 41% (or 30% of all respondents) had mild reservations about buying their property, whereas over half (53%) were not influenced by this (or 38% of all respondents). Similarly, 36% of these respondents (26% of all respondents) were prepared to pay a little less for their property, whereas 53% (38% of all respondents) reported that such knowledge did not influence the price they were willing to pay.

As the response to the question asking respondents to make a choice between a site with a view but with a history of contamination and one with no view but no contamination history indicated that river views in some way compensate for this history, it was considered appropriate to test if respondents that have a river view regard a site's contamination history as less of a concern, than those that do not have a view. To do this, responses were again separated into two groups for those that had a river view and those that did not. Comparing the results between the Mann-Whitney tests from the two groups indicated the responses were significantly different for the variable:

- Whether they would invest in a property within 50 meters of:
  - High-voltage electric transmission lines.
  - A high-traffic street or motorway.
  - A waste treatment plant.

These results did not support the above a priori expectation that respondents with a river view regard a site's contamination history as less of a concern, and instead show that river views affect whether or not respondents would invest in a property within 50 metres of the detrimental land uses listed. While differences in perception toward living on a remediated site may not exist between these two groups, the results show that perceptions towards living near other types of detrimental land uses do vary significantly between the groups.

Those with a river view were more averse than those without a river view to investing in a property within 50 metres of a high-voltage electric transmission line (80% responded "No" v 12.5%) and a high-traffic street or motorway (100% responded "No" v 12.5%). However, those with a river view were less averse than those without a river view to investing in a residence near a waste treatment plant (0% responded "No", though 60% responded "Probably Not" v 50% "No" and 50% "Probably Not").

12.4 Summary and Conclusions

The aim of this research was to estimate the impact of "stigma" on the values or prices of post-remediated residential sites and determine if market perceptions are reflected in market prices. The results from the Market Sales Analysis indicate that a site with a history of contamination has a negative impact on value. This "stigma" effect results in an approximately 30% decrease in sales price of post-remediated residential sites. However, the study also indicates that this can be offset by other factors such as location next to the Swan River (especially with a river view), and additional amenities including cycle-walking pathways, children's playgrounds and the like (as incorporated in the variable "Amenities"). It is not possible to quantify how much each of these factors individually has offset the "stigma" effect from the data available in this study.

While not all residents knew about the site's contamination history before purchasing, the most telling result from the Opinion Survey was that the location's desirability appears to override concerns residents may have about the site's contamination history. The desirable features identified in the study include river views, beach and river access and close proximity to both Fremantle and public transport; together these appear to out-weigh the negative impacts associated with the contamination history of the area.

Although respondents were asked to indicate how the site's contamination history affected the price they were prepared to pay for their property, compared with a similar property in an area unaffected by contamination, no questions were posed to determine residents' estimates of the percentage negative impact on price. Those that responded that it had a negative impact said they were prepared to pay "a little less" yet it is difficult to know how these residents might define "a little less". Therefore, a direct quantitative comparison with the stigma assessment in the Market Sales Analysis was not possible. As a result, only general conclusions can be drawn about whether Opinion Surveys can be used as a proxy for Market Sales Analysis.

From the results it does appear, for example, that the Opinion Survey results are at least consistent with those from the Market Sales Analysis and show the same general direction of impact. Both studies indicate that any negative impact on price caused by the site's contamination history is compensated by the positive impact on price of the location's desirability. This information will be particularly useful to property developers interested in reducing the negative perceptions associated with a site's contamination history and limiting any potential compensation claims. Further, it will aid appraisers in estimating the effect of "stigma" on the value of post-remediated sites.

It must be recognized that stigma effects may vary over time and so the effects reported here of locating on a post-remediated site from 1992 to 1998 may differ in the future. Public perceptions change due to the increased public awareness regarding the potential adverse health and environmental effects of land contamination. Changes in consumers' attitudes to new technology for site testing and remediation may also impact on land value. Thus the perceptions toward post-remediated sites can change either positively or negatively over time. To confirm this, many similar studies of similar design to allow comparison between them need to be conducted over time, and their results made public.

Lastly, it must be kept in mind that these results are the product of a single case study carried out in a specific area at a specific time. Great caution must be used in making generalizations from them or applying them to other areas. Similarly, the case study generally covers only the higher range of the social spectrum. Prior research indicates that social class is an important variable influencing peoples' response to environmental detriments and hence were the study to include neighborhoods with residents of a different social scale the results may have also been different (see for example, King (1973), Thayer et al. (1992), Dale et al. (1999)). To study the effects of social class on stigma, as for the research needed to study stigma-effects over time, many similar studies using a similar design are needed, and their results made public for comparison purposes.

NOTES

[1] As defined by Patchin (1991), Syms (1996), Reichert (1997), Kennedy (1997) and others.

[2] Risk" is defined in the context of contaminated land as the probability or frequency of an occurrence of a defined hazard and the magnitude of the consequences of the hazard (Petts, 1994). The term "risk" as used in this chapter relates to those risks that can be measured or predicted.

[3] "Uncertainty" is the intrinsic risk relating to a defined outcome that is not readily capable of measurement or prediction (Syms, 1997).

[4] As noted by Kinnard and Worzala (1999) remediation and cleanup are not synonymous. Remediation is designed to reduce the actual level of specified on-site contaminants to or below the maximum level established by the relevant environmental agency for the contaminants in question. Cleanup, however, usually involves removing virtually all contaminants from the site. This is frequently neither technically possible nor financially feasible.

[5] Various definitions of "contamination" exist with most relying upon the concept of harm to human and the environment (see, for example, the Environment Act 1995 (UK), and the definition adopted by The European Group of Valuers of Fixed Assets (TEGOVOFA, 1988). The definition adopted for this chapter is that set out in the National Environment Protection Council Service Corporation's "National Environment Protection (Assessment of Site Contamination) Measure", (1999). Here contamination is defined as "the condition of land or water where any chemical substance or waste has been added at above background level and represents, or potentially represents, an adverse health or environmental impact". This definition has legal weight under The National Environment Protection Council Act 1994 (Commonwealth) and corresponding legislation in the other jurisdictions throughout Australia.

[6] The terms "valuer" and "appraiser" have the same meaning ("valuer" is the term used in the UK and NZ, although the term "chartered surveyor" is also used in the UK) and these are used interchangeably throughout this chapter.

[7] Syms (1997) presents various causes for "stigma" including the perceived risk of: inability to effect a total cure; the risk of failure of treatment; compensation payable or receivable; risk of legislation/remedial standards changing; uncertainty etc.

[8] Comparables in this instance are defined in terms of the nature and extent of contamination, rather than the usual features that determine a property's comparability such as site size; location, etc. Properties with the same type of contamination must be used in the comparisons, however.

[9] Yet the problems involved in obtaining data on transactions concerning contaminated property do not appear to be limited to the UK. Patchin recognizes this as a factor for his small collection of case studies also. Subsequent US studies suggest that more and better sales data have become available, (Kinnard & Worzala, 1999).

[10] See for example, Cummings, Harrison and Rustrom (1995), Loomis, Brown, Lucero and Peterson (1996), Champ, Bishop, Brown and McCollum (1996).

[11] See for example, in addition to the Chalmers and Roehr (1993) study mentioned, Randall, Ives, and Eastman (1974), Hanemann (1994), Sanders (1996), McLean and Mundy (1998), and Carson et al. (1998).

[12] A follow-up survey used conjoint analysis, however, reporting the results from this are beyond the scope of this chapter.

[13] Only Dotzour found no significant impact of the discovery of contaminated groundwater on residential house prices. This was likely due to the non-hazardous nature of the contamination where the groundwater was not used for drinking purposes.

[14] See for example Dale et al. (1999), Dotzour (1997), Simons and Sementelli (1997), and Reichert (1997).

[15] AIC is the Akaike Information Criterion, and is a "goodness of fit" measure involving the standard error of the regression adjusted by a penalty factor. The model selected is the one that minimises this criterion, Microsoft (1997).

[16] The SBC is the Schwarz Bayesian Criterion. Like the AIC, SBC takes into account both how well the model fits the observed data, and the number of parameters used in the model. The model selected is the one that adequately describes the series and has the minimum SBC. The SBC is based on Bayesian (maximum-likelihood) considerations, Microsoft (1997).

[17] Real estate agents commonly set the price of property according to what they believe the market will bear but their estimates are not always correct and may be at odds with buyer expectation. Such price setting does not permit the market to act freely to determine this, with the result that the price may be above or below what would otherwise be agreed between market participants.

[18] Much of the information about the site (outlined in this chapter) was sourced from the Fremantle City Council public records; media/newspaper research (Battye library); Land Corp; Valuer General's Office, and the records of Dr. John Rodgers, spokesman of the Minim Cove Action Group.

[19] *Source*: Land Corp (1989). *Proposal to remediate and redevelop the State Engineering Site.*

[20] *Source*: Rockwater Pty Ltd. (1988). Report by A. J. Peck, Principal-hydrologist.

[21] The site clean up standards used were the New South Wales State Pollution Control Commission (NSW SPCC) standards for small children's playing fields. These were the strictest standards at the time that were directly applicable to the redevelopment of contaminated land for residential purposes (DEP, December 1996, *letter to Dr John Rodgers to address his concerns regarding the different clean up criteria used for the SEW site and the Minim Cove development*).

[22] *Source*: Halpern, Glick Maunsell Pty Ltd. (1994, October). *Letter to Landcorp re commitments met.*

[23] Note that all sales prices shown in this chapter are in Australian dollars.

[24] AIC is the Akaike Information Criterion, and is a "goodness of fit" measure involving the standard error of the regression adjusted by a penalty factor. The model selected is the one that minimizes this criterion (Microsoft 1997).

[25] The SBC is the Schwarz Bayesian Criterion. Like the AIC, SBC takes into account both how well the model fits the observed data, and the number of parameters used in the model. The model selected is the one that adequately describes the series and has the minimum SBC. The SBC is based on Bayesian (maximum-likelihood) considerations. (Microsoft 1997).

[26] For full results please contact the author.

[27] The "margin of error" principle is the court's expression of the acceptable level of divergence in valuation. This principle is used in negligence claims against valuers. See for example, Singer and Friedlander Ltd v John D Wood and Co, 243 EG 212 and 295.

[28] Reichert (1999) discusses in detail the appropriate use and predictive accuracy of hedonic modelling in real estate valuation and environmental damages assessment.

[29] The range in coefficients for the variable "Contamination" was from 0.32 to 0.36. Interpretation of these coefficients follows the method advocated by Halvorsen and Palmquist (1980).

[30] Interestingly, McLeod (1984) found a river view adds about 28% to the price of houses (as opposed to vacant land) in Perth, WA in the early 1980's. Fraser, R. and Spencer, G. (1998) found that the best quality ocean view investigated represents 25% of a vacant site's sale price in the period 1990–91. Comparing these results with the 45% result indicated here suggests that ocean views increase vacant sale prices to a lesser extent than do river views. Similarly, as a percentage of sale price, river views increase prices more for vacant sites than they do for improved properties.

[31] For example, Reichert (1997) obtained an adjusted R^2 of 84%; Simons and Sementelli (1997), 78%; Zeiss and Attwater (1989), 73–77%; Abelson (1979), 68%; Dotzour (1997), 56–61%.

[32] Note that the property attributes beach and river access, proximity to public transport and other amenities, were included jointly in the hedonic pricing model in the independent variable *Location*.

[33] *Note*: Heavy metals were present at the case study site prior to remediation.

REFERENCES

Abelson, P. W. (1979). Property Prices and Amenity Values. *Journal of Environmental Economics and Management*, Vol. 6, pp. 11–28.

Blamey, R. K., Bennett, J. W. and Morrison, M. D. (1999). Yea-Saying in Contingent Valuation Surveys. *Land Economics*, Vol. 75, No. 1, pp. 126–141.

Bond, S. G. and Kennedy, P. J. (1998). "Valuers and Contaminated Land: Approaches Used in New Zealand Practice". *New Zealand Valuers' Journal*, November, pp. 50–63.

Bond, S. G., Kinnard, W. N., Worzala, E. M. and Kapplin, S. D. (1998) "Market Participants Reactions Toward Contaminated Property In New Zealand and America". *Journal of Property Valuation and Investment*, Vol. 16, No. 3, pp. 251–272.

Bonz, R. E. and Brinkema, C. B. (1993). "A Transactional Database for Measuring Stigma". *Real Estate Finance*, Vol. 10, No. 2, pp. 23–28.

Carson, R. T. et al. (1998). Referendum Design And Contingent Valuation: The NOAA Panel's No-Vote Recommendation. *Review of Economics and Statistics*, Vol. 80, No. 3, pp. 484–487.

Chalmers, J. A., and Roehr, S. (1993). "Issues in the Valuation of Contaminated Property", *The Appraisal Journal*.

Champ, P. A., Bishop, R. C., Brown, T. C., and McCollum, D. W. (1996). Using Donation Mechanisms To Value Nonuse Benefits From Public Goods. *Journal of Environmental Economics and Management*, Vol. 32, No. 2, pp. 151–174.

Cummings, R. G. Harrison, G. W. and Rustrom, E. E. (1995). Homegrown Values And Hypothetical Surveys: Is The Dichotomous Choice Approach Incentive-Compatible? *American Economic Review*, Vol. 85, No. 1, pp. 260–266.

Dale, L., Murdoch, J. C., Thayer, M. A. and Waddell, P. A. (1999). Do Property Values Rebound From Environmental Stigmas? Evidence From Dallas. *Land Economics*, Vol. 75, No. 2, pp. 311–326.

Department of Environmental Protection (DEP). (1996). Letter to Dr John Rodgers.

Dixon, T. J. (1995). Lessons from America: Appraisal and Lender Liability Issues in Contaminated Real Estate. A research study sponsored by the Jones Lang Wootton Education Trust. College of Estate Management. Reading.

Dotzour, M. (1997, July). "Groundwater Contamination and Residential Property Values." *The Appraisal Journal*: 279–284.

Federal Register (1993). Vol. 58, No. 10, January 15. Proposed Rules, pp. 1401–1614.

Federal Register (1996). Vol. 61, No. 4, January 5. Final Rules and Regulations on Natural Resource and Damage Assessment.

Fraser, R. and Spencer, G. (1998). The Value Of An Ocean View: An Example Of Hedonic Property Amenity Valuation. *Journal of the Institute of Australian Geographers*, Vol. 36, No. 1, pp. 94–98.

Freeman, A. M. III (1979). *The benefits of environmental improvement*. Baltimore, MD: John Hopkins Press.

Hair, J. F. Jr., Anderson, R. E., Tatham, R. L. and Black, W. C. (1995). *Multivariate data analysis with readings,* 4th Ed. Englewood Cliffs, N.J. Prentice Hall.

Halpern, Glick, Maunsell Pty Ltd. (1994, October). *Letter to Land Corp.*

Hanneman, W. M. (1994). Valuing The Environment Through Contingent Valuation. *Journal of Economic Perspectives*, Vol. 8, No. 4, pp. 19–43.

Halvorsen, R. and Palmquist, R. (1980). The Interpretation of Dummy Variables in Semilogarithmic Equations. *American Economic Review*, Vol. 70, No. 3, pp. 474–475.

Kennedy, P. J. (1997). Investment valuation of contaminated land and UK practice: a study with special reference to former gasworks. Unpublished Ph.D. thesis. The Nottingham Trent University.

King, T. A. (1973). *Property Taxes, Amenities and Residential Land Values*. Cambridge, Mass.: Balinger Publishing Co.

Kinnard, W. N. Jr. (1989). "Analyzing the Stigma Effect of Proximity to Hazardous Materials Sites." *Environmental Watch*, Vol. II, No. 4.

Kinnard, W. N. Jr. (1990). Measuring the Effects of Contamination on Property Values: The Focus of the Symposium in the Context of Current Knowledge, *Technical Report*, Chicago, IL: The Appraisal Institute.

Kinnard, W. N. Jr. and Dickey, S. A. (1995). A Primer On Proximity Impact Research: Residential Property. *Real Estate Issues*. Vol. 20, No.1. pg. 23–29.

Kinnard, W. N. Jr. Geckler, M. B. and Dickey, S. A. (1994). *Fear (As a Measure of Damages) Strikes Out: Two Case Studies Comparisons of Actual Market Behavior with Opinion Survey Research.* Paper presented at the American Real Estate Society Conference, Santa Barbara, April.

Kinnard, W. N. Jr. and Worzala, E. W. (1998). *The Valuation of Contaminated Properties and Associated Stigma: A Comparative Review of Practice and Thought in the US, the UK and New Zealand.* Paper presented at The Cutting Edge Conference, Leicester: RICS.

Kinnard, W. N. Jr. and Worzala, E. W. (1999). How North American Appraisers Value Contaminated Property and Associated Stigma. *The Appraisal Journal*, July, pp. 269–279.

Kline, B. (1997). *First Along the River: A Brief History of the U.S. Environmental Movement.* San Fransisco: Acada Books.

Lizieri, C., Palmer, S., Finlay, L., and Charlton, M. (1995). Valuation Methodology and Environmental Legislation: A Research Project for the RICS Education Trust. City University Business School Discussion Paper Series. City University. London.

Loomis, J., Brown, T. C., Lucero, B. and Peterson, G. (1996). Improving Validity Experiments Of Contingent Valuation Methods: Results Of Efforts To Reduce The Disparity Of Hypothetical And Actual Willingness To Pay. *Land Economics*, Vol. 72, November, pp. 450–461.

McLeod (1984). The Demand For Local Amenity: An Hedonic Price Analysis. *Environment and Planning*, Vol. A, No. 16, pp. 389–400.

McLean, D. G. and Mundy, B. "The Addition of Contingent Valuation and Conjoint Analysis to the Required Body of Knowledge for the Estimation of Environmental Damages to Real Property". *Journal of Real Estate Practice and Education*. Vol. 1, No. 1, pp. 1–19.

Microsoft. (1997, 24 February). SPSS Windows Help Guide (9.0.1), [Software package]. Microsoft Windows.

Mundy, B. (1988). "Survey Cites Impacts of Contaminants on Value and Marketability of Real Estate." *News Release*, Chicago, IL: American Society of Real Estate Counselors.

Mundy, B. (1989). *The Impact of Contaminants on Real Property Marketability and Value.* Paper presented at the National Conference of American Society of Real Estate Counselors.

National Environment Protection Council Service Corporation (1999). National Environment Protection (Assessment of Site Contamination) Measure. Adelaide.

Patchin, P. J. (1991). Contaminated Properties-Stigma Revisited. *The Appraisal Journal.* Vol. 59, No. 2, pp. 168–169.

Patchin, P. J. (1992). Valuing Contaminated Properties: Case Studies, *Measuring the Effects of Hazardous Materials Contamination on Real Estate Values: Techniques and Applications,* Chicago, IL: The Appraisal Institute.

Patchin, P. J. (1994). Contaminated Properties and the Sales Comparison Approach. *The Appraisal Journal* Vol. 62, No. 3, pp. 402–409.

Priestley, T. and Ignelzi, P. C. (1989). A Methodology for Assessing Transmission Line Impacts in Residential Communities. Edison Electric Institute, Washington DC, June.

Randall, A., Ives, B. and Eastman, C. (1974). Bidding Games For Valuation Of Aesthetic Environmental Improvements. *Journal of Environmental Economics and Management*, Vol. 1, pp. 134–136.

Richards, T. O. (1995a). "An Analysis of the Impact of Contamination and Stigma on the Valuation of Commercial Property Investment." An unpublished Ph.D. Thesis, College of Estate Management, University of Reading.

Richards, T. O. (1995b). A Changing Landscape: The Valuation of Contaminated Land and Property. College of Estate Management Research Report. Reading.

Richards, T. O. (1996). Valuing Contaminated Land and Property: Theory and Practice. *Journal of Property Valuation and Investment*, Vol. 14, No. 4.

Richards, T. O. (1997). Is it Worth the Risk? The Impact of Environmental Risk on Property Investment Valuation. College of Estate Management Research Report. Reading.

Reichert, A. J. (1997). "Impact of a Toxic Waste Superfund Site on Property Values." *The Appraisal Journal* **65**(4): 381–392.

Rockwater Pty. Ltd. (1988) *Report by A. J. Peck, Principal-hydrologist.*

Rosen, S. (1974) "Hedonic Prices and Implicit Markets: Product Differentiation in Pure Competition. *Journal of Political Economy*, 82: 34–55.

Sanders, M. V. (1996). Post-Repair Diminution in Value from Geotechnical Problems. *The Appraisal Journal*, Vol. 64, No. 1, pp. 59–66.

Simons, R. A. and Sementelli, A. (1997, July). "Liquidity Loss and Delayed Transactions with Leaking Underground Storage Tanks." *The Appraisal Journal*: 255–260.

Slovic, P. (1992). Perceptions of Risk: Reflections on the Psychometric Paradigm. In: *Social Theories of Risk* (eds S. Krimsky & D. Golding), Praeger, Westport, Connecticut.

Syms, P. M. (1994). *The Post-Remediation Values of Contaminated Land*. ISVA Half-Day Seminar, United Kingdom: ISVA.

Syms, P. M. (1995). *Environmental Impairment: An Approach to Valuation*. The Cutting Edge Conference, England: RICS.

Syms, P. M. (1996). The Redevelopment and Value of Contaminated Land. Unpublished Ph.D. thesis. Sheffield Hallam University. Sheffield.

Syms, P. M. (1997). *Contaminated Land: The Practice and Economics of Redevelopment*. Oxford, UK: Blackwell Science Ltd.

TEGOVOFA (1988). Valuation of land subject to soil pollution. *Background Paper BP19*, The European Group of Valuers of Fixed Assets, London.

Thayer, M., Albers, H., and Rahmatian, M. (1992). The benefits of Reducing Exposure to Waste Disposal Sites: A Hedonic Housing Value Approach. *Journal of Real Estate Research*, 7(3), 265–282.

Worzala, E. W. and Kinnard, W. N. Jr. (1997). Investor and Lender Reactions to Alternative Sources of Contamination. *Real Estate Issues*, Vol. 22, No. 2.

Zeiss, C. and Attwater, J. (1989). Waste Facility Impacts on Residential Property Values. *Journal of Urban Planning and Development*, Vol. 115, No. 2, pp. 69–79.

APPENDIX I

Table 3: Descriptive Statistics

Variable	Minimum	Maximum	Mean	Std. deviation
AREA	183.00	748.00	420.4719	116.7765
PRICE	60,000.00	560,000.00	178,494.2910	95,682.5231
LOCATN 2	.00	1.00	.2861	.4525
LOCATN 3	.00	1.00	.2689	.4440
VIEWS	.00	1.00	.1589	.3661
SD1	.00	1.00	.2225	.4164
SD2	.00	1.00	.1051	.3071
SD3	.00	1.00	.2592	.4387
SD4	.00	1.00	.2298	.4212
SD5	.00	1.00	.1491	.3567
Amenities	.00	1.00	.5428	.4988
Contamination	.00	1.00	.1907	.3933
PARK	.00	1.00	6.601E-02	.2486

Table 4: MRA Equation – Linear Model

Model: variables	Without Park		With Park		With view	No view
	Coefficients	T-ratios	Coefficients	T-ratios	Coefficients	Coefficients
Number of sales	409		409		65	344
Location 3	−180,087	−19.59	−183,127	−19.73	−349,638	−138,600
View	98,671	15.47	98,467	15.49		
Amenities	140,203	13.64	142,859	13.83	236,394	92,940
Area	291	11.85	305	11.94	128	290
SD1	124,688	11.20	126,971	11.38	251,009	87,117
SD5	111,972	9.06	114,558	9.25	289,039	96,403
SD4	109,234	9.03	109,642	9.10	287,581	68,783
SD3	101,304	8.33	104,557	8.55	280,695	57,733
SD2	89,303	7.97	91,228	8.15	249,751	61,926
Contamination	−78,767	−7.61	−80,432	−7.77	−27,427	−74,988
Location 2	−54,219	−6.22	−52,575	−6.02	−117,595	−64,689
Constant	−61,718	−3.79	−71,735	−4.23	−68,021	−10,553
Park			20,319	2.005		
R^2	79.5%		79.7%		95.6%	78.3%
Adj. R^2	78.9%		79.1%		94.8%	77.6%
F-statistic	140		129		117	120
Std error	43,939		43,773		33,078	29,724
AIC	9695.66		9697.38		1550.50	7970.82
SBC	9747.83		9753.57		1576.59	8016.90

APPENDIX II

Table 5: MRA Equation – Semi-Log Model

Variables	Coefficients	T-ratios
Number of sales	409	
Constant	6.906	26.79
Location 3	−0.834	−22.66
LN Area	0.752	17.97
View	0.374	15.06
SD1	0.650	14.75
Amenities	0.576	14.17
SD5	0.681	13.95
SD4	0.562	11.83
SD2	0.497	11.26
SD3	0.544	11.26

Table 5: (*Continued*)

Variables	Coefficients	T-ratios
Location 2	−0.324	−9.38
Contamination	−0.362	−8.84
Park	0.121	2.89
Adj. R^2	0.855	
F-test	201	
Std error	0.1731	
AIC	−410	
SBC	−354	

Table 6: Semi-Log Model incl. Interaction Variable

Variables	Coefficients	T-ratios	$100(e^{b_n}-1)$
Number of sales	409		
Constant	7.291	27.55	
Location 2	−0.281	−8.40	−24.5%
Location 3	−0.814	−22.21	−55.7%
LN Area	0.684	15.79	
View	0.463	−15.15	58.9%
Amenities	0.563	14.45	75.6%
SD1	0.657	15.68	92.9%
SD2	0.515	12.22	67.4%
SD3	0.556	12.10	74.4%
SD4	0.561	12.39	75.2%
SD5	0.681	14.52	97.6%
Contamination	−0.346	−8.79	−29%
Park	0.090	2.15	9.4%
Location 2 * View	−0.104	−6.62	−9.9%
Location 3 * View	−0.481	−1.64	−61.8%
R^2	0.873		
Adj. R^2	0.869		
F-test	194		
Std. error, σ	0.1646		
AIC	−431		
SBC	−367		

Appendix III

Table 7: Questionnaire Responses

Variable	Response	Valid percent (%)	N
Occupancy:	Homeowner	97	
	Tenant	3	
Rate Neighbourhood:	Much more desirable	46.4	
	Somewhat more desirable	35.7	
	About the same	10.7	
	Somewhat less desirable	7.1	28
Reasons for desirability:	Access to beach/river	40.9	
	Access to beach/river/public transport	18.2	
	Access to beach/river & views	18.2	22
How long have you lived there?	Less than one year	31	
	1–3 years	44.8	
	More than 4 years	24.1	29
Knowledge of contamination history prior to purchase?	Yes	72.4	
	No	27.6	29
Source of knowledge?	Real Estate Agent (said minor)	26.3	
	Land Corp	21.1	
	Newspaper	15.8	
	Lived in the area	10.5	
	Hearsay	10.5	19
Were you told about contamination history?	Yes	44.8	
	No	55.2	29
Information given	Contaminants removed	42.9	
	No or minor contamination	28.6	
	EPA report	14.3	7
Would you have invested if you knew about the contamination history?	Yes	91.7	
	No	8.3	12
Were you given full details about site clean-up?	Yes	29.6	
	No	70.4	27
Did you seek indemnities?	Yes	0	
	No	100	28
Would indemnities alter concerns?	Yes	7.7	
	Probably	11.5	
	Maybe	42.3	
	Probably Not	26.9	
	No	11.5	26

Table 7: (*Continued*)

Variable	Response	Valid percent (%)	N
Would you invest in a remediated property known to have been contaminated with:			
Underground Storage Tanks	Probably Not or No	27.5	29
Volatile chemicals	Probably Not or No	60.7	28
Toxic chemicals	Probably Not or No	72.4	29
Petroleum products	Probably Not or No	48.3	29
Radioactive materials	Probably Not or No	82.7	29
Asbestos	Probably Not or No	69	29
Heavy Metals	Probably Not or No	65.5	29
Would you invest in property within 50 m of:			
A former defence site	Probably Not or No	25.0	28
High-voltage power lines	Probably Not or No	79.3	29
An industrial landfill	Probably Not or No	64.3	28
A high-traffic street	Probably Not or No	72.4	29
An oil refinery	Probably Not or No	86.2	29
A landfill (non-hazardous)	Probably Not or No	13.7	29
A chemical plant	Probably Not or No	75.9	29
A waste treatment plant	Probably Not or No	79.3	29
A remediated site	Probably Not or No	41.4	29
Do you have a river view?	Yes, full view	17.9	
	Yes, but partially blocked	25	
	Yes, glimpse	28.6	
	No	28.6	28
Choice of view/contamination	View, ex-contaminated	69.2	
	No view, clean site	30.8	26
Choice of clean/contaminated living within 300 m of river	Within 300 m, ex-contaminated	14.8	
	Within 300 m, clean site	85.2	27
Concerns:			
• Possibility of remediation failing:	I do not worry	53.6	
	Worries me somewhat	28.6	
• Not all contamination removed:	I do not worry	57.1	
	Worries me somewhat	28.6	
• Safe "Clean" standards change: change:	I do not worry	64.3	
	Worries me somewhat	21.4	28
Affects of contamination history on decision to buy	Did not know about the site's history	36	
	Mild reservations	28	
	Did not influence me	36	25
Decision influences:	Price	46.7	
	River View	43.3	
	River Access	73.3	

Variable	Response	Valid percent (%)	N
	Cycle Path	53.3	
	Proximity to Fremantle	63.3	30
Affects of contamination history on price paid	Did not know about the site's history	37	
	Pay a little less	22.2	
	Price not influenced	37	27

Valid Percentage: This indicates the percent of those respondents that answered that specific question (it does not include non-responses).

N: This indicates the total number of respondents that answered the question.

IV

PROPERTY TAX ASSESSMENT

Chapter 13

Valuation of Land Using Regression Analysis

Mark A. Sunderman
Department of Economics and Finance, University of Wyoming, Laramie, Wyoming

John W. Birch
Department of Economics and Finance, University of Wyoming, Laramie, Wyoming

13.1 Introduction

Estimating the market value of vacant land is one of the more difficult tasks of current real estate appraisal. The problem applies equally to the appraisal of a single site or to the mass appraisal of land. Appraisal texts list several methods to use for this purpose. Regardless of the method chosen, however, when land sales are sparse, valuation may be reduced to an educated guess.

This paper employs an alternative, regression approach that goes beyond the methods previously recommended.[1] The method is illustrated using a set of observations from a specific assessment district. As detailed later, a test of the resulting predicted land values for a random selection of land sales indicates a significant valuation improvement over the corresponding appraisals based on the old methodology.

The new approach is a general one, and thus applicable to land valuation in other assessment districts. As is the case for the district reported on here, land value tables may be employed in such districts. Without these tables, however, the procedure would simply involve one less step, where land valuation would be estimated directly from the final adjusted regression model.

13.2 Land Valuation

According to the Appraisal Institute, there are four main approaches to the valuation of land. They are the (1) sales comparison, (2) allocation, (3) extraction, and (4) income capitalization methods (Appraisal Institute, 1996, p. 324).[2]

In the sales comparison approach, sales of similar sites are adjusted to provide a value basis for the specific property in each case. "Sales comparison is the most common technique for valuing land and it is the preferred method when comparable sales are available" (Appraisal Institute, 1996, p. 324). Without sufficient comparable sales, this approach is less than effective.

The allocation method assumes that there exists a normal or typical ratio for land value to property value for specific types of real estate in specific locations. "Because of the difficulty of supporting a land-to-property value ratio, allocation is a rarely used land valuation approach" (Appraisal Institute, 1996, p. 324). It is also stated, "The allocation method does not produce conclusive value indications, but it can be used to establish land value when the number of vacant land sales is inadequate" (Appraisal Institute, 1996, p. 326). Here the Appraisal Institute clearly recognizes the shortcomings of the allocation approach.

"Extraction is a method in which land value is extracted from the sales price of an improved property by deducting the value contribution of the improvements, estimated as their depreciated costs. The remainder represents the value of the land" (Appraisal Institute, 1996, p. 326). The weakness in this approach lies in the difficulty of arriving at the depreciated value of the improvements. Unless the value of the improvements are relatively low or easily estimated, not common situations, this method is generally too labor intensive, and accurate results may come at a very high cost.

Last of all, income capitalization procedures encompass several different methods, but each applies to the valuation of income producing property. The methods are thus not applicable, since the concern here is the valuation of residential land.

For an appraiser attempting to value vacant land without sufficient comparable sales, there seems to be no effective approach. Under such a condition, some alternative procedure is apparently desirable.

13.3 Data and Methodology

In this paper we develop a multiple regression analysis (MRA) alternative to the extraction method. Since the market value of a property is composed of the value of land and improvements (buildings, etc.), we can use a multiple regression model to estimate the value of the land, the improvements or both.

Using property sales data, a regression model can be developed with price as a function of land and improvement characteristics, as well as the date of sale. Provided the sales are representative of all properties in the jurisdiction, once the model coefficients have been estimated, the value of any sold (or unsold) property can be predicted. This is accomplished by substituting the appropriate property characteristics for the variables in the fitted model. The result will give an expected sales price for the property in question, which is also an estimate of its market value. Thus, for improved property, we can estimate the land value by deducting the market-estimated values for the improvements from the total estimated market value.

The same regression model can also estimate unimproved land values, by setting the values for all improvement characteristics in the fitted model to zero. To estimate the value for this kind of property, only land characteristics and the date of sale (property valuation date) variables will have nonzero input values when solving the fitted regression.

The data used here are restricted to urban sales from a community in Wyoming.[3] The original observations included 2406 valid sales, of which there are 2252 improved property sales and 154 unimproved (vacant land) sales. They cover the period from January 1991 to October 1996. All non-arms length sales were culled from these observations in developing a final set of data to be used when building the model. Also, some sales were eliminated as they did not appear to be representative of the overall data set. Since the intent of the model was to capture typical land values, a few further deletions were made where improvements were unique and could not be easily controlled for.

The data set includes numerous property characteristics for each property sale used in the analysis. The variables in the model are defined in Table 1 and selected summary statistics for these variables are shown in Table 2.[4]

Table 1: Variable Definitions

Land characteristic	
Ni_p	Lot size in a given neighborhood where "i" represents the neighborhood and "p" represents a power transformation – if the power transformation is 1.0 the "p" term is dropped
Di	Dummy variable capturing any further differential between sales in the neighborhood and sales in the city – "i" represents the neighborhood
VACANT	Dummy variable to represent if the property is vacant land
Date of sale characteristics	
V92 to V97	Weighted time variable for vacant land ONLY
IM92 to IM97	Weighted time variable for improved property ONLY
Style characteristics – Dummy variables	
RANCH	Ranch
BILVL	Bi-Level
TRILVL	Tri-Level
CONTMP	Contemporary construction
CAPE	Cape Cod
COLONL	Colonial
CONDO	Condo
TWNHSE	Townhouse
GLASS	Large use of glass
MODULAR	Modular homes
Exterior wall material – Dummy variables	
FRAME	Frame
ASBEST	Asbestos
MASFR	Masonry and frame
BRICKST	Brick and/or stone
ALMVNL	Aluminum siding
LOG	Log construction
Grade of construction – Dummy variables	
D	D (lowest)
C	C
BA	B and A (highest)
CDU – Condition use factor	
PRA	Square feet of living area in a "poor" CDU property
FRA	Square feet of living area in a "fair" CDU property
AVA	Square feet of living area in a "average" CDU property
GDA	Square feet of living area in a "good" CDU property
VGA	Square feet of living area in a "very good" CDU property
EXA	Square feet of living area in an "excellent" CDU property
Other improvement features	
FINBSMT	Square feet of finished basement area
RECAR	Square feet of a recreation area
AGE1	Age of the improvements taken to the .1 power
TOTFIX1	Total number of plumbing fixtures to the .1 power
MULTIFAM	Dummy variable to represent if the property is multifamily

Other improvement features	
ATGAR	Square feet of attached garage
DETGAR	Square feet of detached garage
DECK	Square feet of deck
PORCH	Square feet of porch
ACGRHS	Square feet of attached solar greenhouse
NFIREPL	Number of fireplaces
BEDRMS	Number of bedrooms
BFULL	Dummy variable for a full basement

Table 2: Selected Summary Statistics Improved Property Only

Variable	Mean	Std dev	Minimum	Maximum
SPRICE (all sales)	75549.44	35367.46	8700.00	378000.00
TOTACRE (all sales)	0.190	0.275	0.01	4.09
RANCH	0.591	0.492	0	1.00
BILVL	0.102	0.302	0	1.00
TRIVL	0.060	0.237	0	1.00
CONTMP	0.019	0.135	0	1.00
CAPE	0.020	0.140	0	1.00
COLONL	0.025	0.156	0	1.00
CONDO	0.036	0.186	0	1.00
TWNHSE	0.134	0.340	0	1.00
GLASS	0.010	0.101	0	1.00
MODULAR	0.004	0.063	0	1.00
FRAME	0.566	0.496	0	1.00
ASBEST	0.067	0.250	0	1.00
MASFR	0.087	0.281	0	1.00
BRICKST	0.065	0.247	0	1.00
ALMVNL	0.075	0.263	0	1.00
LOG	0.003	0.052	0	1.00
D	0.223	0.417	0	1.00
C	0.735	0.441	0	1.00
BA	0.042	0.200	0	1.00
PRA	3.861	57.624	0	1284.00
FRA	24.603	157.840	0	2717.00
AVA	183.752	437.513	0	2678.00
GDA	146.108	429.876	0	4352.00
VGA	705.406	703.856	0	4331.00
EXA	145.199	454.822	0	3551.00
FINBSM	399.185	470.837	0	2303.00
RECAR	83.535	241.490	0	1912.00
AGE	36.759	25.514	0.50	121.00
TOTFIX	7.746	2.272	4.00	23.00
MULTIFAM	0.053	0.224	0	1.00
ATGAR	230.334	230.969	0	1483.00

Table 2: (*Continued*)

Variable	Mean	Std. dev	Minimum	Maximum
DETGAR	102.307	191.353	0	2520.00
DECK	52.181	89.956	0	906.00
ASGRHS	2.663	29.496	0	644.00
NFIREPL	0.384	0.519	0	2.00
BEDRMS	3.020	1.021	1.00	9.00
BFULL	0.553	0.497	0	1.00

13.4 The Specific Model

The model can be briefly discussed. Sales prices are the dependent or predictor variable, to represent market value estimates, and to be predicted by a series of independent or explanatory variables. Several different types of variables are usually employed when multiple regression is used to estimate improved residential property values.[5] The model used follows this practice, and variables include such property characteristics as style of building, type of wall construction, grade and current condition. Also included are variables for other property characteristics, including age of the improvements. In addition to these variables, there is subset of variables (date of sale characteristics) employed to estimate changes in the level of the market from year to year over the time span the data cover. Its use allows predictions of property values at a point in time consistent with the needs of the assessment district.[6] These variables can also be used to estimate market time patterns, although that is not the purpose here.

In addition to improved property characteristics and time of sale variables, there are also three kinds of land characteristic variables included in the model. These variables involve land associated with the sales of improved property, as well as vacant land sales. The first type consists of a set of neighborhood variables, with a variable assigned to each neighborhood.[7] These variables take a value of 0 for sales outside its specific neighborhood. For sales within the neighborhood the variable takes on a value equal to the size of the property. Note also that this variable is raised to some power term p, where p takes on a value between 0 and 1.[8] This permits the model to account for possible neighborhood specific nonlinearity in the price-size relationship. Although there are arguments that the value-size relationship is linear, the overwhelming empirical evidence supports a nonlinear relationship.[9] The advantage of a power transformation for this neighborhood dummy variable is that it allows for both linear and nonlinear relationships in different neighborhoods.

The second set of land characteristic variables involves the estimation of any further typical difference between sales prices within each neighborhood relative to sales prices in the remainder of the community. To control for these affects, 0–1 dummy variables, Dn, were introduced, where n designates the nth neighborhood. Thus, some neighborhoods showed a significant difference between the neighborhood sales prices and those in the rest of the district, having accounted for all other effects, including neighborhood lot size. These Dn variables allow for the measurement of any significant location neighborhood based effects on property sales. Dummy variables are used here only for neighborhoods that showed significant differences in sales prices that could not be explained by any other variables in the model.

A third type of variable was also employed to distinguish vacant land sales from improved property sales. This variable, also a 0–1 dummy, allows the model to pick up any typical difference between the sales price of vacant and improved land that is not already explained by the other characteristics described in the model.[10]

Once the full model was developed and initially fitted, two criteria were used to eliminate a few additional sales from the analysis, with the purpose of improving the final model as a predictor of land values.[11] The first rule was that properties would be removed whose sales prices were more than 3 standard errors above or below their predicted values. Such properties are felt to have characteristics that the model would not properly cover, possibly due to a lack of sufficient information about either the sales price or the property characteristics in such sales, or because of a data reporting error.

The second criteria for deleting some observations, after a preliminary model fit, involved the calculation of Cook's distance for each property sale. An absolute value for Cook's distance greater than or equal to 1.00 indicates that a property sale has an unduly large influence on the overall predicted values coming from the model.[12] Such sales were removed from the analysis.

Using these two criteria resulted in the elimination of approximately 2 percent of all available sales. The final model was generated on the basis of the remaining sales and their associated characteristics.

As a last step before obtaining the final market values, we tested the hypothesis that there was no bias in the predictions of typical sales prices obtained from the model, compared with the actual prices observed. A model with no bias should have predictions centered on actual values over the whole range of actual values. In other words, the linear regression of actual sales prices on the predicted sales prices for the same properties should have an intercept and slope of 0 and 1.00, respectively, or not be significantly different from these parameters. An F test was applied to test the null hypothesis, Ho: Intercept $= 0$; Slope $= 1.00$. Rejection of this hypothesis would mean adjustments to correct for bias. Failure to reject would mean no bias was present and no adjustments would thus be necessary.

13.5 Some Model Results

The chosen model explains most of the variation in sales prices attributable to improved and vacant land sales. The adjusted R^2 has a value of 0.9181. Given the goodness of the model's fit, alternative models are not likely to significantly improve the explanation of sales prices or the accuracy of resulting estimates of market value. A later test of prediction accuracy verifies this expectation. The detailed model results are shown in Table 3.

Table 3: Dependent Variable = Sales Price

Variable	Parameter estimate	Standard error	T-statistic
Intercept	7954.719	9106.203	0.87
N1	25,876**	2520.245	10.27
D1	−4989.319**	1592.465	−3.13
N2_1	−4851.203**	2034.083	−2.38
N3	126,983**	13,350	9.51
N4_1	11,828**	2135.518	5.54
N5	84,813**	11,599	7.31
N6_1	9017.953**	2799.996	3.22
N7	138,637**	9355.741	14.82
N8_1	15,689**	1809.983	8.67
N9_9	91,038**	10,125	8.99
N0_1	−6470.761	4073.077	−1.59
N11	153,490**	71,357	2.15
D11	−15742**	7004.675	−2.25
N12_1	8034.939**	2723.289	2.95
N14_5	280,015**	35,081	7.98
D14	−98716**	17,377	−5.68
N15_7	49,646**	6725.347	7.38
N16	65,284**	15,515	4.21
N17	103,620**	10,195	10.16
N18	114,575**	19,405	5.90
N19_1	9750.658**	3324.397	2.93
N20	61,890**	19,133	3.23
D20	−7180.196**	3218.622	−2.23
N21_5	34,389**	6376.935	5.39
N22	55,643**	8481.330	6.56
N23_1	240,597**	49,706	4.84
D23	−176893**	37,683	−4.69
N24_9	46,959**	8570.766	5.48
N25	84,135**	8144.890	10.33
N26_1	81,908**	22,254	3.68
D26	−58,765**	17,927	−3.28
N27_7	44,200**	5891.396	7.50

Variable	Parameter estimate	Standard error	T-statistic
N28_1	18,281**	2337.819	7.82
N29	22,606**	3194.424	7.08
N30_7	14,051**	1367.327	10.28
N31_1	12,784**	2214.90	5.77
N32_1	6286.408**	2558.223	2.46
V92	10,980	10,072	1.09
V93	17,679**	7770.555	2.28
V94	23,092**	8266.578	2.79
V95	31,492**	7922.721	3.97
V96	25,713**	7886.704	3.26
V97	27,988**	8861.375	3.16
IM92	−731.957	1768.963	−0.41
IM93	2224.578	1464.707	1.52
IM94	16,413**	1473.709	11.14
IM95	22,378**	1481.031	15.11
IM96	29,521**	1510.612	19.54
IM97	41,273**	2012.256	20.51
PRA	6.090	3.729	1.63
FRA	11.301**	1.705	6.63
AVA	13.680**	0.904	15.12
GDA	17.357**	0.892	19.45
VGA	17.106**	0.769	22.26
EXA	18.622**	0.900	20.69
C	3089.532**	629.860	4.91
BA	21,005**	1548.997	13.56
FINBSM	7.267**	0.769	9.46
RECAR	5.930**	1.077	5.51
AGE1	−56620**	3278.513	−17.27
TOTFIX1	72,632**	6223.694	11.67
MULTIFAM	−5778.877**	973.537	−5.94
BILVL	836.695	895.599	0.93
TRILVL	3711.367**	1010.367	3.67
CONTMP	6607.994**	1800.380	3.67
CAPE	−1165.998	1582.798	−0.74
COLONL	2751.264*	1526.325	1.80
CONDO	−17,339**	1596.755	−10.86
TWNHSE	−7025.612**	1129.973	−6.22
GLASS	4612.961**	2282.136	2.02
MODULAR	−14,467**	3409.425	−4.24
ATGAR	14.339**	1.481	9.68
DETGAR	10.374**	1.316	7.88
DECK	17.038**	2.543	6.70
BFULL	2567.834**	676.026	3.80
NFIREPL	4391.795**	486.297	9.03
BEDRMS	873.260**	279.897	3.12
PORCH	11.651**	2.629	4.43

Table 3: (*Continued*)

Variable	Parameter estimate	Standard error	T-statistic
ASGRHS	36.192**	6.967	5.20
ASBEST	−3076.089**	898.067	−3.43
MASFR	2381.427	960.780	2.48
BRICKST	2598.225**	956.064	2.72
STUCCO	−110.082	675.640	−0.16
ALMVNL	−1191.882	839.369	−1.42
LOG	981.186	3970.394	0.25
VACANT	−25,217**	11562	−2.18
Number of Observations		2367	
Adjusted R^2		0.9181	

** Indicates significance at $\alpha = .05$ level or higher.
* Indicates significance between $\alpha = .1$ and $\alpha = .05$.

This model uses a linear functional form. To account for potential non-linear relationships, some of the explanatory variables were modified with power transformations. Attempts were made to modify other variables as well, but the evidence indicated these variables were related to sales prices in a linear way. Given the adequacy of the fit, with the important inclusion of dummy variables, as well as other variables being permitted to take the value of zero, nonlinear forms were not seriously considered[13].

The model as shown in Table 3, includes both improved and vacant land sales. In this way, we ensured that vacant land was encompassed in the analysis of land values. Once the model was developed, applied and tested for adequacy, the results were used to generate values for vacant land for the 31 urban neighborhoods in the study.

The test for the null hypothesis that the actual sales regressed on predicted sales with an intercept and a slope not different from 0 and 1, respectively, was not rejected. The fitted line was very close to this postulated 0–1 "no bias" line. Thus no adjustments were made for predictions from the model.

How well a model predicts the variable of interest is clearly an important way to judge the procedure involved. Thus to test our model, a representative sample of 20 vacant land sales was drawn prior to the analysis. This holdout sample was set aside when building the model and estimating parameters. The resulting model was used to estimate the value for each of these holdout land sales. These estimated market values were then compared with the actual sales prices to see how accurate the predictions were. A comparison was also separately made between the original appraisal values and these actual sales prices.

The coefficient of dispersion (COD) of predicted versus actual holdout sales was calculated, and compared with the same statistic for the original appraisals versus actual holdout sales.[14] The COD values for the predicted sales and for the original appraisals were 21.5 and 28.8, respectively. Since the smaller the COD, the more accurate the estimated market values, the methodology employed here has improved the vacant land value estimates compared with the prior method.

By comparison with ideal standards, as set by the International Association of Assessing Officers, a COD of 20, or less, is desirable for vacant land (IAAO, 1999, p. 57). However, it should be noted that the holdout sample was taken from property sales where properties with unusually large or small appraisal to sales price ratios were not removed prior to the analysis. Removal of these extreme observations is a common practice in assessment work (IAAO, 1999, p. 39). Thus, it could be expected that the COD, under a reasonable trimming scheme, would have been less than the number actually derived, likely within IAAO standards.[15]

Our final model, as shown in Table 3, gives two interesting results relating to land value. First, by observing the V(y) and IM(y) variables it can be seen that the pattern and rate of appreciation is different between vacant land and improved property. Second, within many neighborhoods, we also found that, there was a nonlinear relationship between land value and land size, with value rising more slowly per square foot for larger land parcels.

13.6 Deriving Land Values from the MRA Models

Once the model coefficients were found, the next task was to obtain market values for land sizes within each of the neighborhoods. The fitted model could, of course, be used to obtain values for each parcel directly. However, the neighborhood land tables in use contained only 6 different lot sizes as a base for estimating lot size values. Once the values for these particular lot sizes were estimated, all other land size values could be found by linear interpolation. The 6 different sizes chosen were 2500, 5000, 10,000, 25,000, 40,000 and 60,000 square feet. The smaller differences among the lesser land sizes were used because of the possible greater curvature in the relation between the market value and lot size for smaller lots.

The land values for each of these specified lot sizes were obtained as follows. First, an appropriate table limit or end point value for each explanatory variable was substituted into the fitted model. Thus, for example, when obtaining the land value for a 25,000 square foot lot in a particular neighborhood, we substituted the number 25,000 (after making any needed power transformation) for the "*N*" variable representing that neighborhood. Second, if the neighborhood had a *D* variable, this variable was given the value of 1.

Table 4: Neighborhood Land Tables

Neighborhood 3

Sales	Decrement	Square Feet 2,500.00	Increment	Square Feet 5,000.00	Increment	Square Feet 7,500.00	Increment	Square Feet 15,000.00	Increment	Square Feet 30,000.00	Increment	Square Feet 60,000.00	Increment
Model 106	-1.90	18,013.54	2.92	25,301.36	2.92	32,589.18	2.92	54,452.65	2.92	98,179.58	2.92	185,633.43	3.09
Average CALP	1.50	12,000.00	1.50	15,750.00	1.50	19,500.00	1.50	30,750.00	1.50	53,250.00	1.50	98,250.00	1.50
Recommendation	-4.29	18,014.00	2.91	25,301.00	2.92	32,589.00	2.92	54,453.00	2.92	98,180.00	2.92	185,633.00	3.09

Square Feet –

Range Minimum	Maximum	Mean	Median
871.2	8712.0	4247.1	4573.8

Neighborhood 9

Sales	Decrement	Square Feet 2,500.00	Increment	Square Feet 5,000.00	Increment	Square Feet 7,500.00	Increment	Square Feet 15,000.00	Increment	Square Feet 30,000.00	Increment	Square Feet 60,000.00	Increment
Model 115	-4.29	17,679.00	2.41	23,701.00	2.29	29,415.27	2.16	45,601.65	2.01	75,806.50	1.88	132,170.75	2.20
Average CALP	0.75	12,375.00	0.75	14,250.00	0.75	16,125.00	0.75	21,750.00	0.75	33,000.00	0.75	55,500.00	0.75
Recommendation	-4.29	17,679.00	2.41	23,701.00	2.29	29,415.00	2.16	45,602.00	2.01	75,806.00	1.88	132,171.00	2.20

Square Feet –

Range Minimum	Maximum	Mean	Median
1742.4	10454.4	5180.1	4356.0

All other *N* variables (ones representing other neighborhoods) were given a value of 0. All variables measuring improved property characteristics were also assigned a value of 0, since we were looking for estimated or predicted values for parcels of vacant land. The two exceptions are the date of sale variable for land and the dummy variable for vacant land sales. In this case, the value of 1 was used for the time variable *V*97, representing valuations as of a specified date, January 1, 1997. All other *V* variables were given a value of 0. In this way, we derived a predicted value for 25,000 square feet of vacant land for a given neighborhood as of January 1, 1997.[16]

Since it could be argued that some of the value of improved attributes, positive or negative, is in the fitted model's intercept, we included the vacant land dummy to account for this value effect. For vacant land sales in the regression model, this variable would take the value of 1. Since the coefficient was negative, the vacant land sale predicted was typically lowered slightly.

Land tables could be developed in this way for each neighborhood, for each of the 6 different lot sizes. For illustrative purposes, however, only two neighborhood tables are included in Table 4. At the top of each neighborhood land table, results of the regression model are given for each of the 6 lot sizes.

To determine the value per square foot for actual lot sizes, we interpolated between closest pairs of lot sizes on a linear basis. Values at the extreme ranges were also interpolated after first establishing point dollar values for extremely low and extremely high lot sizes.[17]

Also included in each of the two tables is the existing CALP (computer assisted land price) values that had previously been used for properties in each neighborhood. These were inserted to illustrate and compare the preexisting level of land valuation for the two neighborhoods in question.

For each neighborhood we show a range of land sizes that have been placed within brackets. These are the ranges for which the model results have a solid empirical foundation, based as they are on more than adequate number of sales. In general, most observed property sales fall in these ranges. Additional analysis and/or expertise was recommended for land sizes outside these ranges.[18]

13.7 Conclusions

This paper illustrates a procedure for obtaining land values, either vacant or improved. Sales of similar parcels of land are often unavailable, and valuation tends to be one of the more difficult aspects of a real estate appraisal. However, multiple regression represents a method for obtaining a market based estimate of land value even when sales of vacant land parcels are limited in number. This approach can be used whether or not land value tables are involved. In general, the approach illustrated is a useful alternative when individual land value estimates are needed and land sales are limited.

NOTES

[1] The method illustrated in this paper was employed by the authors to assist a county's assessor in the revaluation of land parcels. In this particular county, land value is based on neighborhood location and size, with each neighborhood identified with a specific land table value. The purpose of this project was to derive a set of updated land table values that could be used to value both improved and vacant land. Most importantly, these values needed to be supported by the market. To the best of our knowledge, the method employed here has no prior history in the field of real estate appraisal.

[2] See for example, chapter 11 in Appraisal Institute (1999) or chapter 9 in Lusht (1997).

[3] The information was provided by the county assessor and consists of the data used by the county to arrive at assessed valuation for the same time point as the regression analysis is applied to.

[4] Since the intent here is to illustrate a method that can be used to arrive at vacant property value and not to report all details for a particular county, we discuss the actual data in summary form only.

[5] For a discussion, see Mark and Goldberg (1988).

[6] To account for market movements we used a set of variables that allows for changes in value over time. The form used was originally employed by Bryan and Colwell (1982). In this method, each date of sale is defined as a linear combination of the end points of the year in which the sale occurs. Date of sale variables, B(y), are the proportionate weights. For example, if a sale occurred on September 30, 1994, then B94 is 0.25, B95 is 0.75 and all other B(y) variables are zero. Since the sale was closer to the beginning of 1995 than to the beginning of 1994, B95 is larger and given more weight than B94. This technique allows the rate of change in prices to be different for each year and allows for a price continuum rather than a step function. In our analysis, the specific method was modified to allow for any difference in the growth rates between vacant land and improved property. This was done by using two sets of variables instead of the single B(y) set. B(y) was replaced with V(y) and IM(y). Thus, V(y) is operational for vacant land sales and IM(y) for improved property sales. This B(y) approach has been applied by Sunderman and Spahr (1994), Spahr and Sunderman (1995, 1998, and 1999), and Colwell et. al. (1998).

[7] The individual neighborhoods were defined by the assessor's office in accord with standard methods for identifying neighborhoods. These neighborhoods have been locally estimated and had been used previously in arriving at assessed valuation.

[8] For example, the variable N6_3 would represent the lot sizes for any neighborhood 6 sold property, raised to the power 0.3. The power transformation number for each neighborhood variable was determined to give the best fit to the data (based on the highest adjusted R^2 for the overall regression model). The INCLUDE, SELECTION, and BEST options in the REG procedure in the SAS statistical package were used. Each neighborhood was allowed to have a different exponent value, since different neighborhood variables were found to have varying exponent value.

[9] For example, see Asaberre and Colwell (1985), Bland (1984), and Keith (1991). For a discussion of potential reasons to expect a nonlinear relationship, see Colwell and Sirmans (1980).

[10] We experimented here, using lot size to some power p, for consistency with earlier neighborhood variables, but found the resulting coefficient was not significant. In the interests of simplicity, we thus returned to a 0–1 dummy variable.

[11] These criteria have also been employed by Spahr and Sunderman (1999).

[12] See Neter et al. (1983, pp. 407–9) for a discussion of this concept.

[13] Nonlinear models that can be linearized via log transforms were not considered, since such transforms are not possible when dummy variables need to be included (Netter et al., 1983, p. 467).

[14] For a description of COD, see IAAO (1999, p. 44).

[15] A reviewer suggested concern with the accuracy of land value predictions, especially as it might relate to multicollinearity among independent variables. Variance Inflation factors were run on all such variables, and almost all had values that were highly acceptable (<10.0). In addition, the vacant land forecast performance reported on suggests that the model was strong enough to overcome any problems from this source.

[16] Note that all IM(y) variables take a value of zero since there are no improvements present.

[17] At the low end we used 0 square feet and at the upper end we used 174,240 square feet (4 acres).

[18] All of this is a caveat that is standard for applied regression results: Beware of extending predictions beyond the observation set.

REFERENCES

1. Appraisal Institute, *Appraising Residential Properties*, 3rd ed. (Chicago: Appraisal Institute, 1999).
2. Appraisal Institute, *The Appraisal of Real Estate*, 11th ed. (Chicago: Appraisal Institute, 1996).
3. Asabere Paul and Peter Colwell, The Relative Lot Size Hypothesis: An Empirical Note, *Urban Studies*, 1985, 22, 355–57.
4. Bland, Robert, The Implicit Price of Housing Attributes: An Explication and Application of the Theory to Mass Appraisal Research, *Property Tax Journal*, 1984, 3:1, 55–65.
5. Bryan, B. Thomas and Peter F. Colwell, "Housing Price Indexes," In C. F. Sirmans, editor, *Research in Real Estate* (Greenwich, CT: JAI Press, 1982), Vol. 2, 57–84.
6. Colwell, Peter, Henry Munneke, and Joseph Trefzger, Chicago's Office Market: Price Indices, Location and Time, *Real Estate Economics*, 1998, 26:1, 83–106.
7. Colwell, Peter and Sirmans, C. F. Nonlinear Urban Land Prices, *Urban Geography*, 1980, 1, 141–52.
8. International Association of Assessing Officers (IAAO), Standard on Ratio Studies, *Assessment Journal*, 1999, 6:5, 23–65.
9. Keith, Tom, Applying Discounted Cash Flow Analyses to Land in Transition, *Appraisal Journal*, 1991, 59:4, 458–70.
10. Lusht, Kenneth, *Real Estate Valuation: Principles and Applications*, (Irwin, 1997).
11. Mark, Jonathan and Michael Goldberg, Multiple Regression Analysis and Mass Assessment: A Review of the Issues, *Appraisal Journal*, 1988, 56:1, 89–109.
12. Neter, John, William Wasserman, and Michael H. Kutner, *Applied Linear Regression Models*, (Homewood, Illinois: Richard D. Irwin, Inc., 1983).
13. Spahr, W. Ronald and Mark A. Sunderman, Additional Evidence on the Homogeneity of the Value of Government Grazing Leases and Changing Attributes for Ranch Values, *Journal of Real Estate Research*, 1995, 10:5, 601–616.
14. Spahr, Ronald W. and Mark A. Sunderman, Property Tax Inequities on Ranch and Farm Properties, *Land Economics*, 1998, 74:3, 374–389.
15. Spahr, Ronald W. and Mark A. Sunderman, Valuation of Agricultural Property Surrounding a Resort Community, *Journal of Real Estate Research*, 1999, 17:2, 227–243.
16. Sunderman, Mark A. and Ronald W. Spahr, Valuation of Government Grazing Leases, *Journal of Real Estate Research*, 1994, 9:2, 179–196.

Chapter 14

Grid-Adjustment Approach – Modern Appraisal Technique

Shwu-huei Huang
Department of Public Finance and Taxation,
National Taichung Institute of Technolog. Taichung, Taiwan.

14.1 Introduction

Appraisers can learn a great deal of information from government assessment reports, especially when the assessment is ideal. In Taiwan, property tax has been separated into land value tax and house tax. Land value tax revenue is the second largest tax revenue (next to the land value increment tax) for local government. The land value increment tax, which takes the increase in land price as the tax base, is very similar to the capital gain tax in the United States. In Taiwan the assessment of land declared price, which is the tax base of the land value tax, is neither efficient nor equitable. The objective of this study is to improve assessment for the land value tax base, which is a very significant data bank for appraisers.

Palmquist (1989) recognized Rosen's (1974) contribution to the hedonic price approach and employed it to calculate implicit prices of real estate characteristics. Since then the hedonic price approach has become a useful tool to evaluate real estate. Bible and Hsieh (1999) applied a geography information system (GIS) to locate real estate transactions and discovered that the distance to the central business district, community population, and zoning had a significant impact on the value of vacant sites in Shreveport and Bossier, Indiana. Furthermore, Detweiler and Radigan (1999) applied a computer-assisted system to enhance the capabilities of the hedonic price approach in Oregon. Kang and Reichert (1991) noted that appraisers are familiar with the traditional appraisal approach, and they combine the traditional with the hedonic price approach to form the grid-adjustment approach.

This chapter is divided into five remaining sections. The second section describes the data source and presents sample statistics. The third explains the assessment results of the market comparison approach. The fourth includes an empirical study of the hedonic price approach. The fifth is the empirical study of grid-adjustment approach. The last section is the conclusion.

14.2 Source of Data and Sample Statistics

Taichung Municipality, with a population of nearly 900,000, is located in the central and the third largest city of Taiwan, and it has been divided into eight administrative districts. Chungshan Land Office, hereafter referred to as Region 1, administers land registration and assessment in the Central, East, West, and South Districts. North and Beitwen Districts are administered by the Chungcheng Land Office, which is known as Region 2. The Sitwen and Nantwen Districts are administered by the Chunghsing Land Office (Region 3). Region 1 is the central city and the remainder is the peripheral area. Vacant land transaction cases analyzed here were collected from the Taiwan Real Estate Transaction Brief (Brief), a quarterly periodical published by the Taiwan Department of Interior. The period examined is from 1994 to 1999, and a total of 764 observations are included. Table 1 presents their geographical distribution.

Sale price for each transaction parcel can be found in the Brief. For a comparison, the corresponding land declared price for each parcel was obtained from the local Land Offices. According to appraisal theory, many parcel characteristics may affect land price. The Brief reveals some characteristics of each parcel, which include roadway width, proximity to major streets, parcel shape, zoning, and land area. To increase the capability of the evaluation

Table 1: Sampled Transaction Cases in Taichung Municipality

Region	Year						Total
	1994	1995	1996	1997	1998	1999	
1	98	60	66	40	54	30	348
2	39	38	44	45	37	14	217
3	12	6	56	59	48	18	199
Taichung	149	104	166	144	139	62	764

model, the proximity of each parcel to the following locations was added: (1) the central business district, (2) sub-centers, such as Fongchia, Beitwen, Chuigwo, Railway Station, and Chungyu, (3) the Municipal Garbage Processing Site and Municipal Funeral Home, and (4) the National Nature Museum. Both locations included in (3), garbage site and funeral home, are NIMBY facilities. They may have the effect of decreasing land price nearby. On the contrary, the Museum may increase land price. All of these characteristics will be listed and explained in more detail in Table 5.

Statistics of the transaction sample are as follows:

(1) The average roadway width 19.47 m and the standard deviation is 8.71 m.
(2) 55.5% of the sample parcels (424 parcels) are proximate to roads, the remainder are proximate to alleyways.
(3) 650 parcels (85.08%) are zoning for residential use, remainder are commercially zoned.
(4) The average parcel land area is 255.95 square meters and the median is 119.50 square meters (SM).
(5) The average sale price was 75.7 thousand NT$/SM and the standard deviation was 46.7 thousand NT$/SM.
(6) The average declared price was 9.5 thousand NT$/SM and the standard deviation is 14.1 NT$/SM.

14.3 Assessment of Government's Traditional Approach

Traditionally, the local government of Taiwan applies the market comparison approach to determine land declared price. The parcels requiring assessment are many. For example, in the Taichung Municipality, there are roughly 351,000 parcels, which require assessment each time. Therefore, the government has divided the entire city into 3,197 land price zones. For each zone, there is a zone price, which is supposed to represent land price for that zone, derived by comparing at least three transaction cases. Then the government forwards all zone prices to the Land Price Examination and Consultant Committee for review, which is an independent semi-public organization composed of representatives from various industries. Most committee members are motivated to reduce the tax burden for their interest. Additionally, the market comparison approach is vulnerable to criticism because it involves subjective elements when it is used to derive the zone price. As a result, zone prices that are forwarded to the Committee are always reduced to an unreasonable level. The land declared price, which is calculated from the zone price via legal procedures, is also underestimated.

Two criteria, efficiency and equity, are employed herein to measure the assessment quality of the land declared price. In this study, efficiency improves as the assessment to sale price ratio (a–s ratio) approaches one. Equity requires the a–s ratio be equal for each parcel of the same value and for other parcels with different values. The coefficient of variation (CV) is used to measure equity. The smaller the coefficient of variation, the greater the assessment equity. Table 2 presents the a–s ratios and the coefficients of variation for the three regions as well as Taichung as a whole during the study period.

Table 2: The Efficiency and Equity Test of Land Declared Price of Taichung

Region	a–s ratio	Fiscal Year						Cumulative
		1994	1995	1996	1997	1998	1999	
1	Mean	0.14	0.15	0.14	0.16	0.15	0.18	0.15
	Standard deviation	0.08	0.09	0.06	0.14	0.07	0.09	0.09
	CV	0.56	0.57	0.44	0.87	0.48	0.52	0.57
2	Mean	0.10	0.09	0.08	0.09	0.09	0.10	0.09
	Standard deviation	0.07	0.05	0.07	0.05	0.05	0.05	0.06
	CV	0.66	0.54	0.89	0.59	0.62	0.49	0.65
3	Mean	0.05	0.04	0.06	0.06	0.06	0.06	0.06
	Standard deviation	0.02	0.01	0.02	0.03	0.02	0.02	0.02
	CV	0.37	0.35	0.39	0.43	0.36	0.27	0.40
Taichung	Mean	0.13	0.12	0.10	0.10	0.10	0.13	0.11
	Standard deviation	0.08	0.08	0.07	0.09	0.07	0.09	0.08
	CV	0.63	0.65	0.70	0.90	0.65	0.68	0.71

Note: Fiscal year starts from July 1 instead of January 1 of every year.

Table 3: A Comparison of a–s Ratios Among Different Countries

Country	Region or type of land	a–s ratio%
Denmark		95
USA		90
Canada	B.C., Manitoba, New Brunswick, and Quebec	90
	Remainder	80
UK		80–84
Sweden		75
Chile	Non-rural land	45
	Rural land	25
South Korea		20–45

Source: UK data is quoted from Kirkwood (1985) and the remainder from Youngman and Maime (1994).

From Table 2, the a–s ratios of the entire city from 1994 to 1999 are merely 13%, 12%, 10%, 10%, 10%, 10%, and 13%, respectively. Furthermore, the cumulative a–s ratios for Regions 1, 2 and 3 for the study period are 15%, 9% and 6%, respectively. Notably, the a–s ratio of the central city (Region 1) is higher than average, while those of the peripheral area are much lower than average (Regions 2 and 3). For comparison, Table 3 presents the a–s ratios for selected countries.

From Table 3, when compared to those of other countries, the a–s ratio of Taichung Municipality is quite low. Additionally, coefficients of variation of the entire city from 1994 to 1999 are 63%, 65%, 70%, 90%, 65% and 68%, respectively, which are lower than Back's criterion of 30% (1970). Furthermore, there are many models, which measure whether an assessment is progressive or regressive, including Paglin and Fogarty (1972), Cheng (1974), IAAO (1978), Kochin and Parks (1982), Bell (1984), Clapp (1990), Sunderman et al. (1990), and Cesare and Ruddock (1998). Of which, only Kochin and Parks view the sale price as the dependent variable and the assessed price as the independent variable. The variation of assessed prices should be lower than the variation of sale prices, since the government controls the former. Therefore, it is best to employ the assessed price as the independent variable. Their model is $P = \beta_0(P')^{\beta_1} e^{\varepsilon}$, where P and P' represent the sale and the assessed prices, respectively, and ε is the error term. The estimation model for this relationship can be presented as $\ln P = \beta_0 + \beta_1 \ln P'$, where ln stands for natural logarithm. The coefficients β_0 and β_1 can be estimated from the sample. If the null hypothesis $\beta_1 = 1$ is accepted, meaning the a–s ratio is equal for each parcel, then it can be concluded that the assessment is consistent. In contrast, if $\beta_1 < 1$ ($\beta_1 > 1$) is accepted, then the assessment is progressive (regressive). Table 4 presents the results of empirical tests of the estimation model.

Table 4: Consistency Tests for Land Declared Price

Parameter	1994	1995	1996	1997	1998	1999
β_0	8.257***	8.254***	7.836***	8.255***	8.357***	7.359***
	(33.109)	(29.439)	(29.954)	(29.429)	(37.379)	(22.171)
β_1	0.395***	0.402***	0.346***	0.370***	0.392***	0.358***
	(19.069)	(18.262)	(24.687)	(21.495)	(24.513)	(13.700)
R^2	0.513	0.597	0.510	0.529	0.645	0.492
$\bar{R}^2$	0.509	0.593	0.507	0.526	0.642	0.484
F	154.6***	151.1***	170.7***	159.6***	248.9***	58.1***

*** Significant at the .01 level.

As shown in Table 4, the alternative hypothesis of $\beta_1 < 1$ is accepted for each year. Therefore, the land value tax is progressive. In sum, assessment of the tax base for the land value tax via the government's traditional approach in Taichung is neither efficient nor equitable. Thus, it must be improved to provide more useful information for both appraisers as well as the government tax office.

14.4 Assessment of the Hedonic Price Approach

This study demonstrates two approaches to improve the assessment. The first is the hedonic price approach and the second is the grid-adjustment approach. The former will be studied in this section. Sale price and land characteristics will exhibit one of the following relationships: (1) linear, (2) semi-log, (3) linear-log, or (4) double log. Independent variables (Xs), which are defined in Table 5, represent the land characteristics; noting that X_2, X_4, X_6, X_8, X_{10}, X_{12}, X_{14}, X_{16}, X_{18}, X_{20}, and X_{22} are discrete (dummy) variables and the rest of them are continuous. Sale price is the dependent variable.

Table 6 displays the empirical results of eight models that were developed with the least squares method. The variables included in Table 6, which are significant in statistical sense, are selected by stepwise regression. In other words, those variables not included in Table 6 are not significant to land price. Model 8, which is a double log function, was chosen because it is the best from the standpoint of Akaike Information Criterion and Press (Lavergne, 1998). However, it had a problem of heteroscedasticity. Therefore, to recalculate Model 8, the weighted least square method (WLS) was applied and Table 7, which is the evaluation model employed herein, presents the results. From Table 7, the Variance Inflated Factor (VIF) of each variable is less than 10, indicating no serious multicollinearity. One statistical dilemma was present, however. Although X_5 is a continuous variable, it is not significant

Table 5: Definition of Variables

Variable	Definition	Measurement
X_1	Distance to the CBD	Meter
X_2	CBD trade area	Extending to 1000 meters
X_3	Distance to Beitwen sub-center	Meter
X_4	Beitwen trade area	Extending to 2000 meters
X_5	Distance to Fongchia sub-center	Meter
X_6	Fongchia trade area	Extending to 2000 meters
X_7	Distance to Chuikwo sub-center	Meter
X_8	Chuikwo trade area	Extending to 3000 meters
X_9	Distance to the rear of rail station	Meter
X_{10}	Rear of rail station trade area	Extending to 1000 meters
X_{11}	Distance to Chungyu sub-center	Meter
X_{12}	Chungyu trade area	Extending to 1000 meters
X_{13}	Distance to National Nature Museum	Meter
X_{14}	National Nature Museum area	Extending to 3000 meters
X_{15}	Distance to Municipal Funeral Home	Meter
X_{16}	Municipal Funeral Home area	Extending to 9000 meters
X_{17}	Distance to Municipal Garbage Processing Site	Meter
X_{18}	Municipal Garbage Site area	Extending to 9000 meters
X_{19}	Width of roadway	Meter
X_{20}	Zoning	Commerce=1, residence=0
X_{21}	Area of parcel	Square meter
X_{22}	Proximity to roadway	Proximate to road=1, Proximate to alley=0
P	Sale price	10000NT$/SM
P'	Land declared price	10000NT$/SM

Table 6: Empirical Results of Various Hedonic Price Approach Models

Model	1	2	3	4	5	6	7	8
Variable Dependent	P	P	P	LNP	LNP	LNP	LNP	LNP
Intercept	6.46370	31.54443	33.65440	1.66140	1.84976	1.72320	3.61307	3.80180
X_1	−0.00086	—	—	−0.00011	−0.00010	−0.00005	—	—
X_2	—	—	—	0.26886	0.20451	0.25004	—	—
X_4	—	—	0.68351	0.28264	—	—	0.29202	0.30021
X_5	−0.00021	−0.00057	—	—	−0.00003	—	—	−0.00003
X_7	—	—	—	—	—	−0.00006	—	—
X_{13}	—	—	—	−0.00011	—	—	—	—
X_{14}	1.20478	—	0.94499	0.12405	0.13616	0.12899	0.14129	0.11633
X_{15}	—	—	—	0.00011	—	—	—	—
X_{19}	0.11754	—	—	0.01176	0.01251	0.01231	—	—

Table 6: (*Continued*)

Model	1	2	3	4	5	6	7	8
Variable Dependent	P	P	P	LNP	LNP	LNP	LNP	LNP
X_{20}	3.21162	1.21185	1.40154	0.14428	0.13203	0.12918	0.11189	0.09350
X_{21}	−0.00070	—	—	−0.00013	−0.00014	−0.00013	—	—
X_{22}	3.52631	3.77109	3.73758	0.45403	0.45714	0.45617	0.45381	0.46116
ln X_1	—	−3.82977	−3.53119	—	—	—	−0.34460	−0.35688
ln X_5	—	—	−1.04604	—	—	—	—	—
ln X_{13}	—	—	—	—	—	—	−0.21576	−0.17710
ln X_{15}	—	—	—	—	—	—	0.20778	0.20151
ln X_{19}	—	2.80908	2.71821	—	—	—	0.24407	0.26342
ln X_{21}	—	−0.24670	—	—	—	—	—	−0.05406
F Value	106.82	205.44	170.33	139.00	157.51	160.90	181.78	154.24
$\bar{R}^2$	0.4972	0.6195	0.6120	0.6486	0.6253	0.6303	0.6583	0.6720
$\sqrt{MSE}$	3.3274	2.8927	2.9232	3.0948	3.0944	3.1292	2.5223	2.4446
AIC(N)	2.41	2.13	2.16	2.27	2.27	2.29	1.86	1.80
PRESS(N)	8585.43	6557.57	6709.74	7415.73	7412.91	7582.44	4965.04	4665.84
Modified Leven Test (*p*-value)	2.9001 (0.0038)	1.9260 (0.0545)	2.0094 (0.0448)	−0.6567 (0.5115)	−3.0050 (0.0027)	−1.6671 (0.0959)	−2.4325 (0.0152)	−2.7369 (0.0064)

when we take natural log form in Model 8, but is significant when in its untransposed form. In order to increase the evaluation capacity, X_5 is does not take a log form in the evaluation model.

As Table 7 shows, the estimation model provides the following results:

(1) As the distance to the CBD, X_1, increases by 1%, land price will decrease by 31.46%. This result is consistent with the differential rent theory; that is, the farther to the CBD, the lower the land price.

(2) Land price rises by 18.79% for those parcels located in Beitwen sub-center (X_4). Since Beitwen sub-center is one of the important community business centers, this result also conforms to theory.

(3) In addition, land price will decrease by 0.003% as the distance to Fongchia sub-center, X_5, is increased by one meter. This is because the Fongchia sub-center is also an important community business center.

(4) As the distance to the National Nature Museum, X_{13}, is extended by 1%, the land price is reduced by 12.77%. The Museum is a sightseeing location with higher nearby land prices. Additionally, those parcels located in the Museum Area, X_{14}, demonstrate a global 10.68% price differential.

(5) As the distance to the Municipal Funeral Home, X_{15}, increases by 1%, the land price increases by 13.71%. Since a funeral home is a NIMBY facility, people generally do not reside nearby.

Table 7: Empirical Results of Hedonic Price Approach (Model 8 WLS)

X	β	VIF	t	P-Value
Intercept	3.55415	—	14.55483	0.00000
X_4	0.18793	2.93147	4.69881	0.00000
X_5	−0.00002	2.54493	−2.32434	0.02037
X_{14}	0.10680	2.79651	3.53682	0.00043
X_{20}	0.11809	1.28201	3.18550	0.00150
X_{22}	0.43775	1.04665	23.54945	0.00000
$\ln(X_1)$	−0.31464	2.80053	−12.62240	0.00000
$\ln(X_{13})$	−0.12774	3.31149	−5.33081	0.00000
$\ln(X_{15})$	0.13706	4.99930	4.09252	0.00005
$\ln(X_{19})$	0.25939	1.13321	10.91014	0.00000
$\ln(X_{21})$	−0.04193	1.14413	−4.07761	0.00005
		$\bar{R}^2 = 0.63927$		
		F=136.21		

(6) As the roadway widens by 1%, X_{19}, the land price increases by 25.94%. Road width pertains to accessibility. Hence, a wider road increases the land price.

(7) For commercial parcels, X_{20}, the land price is 12.53% higher than that for residential parcels. Commercial areas are used more intensively. Consequently they are priced higher. This is one of the proposed functions for zoning.

(8) According to the coefficient of X_{21}, the larger the parcel land area the lower the price. Land price is reduced by 4.19% as the area of a parcel is increased by 1%.

(9) Parcels proximate to roads, X_{22}, are priced 54.92% higher than those proximate to alleyways only.

The evaluation model was applied to appraise each sample parcel and efficiency and equity were measured. Table 8 presents the empirical results.

From Table 8, the a–s ratios for the entire city from 1995 to 1999 are 107%, 110%, 106%, 103% and 121%, respectively. Since the a–s ratios are near one, the hedonic price approach is more efficient than the approach adopted by the government. Notably, the a–s ratios exceed 100% slightly due to a depressed real estate cycle in Taiwan during the past decade causing the price in previous year to exceed the current price. Coefficients of variation for the entire city in the same period are 29%, 32%, 31%, 34% and 42%, respectively, which are very close to Back's criterion. Therefore, the assessment is more equitable. Kochin and Parks model was also employed to evaluate consistency (Table 9).

Table 8: The Efficiency and Equity Test for Hedonic Price Approach

Region	a–s ratio	Year					Cumulative
		1995	1996	1997	1998	1999	
1	Mean	1.05	1.16	1.02	1.09	1.24	1.10
	Standard deviation	0.33	0.34	0.35	0.37	0.39	0.36
	C.V.	0.32	0.30	0.34	0.34	0.32	0.32
2	Mean	1.11	1.03	1.14	1.06	1.41	1.11
	Standard deviation	0.28	0.36	0.40	0.43	0.81	0.43
	C.V.	0.25	0.35	0.35	0.41	0.58	0.39
3	Mean	0.98	1.09	1.02	0.94	0.99	1.01
	Standard deviation	0.28	0.32	0.23	0.23	0.20	0.27
	C.V.	0.28	0.32	0.23	0.23	0.20	0.27
Taichung	Mean	1.07	1.10	1.06	1.03	1.21	1.08
	Standard deviation	0.31	0.35	0.33	0.35	0.50	0.36
	C.V.	0.29	0.32	0.31	0.34	0.42	0.33

Table 9: Progressive and Regressive Test for the Hedonic Price Approach

Parameter	1995	1996	1997	1998	1999
β_0	0.936***	0.968***	0.905***	1.230***	1.075***
	(6.991)	(8.857)	(9.077)	(7.663)	(3.949)
β_1	1.020	0.991	1.043	0.900	0.898
	(0.295)	(0.145)	(0.745)	(1.476)	(0.804)
R^2	0.679	0.624	0.695	0.561	0.455
$\bar{R}^2$	0.676	0.622	0.693	0.558	0.446
F	216.0***	272.4***	323.2***	175.3***	50.2***

*** Significant at the .01 level.

From Table 9, the null hypothesis of $\beta_1 = 1$ is accepted for each year. Consequently, the assessment conducted via the hedonic price approach is consistent.

14.5 Assessment of the Grid-Adjustment Approach

Although hedonic price approach has several advantages over the approach adopted by the government, government appraisers are more familiar with the market comparison approach. As a result, a grid-adjustment approach combining the hedonic price approach and the market comparison approach may be beneficial in Taiwan. The appraisal procedures of the grid-adjustment approach can be separated into the following steps. (1) Although an appraiser still needs to choose properties with characteristics similar to the subject property, they do not select comparable properties subjectively. Instead, comparable properties selected within the grid-adjustment approach meet predetermined conditions, such as location, roadway, or zoning. In addition, the absolute value of the net adjustment factor is used to select comparable properties from the numerous transactions (Kang and Reichert, 1991). (2) Instead of evaluating each real property characteristic according to the market comparison approach, the grid-adjustment approach employs an hedonic price equation (Model 8 of Section IV of this paper) to estimate the implicit price of each land characteristic. (3) The grid-adjustment approach incorporates a weighting method to calculate the mean of the adjusted prices for comparable properties, which is the estimated price of the subject property (Cannaday, Colwell, and Wu, 1984). Table 10 presents the mean, standard deviation, and coefficient of variation of the estimated sample prices grouped by area.

From Table 10, a–s ratios for the entire city from 1995 to 1999 are 105%, 108%, 107%, 105% and 113%, respectively. The grid-adjustment assessment

Table 10: The Efficiency and Equity Test for the Grid-adjustment Approach

Region	Statistics	Year					Cumulative
		1995	1996	1997	1998	1999	
1	Mean	1.03	1.08	1.06	1.04	1.20	1.07
	Standard deviation	0.24	0.31	0.20	0.36	0.38	0.30
	C.V.	0.23	0.28	0.19	0.34	0.32	0.28
2	Mean	1.10	1.06	1.07	1.13	1.05	1.08
	Standard deviation	0.17	0.22	0.38	0.29	0.16	0.28
	C.V.	0.15	0.21	0.35	0.26	0.15	0.26
3	Mean		1.09	1.08	0.99	1.04	1.05
	Standard deviation		0.23	0.21	0.18	0.21	0.20
	C.V.		0.21	0.21	0.18	0.21	0.20
Taichung	Mean	1.05	1.08	1.07	1.05	1.13	1.07
	Standard deviation	0.22	0.27	0.28	0.29	0.32	0.27
	C.V.	0.21	0.25	0.26	0.28	0.28	0.26

is efficient as these ratios are close to one. In addition, coefficients of variation of the entire city during the same periods are 22%, 27%, 28%, 29% and 32%, respectively. Therefore, the assessment is equitable because they mostly satisfy Back's criterion. Table 11 presents the results of the Kochin and Parks model. According to Table 11, the assessment is mostly consistent as the null

Table 11: Progressive and Regressive Test for the Grid-Adjustment Approach

Parameter	1995	1996	1997	1998	1999
β_0	0.916***	1.109***	1.038***	1.219***	1.608***
	(8.406)	(8.833)	(10.076)	(7.931)	(4.917)
β_1	1.032	0.923	0.959	0.888*	0.709***
	(0.543)	(1.309)	(0.803)	(1.703)	(2.810)
R^2	0.821	0.672	0.772	0.624	0.516
$\bar{R}^2$	0.818	0.669	0.770	0.620	0.505
F	310.9***	244.0***	348.6***	180.8***	46.9***

*** Significant at the .01 level.
  * Significant at the .10 level.

Table 12: A Comparison of Market Comparison, Hedonic Price and Grid-Adjustment Approaches

	Year	Market Comparison Approach	Hedonic Price Approach	Grid-Adjustment Approach
a–s ratio	1994	.13		
	1995	.12	1.07	1.05
	1996	.10	1.10	1.08
	1997	.10	1.06	1.07
	1998	.10	1.03	1.05
	1999	.13	1.21	1.13
	Cumulative	.11	1.08	1.07
Coefficient of Variation	1994	.63		
	1995	.65	.29	.21
	1996	.70	.32	.25
	1997	.90	.31	.26
	1998	.65	.34	.28
	1999	.68	.42	.28
	Cumulative	.71	.33	.26
Progressive or Regressive Test		Progressive	Consistent	Consistent for most cases

hypothesis of $\beta_1 = 1$ is accepted for each year except 1998 and 1999. The grid-adjustment approach does not appear to be superior to the hedonic price approach in every respect. For example, the a–s ratio is inferior for 1997 and 1998, and the result is progressive in 1998 and 1999. However, it is one of the latest appraisal techniques, and may be more accepted by appraisal officials because it is an extension of the market comparison approach.

The assessment results from the three approaches are compared in Table 12.

14.6 Conclusion

Appraisal techniques are continuously improving, and many mass appraisal approaches have been introduced. This paper takes Taichung Municipality of Taiwan as an example to test some of the new techniques. When the hedonic price approach is compared with the market comparison approach, the former has the following merits: (1) The hedonic price approach can employ all transaction cases within a city as a sample to evaluate the subject property. Therefore, it is more reliable due to its higher degrees of freedom. (2) An evaluation model can be employed to calculate the implicit price of each real estate characteristic, resulting in an objective value estimate. As a result, the value is less apt to be criticized or changed when forwarded to a land price examination and consultant committee. (3) The relative contribution of each characteristic is revealed from the implicit price, rather than evaluating them by experience.

However, empirical evidence suggests that, considering either efficiency or equity, the grid-adjustment approach is superior to the hedonic price approach in most cases. In addition, most appraisers are familiar with the procedure because it is an extension of market comparison approach. Thus, this study recommends the grid-adjustment approach.

ACKNOWLEDGEMENT

I would like to thank an anonymous refree for her (his) helpful Comments. However, any errors are mine.

REFERENCES

Back, Kenneth, "Land Value Taxation in Light of Current Assessment Theory and Practice," selected in Daniel M. Holland, *The Assessment of Land Value* (Madison, Milwaukee: University of Wisconsin Press, 1970), 37–54.

Bell, Earl J., "Administrative Inequity and Property: The Case for the Traditional Approach". *Property Tax Journal* 3 (1984): 123–131.

Bible, Douglas S. and Chengho Hsieh, "Determinants of Vacant Land Values and Implications for Appraisers," *The Appraisal Journal* (July 1999): 264–268.

Cannaday, R., Colwell, P. and Wu, C. "Weighting Schemes for Adjustment Grid Methods of Appraisal", *Appraisal Review Journal* 7(1) (Summer 1984): 24–31.

Cesare, Claudia M. and Les Ruddock, "A New Approach to the Analysis of Assessment Equity," *Assessment Journal* (Mar/Apr 1998): 57–69.

Pao L. Cheng, "Property Taxation, Assessment Performance, and its Measurement", *Public Finance* 29:3–4 (1974): 268–284.

Clapp, John M, "A New Test for Equitable Real Estate Tax Assessment," *Journal of Real Estate Finance and Economics* 3 (1990): 233–249.

John H. Detweiler, and Ronald E. Radigan, "Computer-Assisted Real Estate Appraisal: A Tool for the Practicing Appraiser," *The Appraisal Journal* (July 1999): 280–286.

International Association of Assessing Officers, *Improving Real Property Assessment: A Reference Manual* (Chicago: IAAO, 1978), 121–155.

Kang, Han-Bin and Alan K. Reichert, "An Empirical Analysis of Hedonic Regression and Grid-Adjustment Techniques in Real Estate Appraisal", *Journal of American Real Estate and Urban Economics Association* 19–1 (1991): 70–91.

John S. Kirkwood, "Information Technology: Its Impact On Real Estate Valuation and Management", in Arlo Woolery and Sharon Shea (ed.), *Introduction To Computer Assisted Valuation* (Boston: Lincoln Institute of Land Policy, 1985), 1–16.

Lewis A. Kochin, and Richard W. Parks, "Vertical Equity in Real Estate Assessment: A Fair Appraisal", *Economic Inquiry* 20:4 (1982): 511–531.

Lavergne, Pascal, "Selection of Regressors in Econometrics: Parametric and Nonparametric Methods," *Econometric Review* 17(3) (1998): 227–273.

Paglin, Morton and Michael Fogarty, "Equity and the Property Tax: A New Conceptual Performance Focus", *National Tax Journal* 25:4 (1972) 557–65.

Palmquist, R. B., "Land as a Differentiated Factor of Production", *Land Economics* 65–1 (1989).

Rosen, S., "Hedonic Prices and Implicit Markets: Product Differentiation in Pure Competition", *Journal of Political Economy*, 82 (1974): 34–55.

Sunderman, Mark, A. et al., "Testing for Vertical Inequity in Property Tax Systems," *Journal of Real Estate Research* 5 (1990): 319–334.

Youngman, J. M. and Maime, J. H., *An International Survey of Taxes on Land and Buildings* (Boston: Kluwer Law and Taxation Publishers, 1994).

V

NEW PERSPECTIVES ON TRADITIONAL APPRAISAL METHODS

Chapter 15

The Unit-comparison Cost Approach in Residential Appraisal

Peter F. Colwell
University of Illinois at Urbana-Champaign, Urbana, Illinois

David W. Marshall
School of Business Administration, Miami University, Oxford, Ohio

The cost approach has not received much attention in academic journals. However, this lack of attention is undeserved. Cost functions represent one side of the market and may constrain the form of hedonic equations and the type of grid used in the market approach. Of course, cost functions can play a role in appraisals. A theory of cost functions is developed in this chapter. This theory accomplishes several purposes. First, it provides a link between unit-in-place costs and cost comparisons using square footage. Second, it provides the foundation for developing an alternative, non-tabular approach to cost estimation.

Finally, it provides some analytical principles regarding the shape of cost functions so as to inform hedonic analysis.

The functional approach developed in this chapter is subject to some of the same limitations that affect cost manuals. An implicit assumption in cost manuals is that all firms have access to the same technology and competitive input markets. That is, the production function and the input prices are the same for all firms. Furthermore, economies and diseconomies of scale are ignored by the manuals possibly by assuming that the optimal scale is achieved for each set of house attributes or by assuming that there are constant returns to scale. This chapter assumes competitive input markets, constant technology across producers and constant returns to scale.

The approach developed in this chapter avoids some of the limitations found in unit comparison cost tables. Specifically, the functional approach is more flexible regarding house shape. While we specifically consider L-shaped houses, it is a simple extension to include U-shaped and H-shaped houses. Like most cost tables, the approach developed here can handle two story houses (considered explicitly) and other configurations such as the tri-level and the bi-level.

The focus of this chapter is on the unit-comparison cost approach. This approach can be defined as one in which cost estimates are related to a measure of building size such as square footage or cubic footage. The unit-comparison, unit-in-place, and quantity survey cost approaches can be thought of as being related. The unit-comparison represents the highest level of aggregation among these three approaches, while the quantity survey represents the lowest level of aggregation. A theory is developed which derives the unit-comparison approach out of unit-in-place estimates (e.g., roof costs per square foot or wall costs per linear foot), just as unit-in-place estimates are derived from quantity survey estimates (e.g., the cost of a brick or a sheet of gypsum board). The theory directly leads to the economic meaning of parameters of functions relating cost to the square feet of living area. The functional form depends on certain geometrical principles relating units-in-place such as roofs, floors, and walls to living area, and the parameters depend on the physical configuration of the house and the materials used. Cost and cost per square foot tables similar to those found in cost manuals can be derived from these functions. Alternatively, the functions provide so much flexibility by themselves that nothing may be gained and something lost by creating tables. That is, one can develop total cost or cost per square foot estimates that relate to a specific house directly from the functions.

This chapter first turns to a theory of cost functions. Three cost components are developed which relate to living area and shape. Next, several of many possible details are handled: foundation walls, interior walls, quality, and style. Additional details such as heating and cooling equipment and roof pitch are handled in an appendix. An empirical section explores estimating the functions two ways: from actual cost data and from cost manual "data." A section of conclusions is at the end of this chapter.

15.1 A Theory of Costs

There are a number of key articles in the literature on building cost functions. While some authors have opined that there are no restrictions on the shape of hedonic functions (Rosen [1974]), this may not be completely true. Colwell [1993] has shown that a concave cost function imposed concavity on the hedonic function. Colwell and Ebrahim [1993] assumed that the cost function for office buildings is concave in the footprint area but convex in building height. Gat [1995] postulated that the cost function is convex in building area. He wrote that "In the construction of a building on a given site, as more floor space is added to the site, vertical stacking of floors takes place and causes marginal costs to rise." Doiron, Shilling, and Sirmans [1992] used a cost function that was neither strictly concave nor convex. Tan [1999] used a simple neoclassical production function model to identify the impacts of particular variables more explicitly as building height increases. Of course, this paper is focused on rather simple buildings, single-family, detached houses. The complexities associated with the costs of tall buildings are not likely to be found in this context. If it can be shown that the cost of houses is concave in square footage, then there are strong implications for the shape of hedonic functions.

This theory of costs takes unit-in-place costs as its starting point. Then it explores the implications for the relationship between total cost and the square footage of living area. This is not a theory of human behavior. Instead, it is a theory of the engineering economics relationships between the major features of house design and construction cost. It is discovered that when relating total costs to the living area of a house, three distinct cost components emerge. A table of cost, or cost per square foot, must recognize the role of each of these three components. Otherwise, estimates of total costs for houses of various sizes may drift dramatically from the actual costs. The next section shows that the three components of the cost function are (1) costs that do not change as living area increases (constant costs), (2) costs that increase at a constant rate as living area increases (linear costs), and (3) costs that increase at a decreasing rate as living area increases (square root costs).

15.1.1 The Three Components

Constant costs represent the contribution to cost of items that a base house would have regardless of its size. Cost manuals typically refer to a list of features in a base house. Deviations from this list in the subject property require the addition (subtraction) of the unit-in-place costs for the extra (missing) items. We assume, as do the cost manuals, that the base house includes a certain number of plumbing fixtures, a front door, some aspects of heating and cooling equipment, and so forth. The number and cost of these features is supposed to be constant for a column in a cost or cost per square foot table. Thus, these features are referred to as constant costs in this chapter. It should be understood that there is no problem in allowing these "constant" cost items to change, they are only "constant" in the sense that they do not change automatically as square footage changes.

A linear cost component represents costs associated with square footage such as floors, ceilings, and roofs (holding the pitch, materials, and the design type of the roof constant). The slope of the linear portion of the cost function is simply the sum of the unit-in-place costs for those building elements that are linearly related to living area. For example, as living area increases by some factor, the roof and ceiling areas increase by the same factor. Unit-in-place costs are related to roof and ceiling areas, so living area is related to this dimension of costs.

The third cost component is a square root function. The costs of certain building elements do not rise in direct proportion to living area. We conclude that these costs rise at a declining rate as square footage increases. An example of this would be the exterior walls of a house. Generally, wall length is a smaller proportion of the living area of larger houses. This geometrical principle gives rise to the need for this third cost component. The fact of this cost component makes the cost a concave function of living area. So it is this feature of the cost function that constrains hedonic models to being concave in the variable living area.

The rationale for the square root function is probably the least obvious of the three components. The square root function may be derived by holding the configuration of the floor plan constant in some sense while allowing the area to vary. For example, suppose houses are rectangular with the ratio of width to length as

$$\frac{W}{L} = a. \tag{1}$$

The living area of the house is given by

$$WL = A. \tag{2}$$

Dividing equation (2) by L^2 yields

$$\frac{W}{L} = \frac{A}{L^2}. \tag{3}$$

Substituting from equation (1) into equation (3) and solving for L yields

$$L = \left(\frac{A}{a}\right)^{.5}. \tag{4}$$

The exterior perimeter of the rectangular house is

$$2L + 2W. \tag{5}$$

Substituting from equations (1) and (4) into (5) and multiplying by wall height provides the following statement of exterior wall area:

$$\frac{2h(1 + a)A^{.5}}{a^{.5}} \tag{6}$$

where h = wall height.

Multiplying (6) by the unit-in-place cost of exterior walls (i.e., the cost per square foot) yields the exterior wall cost,

$$\frac{2p_x h(1 + a)A^{.5}}{a^{.5}}, \tag{7}$$

where p_x = the unit-in-place cost of exterior walls per square foot.

Statement (7) provides the proof that exterior wall cost is proportional to the square root of living area. Thus, the groundwork has been laid for combining the square root cost component with the constant and linear components to derive the total cost function.

15.1.2 The Cost Function

The ideal total cost function would be the sum of the three components: constant costs, costs which are linearly related to living area, and costs which are related to the square root of area. This cost function may be written as

$$C = B_0 + B_1 A + B_2 A^{.5} \tag{8}$$

where

C = total costs,
B_0 = the sum of the unit-in-place costs of the base house features,
B_1 = the sum of the unit-in-place costs of floors, ceilings, and roofs, and
B_2 = a function of the unit-in-place price of the walls based on house shape.

Assuming a completely open plan (i.e., no interior walls) and a slab (i.e., no footings or foundation walls), the parameter B_2 in equation (8) can be defined by referring to equation (7) as

$$\frac{2p_xh(1 + a)}{a^{.5}} \qquad (9)$$

15.1.3 L-shaped Houses

The parameter B_2 has only been defined for rectangular houses. For an L-shaped house as shown in Figure 1, living area and length are as follows:

$$A = aL^2 + gbL^2, \qquad (10)$$

and

$$L = \frac{A^{.5}}{(a + gb)^{.5}} \qquad (11)$$

where a, g, and b are shape parameters as shown in Figure 1.
The exterior wall length is

$$2L(1 + a + g). \qquad (12)$$

Substituting for L from equation (11) in equation (12) and multiplying by the unit-in-place cost of interior walls, p_x, and the height of the walls, h, yields the exterior wall cost,

$$\frac{2p_xh(1 + a + g)A^{.5}}{(a + gb)^{.5}}. \qquad (13)$$

Figure 1:

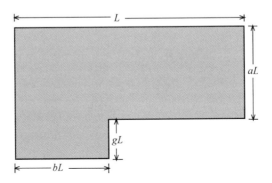

Again, considering a completely open plan built on a slab but L-shaped,

$$B_2 = \frac{2p_x h(1 + a + g)}{(a + gb)^{.5}}. \tag{14}$$

The variation introduced into the square root component of the cost function by variations in configurations is clear from equation (14). This variation leads to insoluble problems with unit-comparison data presented in tabular form. That is, it is impractical to have a different table for each basic shape and set of parameter values (e.g., parameters a, b, and g). However, it is not much of a problem if functions are substituted for tables. This is one important reason why the functional approach is more flexible than the tabular approach. Just like equation (9), equation (14) begins to provide some detail for understanding the key parameter that gives rise to concavity in the cost function.

15.1.4 Foundation Walls, Footings, and Basements

The costs of foundation walls and footings only affect the B_2 term. The foundation wall length is the same as the exterior wall length,

$$\frac{2(1 + a + g)A^{.5}}{(a + gb)^{.5}}.$$

Thus the foundation wall cost is simply the product of the length, the height, h_f, and the price of the foundation wall per square foot of foundation wall, p_f,

$$\frac{2p_f h_f(1 + a + g)A^{.5}}{(a + gb)^{.5}}, \tag{15}$$

where

p_f = the cost of foundation wall per square foot, and
h_f = the height of the foundation wall.

Similarly, the cost of footings is

$$\frac{2p_o(1 + a + g)A^{.5}}{(a + gb)^{.5}} \tag{16}$$

where p_o = the cost of footings per linear foot.

Thus, the magnitude of the parameter B_2 is increased over what is seen in (14) to

$$B_2 = \frac{2(p_x h + p_f h_f + p_o)(1 + a + g)}{(a + gb)^{.5}}. \tag{17}$$

The cost of a basement is more complex. It affects all three parameters of the cost function. The stairway has an impact on B_0. That is, the size and cost of the basement stairway is unaffected by the square footage of living area. Of course as with any of the constant cost features, one can imagine and compute the impact on cost of changing the quality or the size (i.e., width) of the stairway. Such changes shift the height of the total cost function but do not change the derivatives of the function. The basement floor has an impact on B_1 because of the perfect correlation of the basement floor area with the living area (i.e., assuming a full basement and a one story house). Finally the increment in wall height beyond a foundation wall has an impact on B_2. The parameter B_2 is further increased to

$$B_2 = \frac{2(p_x h + p_f h_f + p_o + \hat{b}p_f h_b)(1 + a + g)}{(a + gb)^{.5}}, \tag{18}$$

where

$h_{\hat{b}}$ = the incremental height of the basement wall over the standard foundation wall, and

$\hat{b}$ = a dummy variable indicating whether there is a basement.

Thus, equation (18) continues adding to the building detail that gives rise to concave cost functions.

15.1.5 Interior Wall Length

The assumption of a completely open floor plan cannot be maintained. Any coherent cost function must take interior walls into account. Frequently, the ratio of interior to exterior wall length is approximately unity. However, one should probably allow this ratio to become a parameter in the cost function, because house style and age can play a significant role in generating differences in this ratio. Thus, the cost of exterior and interior walls becomes

$$\frac{2(p_x + p_i k)h(1 + a + g)A^{.5}}{(a + gb)^{.5}}, \tag{19}$$

where

p_i = the unit-in-place cost of interior walls per square foot, and

k = the ratio of interior to exterior wall length.

Thus, the parameter B_2 becomes

$$B_2 = \frac{2((p_x + p_i k)h + p_f h_f + p_o + bp_f h_b)(1 + a + g)}{(a + gb)^{.5}}. \tag{20}$$

Once again, we emphasize the parameter, B_2, that produces concavity in the cost function.

15.1.6 Quality and Style

Total costs differ for different quality levels (e.g., finish and materials) and house styles (e.g., ranch vs. two-story). It is these differences that have traditionally given rise to the need for different columns in cost manuals. Differences in quality levels correspond to shifts in each of the three cost function components. An example would be two houses with the same size and style, but one of them built as a higher quality house. A higher quality implies better workmanship and higher priced materials. It may also imply more base features (e.g., plumbing fixtures). This would be reflected in the cost functions by increased parameters for the base house (B_0), the roof, ceiling, and floors (B_1), and walls etc. (B_2). Perhaps all three parameters should be increased by the same percentage. This would mean that quality differences can be handled by multiplying a column in a table by a constant quality adjustment factor as would be common practice. In terms of the total cost function developed in this chapter, it would mean multiplying the entire function by a constant.

Different cost functions would also have to be used for various styles of houses. An example of this would be a two-story house versus a one-story house, each having the same square footage. The two-story house would have less roof and foundation or basement, but more exterior walls and a stairway. To account for these differences, the parameter on the square root of living area for the two-story house should be larger than for the one-story house because of the difference in wall length even considering the reduced foundation length. That is, the two-story house cost function is more concave. Also, B_1 for the two-story house should be less than for the one-story because of the difference in roof area. Finally, the constant term, B_0, would be higher for the two-story because of the stairway.

15.1.7 Empirical Implications

From the analysis above, it is possible to develop a regression equation that one could use to estimate costs for one story houses of a given quality level where the data are ideal. Unfortunately, data are likely to be far from ideal, and a detailed equation is not likely to admit to estimation. The best available house cost data were developed from invoices in a large building company by Somerville [1996, 1999]. It is possible to use this data to estimate a much simpler equation. We use only a small portion of the Somerville data, data from a single metropolitan area and a single year (1991) with a total of 383 observations.

We begin with equation (8),

$$C = B_0 + B_1A + B_2A^{.5}, \tag{8}$$

where the parameters contain information on the typical configuration along with unit-in-place pricing. The next step is to deal with quality, because builders tend to increase quality for larger houses. Thus, the curvature of the cost function will be wrong unless there is a way to control for quality. This issue is described in Colwell [1993]. The function that we estimate uses land value as a quality indicator. It does so by interacting with the square root of area (i.e., the critical curvature variable), as follows:

$$hcst - ocst = B_0 + K_0gat + K_1bsmt + B_1A + B_2 \frac{lcst}{1000} A^{.5}, \tag{21}$$

where

$hscst - ocst$	= housing cost minus options cost or the cost of the basic house,
gat	= a dummy variable for attached garage (treated here as a constant cost item),
$bsmt$	= a dummy variable for a basement (a second constant cost item in this equation); and
$lcst$	= land cost.

The cost function was estimated using OLS, and the results are as follows:

$$hcst - ocst = -566.18 + 6406.0gat + 10007bsmt$$
$$+ 24.226A + 2.9897 \frac{lcst}{1000} A^{.5}. \tag{22}$$

All estimated coefficients on the variables have t-ratios in excess of 4.75, so each is significantly different from zero at any conventional level of confidence one might choose (the intercept term with a t-ratio of $-.24$ is not significantly different from zero). The overall explanatory power of the equation is very high with the adjusted R^2 at .808. The sign of the coefficient on each of the variables is as one would expect. Even the magnitudes of the coefficients are sensible. The constant cost features (i.e., the constant term plus the attached garage and basement coefficient) are approximately $16,000 with the basement costing about $10,000 and the garage about $6,500. The marginal costs depend on the quality indicator and the living area. For example, evaluating the marginal cost at the average lot cost (i.e., $54,818) and the average living area (i.e., 1,934 square feet) yields $26.09 as the cost of an extra square foot. The concavity (i.e., the second derivative) evaluated at the same house size is $-.00048$. Regardless of there being positive things to report regarding the regression estimate, it is necessary to say that these sorts of results are not robust across changes in the specification. There are two econometric problems. One problem is that the data are not spread widely over a large range of house sizes, so that there is danger in extrapolating, say, to the origin in order to interpret the constant term. The other problem seems to be the measurement of quality; one might wish for a variable that measures the cost of a single toilet or the cost per square foot of kitchen and bath countertops as indices of quality. Instead, we have land value. Intuitively, this seems like an interesting quality measure, but there is no previous empirical work of which we are aware that provides support for this use of land value.

It is possible to use this sort of structure to evaluate cost manuals. To illustrate this procedure, we have used a well-known cost manual to determine the cost of a good quality, two-story, wood sided house with and without a basement as well as with and without a two-car, attached garage (33 houses in all). We did this "as of" September 1991 (recall that the Somerville data we used was for 1991 construction). Equation (22), minus the quality indicator was then estimated using this data. The results are as follows:

$$hcst = -18,248 + 7060gat + 12,326bsmt + 21.108A + 1472A^{.5}. \quad (23)$$

The adjusted R^2 is .9974. Of course, the R^2 is expected to be very high in this context. The primary reason it is not perfect (i.e., 1.0) is that basement is handled like a constant cost item instead of also being affected by area and the square root of area. Actually the R^2 is irrelevant here, we should focus instead on the magnitudes of the parameters. Although the constant term is very large in absolute value, its t-ratio is -1.933. Thus, it would not be significantly different from zero at the 95% level of confidence. Each of the coefficients on the variables is significantly different from zero with t-ratios all larger than 3.5. Note that the garage cost and the basement cost are slightly higher in this experiment than they were with the actual data. The linear portion of the square foot costs are a little lower here. But the way to really compare would be to evaluate the marginal cost at the same square footage as before, 1,934. The marginal cost at this square footage is $37.84. So what we see is a cost manual function with a lower intercept term but one that is much steeper than the one based on real data. The concavity measure is $-.00433$ evaluated at the same square footage. So the function that is implied in the manual is also more concave than the function estimated from actual data. Although this is an early stage of analyzing these sorts of issues, it appears that questions might arise about the accuracy of cost manuals that might ultimately be addressed in a similar fashion to what we have done here. For example, one might question how cost manuals handle style or quality. Are higher levels of quality associated with all parameters being larger? If the analyst shifts from one story to two story houses, does the parameter on the linear term decline while the parameter on the square root term increases? That is, do the manuals produce sensible results when viewed from the basic model developed in this chapter?

15.2 Conclusions

Total housing cost was shown to be a function of living area. This function consists of three different cost components. A constant cost component represents the attributes of the base house. A linear component represents the cost of the roof, ceiling, floors, and some aspects of the heating and cooling systems. A square root cost component represents the cost of the walls, footings, and foundation as well as other aspects of the heating and cooling systems.

The theory in this chapter suggests that costs should change across different living areas, quality level, styles, or exterior materials according to a specific scheme. For example, a graph of costs against living area (holding other things constant) should have a positive intercept to reflect the costs of the base house and a positive but diminishing slope to reflect both the linear and square root components. See Figure 2. If another graph were drawn for a house of the same style, but a higher level of quality, the new function should have a higher vertical intercept and a steeper slope at each particular living area. The functions for different styles should reveal more complex differences. One style may well have a lower intercept but a steeper slope, or the degree of concavity may differ across styles. It is especially because of style and shape differences that cost tables will necessarily fall short of what can be accomplished with a non-tabular approach.

If costs are a concave function of square footage, then it is sure that hedonic functions are concave in this variable. Thus the work in this chapter which develops a rationale for concave cost functions is critical for the construction of hedonic functional forms. If one finds that a hedonic function is convex in square footage, it is probably the result of some excluded variable(s) correlated with square footage.

It was found that it is remarkably simple to develop a cost function that utilizes parameters for structural detail that is not handled by the unit comparison tables in cost manuals. Examples include the interior to exterior wall length ratio and the roof pitch as well as house shape parameters. Because the functions are so descriptively rich compared to the tables while maintaining a great deal of simplicity, it is suggested that the tables be abandoned in favor

Figure 2:

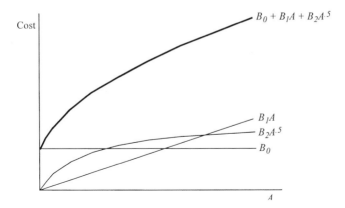

of the functions. Of course, the function can be transparent to the user of a cost service. The user need only enter the structural parameters and a computer can utilize the function to produce the cost estimate.

An empirical section takes two directions. First, we estimate cost as a function of square footage using actual invoice data. This approach shows that the function works, if we can find an appropriate indicator of quality. We use lot cost as an indicator of quality and it seems to "work" after a fashion. The function estimated from actual data exhibits some small degree of concavity. The second direction we take is to estimate the function found in a cost manual. Quality is supposed to be held constant in this context, and we find that the cost manual can be well represented with function developed in this chapter. The cost manual function is more concave than the function estimated from real data. We offer a couple of experiments that could be performed in order for others to judge whether cost manuals make sense.

ACKNOWLEDGEMENT

The authors are especially grateful to C. Tsuriel Somerville who graciously shared his cost data.

REFERENCES

Colwell, Peter, Semiparametric Estimates of the Marginal Price of Floorspace, *The Journal of Real Estate Finance and Economics* (1993), 7: 73–75.

Colwell, Peter F. and Shahid Ebrahim, M. A Note on the Optimal Design of an Office Building, *Journal of Real Estate Research* (1997), 14: 169–174.

Doiron, J. C., Shilling, J. D., and Sirmans, C. F. Do Market Rents Reflect the Value of Special building Features? The Case of Office Atriums, *Journal of Real Estate Research* (1992), 7: 147–156.

Gat, D. Optional Development of a Building Site, *Journal of Real Estate Finance and Economics* (1995), 11: 77–84.

Rosen and Sherwin. Hedonic Prices and Implicit Markets: Product Differentiation in Pure Competition, *Journal of Political Economy* (1974), 82: 34–55.

Somerville, Tsur. Residential Construction Costs and the Supply of New Housing: Finding Consistent Effects of Structure Costs on Homebuilding Activity. *Journal of Real Estate Finance and Economics*. 18(1), 43–62, 1999.

Somerville, Tsur. The Contribution of Land and Structure to Builder Profits and House Prices. *Journal of Housing Research*, 7(1), 127–141 (1996).

Swaffield, L. M. and Pasquire, C. L. Examination of Relationships Between Building Form and Function, and the Cost of Mechanical and Electrical Services, *Construction Management and Economics* (1999), 17: 483–492.

Tan and Willie Construction Cost and Building Height, *Construction Management and Economics* (1999), 17: 129–132.

APPENDIX

Several additional details are developed in this appendix. In each case, the point is that these details can be structured in terms of cost as a function of living area. As in the body of the chapter, this function has three terms: a constant term, a linear term, and a square root term.

Heating and Cooling Systems

So far, we have not discussed the impact of heating and cooling (HVAC) equipment cost on the cost functions. An earlier study that supports the finding that mechanical and electrical services and their costs relate to building parameters such as perimeter of external walls, story heights, and buildings of different functions (commercial, industrial, and residential) is Swaffield and Pasquire [1999]. Perhaps the most simple way to handle this issue is to argue that the distribution system costs are already built in to the unit-in-place wall costs. This argument may not be completely satisfactory, so it is probably better to deal with HVAC explicitly. One way to simplify the cost estimation of heating and cooling equipment is to separate the estimate for the equipment from that of the distribution system (e.g., the ductwork in a forced air system). Turning first to the equipment, its required capacity to provide heating or cooling depends most importantly on the area of the envelope through which heat can be transferred. However, not all elements of the envelope resist the transfer of heat equally. One might, for example, find it useful to make a broad distinction between the resistance to heat transfer of the ceiling with that of the exterior walls. Momentarily considering only a single story house, the area of the exterior walls would be

$$\frac{2h(1 + a + g)A^{.5}}{(a + gb)^{.5}},$$

(A1)

and the relevant ceiling area would simply be the living area, A. The BTU requirements for the exterior wall and ceiling elements of the envelope are

$$\frac{2h(m/R_w)(1 + a + g)A^{.5}}{(a + gb)^{.5}}, \tag{A2}$$

and

$$\left(\frac{m}{R_c}\right)A, \text{ respectively, where} \tag{A3}$$

m = the BTU requirement per square foot when $R = 1$ given the maximum temperature differential between interior and exterior temperature,

R_w = the average resistance to heat transfer of the exterior wall, or in technical terms, R is the number of hours it takes for 1 BTU to get from one side of a 1 square foot surface to the other given a temperature difference of 1 degree, and

R_c = the average resistance to heat transfer of the ceiling.

Of course, some details have been glossed over here. For example, air infiltration has been ignored, and the parameter m would differ for heating and cooling equipment. Continuing in this vein and assuming that equipment cost is a linear function of the BTU requirement, one can derive the following statement of equipment cost:

$$p_E + \frac{p_e mA}{R_c} + \frac{2hp_e m(1 + a + g)A^{.5}}{R_w(a + gb)^{.5}} \tag{A4}$$

where

p_E = partly the installation cost and partly a constant cost component of the equipment cost itself, and

p_e = the marginal cost associated with an increase of 1 BTU capacity.

In point of fact, the cost of some boilers appears to be an exponential function of BTU capacity. In any event, we believe that the assumption of a linear function is fairly accurate assuming further that p_E is large and p_e is very small.

The cost of the distribution system is perhaps less complex. Doubling the exterior wall length typically causes the cost of the distribution system to be squared as both the number of outlets and the length of, say, ducts double. An easy way to conceive of this relationship is in terms of a circular house in which outlets are placed at a constant interval along the exterior wall. Clearly, doubling the diameter causes the number of outlets to double because the circumference will have doubled and the length of the ducts from centrally located equipment will double by definition. Therefore, the total length of the distribution system will be the square of the exterior wall length multiplied by the average number of outlets per foot and the average length of a duct per foot of exterior wall length.

$$\frac{4nq(1 + a + g)^2 A}{(a + gb)} \tag{A5}$$

where

n = the average number of outlets per foot of exterior wall, and
q = the average length of a duct per foot of exterior wall length.

Assuming that the cost of the distribution system is a linear function of its length yields the following statement of distribution system costs:

$$p_z + \frac{4p_d nq(1 + a + g)^2 A}{(a + gb)} \tag{A6}$$

where p_z = the costs which are unrelated to living area or the size of the distribution system, and p_d = the marginal cost of the distribution system as the length of the system grows.

Again, we are glossing over details here. For example, super-insulated houses will not need outlets along the exterior wall. Also, the number of outlets should probably be a function of the number of rooms as well as the length of the exterior wall. Nevertheless, we have focused on the more important aspects of the distribution cost function in statement (A6).

The total HVAC system costs would be the sum of (A4) and (A6). That is, total system costs would have constant, linear, and square root components. Unfortunately, our casual empiricism has suggested that there is both a constant term and a square root term in the system cost functions but no linear term. This empiricism has amounted to calling contractors and asking them to estimate the cost of installed equipment for houses of various sizes and then utilizing regression analysis to estimate the system cost functions. Although we found no significant linear term, we consider the question to be open, given the strong theoretical indication that there should be a linear term to handle both the distribution system and the equipment. In any event, the importance of the square root term, the term that gives rise to concavity, is confirmed by this casual empiricism.

Roof Pitch

To this point, we have assumed that the pitch or slope of the roof is constant across houses. However, it is possible to build-in a parameter for pitch thereby directly allowing for pitch variation. The area of the roof is

$$\frac{(j^2 + 144)^{.5} A}{12} \tag{A7}$$

where j = the pitch in terms of the number of inches in rise given a 12 inch run.

Assuming that the cost of the roof sheathing and structural elements are proportional to roof area yields a roof cost as follows:

$$\frac{p_r(j^2 + 144)^{.5} A}{12} \tag{A8}$$

where p_r = the roof cost per square foot of roof area (i.e., it would be conventional in the trade to speak of the cost per "square" meaning 100 square feet). Thus, the cost function parameter B_1 contains the term, $p_r(j^2 + 144)^{.5} A / 12$, which is the roof cost per square foot of living area. While roof pitch adds interesting detail, it does nothing to contribute to the concavity of the cost function.

Chapter 16

The Long-run Equilibrium Relationship among Equity Capitalization Rates For Retail, Apartment, Office, and Industrial Real Estate

Michael Devaney
Department of Accounting and Finance, Donald Harrison College of Business, Southeast Missouri State University, Cape Girardeau

16.1 Introduction

Under the income approach, the value of a property is found by discounting the property's expected future net cash receipts to their present value. This process of converting a property's expected future net operating income into an estimate of current market value by discounting is referred to as capitalization.

In direct capitalization, the capitalization rate can be derived by dividing the net operating income of the property by the sale price.[1]

The ratio of NOI/Value is conceptually similar to the reciprocal of the P/E or price-earnings ratio used by financial analysts to evaluate stocks. Security analysts focus on the magnitude of the P/E ratio as well as the P/E relationship vis a vis stocks in other sectors. Stocks in a sector may be characterized as "over priced" if existing P/E ratios are high relative to the historical P/E. Investors are expected to purchase stocks in "under-priced" sectors while selling stocks in "over-priced" sectors such that sector P/E ratios return to their historical relationship.[2]

The premise that equity capitalization rates across different types of high quality investment grade real estate will share a common, long-run equilibrium relationship similar to P/E ratios for common stocks has a basis in both appraisal theory and investment. The appraisal principle of "substitution" suggests that equity investors will pay no more for a property than they would pay for a substitute property that delivers an identical expected cash flow. Presumably, investors substitute both within and across property type if the competing property type is temporarily mis-priced and is expected to return to its long-run equilibrium price path.

Although the magnitude of equity cap rates by property type may still vary because of risk premiums, short-run deviations from the long-run relationship will tend to be restored if equity capitalization rates across property type are cointegrated. A characteristic of cointegrated series is that their time paths are influenced by any deviation from the long-run relationship. Without a full dynamic specification it is impossible to determine how equilibrium is restored. Chaudry et al. (1999) and Tarbert (1998) test for cointegration among property types but stop short of using the cointegrating vectors to develop an error correction model.

In this research I test the null hypothesis that equity capitalization rates for different types of commercial real estate do not share a common long-run equilibrium relationship. An error correction model is estimated using American Council of Life Insurance (ACLI) quarterly data for retail (RET), office (OFF), apartment (APT), and industrial (IND) properties for the period 1975 to 1997.

The results have implications for both appraisal practice and real estate investment. If equity capitalization rates for different property types are cointegrated, then an error correction model utilizing the cointegrating vectors may be employed to forecast future rates and the time required for equilibrium to be restored.

The next section briefly reviews the literature on ACLI capitalization rates and the cointegration among property types. The following section describes how equity rates were extracted from over-all capitalization rates and the characteristics of the ACLI data. Section III discusses the methodology and section IV analyzes the results. The final section is a summary of conclusions.

16.2 ACLI Capitalization Rate Literature

Much of the literature has examined the relationship between ACLI capitalization rates and national capital markets. Froland (1987) and Evans (1990) found that ACLI cap rates were related to national capital markets. In contrast, Liu, Hartzell, Grieg and Grissom (1990) found that ACLI cap rates are segmented from the stock market. Ambrose and Nourse (1993) also found no relation between the stock market and ACLI capitalization rates and suggest that results could be biased by the use of an aggregated capitalization rate that does not allow for property type variation. Jud and Winkler (1995) test the relationship between capitalization rates, returns on the S&P 500 and a bond market index and conclude that real estate markets are not fully integrated with national capital markets.

Cointegration tests of real estate property type and geographic region have examined real estate property indices such as Russell-NCREIF and the Hillier Parker Investment Property Databank rather than ACLI capitalization rates. Chaudry, Myer and Webb (1999) use the Russell-NCREIF index and reject the hypothesis of no cointegration for real estate property types. The hypothesis of no cointegration by region is weakly rejected at the 10% level based on the L-Max statistic but is rejected by the Trace test.

Tarbert (1998) characterizes the London office property market as "international" in nature. Based on Hillier Parker data, she found cointegration among properties in different regions of the United Kingdom and concludes that this result conflicts with the conventional wisdom that assumes substantial benefits from geographic diversification. Although cointegrated by region, Tarbert found evidence of segmentation by property type. Industrial property was not cointegrated with either retail or office property. Neither Chaudry et al. (1999) nor Tarbert (1998) utilize the cointegrating vectors to construct an error correction model that identifies the dynamics of the long-run relationship among property type and/or region.

Hendershott and Kane (1995) argue that qualitative differences in property traded at different stages in the real estate cycle may bias Russell-NCREIF data. The finding of cointegration among ACLI property types does not ensure that real estate of a different quality is also cointegrated across property type. ACLI data represents "high quality, investment grade property suitable for institutional investment portfolios". Fulman (1999) indicates that the market for high quality real estate in urban areas that institutional investors characterize as "24/7 Cities" is more likely to be national in scope.

16.3 The Data

The American Council of Life Insurance companies publishes a quarterly *Investment Bulletin* that tracks mortgage data for the U.S. life insurance industry by property type and geographic region. Data items reported each quarter include the number of new loans, the total amount committed, the average contract interest rate (weighted by dollars and number), the mean over-all capitalization rate (R_o), the mean loan-to-value ratio (LTV), and the mean mortgage constant (MC) for apartments, retail, office, industrial, FHA and NHA apartments, commercial services, institutional and recreational, and hotels and motels.

When the number of transactions is too small to be reliable, gaps appear in the ACLI regional data as well as the latter four property types (i.e., FHA and NHA apartments, commercial services, institutional and recreational, hotel and motel) and render them inappropriate for long-run time series analyses. While many time series packages can adjust the analysis for a small number of missing observations, the problem becomes intractable for larger numbers of missing items.

To overcome the problem of missing regional data, Ambrose and Nourse (1993) aggregate the ACLI regional data into five location variables but report insignificant results from their panel data model on location factors and conclude that this finding may be the result of their "crude measure of location." Given the incomplete regional data, the results on the location variables in the Ambrose and Nourse study, and the need to control for the number of parameters in the vector error correction model, this study will examine equity capitalization rates for retail, office, apartment and industrial property without reference to regional location.[3]

Based on a band of investment approach, the over-all capitalization rate within each property type can be defined as:

$$R_o = [LTV * MC] + [(1 - LTV) * R_e] \qquad (1)$$

where R_o is the over-all capitalization rate, LTV is the loan-to-value ratio, MC is the mortgage constant and R_e is the equity capitalization rate. The over-all capitalization rate is familiar to real estate appraisers and conceptually similar to the weighted average cost of capital concept in corporate finance.

Rearranging (1) and solving for R_e results in:

$$R_e = \frac{R_o - (LTV * MC)}{(1 - LTV)} \qquad (2)$$

Unlike the over-all capitalization rate which incorporates the cost of mortgage finance, equity rates focus exclusively on the return to equity investors.

Accordingly, equity cap rates were extracted for retail (RET), office (OFF), apartment (APT) and industrial (IND) property for the first quarter of 1975 thru the second quarter of 1997.

Figure 1 graphs each of the four time series in their level form and descriptive statistics appear in Table 1. Because four quarterly periods for APT and one for RET are missing in the early 1980s, the time series package adjusts for missing data items in APT and RET by excluding contemporaneous values of OFF and IND so that the total number of quarterly observations utilized in the data analysis is reduced to 86 for each category of property.

Mean equity capitalization rates for RET, OFF, APT and IND over the 23 year period are 7.34%, 7.78%, 7.17% and 7.13%, respectively. OFF had the largest mean, the largest standard deviation, and the largest range between maximum and minimum values. Because cointegration tests have been found to be sensitive to violations of the normality assumption, the Jarque-Bera statistic is used to test departures from normality.

The normal distribution has a skewness of 0 and kurtosis of 3. All four distributions exhibit moderate skewness while APT, RET and OFF show excess kurtosis. The Jarque-Bera test statistic measures the difference of the skewness and kurtosis of the series with those of the normal distribution. Under the null hypothesis of a normal distribution, the Jarque-Bera statistic is distributed X^2 with 2 degrees of freedom. For all four distributions, the Jarque-Bera statistic does not allow the rejection of the null hypothesis of a normal distribution. Unlike stock market return series which typically exhibit a high degree of kurtosis that results in a Jarque-Bera statistic that leads to the rejection of normality, the distributional characteristics of equity capitalization rates for all four property types conform closely to a normal distribution.

Table 1: Descriptive Statistics For Apartment – Retail – Office – Industrial Equity Capitalization Rates

	RET	OFF	APT	IND
# of Observations	86	86	86	86
Mean	7.34	7.78	7.17	7.13
Std. Deviation	1.70	2.03	1.84	1.77
Maximum	13.27	14.50	10.90	11.84
Minimum	3.10	3.55	2.95	2.90
Skewness	.274	.422	−.025	−.209
Kurtosis	3.85	3.71	2.02	2.72
Jarque-Bera	3.68	4.38	3.39	.91
Probability	(.15)	(.11)	(.18)	(.63)

16.4 Unit Root, Cointegration, And Error Correction

The stationarity of the four series are examined using both the Augmented Dickey-Fuller test and the Phillips-Perron test to determine whether they are integrated of the same order. To illustrate the Dickey-Fuller test consider an AR(1) process:

$$y_t = \delta + \alpha y_{t-1} + \xi_t \tag{3}$$

where δ and α are parameters and ξ_t is assumed to be white noise. y is a stationary series if $-1 < \alpha < 1$. If $\alpha = 1$, y is a nonstationary series. The hypothesis of a stationary series is evaluated by testing whether the absolute value of α is less than one. The Dickey-Fuller test is implemented by estimating the following equation where y is the series to be tested.

$$\Delta y_t = \delta + \gamma y_{t-1} + \xi_t \tag{4}$$

Dickey and Fuller (1979) have shown that the estimated γ for testing the unit root does not follow the t-distribution and simulated the critical values for selected sample sizes. More recently, MacKinnon (1991) has implemented a much larger set of simulations and it is the MacKinnon critical values that are used in many statistical software packages and reported here.

The ADF tests appearing in Table 2 utilized 4 lags. Also appearing Table 2 are the results of the Phillips-Perron unit root test. The Phillips-Perron test makes a correction in the t-statistic of the AR(1) regression to account for serial correlation in the errors. The correction is nonparametric and is based on the Newey-West heteroskedasticity autocorrelation consistent estimate. Both ADF and PP tests indicate that all four equity capitalization series are nonstationary in level form and that nonstationarity is removed by first differencing. APT, RET, OFF and IND are determined to be integrated of order one I(1).

Inders (1993) and Noriego-Muro (1993) demonstrate that the Engle and Granger procedure for testing cointegration suffers from low empirical power and sensitivity to non-normality and that the Johansen method overcomes these problems. (also see Gonzalo, 1994; Enders, 1995) Because equity capitalization rates for all four property types are integrated of the same order, cointegration tests are appropriate. Results of the Johansen test for the number of cointegrating equations appear in Table 3. In a four variable system (n) there are at most three cointegrating regressions $(n-1)$. Critical values for the Johansen test indicate the existence of two cointegrating equations at 5% significance.

Also appearing in Table 3 are the normalized cointegrating coefficients for the two significant cointegrating equations. The asymptotic standard error appears in parentheses below the estimated coefficients. The appearance of

Table 2: Augmented Dickey-Fuller And Phillips-Perron Tests for Unit Root in the Equity Capitalization Rate for Retail – Office – Apartment – Industrial Real Estate

Variable	Augmented Dickey-Fuller Test (4) (Level From)	Augmented Dickey-Fuller Test (4) (First Difference)
Retail (RET)	−2.148	−7.343*
Office (OFF)	−1.999	−9.122*
Apartment (APT)	−1.393	−6.196*
Industrial (IND)	−2.021	−6.634*

MacKinnon critical values for rejection of the unit root hypothesis at 1%*, 5%**, and 10%*** are −3.507, −2.895 and −2.584.

Variable	Phillips-Perron (Level From)	Phillips-Perron (First Difference)
Retail (RET)	−.617	−19.77*
Office (OFF)	−.693	−25.69*
Apartment (APT)	−.496	−17.28*
Industrial (IND)	−.592	−14.36*

Critical values for rejection of the Phillips-Perron unit root hypothesis at 1%*, 5%**, and 10%*** are −2.591, −1.944 and −1.617.

Table 3: Johansen Test for Cointegration in Equity Capitalization Rates of Retail-Office-Apartment-Industrial Property

Eigenvalue	Likelihood Ratio	5 Percent Critical Value	Hypothesized No. of CE(s)
0.3744	73.06	47.21	none**
0.3083	36.94	29.68	At most 1**
0.0860	8.55	15.41	At most 2
0.0209	1.62	3.76	At most 3

**L.R. test indicate 2 cointegrating equations (CE) at 5% significance.

Normalized Cointegrating Coefficients: 2 Cointegrating Equations Parentheses under the estimated coefficients are the asymptotic standard errors.

RET	OFF	APT	IND	C
1.000	0.000	−.679 (0.139)	−.122 (0.172)	−1.434
0.000	1.000	.467 (0.300)	−1.725 (0.369)	1.008

Log likelihood −430.19.

the cointegrating relations depends on how the series are ordered since the time series package normalizes the first series listed to equal one. Of course, nothing of substance is affected since any linear combination of the cointegrating relations is also a cointegrating relation.

A vector error correction model was estimated using the two cointegration equations as well as lagged and contemporaneous values of the differenced equity capitalization rates. The four endogenous variables are the first difference of the contemporaneous values of RET, OFF, APT and IND. The model can be summarized by equations 7–10.

$$\Delta RET_t = \alpha_0 + \alpha_1 CI_1 + \alpha_2 CI_2 + \sum \alpha_3 (i) \Delta RET_{t-1}$$
$$+ \sum \alpha_4 (i) \Delta ER_{j,t-1} + \xi_{R,t} \tag{7}$$

$$\Delta OFF_t = \alpha_0 + \alpha_1 CI_1 + \alpha_2 CI_2 + \sum \alpha_3 (i) \Delta OFF_{t-1}$$
$$+ \sum \alpha_4 (i) \Delta ER_{j,t-1} + \xi_{o,t} \tag{8}$$

$$\Delta APT_t = \alpha_0 + \alpha_1 CI_1 + \alpha_2 CI_2 + \sum \alpha_3 (i) \Delta APT_{t-1}$$
$$+ \sum \alpha_4 (i) \Delta ER_{j,t-1} + \xi_{A,t} \tag{9}$$

$$\Delta IND_t = \alpha_0 + \alpha_1 CI_1 + \alpha_2 CI_2 + \sum \alpha_3 (i) \Delta IND_{t-1}$$
$$+ \sum \alpha_4 (i) \Delta ER_{j,t-1} + \xi_{I,t} \tag{10}$$

where α_1 and α_2 are speed of adjustment coefficients on the cointegrating equations, α_3 are coefficients on lagged differences of the endogenous variables own value and α_4 are coefficients on the other three differenced and lagged equity rates ($\Delta ER_{j,t-1}$) not on the left hand side of each equation. ξ is an error term.

By starting with five lags and testing down one lag at a time, a two period lag structure was identified based on the Akaike (AIC) and Schwartz (SC) criteria. Q-statistics for the residuals of equation 7–10 were calculated for 12 and 18 period lags. The Q-statistics indicate that the residuals follow a white noise process.

16.5 Results

Of particular interest are the size and significance of the "speed of adjustment" parameters, α_1 and α_2, since they dictate how equity capitalization rates

Table 4: Vector Error Correction Model of Retail – Office – Apartment Industrial Equity Capitalization Rates (Standard Errors and t-test In Parentheses)

	ΔRET	ΔOFF	ΔAPT	ΔIND
α_1	−.623	−.019	.613	.081
	(.164)	(.255)	(.171)	(.177)
	(3.793)	(.078)	(3.576)	(.458)
α_2	−.115	−.254	−.186	.370
	(.087)	(.136)	(.091)	(.094)
	(1.317)	(1.866)	(2.035)	(3.903)
ΔRET$_{t-1}$	−.336	−.050	−.316	.124
	(.132)	(.206)	(.138)	(.143)
	(2.530)	(.244)	(2.281)	(.862)
ΔRET$_{t-2}$	−.053	−.256	−.082	.241
	(.096)	(.150)	(.101)	(.104)
	(.550)	(1.701)	(.813)	(2.303)
ΔOFF$_{t-1}$	.244	−.720	.286	−.216
	(.101)	(.157)	(.105)	(.109)
	(2.410)	(4.566)	(2.706)	(1.967)
ΔOFF$_{t-2}$	.081	−.238	.121	−.067
	(.084)	(.131)	(.087)	(.091)
	(.968)	(1.820)	(1.378)	(.739)
ΔAPT$_{t-1}$	−.185	.350	−.418	−.050
	(.125)	(.195)	(.131)	(.136)
	(1.472)	(1.792)	(3.185)	(.371)
ΔAPT$_{t-2}$	−.017	.387	−.111	−.020
	(.110)	(.171)	(.115)	(.119)
	(.158)	(2.257)	(.966)	(.172)
ΔIND$_{t-1}$	−.159	−.229	.071	−.074
	(.136)	(.212)	(.142)	(.148)
	(1.170)	(1.077)	(.500)	(.505)
ΔIND$_{t-2}$	−.074	.027	.039	.013
	(.112)	(.175)	(.117)	(.121)
	(.665)	(.154)	(.335)	(.107)
α_0	.015	.015	−.013	.092
	(.109)	(.170)	(.144)	(.118)
	(.137)	(.088)	(.114)	(.783)

are restored to their long-run equilibrium path. Results of the VEC model are reported in Table 4. All speed of adjustment parameters have an absolute value between 0 and 1. The α_1 parameter was negative for RET and OFF and positive for APT and IND. While a mix of positive and negative signs on the speed of adjustment coefficients is consistent with convergence toward the long-run equilibrium, adjustment parameters were only statistically significant in the first cointegrating equation for RET and APT. The size of the coefficients, $-.62$ and .61, indicate that in the presence of a one unit deviation from the long-run relationship in equity capitalization rates in period $t-1$, the RET rate falls by .62 units while APT rate rises by .61 units. Both of these changes in period t act to eliminate the discrepancy from long-run equilibrium in period $t-1$.

The coefficients for the second cointegration equation (α_2) were negative for RET, OFF, APT, and positive for IND and were substantially smaller than the speed of adjustment coefficients in the first cointegration equation. Coefficients for RET and OFF were insignificant while those for APT and IND were significant at 5%. IND had a speed of adjustment coefficient in the second cointegration equation equal to .37 while the adjustment coefficient for APT was $-.18$.

The results of the vector error correction model indicate that deviations from the long-run equilibrium time path represented by the model in equation 7–10, are restored primarily by large unit adjustments in APT and RET, and smaller adjustment in IND equity rates. The speed of adjustment coefficients for OFF were small and insignificant.

Adjustments in ACLI equity cap rates of RET, APT, and IND are consistent with a long-run equilibrium relationship among these three property types while the equity capitalization rates for OFF appear to be segmented from other commercial real estate. An examination of Figure 1 indicates a pattern of higher volatility in OFF rates for the early 1990s. In 1993, the OFF rate ranged from a low of 3.5% to a high of 14.5% in a single year.

Although there is not a test statistic on which to evaluate differences in variance decomposition for assets which share a long-run equilibrium relationship, Seth (1996) suggests that differences in variance decomposition from the error correction model lend some insight into the "substitutability" of competing property types. Each of the variance decomposition panels shown in Table 5 represents the percentage of the variance of forecast errors

Table 5: Variance Decomposition For the Vector Error Correction Model

Period	S.E.	RET	OFF	APT	IND
Variance Decomposition of OFF					
1	1.365	.35	99.64	.00	.00
2	1.408	.33	94.05	3.77	1.82
3	1.646	.24	90.03	3.86	5.84
4	1.739	3.69	86.15	3.69	6.45
5	1.867	3.20	84.64	5.02	7.12
6	1.959	3.60	83.24	4.61	8.52

Table 5: *(Continued)*

Period	S.E.	RET	OFF	APT	IND
7	2.051	3.46	82.44	4.69	9.38
8	2.137	3.57	81.77	4.57	10.06
9	2.223	3.49	81.28	4.52	10.69
10	2.302	3.50	80.76	4.50	11.23
Variance Decomposition of APT					
1	0.915	6.52	6.72	86.74	.00
2	1.034	13.85	8.01	70.53	7.59
3	1.178	21.43	6.17	65.47	6.91
4	1.305	27.14	5.63	59.09	8.12
5	1.405	30.37	5.05	55.57	8.99
6	1.516	32.54	4.38	53.32	9.74
7	1.611	34.39	4.07	50.94	10.58
8	1.704	35.84	3.70	49.45	10.99
9	1.792	36.71	3.46	48.33	11.48
10	1.87	37.67	3.24	47.23	11.84
Variance Decomposition of IND					
1	0.950	.38	.27	10.28	89.06
2	1.045	4.95	5.49	10.33	79.21
3	1.162	7.95	13.70	10.85	67.48
4	1.262	6.74	19.75	13.19	60.30
5	1.340	7.93	21.92	13.48	56.65
6	1.418	8.23	25.93	13.17	52.64
7	1.483	8.93	28.00	13.28	49.76
8	1.551	9.05	30.19	13.33	47.40
9	1.612	9.58	31.64	13.22	45.54
10	1.673	9.84	33.08	13.23	43.83
Variance Decomposition of RET					
1	.877	100.00	.00	.00	.00
2	.937	88.78	5.78	4.20	1.22
3	1.060	81.37	5.35	9.23	4.03
4	1.143	74.99	5.89	11.43	7.67
5	1.221	73.59	5.20	13.04	8.14
6	1.293	68.90	5.22	16.50	9.37
7	1.358	67.01	4.94	17.76	10.27
8	1.422	64.74	4.80	19.55	10.89
9	1.482	63.21	4.70	20.68	11.39
10	1.539	61.72	4.60	21.82	11.83

that is attributable to innovations in the type of real estate listed at the top of the columns. The percentages across each row must total 100% for each step. Consistent with the strong observed autocorrelation in the data, the largest percentage of forecast error variance is explained by innovations in the real estate type's own value in previous quarters. This is especially true for RET and OFF both of which explain approximately 100% of their own error variance in the first quarter while the proportion explained by APT and IND is 86% and 89%, respectively.

The explanatory power of real estate cap rates other than the cap rates own value tends to increase substantially in subsequent quarters for all real estate categories except OFF. After 10 quarters OFF still explains approximately 80% of its own forecast error while RET explains 61%, and APT and IND explain 47% and 43%, respectively. The variance decomposition for the OFF cap rate is consistent with market segmentation in office equity capitalization rates. Even after 10 quarters or 2.5 years, more than 80% of forecast error variance in OFF is explained by innovations in OFF's own value.

These results are similar to Hendershott and Kane (1995) who examine the Office component of NCREIF and conclude that the distortions could be caused by qualitative differences in the character and condition of office properties that trade at different stages of the real estate cycle. Similarly, Seth (1996) found that innovations in the level of economic activity were incorporated into the NCREIF Office Index at a much slower rate than was the case for other property types.

Standard errors and t-tests for the other variables in the VEC model indicate large and significant values for the one period lag of the endogenous variable on itself. The only exception is the equity capitalization rate for IND lagged one period. The second lag of the endogenous variable on itself were less frequently significant. In some cases the two period lag had more explanatory power than the one period lag. This is true of APT on OFF and RET on IND. In an attempt to test the stability of model parameters, the sample period was divided in half and re-estimated. The cointegration results were determined to be weaker for the shorter time horizons.[4]

16.6 Conclusions

This research examines equity capitalization rates of retail, office, apartment and industrial property for evidence of a long-run equilibrium relationship. Error correction speed of adjustment parameters indicate market integration for retail, apartments and industrial property since unit changes in the equity capitalization rate of all three property types in period t act to remove discrepancy from the long- run equilibrium present in t−1. In contrast, only OFF cap rates failed to adjust. The variance decomposition of the VEC model suggest that even after 10 quarters, more than 80% of the forecast error in OFF is explained by its own value.

The small and insignificant coefficients on the speed of adjustment parameters of the cointegration equations, as well as the variance decomposition for the VEC model, are consistent with segmentation in the equity capitalization rates of ACLI office property. The finding of non-cointegration for office may reflect regional or qualitative differences in ACLI office market data, however, it is not clear why qualitative differences in property exchanged over the real estate cycle would preclude cointegration of OFF and not APT, RET, and IND.

The 1980s and early 1990s was a turbulent period for all types of commercial real estate. A chronology of events including financial institution disintermediation in the early 1980s, changes in the 1986 tax law, and the enactment of the Financial Institutions Reform, Recovery and Enforcement Act of 1989 may have disrupted long-established credit channels of many real estate developers and mortgage borrowers.

Institutional differences and/or greater imbalances in the supply and demand of office property may have caused the cumulative turmoil to have more of an impact on office property valuations than other types of commercial real estate. In which case, the finding of office market segmentation may be a period specific market anomaly that will disappear or become less apparent during more tranquil times.

NOTES

[1] Under direct capitalization, real estate value is determined by capitalizing net operating income (NOI) with an over all capitalization rate (R_o):

$$\text{Value} = \text{NOI}/R_o$$

The over all capitalization rate R_o can be calculated using the band-of-investment approach:

$$R_o = [\text{LTV*MC}] + [(1 - \text{LTV}) *R_e]$$

where LTV is the loan-to-value ratio, MC is the mortgage constant and R_e is the equity capitalization rate also called the equity dividend yield. The over all capitalization rate is familiar to real estate appraisers and conceptually similar to the weighted average cost of capital. See the *Appraisal of Real Estate* for a detailed discussion of direct capitalization and band-of-investment.

[2] The literature on stock P/E earnings multiples is extensive. For a practitioner interpretation of P/E mispricing see G. Gray, P. Cusatis and J. Woolridge. 1999. *Streetsmart Guide to Valuing a Stock*, McGraw-Hill, NY. In the financial press see Jeremy Siegel, "Big Cap

Tech Stocks Are a Sucker Bet", *The Wall Street Journal*, March 14, 2000 and J. Chernoff, "Flaws In Forecasts: Researchers Say P/E, Dividend Yield Make Poor Prognosticators", *Pensions & Investments*. July 10, 2000. For an extended discussion of historical P/E ratios see Robert Shiller, *Irrational Exuberance*, Princeton University Press, Princeton, New Jersey, 2000 and E. Elton and M. Gruber. 1987. *Modern Portfolio Theory and Investments Analysis*, John Wiley & Sons, New York, NY.

[3] Chaudry et al. (1999) and Tarbert (1998) provide conflicting results on the importance of region in cointegration tests. Unfortunately, insufficient ACLI data preclude regional cointegration tests. The finding of cointegration for ACLI property types may not be extended to real estate of substantially different quality than the property represented in the ACLI data set. However, the market for high quality institutional grade property is more likely to be national in scope. See Fulman (1999) for a discussion of how institutional investors characterize the U.S. real estate market.

[4] Because standard time series packages do not provide parameter stability tests such as the Cusum Test or Break point Chow for VAR or VEC models, an attempt was made to test the stability of the VEC model by dividing the time horizon in half and re-estimating the model. In the short horizon models, the number of cointegrating equations decreased and speed of adjustment parameters were insignificant for both office and retail. The results are not reported here but are available from the author.

REFERENCES

Ambrose, B. and Nourse. H. 1993. "Factors Influencing Capitalization Rates," *Journal of Real Estate Research*, 8,2. 221–237.

American Council of Life Insurance. Commitments on Mutli-family and Non-residential Properties. *Investment Bulletin*. 1975–1997.

Chaudhry, M., Myer, F., and Webb, J. 1999. "Stationarity and Cointegration in Systems with Real Estate and Financial Assets," *Journal of Real Estate Finance and Economics*, 18:3,339–349.

Elton, E. and Gruber, M. 1987. *Modern Portfolio Theory and Investments Analysis*. John Wiley & Sons, New York, NY.

Enders, W. 1995. *Applied Econometric Time Series*, New York: John Wiley & Sons, Inc.

Evans, R. 1990. A Transfer Function Analysis of Real Estate Capitalization Rates," *Journal of Real Estate Research*. 5,3. 371–380.

Engle, R. and Granger, C. 1987. "Co-integration and Error Correction Representation, Estimation and Testing," *Econometrica*, Vol. 55, No. 2, March.

Engle, R. and Yoo, B. 1987. "Forecasting and Testing in Co-integrated Systems," *Journal of Econometrics*, Vol. 35, May, pp. 143–159.

Fergus, J. and Goodman, J. 1994. "The 1989–1992 Credit Crunch for Real Estate: A Perspective," *AREUEA Journal*, 22,1. 5–32.

Froland, C. 1987. "What Determines Cap Rates on Real Estate," *Journal of Portfolio Management*, 13, 77–83.

Fuller, W. 1976. *Introduction to Statistical Time Series*, Wiley Publications, New York, NY.

Fulman, R. 1999. "24/7 Cities Forecasted As Real Estate Focus In 2000," *Pensions & Investments*, November 1, 1999, 52–53.

Gonzalo, J. 1994. "Five Alternative Methods of Estimating Long-Run Equilibrium Relationships," *Journal of Econometrics*, 60, 203–233.

Granger, C. 1969. "Investigating Causal Relations by Econometric Models and Cross-Spectral Methods," *Econometrica*, July.

Hartzell, D. J. Hekman, and Miles, M. 1986. "Diversification Categories In Investment Real Estate," *AREUEA Journal*. 14.2 230–254.

Hendershott, P. and Kane, E. 1992. "Causes and Consequences of the 1980s Commercial Construction Boom," *Journal of Applied Corporate Finance*.

Hendershott, P. and Kane, E. 1995. "U.S. Office Market Values During the Past Decade: How Distorted Have Appraisals Been?" *Real Estate Economics*, 23, 2. 101–116.

Inders, B. 1993. "Estimating Long-Run Relationships In Econometrics: A Comparison of Different Approaches," *Journal of Econometrics*, 57, 53–68.

Johansen, D. 1988. "Statistical Analysis of Cointegrated Vectors," *Journal of Economic Dynamics and Control*, 12, 231–254.

Jud, G. and Winkler, D. 1995. "The Capitalization Rate of Commercial Properties and Market Returns," *Journal of Real Estate Research*, 10,5. 509–518.

MacKinnon, J. 1991. "Critical Values for Cointegration Tests," Chapter 13 in *Long Run Economic Relationships: Readings in Cointegration*, edited by R. Engle and C. Granger, Oxford University Press.

Noriega-Muro, A. 1993. *Nonstationary and Structural Breaks in Economic Time Series*, New York: Avebury.

Quan, D. and Titman, S. 1999. "Do Real Estate Prices and Stock Prices Move Together? An International Analysis," *Real Estate Economics*. 27.2:183–207.

Seck, D. 1996. "The Substitutability of Real Estate Assets," *Real Estate Economics*,". 24.1:75–95.

Tarbert, H. 1998. "The Long-run Diversification Benefits Available From Investing Across Geographical Regions and Property Type: Evidence From Cointegration Tests," *Economic Modelling*, 15, 1:49–65.

Weber, W. and Devaney, M. 1999. "Bank Efficiency, Risk-Based Capital, and Real Estate Exposure: The Credit Crunch Revisited," *Real Estate Economics*, 27, 1. 1–25.

Chapter 17

A Fuzzy Discounted Cash Flow Analysis for Real Estate Investment

Tien Foo Sing
Department of Real Estate, National University of Singapore, Singapore

David Kim Hin Ho
Department of Real Estate, National University of Singapore, Singapore

Danny Poh Huat Tay
Alcatel Australia Limited, Australia

17.1 Introduction

In a discounted cash flow (DCF) analysis, reliability and credibility of results are strictly dependent on the prediction of key input variables. There are two approaches at which these inputs can be rigorously determined. The first approach involves the use of standard statistical tools such as the multiple regression analysis and the Box-Jenkin's time series models. These tools are not foolproof and are fettered by inherent statistical weaknesses. Based on probabilistic assumptions, results of the statistical analysis are bounded by occurrences of *ex-post* random events or observations. In a complex world, randomness alone is insufficient to capture dynamics and changes in real world events. *Ex-ante* expert judgement of events in a near future,[1] which does not rely on probabilities of *ex-post* events or information, offers an alternative way to arrive at a prediction of the input variables.

Experts with sufficient information and reasonable knowledge of the market are able to intuitively judge and predict the performance of a real asset within an acceptable confidence interval. The expert knowledge, if uninhibited with judgemental biases, could be relied upon to arrive at predictions that are intuitively more reliable than those obtained using *ex-post* probabilistic models (Makridakis and Wheelwright, 1979). Expression of expert knowledge in reality is constrained by the complexity and uncertainty of information (Zadeh, 1977). Experts tend to express their judgemental knowledge in cognitively vague and imprecise forms (von Winterfeldt and Edward, 1986). The representation of the expert knowledge is, in most instances, incompatible with the corresponding expression in mathematical models (Fischhoff, 1989). They tend to avoid making an exact point estimate. For example, instead of predicting that the current average rental is S$70 per square meter (psm) for the prime office space, they are more inclined to express their judgement in a less precise way by saying that the current prime office market is "weak" or the current unit rental ranges between S$60 psm and S$80 psm for prime office space. Similarly, investors are also not likely to represent their risk and return preference in an unambiguous form. When they perceive themselves to be risk-averse, they may have set in mind a threshold return for their investment of not less than 8% with a standard deviation of 0.5%. This "not less than 8%" expectation may imply that they are indifferent with a return of 8% per annual, but they may reject outright a return of below 5%, for example.

The cognitive uncertainty associated with the subjectivity of human thinking and reasoning is collectively known as "fuzziness." Fuzzy set theory first introduced by Zadeh in 1965, is a new theoretical construct that trades-off precision for vagueness in information in an attempt to arrive at an intuitively sound result (Klir and Folger, 1992). In the DCF analysis, expert inputs are rigidly translated into crisp but imprecise cash flow projections at the expense of accuracy. Information, which is relevant but too vague to be fitted into the rigid probabilistic structure of projection, is eliminated. Fuzzy set theory offers an alternative but conceptually more natural way of generalizing the expert knowledge in the cash flow projection. By compromising the precision and crispness in the representation of expert knowledge, vague and ambiguous information can be incorporated in the process.

Buckley (1987) demonstrates how the "precision" of input estimates in the traditional DCF analysis can be represented using inexact "fuzzy" numbers without compromising the quality of the cash flow streams, and hence, the reliability of the DCF outcome. He generalizes the compound interest concept by using fuzzified variables for the interest rate and the cash amounts, and a set of positive discrete fuzzy duration of investment. This paper aims to apply the proposed fuzzy DCF model to analyse a real estate development project. We can first "defuzzify" the fuzzy solutions using the "centroid defuzzification" methodology to arrive at an approximated non-fuzzy NPV. Assuming the crisp DCF as being a subset of the fuzzy DCF estimates with a full membership value, the difference in the NPV values between the classical and the fuzzy DCF models measures the effects of "fuzzification" of the cash flow variables.

The paper is organized into five sections. Section 17.2 highlights the importance of the concepts of "fuzziness" and the differences vis-à-vis the traditional DCF technique that does not contain imprecise and vague information in the projection of essential variables. Section 17.3 conceptualises the fuzzy compound interest formula, and Section 17.4 defines the decision criteria of the fuzzy DCF model proposed by Buckley (1987). A comparison of the results obtained by the fuzzy and traditional DCF models is illustrated in Section 17.5 and 17.6 using a case study of an office development project in Singapore. Section 17.7 concludes the analyses.

17.2 Fuzzification of Cash Flows

There are two conceptually different ways of quantifying uncertainty in the cash flow projection and forecast. The probabilistic approach that relies on past events is a more common way of analysing risks in investment vis-à-vis the fuzzy approach (or sometimes known as possibilistic approach). In the probabilistic approach, risk is normally considered in the light of how likely an investment outcome will be in line with the investor's expectation. The outcome of an investment prediction is assumed to be an independently and identically distributed random event. Based on a large number of past observations, the likelihood of occurrence of an outcome can be represented by a bell-shaped distribution where the further away the outcome is from the mean value the less likely is its occurrence. For unique events or events with infrequent recurrences, the statistical properties of the bell-shaped distribution will not strictly be adhered to, and errors of estimates may arise because of possible skews in the distribution. However, in the subjective probability approach, it is believed that with a good knowledge of the market, an expert is some-times able to make good *ex-ante* judgements of the occurrence of an event and also to adjust for possible skewed event that may widen the deviation of prob-ability space.

In the probabilistic framework, there is a crisp division between the prob-able and the non-probable events, which as a result leads to *a-priori* elimina-tion of useful information in the process of making inference or prediction. Consider the criminal trial example given by Klir and Folger (1992), where the jury faces uncertainty in making verdicts on whether defendants are found guilty or innocent. If there is perfect evidence, the jury could with full confi-dence determine whether the defendants should fall within the crisp boundary of either the guilty group or the innocent group. When the evidence is imper-fect, the boundary between the guilt and innocence of the defendants becomes blurred, and thus increases the chance of making a flawed judgement. An alternative way of quantifying this uncertainty associated with imperfect information is to indicate the possibility, or known in a more technical term as the membership, of the defendant being judged guilty or innocent. In other words, we assign all the prosecuted defendants with different memberships with respect to the possibility of either being convicted as guilty or acquitted for being innocent independently with vague boundaries. The latter way of assigning membership grades to the defendant is known as a fuzzy measure.

Using the same analogy, we may assign membership values to indicate the "feasibility" of different projects based on their respective net cash flow esti-mates. There is no crisp classification for a project of being either feasible or not feasible. For example, consider three different projects with estimated internal rate of returns (IRRs) of 4.0%, 6.0% and 10.0%. Given an investor's expected rate of return of 6%, it would be easily concluded with confidence that project with 4% IRR will be rejected, and that with 10% IRR will be accepted. The investor, however, will be indifferent with the second project with 6% IRR. The results are straightforward as long as there is no uncer-tainty, or more specifically fuzziness, associated with the inputs used in the IRR estimation. However, for a unique project with no previous statistics to be relied on for cost and revenue projections, the rigid and crisp way of deter-mining the project feasibility based on IRR estimates is prone to various sta-tistical errors. In an imperfect information condition, the errors may be compounded if the *ex-post* cash flow projection is imprecise and vague. An alternative way of analysing the investment feasibility using the fuzzy measure/concept is suggested. In the proposed fuzzy framework, no absolute conclusion should be assigned to each of the project. Instead, *ex-ante* knowl-edge of an expert would be relied upon in assigning membership of say 0.50, 0.85 and 1.00 for projects with IRRs of 4.0%, 6.0% and 10.0% respectively, to reflect different level of feasibility of the projects. In the non-feasibility rating, the membership may take the values of 0.96, 0.60 and 0.2, for example, for the respective projects.

The fuzzy measure is advocated merely as an alternative way of quantifying uncertainty in a market where information is complex and imperfect. It should not be considered as a substitute to the probabilistic way of predicting the cash flow variables. By incorporating the fuzzy cash flow projection in a DCF framework, an outcome that is totally different from that obtained under the probabilistic framework could be derived. However, the result should not be construed as being a superior yardstick of investment feasibility than the traditional DCF estimate.

Since there is no straightforward way of comparing the results of the crisp and the fuzzy DCF models, the defuzzification process is carried out to translate the fuzzy solution space into a crisp representation. Assuming that the crisp DCF result is a subset of the fuzzy solution space with a full membership value, the difference between the two estimates, i.e. the crisp DCF and the fuzzy DCF models, simply implies a value for fuzzifying or relaxing the crispness of the membership functions of the cash flow input variables. It is important to reiterate that the results of the two DCF models should not be interpreted as giving contrasting or inconsistent recommendation to investors. The margin between the two estimates highlights only the difference in the properties of the two measures. Given that the crisp DCF estimate (y_0) is a subset of the fuzzy DCF estimate (NPV) with a full membership value, $\mu(y_0|\text{NPV}) = 1.0$, the higher value obtained for the fuzzy DCF model is deemed to be a trade-off for the fuzziness when the crisp membership estimate is extended to incorporate n possible outcomes that are vaguely or imprecisely identified in the fuzzy set, i.e. $\text{NPV} = \{y_0/\mu_0, y_i/\mu_i\}$ where $i = (1, ..., n)$.

There are three basic differences between the probabilistic and fuzzy measures. In a probability-based model, an expected outcome of random events is predicted by limiting the boundary of error within a crisp level of significance. For example, a mean office rental of S$70 psm can be inferred with a 95% level of confidence if *ex-post* rentals were within the critical range of S$60 psm to S$80 psm and the standard deviation of rental is S$5 psm. Rents on either sides of the crisp boundary, for example S$55 psm and S$85 psm, are discretely eliminated. In a fuzzy-based model, it is not merely concerned with the membership of a point in a set, it also relates to the gradual progression from a membership to a non-membership function (Gupta, 1977). Memberships could be assigned to rents on both sides of the critical range, i.e. (< S$60 psm) and (> S$80 psm), to offer a "possibility" dimension to the information, which is conceptually different from the probabilistic angle that emphasises the crispness and precision of representation. In this framework, the possibility of achieving above-average rental of S$85 psm and the outcome of obtaining a below market rent of S$55 psm are not rejected outright.

Another unique difference between the probabilistic and fuzzy models is concerned with the measurement of randomness and fuzziness. In the probabilistic measurement process, independent and identical random events in the past are collected in a so-called probability sample space, and the frequency of occurrence of each random event is translated into a probability density function. Events that are not within the probability sample space will be eliminated as outliers. The probability density function of the collection of random events in the sample space must sum up to unity. However, the sample space of the fuzzy measurement is not restricted to the occurrence of past events. An event that is possible but not observed in the past could be included in the fuzzy sample set. A possibility density function is defined for each event in the fuzzy set with respect to a fuzzy phenomenon being measured. The possibility functions need not sum up to unity. The two types of measurement are mutually exclusive and independent from each other. Let us consider a hypothetical event of "asset return ($x\%$) in year n" having a sample space defined as $x\% = \{11\%, 12\%, 13\%, 14\%, 15\%, 16\%, 17\%, 18\%\}$. The probability distribution of x, i.e. P(x), which is *a-priori* determined from historical observation is summarized in Table 1, alongside with the possibility distribution, i.e. $\mu(x)$, which is defined by vague judgement of experts. The results show that a high degree of probability of an event may imply a high possibility of the same event occurring, but the opposite does not hold. Therefore, being a subset of fuzzy measure, the event that is impossible is bound to be improbable, but the reverse is not true.

The third difference between the two concepts is related to the definition of the "linguistic variable[2]." The concept of attaching linguistic measures to the variable varies between the two models. A probabilistic linguistic variable is determined, if possible, by the subjective judgement of expert based on his/her *a-priori* knowledge of the variable or event, whereas a fuzzy linguistic variable is characterised by a compatibility function that has an interval of [0, 1]. For example, when we assign a fuzzy value to an event defined as "good investment," compatibility of stocks with returns of 5%, 10% and 20% could be measured by a membership value of 0.1, 0.6 and 1.0 respectively. Another peculiar feature of fuzzy linguistic variable is the flexibility to modify the meaning of the variable through connectives (and, or), negation (not) and hedge (more or less, approximately) operators.

Table 1: Probability and Possibility Distribution Associated with Asset Return (x) in Year n

$x\%$	11%	12%	13%	14%	15%	16%	17%	18%
P(x)	0.1	0.8	0.1	0.0	0.0	0.0	0.0	0.0
$\mu(x)$	1.0	1.0	1.0	1.0	0.8	0.6	0.4	0.2

As the concept of the fuzzy measure and its application to investment analysis is new and not widely explored, it is, therefore, imperative to include this section to explain the theoretical properties of the fuzzy measure and make a comparison with respect to the probabilistic measure. By highlighting the conceptual differences between the two measures, it would help to shed meaningful light on the interpretation of results in the subsequent case study. It should be stressed that the fuzzy measure offers only a different view on uncertainty that is attributable to imprecise and vague information. It does not, however, advocate that the fuzzy DCF is better or more correct in the analysis of an investment vis-à-vis the traditional DCF model. Hence, if the concept of the fuzzy measure is not disputed, we should then not reject the fuzzy DCF model as an alternative way of looking at investment feasibility from a conceptually different perspective.

17.3 Concepts of the Fuzzy Compound Interest

In the fuzzy DCF model, three fuzzy compound interest concepts are introduced: the fuzzy future value, the fuzzy present value, and the fuzzy present value of annuity. The fuzzy compound interest factors are defined as functions of four essential variables: fuzzy present value $(\bar{A})$, fuzzy future value $(\bar{S})$, fuzzy interest rate per period $(\bar{r})$, and number of compounding periods, which can either be a crisp number (n) or a discrete positive fuzzy number $(\bar{n})$ with a membership function of $\mu(n_i|\bar{n}) = \lambda_i$, where $0 \le \lambda_i \le 1$ and $1 \le i \le k$ such that k is the collection of the fuzzy number n_i, $\mu(x|\bar{n}) = 0$ for $x \ne n_i$. The value of λ measures the possibility of a compounding period being n_i given that $\bar{n}$ is a fuzzy number.

In the formulation of the fuzzy compound interest factors, we adopt the LR-type (Left-Right) representation for a fuzzy number $\bar{M} = (m_1/m_2, m_3/m_4)$, which is consistent with that used by Buckley (1987). The memberships of fuzzy number $\bar{M}$ are defined by an increasing function $f_1(y|\bar{M})$ from m_1 to m_2, and a decreasing function $f_2(y|\bar{M})$ from m_3 to m_4. Figure 1 shows the membership function for $\bar{M}$ with zero memberships at points m_1 and m_4, i.e. $f_1(y|m_1) = 0$ and $f_2(y|m_4) = 0$, which is mathematically represented as:

$$\mu(x|\bar{M}) = [m_1, f_1(y|\bar{M})/m_2, m_3/f_2(y|\bar{M}), m_4] \tag{1}$$

17.3.1 Fuzzy Future Value

Fuzzy future value is a fuzzy lump sum $(\bar{S}_n)$ that a fuzzy amount of $\bar{A}$ invested today will accumulate to in period n in the future at a fuzzy

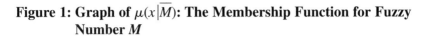

Figure 1: Graph of $\mu(x|\overline{M})$: The Membership Function for Fuzzy Number M

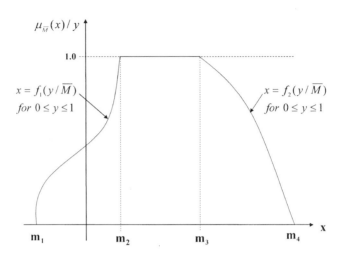

compounding interest rate of $\overline{r}$. Given that $\overline{A}$ and $\overline{r}$ are fuzzy positive numbers, the fuzzy lump sum future value is defined as,

$$\overline{S}_n = \overline{A} \otimes (1 \oplus \overline{r})^n \tag{2}$$

where $\otimes$ and $\oplus$ are the extended fuzzy multiplication and addition operators.[3] The membership function for $\overline{S}_n$ is represented as,

$$\mu(x|\overline{S}_n) = (s_{n1}, f_{n1}(y|\overline{S}_n)/s_{n2}, s_{n3}/f_{n2}(y|\overline{S}_n), s_{n4}) \tag{3}$$

If the compounding period $\overline{n}$ is also a fuzzy number, the membership function of the fuzzy future value is then defined by

$$\mu(x|\overline{S}) = \max_{1 \leq i \leq k} [\min(\mu(x|\overline{S}_{ni}), \lambda_i)] \tag{4}$$

where λ denotes the membership function of the compounding period n_i. Equation (4) modifies the membership function of $\overline{S}_{ni}$ in equation (2) where the membership function is tapered-off at a height of λ_i.

For illustration, let the future worth of an asset $\overline{S}_2$ with a current market value of $\overline{A}$ that is growing at a compounding rate of $\overline{r}$ in two year time be a fuzzy number, which can be determined as follows:

Market Value $(\bar{A})$ = ($239,450,000/$239,500,000, $240,000,000/ $240,100,000)

Compound Interest Rate $(\bar{r})$ = (2.5%/3%, 4%/4.2%)

Market Value in Year 2 $(\bar{S}_2)$

$\bar{S}_2$ = ($239,450,000/$239,500,000, $240,000,000/$240,100,000)

$\qquad \otimes[1 \oplus (2.5\%/3\%, 4\%/4.2\%)]^2$

$\bar{S}_2$ = ($253,046,929/$253,099,768, $260,583,360/$260,691,936)

If $\bar{n}$ is a fuzzy number with a membership value of $\lambda = 0.85$, the membership function of the fuzzy future value for the asset in year two is cut-off at 0.85. Assuming that the increasing $f_1(y|\bar{S}_n)$ and the decreasing $f_2(y|\bar{S}_n)$ parts of $\mu_2(x|\bar{S}_n, \bar{n})$ are linear functions, x_1 and x_2 can be determined as follows:

$$x_1 = (\bar{S}_2 - \bar{S}_1)y + \bar{S}_1, \tag{5a}$$

$$x_2 = (\bar{S}_3 - \bar{S}_4)y + \bar{S}_4. \tag{5b}$$

At the cut-off point where the membership value of λ is 0.85 (i.e. $y = 0.85$), x_1 and x_2 are calculated as $253,091,842 and $260,599,646 respectively (Figure 2).

Figure 2: Fuzzy Market Value in Year Two

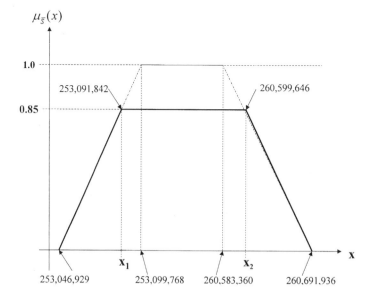

17.3.2 Fuzzy Present Value

A fuzzy present value $\overline{A}$ is defined as the current worth of a fuzzy lump sum $\overline{S}$ received in period n in the future. Given a fuzzy discount rate per period of $\overline{r}$, there are two definitions for the fuzzy present value ($\overline{A}$) depending on whether $\overline{S}$ is a positive or a negative fuzzy variable.

Definition 1:

$PV_1(\overline{S}, n) = \overline{A}$ if and only if (iff) $\overline{A}$ is a fuzzy number and $\overline{A} \otimes (1 \oplus \overline{r})^n = \overline{S}$, such that $\overline{S}$ is negative. Thus

$$PV_1(\overline{S}, n) \otimes (1 \oplus \overline{r})^n = \overline{S}. \tag{6}$$

The membership function $\mu_1(x|\overline{S}, n)$ for $PV_1(\overline{S}, n)$ with negative $\overline{S}$ is determined by

$$f_i(y|\overline{A}) = f_i(y|\overline{S}) * [1 + f_i(y|\overline{r})]^{-n} \tag{7}$$

for $i = 1, 2$ and $a_1 = f_1(0|\overline{A})$, $a_2 = f_1(1|\overline{A})$, $a_3 = f_2(1|\overline{A})$, $a_4 = f_2(0|\overline{A})$. Then $PV_1(\overline{S}, n) = \overline{A}$, iff $f_1(y|\overline{A})$ is increasing and $f_2(y|\overline{A})$ is decreasing and $a_2 \leq a_3$.

Definition 2:

$PV_2(\overline{S}, n) = \overline{A}$ if and only if $\overline{A}$ is a fuzzy number and $\overline{A} = \overline{S} \otimes (1 \oplus \overline{r})^{-n}$, such that $\overline{S}$ is positive. Thus

$$PV_2(\overline{S}, n) \otimes (1 \oplus \overline{r})^n \cong \overline{S}. \tag{8}$$

The membership function of $\mu_2(x|\overline{S}, n)$ for $PV_2(\overline{S}, n)$ with positive $\overline{S}$ is determined by

$$f_i(y|\overline{A}) = f_i(y|\overline{S}) * [1 + f_{3-i}(y|\overline{r})]^{-n} \tag{9}$$

for $i = 1, 2$ and $a_1 = f_1(0|\overline{A})$, $a_2 = f_1(1|\overline{A})$, $a_3 = f_2(1|\overline{A})$, $a_4 = f_2(0|\overline{A})$. Then $PV_2(\overline{S}, n) = \overline{A}$, a fuzzy number, iff $f_1(y|\overline{A})$ is increasing and $f_2(y|\overline{A})$ is decreasing and $a_2 \leq a_3$.

If $\overline{n}$ is a fuzzy number then the membership functions for both the present value $PV_1(\overline{S}, n)$ and $PV_2(\overline{S}, n)$ are defined by

$$\mu(x|\overline{S}) = \max_{1 \leq i \leq k} [\min(\mu(x|\overline{S}, \overline{n}), \lambda_i)]. \tag{10}$$

Based on equation (8), the computation of the present value of a fuzzy lump sum of $\overline{S}_3$ in year three in the future discounted at a fuzzy rate of $\overline{r}$ is illustrated as follows:

Lump sum value in Year 3 $(\bar{S}_3)$
$\bar{S}_3 = (\$65,095,958/\$68,214,193, \$85,527,659/\$88,818,865)$
Discount rate $(\bar{r}) = (8\%/9\%, 9\%/12\%)$

$PV_2(\bar{S}|n_3) \cong (\$65,095,958/\$68,214,193, \$85,527,659/\$88,818,865)$
$\otimes [1 \oplus (8\%/9\%, 9\%/12\%)]^{-3}$

$PV_2(\bar{S}|n_3) \cong (\$46,334,017/\$48,553,515, \$67,894,613/\$70,507,079)$

Assuming that the membership function of n_3 is 1.0, then, $\min(\mu(x|\bar{S}, n_3), \lambda_3)$ is equivalent to $\mu(x|\bar{S}, n_3)$. The possibility distribution for the fuzzy present value is shown in Figure 3.

17.3.3 Fuzzy Present Value of Annuity

Let $\bar{A}_n = (a_{n1}/a_{n2}, a_{n3}/a_{n4})$ represent the present worth of a stream of fuzzy payments P, which is made at the end of each period for n periods at a fuzzy interest rate of $\bar{r}$. If both $\bar{P}$ and $\bar{r}$ are positive fuzzy number, the present value of the fuzzy cash flow is given as,

$$\bar{A}_n = \bar{P} \otimes \gamma(n, \bar{r}) \tag{11}$$

Figure 3: Fuzzy Present Value For Year 3 Terminal Cash Flow

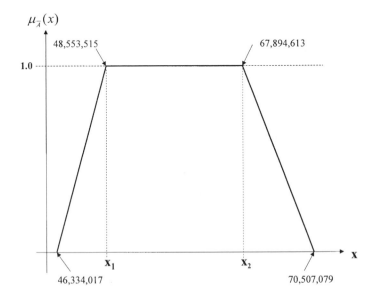

$\gamma(n, \bar{r})$ is the fuzzy present value factor defined as

$$\gamma(n, \bar{r}) = [1 \ominus (1 \oplus \bar{r})^{-n}] \otimes \bar{r}^{-1} \qquad (12)$$

where $\ominus$ is the extended fuzzy subtraction operator. The membership function $\mu(x|\bar{A}_n)$ for $\bar{A}_n$ is determined by,

$$f_{ni}(y|\bar{A}_n) = f_i(y|\bar{P}) * \gamma[n, f_i(y|\bar{r})] \qquad (13)$$

for $i = 1, 2$ where $a_{n1} = f_{n1}(0|\bar{A}_n)$, $a_{n2} = f_{n1}(1|\bar{A}_n)$, $a_{n3} = f_{n2}(1|\bar{A}_n)$, and $a_{n4} = f_{n2}(0|\bar{A}_n)$.

If the number of payment periods $\bar{n}$ is a fuzzy number with a membership function of $\mu(n_i|\bar{n}) = \lambda_i$, the membership function of $\bar{A}_n$ can be defined as,

$$\mu(x|\bar{A}) = \max_{1 \leq i \leq k} [\min(\mu(x|\bar{A}_n), \lambda_i)]. \qquad (14)$$

To illustrate the concept of the fuzzy present value of annuity, the calculation of the fuzzy annual debt service for a 20-year mortgage loan that is equivalent to 80% of an asset market value of $\bar{A}$ is shown below. The interest rate (r) is assumed in this illustration to be a non-fuzzy value of 6.5%.

Term of Loan (n) = 20 years
Loan to Value ratio = 80%
Interest Rate (r) = 6.5%
Market Value of an asset $(\bar{A})$
 = ($\$,239,450,000/\$239,500,000, \$240,000,000/\$240,100,000$)
Loan Principal
 = $0.8 \otimes \bar{A}$ = ($\$191,560,000/\$191,600,000, \$192,000,000/\$192,080,000$)

Annual Debt Service $(\bar{P})$ = $(0.8 \otimes \bar{A}) \otimes \gamma(n, r)$
$\bar{P}$ = ($\$191,560,000/\$191,600,000,\$192,000,000/\$192,080,000$)
  $\otimes [(1 - 1.065^{-20})/0.065]$
$\bar{P}$ = (**$\$17,385,295/\$17,388,925, \$17,425,228/\$17,432,488$**).

17.4 Fuzzy Discounted Cash Flow (Fuzzy DCF) Models

Fuzzy DCF models involve discounting a stream of fuzzy net cash flows over n holding periods by a fuzzy interest rate $\bar{r}$. There are two types of fuzzy DCF models: fuzzy net present value (NPV) and fuzzy internal rate of return (IRR)[4]. In a fuzzy NPV model, consider a fuzzy net cash flow stream of $\bar{\Lambda} = \bar{A}_0, ..., \bar{A}_n$, where $\bar{A}_0$ is a negative fuzzy number and the other $\bar{A}_i$ are either positive of negative fuzzy numbers. A positive $\bar{A}_i$ indicates net revenue generated from a project whereas a negative $\bar{A}_i$ represents net investment outlays at the end of period i.

The membership function $\mu(x|\bar{A}_i)$ for the fuzzy number $\bar{A}_i$ is defined as,

$$\mu(x|\bar{A}_i) = (a_{i1}, f_{i1})y|\bar{A}(/a_{i2}, a_{i3}/f_{i2}(y|\bar{A}_i), a_{i4}) \tag{15}$$

for $i = 0, 1, ..., n$. The net present value of the fuzzy cash flow stream $\bar{\Lambda}$ is given as,

$$NPV(\bar{\Lambda}, n) = \bar{A}_0 \oplus \sum_{i=1}^{n} PV_{k(i)}(\bar{A}_i, i) \tag{16}$$

where Σ is the fuzzy summation. $k(i) = 1$ when $\bar{A}_i$ is negative and $K(i) = 2$ for a positive $\bar{A}_i$.

The membership function $\mu(x|\bar{\Lambda}, n)$ for the NPV$(\bar{\Lambda}, n)$ is defined by

$$\mu(x|\bar{A}, n) = (\alpha_{ni}, f_{ni}(y|\bar{A})/\alpha_{n2}, \alpha_{n3}/f_{n2}(y|\bar{A}), \alpha_{n4}) \tag{17}$$

where

$$f_{ni}(y|\bar{A}) = \sum_{j=0}^{n} f_{ji}(y|\bar{A}_j) * [1 + f_{k(j)}(y|\bar{r})]^{-j} \tag{18}$$

for $i = 1, 2$, where $k(j) = 1$ for a negative $\bar{A}_j$ and $K(j) = (3 - i)$ for positive $\bar{A}_j$, so that $\alpha_{n1} = f_{n1}(0|\bar{\Lambda})$, $\alpha_{n2} = f_{n1}(1|\bar{\Lambda})$, $\alpha_{n3} = f_{n2}(1|\bar{\Lambda})$, $\alpha_{n4} = f_{n2}(0|\bar{\Lambda})$.

If the expected holding period is a discrete positive fuzzy number $\bar{n}$, the membership function of the fuzzy net present value NPV$(\bar{\Lambda}, \bar{n})$ is generalised as follows,

$$\mu(x|\bar{\Lambda}) = \max_{1 \le i \le k} [min(\mu(x|\bar{\Lambda}, n_i), \lambda_i)]. \tag{19}$$

The decision making rule under fuzzy NPV requires that the NPV exceed $\bar{0}$ for a project to be accepted, where $\bar{0}$ is an appropriate representation of fuzzy zero. Therefore,

if the fuzzy NPV is positive [i.e. NPV$(\bar{\Lambda}, \bar{n}) \ge \bar{0}]$, *then the project is accepted; and*
if the fuzzy NPV is negative [i.e. NPV$(\bar{\Lambda}, \bar{n}) \le \bar{0}]$, *then reject the project.*

17.5 Case Illustration: An Office-Cum-Retail Development

Using an office-cum-retail development as a case study, the feasibility of the investment is first analysed under the classical DCF model based on key input variables. Assumptions for selected variables are then "fuzzified" and the NPV based on the projected fuzzy cash flows is computed. The results of the two DCF models are compared and the effects of cognitive uncertainty as reflected by the differences in the two NPV estimates are discussed.

17.5.1 Case Facts and Assumptions

The subject property is a 10-storey office-cum-retail development located in the Central Business District of Singapore. The subject property comprises 8 floors of offices with a total net lettable area of 26,092.3 square meters (sqm). Several shops with a total floor area of 1,760.6 sqm and a restaurant of 1,342.2 sqm occupy the first two floors of the subject property. The subject property was built in 1973 on a 6,147.9 sqm land with a leasehold interest of 99 years. Based on our site surveys and market analysis, the following information is collected:

(i) The market value of the subject property is estimated at S$240,000,000. The costs of acquisition and disposal, which include legal fees, professional fees and stamp duty, are assumed to be 4% of the transaction price. The capital appreciation rate is assumed at 3.4%.

(ii) A 20-year term loan is obtained from a bank at a fixed interest rate of 6.5% compounded annually. The permissible loan amount is subject to a maximum loan to value cap of 80%, i.e. the loan principal for the acquisition is computed at $192,000,000. The annual debt service is calculated as S$17,425,228.

(iii) The current gross office rental is S$53.80 psm per month, whereas the average gross monthly rentals for the shop and restaurant are S$207.60 psm. A 5% vacancy rate is assumed at the time of analysis. The leases are subject to a 3-year rent revision term at an annual rate of 3.4%.

(iv) The four-storey basement carpark is expected to generate a revenue of S$600,000 per annum net.

(v) The operating expenses are 15% of the gross revenue. The property tax rate is 16% of the effective gross rental[5] and the corporate tax is 30% of the before tax cash flow.

(vi) The expected rate of return of the investor is assumed to be 9% per annum, and he will hold the property for a period of 5 years.

17.5.2 Assumptions for Fuzzy Input Variables

For the Fuzzy DCF analysis, the after-tax cash flows (ATCF) are projected based on the following selected *fuzzified* variables, i.e. variables that are expressed vaguely and imprecisely by fuzzy numbers,

(i) The market value is *around $239,500,000 to $240,000,000* and the rate of capital appreciation is *not more than 4% and not less than 3%*. The costs of acquisition and disposal are *about 4%*.

(ii) The gross monthly rental for office is *about $54 psm*, whereas the gross monthly rental for retail and restaurant ranges *approximately between $200 psm and $210 psm*. The vacancy rate remains at *around 5%, but will not be more than 6%*. The annual rental growth rate is *approximately 3.4%*.

(iii) The carpark revenue is *more or less $600,000 per annum*.

(iv) The operating expenses *are more than 10%*.

(v) The holding period of the investment *will not be more than 6 years* with the possibility of each period being indicated by λ_i in Table 2.

(vi) The expected rate of return *is not less than 8%*.

Other variables like the property tax rate and the loan terms are assumed to be deterministic and they are represented by the same crisp numbers given in the earlier section. The fuzzy variables can be translated into LR-type fuzzy numbers with linear continuous monotone increasing and decreasing functions, and they are summarized in Table 3. Figure 4 shows the possibility distributions of the selected fuzzy variables.

Table 2: Possibility Distribution of the Number of Holding Period in Year

n	1	2	3	4	5	6
λ_i	0.8	0.85	1.0	1.0	0.9	0.7

Table 3: Fuzzy Variables and their LR Fuzzy Representations

Input Variables	The LR Fuzzy Representation
Market value ($ million)	($239.45, $239.50, $240.00, $240.10)
Capital appreciation rate (% per annum)	(2.50%, 3.00%, 4.00%, 4.20%)
Gross monthly rental for offices ($psm)	($50.00, $54,00, $54.00, $59.00)
Gross monthly rental for retail & restaurant ($psm)	($195.00, $200.00, $210.00, $220.00)
Vacancy rate (%)	(4.00%, 5.00%, 6.00%, 6.50%)
Rental growth rate (% per annum)	(3.00%, 3.40%, 3.40%, 4.00%)
Net carpark revenue ($'000)	($560.00, $600.00, $600.00, $650.00)
Operating expenses (% of gross revenue)	(10.00%, 11.00%, 11.00%, 15.00%)
Expected rate of return (%)	(8.00%, 9.00%, 9.00%, 12.00%)
Costs of acquisition and sale (% agreed prices)	(3.80%, 4.00%, 4.00%, 4.50%)

Figure 4: The Decision Space of the Fuzzy Solution

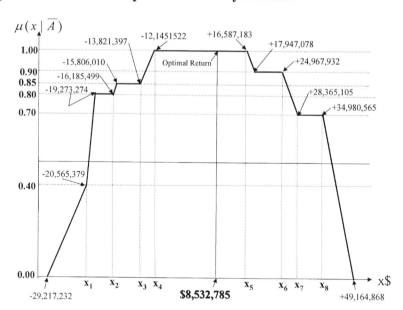

17.6 Cash Flow Projections and Decision Criteria

17.6.1 Classical DCF Analysis

Based on the assumptions in Section 17.4, the feasibility of investing in the subject property is evaluated using two criteria: Net Present Value on equity (NPV_e) and Internal Rate of Return on equity (IRR_e) as represented by equations (20) and (21) below,

$$\text{NPV}_e = \sum_{t=1}^{n} \frac{\text{ATCF}_t}{(1+K_e)^t} + \left[\frac{\text{ATER}_n}{(1+K_e)^n} - I_0 \right] \tag{20}$$

$$0 = \sum_{t=1}^{n} \frac{\text{ATCF}_t}{(1+\text{IRR}_e)^t} + \left[\frac{\text{ATER}_n}{(1+\text{IRR}_e)^n} - I_0 \right] \tag{21}$$

ATCF = After-Tax Cash Flow;
ATER = After-Tax Equity Reversion;
k_e = Required rate of return on Investment;
n = Investment holding period in year;
I_0 = Initial equity outlay.

The results show a positive NPV of $5,563,288 and an IRR of 10.9%, which is greater than the expected return of 9%. Therefore, the investment is feasible based on the classical DCF analysis.

17.6.2 Fuzzy DCF Analysis

There are basically three steps involved in the computation of the fuzzy NPV. First, the fuzzy cash flows are projected for n_i holding periods, where $n_i = \{1, 2, 3, 4, 5, 6\}$. Table 4 shows a typical fuzzy cash flow pro-forma for years 0 and 1, which includes the equity revision if the holding period n_i is assumed to be 1. The cash flows are discounted at a fuzzy discount rate of $\bar{r}$ and the fuzzy NPVs for the respective n_i holding periods are summarized in Table 5. The fuzzy NPV is then calculated as the fuzzy summation of the discounted fuzzy cash flow using equation (16), which is re-written as follows,

$$NPV(\bar{A}, n) = \bar{A}_0 \oplus \sum_{i=1}^{n} PV_{k(i)}(\bar{A}_i, i) \tag{16}$$

As the holding periods $\bar{n}_i$ is a collection of positive discrete fuzzy numbers with possibility distributions (λ_i) given in Table 2, the second step of the computation is to determine the membership function of the fuzzy NPV at each n_i taking into consideration the cut-off level of λ_i. The membership function of the fuzzy set is determined using the minimum operator as,

$$\mu(x|\bar{A}, n_i) = \min[\mu(x|\bar{A}, n_i), \lambda_i]. \tag{22}$$

Assuming that $f_1(y|NPV)$ and $f_2(y|NPV)$ are two monotonous linear functions, the intersection points (x_1, x_2) between the $\mu(x|\bar{A}, n_i)$ and λ_i are calculated as follows:

$$x_1 = (NPV_2 - NPV_1) * y + NPV_1 \tag{23a}$$

$$x_2 = (NPV_3 - NPV_4) * y + NPV_4 \tag{23b}$$

After determining the fuzzy $NPV(\bar{A}, n_i)$ (Table 5) and their respective membership functions, the last step involves the aggregation of the membership functions of the fuzzy NPVs from periods n_1 to n_6. The maximum operator given by equation (19) is used in this case to form the fuzzy decision space, which is graphically shown in Figure 4.

$$\mu(x|\bar{A}) = \max_{1 \le i \le k} [\min(\mu(x|\bar{A}, n_i), \lambda_i)] \tag{19}$$

Table 4: Fuzzy Cash Flow Projection for the Investment

Year Fuzzy number representation:	Year 0				Year 1			
	$x_{year=0,1}$	$x_{year=0,2}$	$x_{year=0,3}$	$x_{year=0,4}$	$x_{year=1,1}$	$x_{year=1,2}$	$x_{year=1,3}$	$x_{year=1,4}$
Initial Cash Outlay:								
Equity on Purchase Price	($48,020,000.0)	($48,000,000.0)	($47,900,000.0)	($47,890,000.0)				
Cost of Acquisition	($10,804,500.0)	($10,800,000.0)	($9,101,000.0)	($9,099,100.0)				
Potential Gross Rental					$22,915,932.0	$24,354,530.0	$24,726,866.0	$26,664,740.0
Less Vacancy					($1,733,208.0)	($1,607,246.0)	($974,181.0)	($916,637.0)
Effective Gross Rental					$21,182,724.0	$22,747,284.0	$23,752,685.0	$25,748,103.0
Gross Carpark Revenue					$560,000.0	$600,000.0	$600,000.0	$650,000.0
Effective Gross Income					$21,742,724.0	$23,347,284.0	$24,352,685.0	$26,398,103.0
Less Operating Expenses					($3,959,715.0)	($3,652,903.0)	($2,334,728.0)	($2,174,272.0)
Less Property Tax (16%)					($4,223,696.0)	($3,896,430.0)	($3,735,565.0)	($3,478,836.0)
Net Operating Income					$13,559,313.0	$15,797,951.0	$18,282,392.0	$20,744,995.0
Less Annual Debt Service					($17,432,488.0)	($17,425,228.0)	($17,388,925.0)	($17,385,295.0)
Before Tax Cash Flow					($3,873,175.0)	($1,627,277.0)	$893,467.0	$3,359,700.0
Less Corporate Tax (30%)					($2,488,078.0)	($1,748,518.0)	($995,385.0)	($322,234.0)
After Tax Cash Flow	($58,824,500.0)	($58,800,000.0)	($57,001,000.0)	($56,989,100.0)	($6,361,253.0)	($3,375,795.0)	($101,918.0)	($3,037,466.0)
Equity Reversion At the end of year 1					$47,763,600.0	$47,164,296.0	$54,059,097.0	$54,204,220.0
Terminal Cash Flow at year 1	*$58,824,500.0*	*$58,800,000.0*	*$57,001,000.0*	*$56,989,100.0*	*$41,402,347.0*	*$43,788,501.0*	*$53,957,179.0*	*$57,241,686.0*

Table 5: Fuzzy Net Present Value for n_i Holding Periods

Holding Periods n_i Year	Fuzzy Net Present Value
1	$(-21{,}858{,}120/-18{,}627{,}063,\ -7{,}499{,}001/-3{,}987{,}539)$
2	$(-22{,}257{,}317/-14{,}667{,}544,\ +1{,}282{,}604/+8{,}105{,}296)$
3	$(-23{,}318{,}025/-12{,}145{,}522,\ +8{,}739{,}897/+18{,}852{,}075)$
4	$(-24{,}870{,}682/-10{,}026{,}734,\ +16{,}587{,}183/+30{,}186{,}131)$
5	$(-26{,}866{,}944/-8{,}533{,}056,\ +23{,}269{,}346/+40{,}255{,}209)$
6	$(-29{,}217{,}232/-7{,}592{,}921,\ +28{,}901{,}578/+49{,}164{,}868)$

The cut-off points x_i in Figure 4, where $i = \{1, 2, ..., 8\}$, are calculated based on equation (23). Let x_1 be the intersection points of the increasing segments of $f_1(y|\text{NPV}_1)$ and $f_1(y|\text{NPV}_6)$ and y be the height of $\mu(x_1|\bar{A})$. At the cut-off point defined by $(x_1|y)$ where x_1 is the fuzzy NPV and y is the corresponding membership, which can be jointly estimated at the two intersection junctions below,

at function $f_1(y|\text{NPV}_1)$,

$$x_1 = \$3{,}231{,}057 * y - \$21{,}858{,}120 \tag{24}$$

at function $f_1(y|\text{NPV}_6)$

$$x_1 = \$21{,}624{,}311 * y - \$29{,}217{,}232 \tag{25}$$

the value of x_1 and the height of the membership function (y) are respectively estimated at $-\$20{,}565{,}697$ and 0.4 by solving equations (24) and (25) simultaneously.

By repeating the computation of x_i for $i = \{1, 2, ..., 8\}$, the membership characteristic of the fuzzy solution space as shown by Figure 4 is obtained, which has a complex form that is not easily interpretable. The fuzzy solution is constituted of an array of fuzzy net present values ranging from $-\$29{,}217{,}232$ to $+\$49{,}164{,}868$ with a distribution of membership values. A comparison of the results with that estimated by the traditional DCF model is necessary to reflect the effects of fuzzification of the cash flow variables. Hence, a 'defuzzification' process is carried out using the 'Centroid' method (Reynolds, Kent and Lazenby, 1973), and the 'defuzzified' NPV yields a crisp and non-fuzzy solution of $\$8{,}532{,}785$. The positive defuzzified value is consistent with that suggested by the crisp DCF model, and both results recommend acceptance of the investment.

The non-fuzzy result of the fuzzy DCF model is expected to be higher than that of the classical model because of the uncertainty involved in the fuzzy solution. The variance between the fuzzy NPV of $\$8{,}532{,}785$ and the traditional discounted NPV of $5,563,288 is found to be $2,909,497 or +53.8%. This variance is partly attributable to the trade-off in generalising the crisp membership of the classical model via the use of "fuzzified" inputs. Taking the crisp DCF estimate as a subset of the fuzzy DCF with a membership value of unity, the difference of S$2,909,497 or 53.8%, between the two estimates simply implies the value, or technically defined as the fuzzy risk premium, for relaxing the crisp measure to incorporate the uncertainty of vague and imperfect information. The margin of the variance is dependent on the subjective judgement made by experts with respect to "fuzzification" of the selected input variables.

It is important to stress that the higher value of the fuzzy NPV estimate does not imply that the fuzzy model is superior to the traditional NPV model. As discussed in Section 17.2, the results should be construed in the light that the crisp NPV estimate is deemed to be a subset of the fuzzy solution that has a membership of unity. The defuzzified solution simply means that when the membership boundary of the crisp NPV is relaxed, the fuzzy NPV value increases correspondingly as a countermand to the incorporation of vague and imprecise predictions. The decision based on the estimation results is not expected to deviate widely from a conclusion obtained in the traditional DCF model if the cash flow is adequately projected. The two approaches offer no more than just two different ways of analysing uncertainty. The final outcome is still largely subject to market knowledge, the judgement of the expert, and also how the expert transforms this knowledge or information into reliable inputs either by a probabilistic or a fuzzy measure.

17.7 Conclusion

In a highly volatile market with limited historical data, it is extremely difficult to predict cash flows with sufficient confidence by purely relying on *ex-post* observations. The point estimates of the classical DCF are highly susceptible to errors due to the not-so-random-walk properties of the market. The ability to translate expert's experience and market knowledge into useful *ex-ante* judgement is more realistic and reliable than the *ex-post* forecasts under this type of market condition. However, when market information is imperfect, the representation of the expert's judgment using probabilistic approach is hindered by imprecise and vague information. This form of uncertainty, which is also known as "fuzziness," is the main research issue that this paper attempts to address via the proposed fuzzy DCF model.

Fuzzy DCF model provides a natural and intuitive way of dealing with cognitive uncertainty associated imprecise and vague information. It relaxes the precision and crispness imposed on a rigid model for a somewhat inexact and vague but robust representation of market knowledge. In this framework, investors and analysts are allowed to make imprecise but reliable predictions in lieu of data-intensive statistical analyses. Based on a set of fuzzy inputs, the fuzzy NPV can be calculated to provide an approximated evaluation of the investment interest. With the membership characteristics of the fuzzy NPVs, the uncertainty of each outcome is concurrently captured and reflected. This approximative model merges two limbs of an investment analysis: return and risk evaluation, in a fuzzy solution space, which is defined by a set of fuzzy NPV estimates and the respective memberships.

In a case illustration using an actual office-cum-retail building in Singapore, the NPV of the classical DFC model based on crisp and precise inputs is estimated at $5,563,288. When the input variables are fuzzified with different possibility distributions, the fuzzy NPV, after the centroid defuzzification process, yields a crisp value of $8,532,785. A comparison of the results shows that an increase in the NPV of 53.38% was obtained by the fuzzy DCF vis-à-vis the classical NPV. Taking the crisp DCF estimate as a subset of the fuzzy DCF, this variance is attributable to the trade-off that is needed to generalise the classical model. The margin of the variance is to a large extent dependent on the subjective judgement made by the experts in the "fuzzification" of selected input variables.

It is important to stress that the higher value of the fuzzy NPV estimate does not imply that the fuzzy model is superior to the traditional NPV model. The defuzzified solution simply means that when the membership boundary of the crisp NPV is relaxed, the fuzzy NPV value increases correspondingly as a countermand to the incorporation of vague and imprecise predictions. The two approaches offer no more than just two different ways of analysing uncertainty. The fuzzy DCF model is not a substitute rather it is a complement to the traditional DCF in investment analysis.

Cognitive uncertainty has long been overlooked in the past. As the market moves away from randomness, the ability to deal with this form of uncertainty will ultimately distinguish the better investors. The application of the fuzzy DCF would suggest a competitive edge for the enlightened investor.

NOTES

[1] The *ex-ante* judgemental approach in this context is distinguished from the methods that rely on subjective probability of an event. The *ex-ante* judgemental is referred, in this context, to the expert's intuitive but measured view, which may be vaguely represented by descriptive or qualitative comments, on the possible outcome of a near future event.

[2] Zadeh (1975) defines a "linguistic variable" as a variable whose values are words or sentences in a natural or artificial language. It is used to express both fuzzy and probabilistic events.

[3] Please refer to Dubois and Parade (1979) for the technical details of the extended fuzzy arithmetic operations.

[4] The fuzzy IRR model has been shown to be an inappropriate extension of cash flow analysis under fuzzy representation by Buckley (1987).

[5] The 16% property tax rate is applicable at the date of the analysis, and the current property tax rate has been reduced to 12%.

REFERENCES

Buckley, J. J. The Fuzzy Mathematics of Finance, *Fuzzy Sets and Systems*, 1987, 21, 257–273.

Dubois, D. and Parade, H. Fuzzy Real Algebra- Some Results, *Fuzzy Sets and System*, 1979, 2, 327–348.

Fischhoff, B. Eliciting Knowledge for Analytical Representations, *IEEE Transactions on Systems, Man and Cybernetics*, 1989, 19, 98–99.

Gupta, M. M. "Fuzzy-ism", The First Decade, in M. M. Gupta, G. N. Saridis and B. R. Gaines, editors, *Fuzzy Automata and Decision Processes*, Elsevier Notrth-Holland, 1977, 5–10.

Klir, G. F. and Folger, T. A. *Fuzzy Sets, Uncertainty and Information*, Prentice Hall, International Edition, 1992.

Makridakis, S. and Wheelwright, S. C. editors, Forecasting the future and the future of forecasting, in *Managerial Sciences: Vol 12, Forecasting*, Amsterdam: North Holland, 1979.

Reynolds, T. J., Kent L. E., and Lazenby, D. W. *Introduction to Structural Mechanics*, London: Hodder and Stoughton, 1977.

von Winterfeldt, D. and Edward, W. *Decision Analysis and Behavioural Research*, New York, Cambridge University Press, 1986.

Zadeh, L. A. Fuzzy Sets, *Information and Control*, 1965, 8, 338–353.

Zadeh, L. A. The Concept of a Linguistic Variable and its Application to Approximate Reasoning – Part I, *Information Science*, 1975, 8:3, 199–249.

Zadeh, L. A. Fuzzy Set Theory – A Perspective, in M. M. Gupta, G. N. Saridis and B. R. Gaines, editors, *Fuzzy Automata and Decision Processes*, Elsevier North-Holland, 1977, 3–4.

Chapter 18

Real Options and Real Estate: A Review and Valuation Illustration*

Steven H. Ott
Belk College of Business Administration, University of North Carolina at Charlotte, Charlotte, NC 28223-0001

18.1 Introduction

The traditional capital budgeting and valuation framework for a land development investment opportunity involves determining the project's net present value (NPV). The first step in an NPV analysis is to forecast cash flows over time and discount these cash flows at the appropriate required rate-of-return, where the required rate-of-return is based on the systematic risk of these cash flows. The NPV is the difference between the present value of the expected future cash inflows and the present value of the expected cost outflows. When the NPV is zero or positive, the project is accepted. When the NPV is negative, the project is rejected.

This simple NPV decision rule ignores the changing dynamics of the actual marketplace. For example, cash flows may differ from what management originally expects, and management may have flexibility to alter its original strategy by expanding, contracting, changing the tenant mix, or redeveloping real estate projects to capitalize on opportunities or to mitigate potential losses. These and other examples of management's inherent flexibility to adapt its future actions to market conditions are termed real options (i.e., options on *real* assets such as real estate, as opposed to options on financial assets such as stock). Real-option analysis recognizes that investment opportunities often have valuable managerial (strategic) flexibility. Managers that identify and effectively value these real options gain a competitive advantage due to a more accurate analysis of the investment opportunity (see Dixit and Pindyck (1994) for a review of valuation and decision-making using real option analysis, and Amram and Kulatilaka (1999) for a discussion of the link between managerial strategy and investment decisions).

Real options often have characteristics that are similar to standard financial options (i.e., puts and calls on stocks, financial indices, etc.), and can often be valued utilizing existing option-pricing methodology. As with financial options, the longer the option lasts before it expires and the more volatile the value of the underlying asset, the more the option is worth. By synthesizing the characteristics of options within a real investment opportunity, and using an appropriate option-pricing valuation methodology, it is possible to estimate the value of any inherent options attached to an investment opportunity. Option valuation can then be linked to the traditional capital budgeting (NPV) analysis to reflect both the project's static NPV valuation and the option value of any management operating or strategic flexibility.

It has been recognized in the academic literature that real options exist within many real estate and land development projects. The next section reviews the literature that has specifically examined this link between real options and real estate.

18.2 Real Options and Real Estate: A Review of the Literature

The holding of vacant land has been recognized as an option to develop a completed building at a future date. Titman (1985), Capozza and Helsley (1990), Williams (1991) and Grenadier (1995), among others, have used this analogy to develop models to explain the valuation of land and the factors that affect the development decision. These models show that the source of vacant land value derives from the right, but not the obligation, to develop an underlying asset (a completed building) by paying the relevant exercise price (costs of construction).

These land option models have revealed the importance of uncertainty in determining the optimal development decision. Uncertainty is relevant because the developer often has an option to wait to develop the property, and the value of this option increases with increases in uncertainty about the future value of the built property. The option to wait is valuable, because as time passes the developer can gain additional information about the evolving value of the property. For example, if property values increase, the developer is more certain that it is worthwhile to proceed with construction of the project. Conversely, if values decline, the developer has avoided, by deferring construction, a potential loss on the investment in the project. Thus, the combination of asset value uncertainty, irreversible development and the flexibility to wait suggests that the development of land will not occur until the value of the completed property exceeds the cost of construction by a "waiting-time" option premium.[1]

The land option models determine a development hurdle ratio, defined as P/K, where P is the value of the completed development project (both land and building) and K is the cost of construction. These models predict that there is a critical development hurdle ratio (greater than the traditional NPV hurdle of one), above which it is optimal to proceed with development immediately, and below which it is optimal to defer investment in the project.

Several empirical studies have tested and validated the real-option model for land valuation and development decision-making. Holland, Ott and Riddiough (2000) and Ott and Yi (2001) specify and empirically estimate structural models of real estate asset market equilibrium. Using aggregate U.S. and regional commercial real estate time series data, these papers find that the real-option model and the uncertainty variable in particular, have significant power in explaining commercial real estate investment and development cycles. Thus, their empirical results generally favor the predictions of the real-option model, and also suggest that irreversibility and the option to wait are important considerations to investors. Other related empirical work includes a study by Sivitanidou and Sivitanides (2000). Examining investment over time for the U.S. office market, they find results consistent with those of Holland, Ott and Riddiough. An earlier study by Quigg (1993) who empirically studies land transactions in Seattle, finds that the land-option model has explanatory power for predicting land transaction prices. She finds that the option to wait represents 6% of the undeveloped land value.

The basic land valuation option model discussed above has been extended to examine strategic real estate development, i.e. the situation where developers compete with each other (see Grenadier (1996)). Grenadier's model shows that investment timing options for projects held by these competitors, combined with the strategically optimal exercise of these options, can explain both simultaneous investment in competing projects and long lag times between investments. Research by Grenadier (1999) and Childs, Ott and Riddiough (2002) extend this strategic stetting, to one where there is either asymmetric or incomplete information among the competing developers. In these models actual development reveals information to competitors. This work provides further explanation as to why supply boom and bust patterns are observed in many localized real estate markets.

In addition to the real-option land valuation model and its extensions, several papers have examined the impact of operational flexibility in real estate investment and redevelopment decisions. Specifically, they examine options for repeated redevelopment, and for determining the building's optimal tenant mix. They find that the values of these options are significant, and are reflected in the value of the land and the completed building. The presence of these options can explain continuing investment patterns over time in existing (already developed) real estate assets (see Capozza and Sick (1991); Capozza and Li (1994); Geltner, Riddiough and Stojanovich (1996); Childs, Riddiough and Triantis (1996); Williams (1997)).

18.3 The Practical Use of Real Options for Real Estate Investment and Development Decisions

As a result of the academic literature on real options and real estate, it is becoming increasingly recognized by real estate practitioners that the use of real options analysis can enhance real estate valuation and investment decision-making (see e.g., Steinfeld and Zisler (2000)). Discussion of real options is also becoming part of the standard material in textbooks that are intended for graduate students in real estate (see e.g., Geltner and Miller (2001)). Despite this progress, a significant gap exists between the theory of real options and the practical application of these ideas. In order to help bridge this gap, the remainder of the paper provides an illustration of how to practically apply the use of real options analysis into the real estate investment decision-making process.

To expand upon the types of real estate related options that have been previously discussed in literature, the illustration that follows focuses on a real *growth* option where an initial investment in a development may set the path for potential expansion of investment opportunities. In essence, the initial investment fosters a possible chain of interrelated investments. Specifically, developing the initial real estate project allows for the option to replicate of the initial development. This option would be exercised only *if* the initial investment was financially successful. Therefore, this is a growth option to invest in another project. In the capital budgeting framework for this problem, real option valuation can be linked to the NPV analysis to reflect both the project's NPV valuation and the option value of strategic flexibility. This practical illustration is based on an actual land development project that is currently being developed in Charlotte, North Carolina.

18.4 Real Option and Real Estate: An Illustration

18.4.1 Description of the Land Development Project

The development project for this illustration is located in Charlotte, North Carolina, one of the fastest growing cities in the Southeast. It consists of approximately 200 units on 20+ acres and was designed primarily to appeal to the busy professional. It features detached, cluster homes in a courtyard setting. Homes are located on private courtyard drives creating privacy and a safe, secure atmosphere. The homeowner's association maintains the grounds. The property is located within the larger master-planned neighborhood that hosts a number of amenities including swimming, tennis and golf.

An executive from a Charlotte regional development firm was evaluating a proposal to replicate a unique project that had been successful in Atlanta, Georgia. The Atlanta development was comprised primarily of low-maintenance patio homes that featured maintenance-free front and side lawns and required little external upkeep. Given the high concentration of single, professional people in Atlanta, the development was a natural "fit" for Atlanta's demographic mix.

The project turned out to be extremely successful in Atlanta, and this type of development would seem to fit well within the context of the Charlotte region's growing population and changing demographic mix. Thus, the firm was particularly motivated to develop a project of this type in Charlotte. The developer would develop the land into buildable lots exclusively for this unique product, and then sell these lots to homebuilders. If a project of this type was financially successful in Charlotte, the developer felt that they would have the flexibility and know-how to replicate this success elsewhere in the metropolitan area. This flexibility can be construed as a real option. Specifically, the option would be considered a growth option, in that, the developer has the right, but not the obligation, to invest in another project of this type, once the initial project was completed and demand for this type of housing product was revealed.

There are many uncertainties inherent in the project development. Since this type of development had not yet been attempted in Charlotte, the costs to prepare the land for development (the development of the lots) were highly uncertain. There were several reasons for this cost uncertainty. First, greater design difficulty such as grading and utility conflicts resulting from the higher density created fewer margins for error. Second, design tolerances were small (i.e., curbs poured at 1% slope) which can lead to difficulty with workmanship quality and several re-pours to achieve positive drainage. Third, excessive earth moving amplified the grading risk. All of these challenges resulted in an *expectation* of total development costs of $30,000 per lot, thus creating a 30% lot-to-finished home price ratio. According to the developer, "This ratio, relative to the size of the lot, is unprecedented for Charlotte."

Other uncertainties existed with respect to the timing and sale price of the completed lots. For example, the builder (the prospective purchaser of the lots) was a new entrant to the Charlotte market. They lacked a record of acceptance within the Charlotte market, and the specialized nature of the development made difficult the possibility of bringing in an alternative builder if they decided to abandon the project. Also, most importantly, this new type of housing product resulted in uncertain product demand. Thus, in addition to cost uncertainty, the success of the project depended upon the uncertain timing and selling price of the lots, which in turn, depended on uncertain demand for a new type of housing product in the market.

In determining the financial feasibility for this project, the developer wanted to account for the multiple uncertainties that existed. Additionally, the developer was interested in incorporating the value of the growth option into the financial analysis and decision-making process.

18.4.2 Financial Analysis of the Development

In order to properly undertake the financial analysis of the project, it must be accomplished in two steps. Initially, the project should be valued using the traditional NPV approach. After the NPV valuation, the value of the growth option will be calculated and linked to the NPV valuation to determine the overall valuation of the investment opportunity.

18.4.2.1 NPV Analysis

NPV analysis begins by finding the expected net present value of the project assuming that the project has no real options. The expected NPV is found by calculating the present value for each of the potential outcomes (scenarios) and then using the associated subjective probabilities for each scenario to calculate an expectation. Since the outcome of the project is highly uncertain, scenario analysis can help quantify the associated risks (uncertainties) connected to the project. Scenario analysis also allows for the calculation of the variance of the values, as these variances will be needed for calculating the value of the growth option. The probabilities and explanations of the scenarios for the project are shown in Table 1.

The first step for calculating the NPV of the project is to determine the project's expected revenues and costs for each scenario. Traditional capital budgeting theory stipulates that a project's NPV is the present value of its future cash inflows, subtracted from the present value of the project's expected cash outflows (costs). Both the cash inflows and outflows are discounted at a rate that reflects the systematic risk of these expected future cash flows. Table 2 shows the summary of the present value of revenues and costs as well as the corresponding probability-weighted expected NPV calculation for the project.

Table 1: Probability Distribution Table for the Project

Scenario	Probability Weight (%)	Explanation
Very optimistic	15	Project is very successful
Optimistic	20	Project is successful
Base case	30	Project meets basic revenue and cost expectations
Pessimistic	20	Project performs below expectations
Very pessimistic	15	Project is very unsuccessful

Table 2: Present Value Calculation of Revenues and Costs for the Project

Scenario	Probability Weight (%)	PV of Lot Sale Revenues	PV of Development Costs
Very optimistic	15.00	$6,409,826	$3,346,165
Optimistic	20.00	$4,273,217	$3,691,101
Base case	30.00	$4,138,809	$3,990,728
Pessimistic	20.00	$2,574,837	$4,241,336
Very pessimistic	15.00	$1,685,679	$4,495,500
Expected Present Value		**$3,825,579**	**$3,959,956**

Based on investor surveys for similar unlevered land development investments, and an estimate of the *systematic* risk associated with the lot sales, an annualized discount rate of 11.5% was used in calculating the present value of the lot sale revenues. Because the uncertainty in the costs was considered project-specific (unsystematic), an annualized discount rate of 6%, the risk-free rate, was used in calculating the present value of costs.

The traditional NPV for the project is $-\$134,377$ ($\$3,825,579-\$3,959,956$). Thus, under the traditional NPV decision rule, the project should be rejected. However, considering the flexibility that management has to replicate the project if it is successful, there is additional value embedded in the project. Real-option analysis can be used to determine this additional value. After calculating the value of the option, the NPV and option analysis can be linked to ascertain the overall valuation of the project.

18.4.2.2 Real Options Analysis – Valuation of the Growth Option

The next step in the analysis is to value the growth option attached to the initial development of the project. Since options on real assets behave similarly to options on financial assets, the value of real options can be ascertained using similar valuation methodologies used for options on financial assets. Table 3 shows the analogies between a typical financial call option on a stock and the land development project's real growth option in this case.

Because in this case the value of the completed project *and* the development costs are uncertain, the growth option will be valued using a variant of the Black-Scholes Option Pricing Model; specifically, the formula for an exchange option will be used. The growth option attached to the project,

Table 3: Analogies Between a Call Option on a Stock and the Project's Real Growth Option

Financial Option	Real Growth Option
Underlying Stock Price (S)	The present value of the replicated project's cash inflows (i.e., the revenues that determine the value of the completed project)
Stock Exercise Price (X)	The present value of the cash outflows required to replicate the project (the development costs)
Option time to expiration (T)	The length of time that the firm can defer a decision with respect to commencing the investment in the replicated project
Variance of returns on the stock (σ)	The variance of the completed project's value

denoted as G, will be valued using the standard exchange-option formula:

$$G = S_0 N(d1) - X_0 N(d2)$$

where,

S_0 = the time-zero expected present value of the replicated project's cash inflows.

X_0 = the time-zero present value of the cash outflows, i.e., the expected development costs required to replicate the project.

N = the cumulative standard normal distribution function.

$$d1 = \frac{\ln(S_0/X_0) + 1/2\, \hat{\sigma}^2 T}{\hat{\sigma} \sqrt{T}}$$

$$d2 = d1 - \hat{\sigma} \sqrt{T}$$

T = the length of time that the firm can defer a decision with respect to commencing an investment in the replicated project.

$\hat{\sigma} = \sqrt{\sigma_S^2 + \sigma_X^2 - 2\rho\sigma_S\sigma_X}$, is the standard deviation of the ratio of revenues to costs.

σ_S = the annualized standard deviation of the return on the value of the replicated project, S.

σ_X = the annualized standard deviation of the return on the value of the costs, X.

ρ = the correlation between the return on value, S, and the return on costs, X.

The present values of cash inflows and costs for the project that were calculated earlier and displayed in Table 3 are noted below:

$$S_0 = \$3,825,579$$
$$X_0 = \$3,959,956$$

T corresponds to the amount of time in years that the firm has to exercise the growth option with respect to the project. Given that the average time frame to complete the initial project is 3 years, a minimum of 3 years is needed to determine demand for the lots and the financial success of the project. The maximum time to exercise the option is typically finite due to competitive forces that can enter the market reduce or eliminate positive NPV opportunities. For this project, it is estimated that 5 years is the "window of opportunity" available to exercise this option.

Standard deviations for the returns on revenues and costs are obtained by calculating internal rates of return (IRR's) on the cash flows for each scenario. The initial cash flow in the calculation of IRR assumes that revenues and costs can be theoretically "purchased" (i.e., a cash outflow is incurred) for their time zero expected values, i.e., $S_0 = \$3,825,579$ and $X_0 = \$3,959,956$. Subsequent cash flows are than based on the projected revenues and costs for each scenario. Once the IRRs are determined for the scenarios, annualized standard deviations for these returns can be calculated. A summary of the IRR's is shown in Tables 4 and 5.

The net revenues from the sale of the lots are based on market demand for the built housing product; therefore, these revenues are not related to the costs of developing the lots for sale. Thus, it is assumed that the correlation between the return on value and the return on costs, ρ, is 0.

After obtaining values for d1 and d2, the respective values are used to obtain values for $N(d1)$ and $N(d2)$. $N(d1)$ and $N(d2)$ represent areas under a standard normal distribution function. The values of the normal distribution

Table 4: Inputs for the Calculation of the Annualized Standard Deviation of the Return on Completed Project Value

Scenario	Probability (%)	IRR(%)
Very Optimistic	15.00	32.86
Optimistic	20.00	26.83
Base Case	30.00	14.24
Pessimistic	20.00	−2.11
Very Pessimistic	15.00	−16.28
Expected Revenue IRR		**11.70**

Table 5: Inputs for the Calculation of the Annualized Standard Deviation of the Return on Development Costs

Scenario	Probability (%)	IRR(%)
Very Optimistic	15.00	−7.32
Optimistic	20.00	0.47
Base Case	30.00	6.59
Pessimistic	20.00	11.24
Very Pessimistic	15.00	15.72
Expected Cost IRR		**5.58**

can be readily obtained from many statistic textbooks or can be found using an Excel spreadsheet program.

18.4.2.3 Calculating the Value of the Growth Option

Table 6 shows all of the necessary inputs to obtain a valuation of the growth option along with the final calculated value of the growth option. Note that after calculating the standard deviation of the return on revenues and costs using the data from Tables 4 and 5, this result must be annualized by dividing by the square root of the time for initial project completion (3 years).

The value of the option based on the underlying assumptions and the corresponding inputs is $296,142.

The final present value of the development project, including the growth option, is found by simply summing the traditional NPV value and the value of the growth option. Table 7 summarizes this calculation.

18.4.3.4 The Investment Decision

The analysis shows that the option value represents approximately 8% of the completed project value, S_0. While the traditional NPV of the project is negative and indicates that it should not be undertaken, the inclusion of the

Table 6: Growth Option Valuation Model for the Project

Present Value of Sales Revenues S_0	$3,825,579
Present Value of Costs X_0	$3,959,956
Time to exercise the option T	5 years
Annualized Standard Deviation of Revenues σ_S	9.49%
Annualized Standard Deviation of Costs σ_X	4.18%
Correlation between Revenues and Costs ρ	0
Standard Deviation of the ratio of revenues to costs $\hat{\sigma}$	10.37%
$d1$	−.0329
$d2$	−.2648
$N(d1)$	.4869
$N(d2)$	.3956
Calculated Value of the Growth Option G	$296,142

Table 7: Linking the Growth Option to NPV analysis

NPV of Project without growth option	−$134,377
Value of growth option	$296,142
NPV including growth option	$161,765

growth option in the analysis changes this decision. Indeed, with the growth option, the project has a positive NPV. In this case, the development and investment in the new project provides the developer with valuable information that may be able to be used to undertake an additional positive NPV project. The value of this future investment opportunity overcomes the initial project's negative NPV. By strategically recognizing this future growth opportunity (option), real-options analysis can change decisions that would have been made using only the traditional NPV approach; therefore, incorporating real options into the analysis allows for more informed, wealth enhancing, and accurate valuation assessment.

18.5 Summary

Real estate practitioners are recognizing real options exist as part of many real estate development projects. However, the practical application of real options theory to actual real estate valuations remains somewhat elusive. This paper provides an illustration of how to practically apply the use of real options analysis into the real estate investment decision-making process. This illustration shows how option pricing can be used, in conjunction with traditional discounted cash flow analysis (NPV), to uncover the value of real growth options that may be part of a real estate development. Option-pricing methodology is employed to uncover the value of a real growth option that is part of a land development project. The development project is first analyzed using the familiar traditional discounted cash flow approach (NPV). Next, the necessary parameter values for real-option valuation are determined within the traditional NPV framework. Finally, the value of the real option is calculated and linked to the NPV value to determine the overall project value and the investment decision. This illustration shows that an analysis that recognizes and incorporates real options may change decisions that are based solely on the traditional approach.

Notes

[*] Steven H. Ott is an Associate Professor of Real Estate Finance in the Department of Finance and Business Law, University of North Carolina Charlotte, Charlotte, North Carolina. He would like to thank Paul Childs, Timothy Riddiough, Ko Wang and James Webb for helpful comments and suggestions. He would also like to thank Maurice Clark, an MBA graduate from UNC-Charlotte, who provided research assistance.

[1] An investment is irreversible if the initial investment is a sunk cost; thus, it cannot be fully recovered. For real estate, investment irreversibility is the typical scenario, i.e., the property can be sold for its market value, but this value has no relationship to the investment made.

REFERENCES

Amram, Martha and Nalin Kulatilaka, Disciplined Decisions: Aligning Strategy with the Financial Markets, *Harvard Business Review*, January–February 1999, 95–105.

Capozza, Dennis and Robert W. Helsley, 1990, The Stochastic City, *Journal of Urban Economics* 28, 187–203.

Capozza, Dennis and Y. Li, 1994. The Timing and Intensity of Investment: The Case of Land, *American Economic Review*, 84, 889–904.

Capozza, Dennis and Gordon Sick, 1991. Valuing Long Term Leases: The Option to Redevelop, *Journal of Real Estate Finance and Economics*, 4, 209–223.

Childs, Paul D., Steven H. Ott, and Timothy J. Riddiough, 2002. Optimal Valuation of Claims on Noisy Real Assets: Theory & an Application. Forthcoming, *Real Estate Economics*.

Childs, Paul D., Timothy J. Riddiough, and Alexander J. Triantis, 1996. Mixed Uses and the Redevelopment Option, *Real Estate Economics*, 24, 317–339.

Dixit, Avinash K. and Robert S. Pindyck, 1994. *Investment Under Uncertainty*, Princeton University Press, Princeton, NJ.

Geltner, David and Norman G. Miller. Commercial Real Estate Analysis and Investments, Prentice Hall (2001), Chapters 28 and 29.

Geltner, David, Timothy J. Riddiough, and Srdjan Stojanovich, 1996. Insights on the Effect of Land Use Choice: The Perpetual Option on the Best of Two Underlying Assets, *Journal of Urban Economics*, 39(1), 20–50.

Grenadier, Steven R., 1995. The Persistence of Real Estate Cycles, *Journal of Real Estate Finance and Economics* 10, 95–119.

Grenadier, Steven R., 1996. The Strategic Exercise of Options: Development Cascades and Overbuilding in Real Estate Markets, *Journal of Finance*, 51, 1653–1679.

Grenadier, Steven R., 1999. Information Revelation Through Option Exercise, *The Review of Financial Studies* 12(1), 95–129.

Holland, Steven, Steven Ott and Tim Riddiough, 2000. The Role of Uncertainty in Investment: An Examination of Competing Investment Models Using Commercial Real Estate Data, *Real Estate Economics*, 28(1), 33–64.

Ott, Steven H. and Ha-Chin Yi, 2001. Real Options and Development: A Model of Regional Supply and Demand, *Real Estate Finance*, 18(1), 47–55.

Sivitanidou, Rena and Petros Sivitanides, 2000. Does the Theory of Irreversible Investments Help Explain Movements in Office-Commercial Real Estate? *Real Estate Economics*, 28 (4), 623–661.

Steinfeld, Bart R. and Randall C. Zisler, February 2000. Uncovering Hidden Value in Real Estate: Modifying the NPV Approach, *The Real Estate Capital Markets Review*, published by Cushman and Wakefield and Apogee Associates, LLC.

Titman, Sheridan, 1985. Urban Land Prices Under Uncertainty, *American Economic Review*, 75, 505–514.

Quigg, Laura, 1993. Empirical Testing of Real Option-Pricing Models, *Journal of Finance*, 48, 621–640.

Williams, Joseph T., 1991. Real Estate Development as an Option, *Journal of Real Estate Finance and Economics*, 4, 191–208.

Williams, Joseph T., 1997. Redevelopment of Real Assets, *Real Estate Economics*, 25, 387–407.

Index